W9-AXY-984

# Frommer's
3rd Edition

# Virgin Islands

**by Darwin Porter
& Danforth Prince**

Macmillan • USA

## MACMILLAN TRAVEL

A Simon & Schuster Macmillan Company
1633 Broadway
New York, NY 10019

ISBN 0-02-860644-2
ISSN 1055-5447

Editor: Blythe Grossberg
Map Editor: Doug Stallings
Design by Michele Laseau
Digital Cartography by Jim Moore

### SPECIAL SALES

Bulk purchases (10+ copies) of Frommer's travel guides are available to corporations at special discounts. The Special Sales Department can produce custom editions to be used as premiums and/or for sales promotion to suit individual needs. Existing editions can be produced with custom cover imprints such as corporate logos. For more information write to: Special Sales, Simon & Schuster, 1230 Avenue of the Americas, New York, NY 10020.

Manufactured in the United States of America

# Contents

### 4   The U.S. Virgin Islands: St. Thomas   71

# List of Maps

## An Invitation to the Reader

In researching this book, we discovered many wonderful places—hotels, restaurants, shops, and more. We're sure you'll find others. Please tell us about them, so we can share the information with your fellow travelers in upcoming editions. If you were disappointed with a recommendation, we'd love to know that, too. Please write to:

Darwin Porter/Danforth Prince
*Frommer's The Virgin Islands,* 3rd Edition
Macmillan Travel
1633 Broadway
New York, NY 10019

## An Additional Note

Please be advised that travel information is subject to change at any time—and this is especially true of prices. We therefore suggest that you write or call ahead for confirmation when making your travel plans. The authors, editors, and publisher cannot be held responsible for the experiences of readers while traveling. Your safety is important to us, however, so we encourage you to stay alert and be aware of your surroundings. Keep a close eye on cameras, purses, and wallets, all favorite targets of thieves and pickpockets.

## What the Symbols mean

**✪ Frommer's Favorites**

Hotels, restaurants, attractions, and entertainments you should not miss.

**Ⓢ Super-Special Values**

Hotels and restaurants that offer great value for your money.

The following abbreviations are used for credit cards:

| | | | |
|---|---|---|---|
| AE | American Express | EU | Eurocard |
| CB | Carte Blanche | JCB | Japan Credit Bank |
| DC | Diners Club | MC | MasterCard |
| DISC | Discover | V | Visa |

# The Best of the Virgin Islands

You've come to the Virgin Islands to relax—not to exhaust yourself searching for the best deals and most eclectic experiences. With this guide in hand, you can spend your vacation in peace and let us do the work. Below you'll find our carefully compiled lists of the islands' superlative beaches, hotels, restaurants, shopping, sightseeing, and nearly anything else your heart might desire.

## 1 The Best Beaches

Both the U.S. and the British Vilrgin Islands are known for their white, sandy beaches. This is not true of all islands in the Caribbean, many of which have only jagged coral outcroppings or beaches with black volcanic sand (which gets very hot in the noonday sun). Best of all, every beach in the Virgin Islands is open to the public, although in some cases, you'll have to walk across the grounds of a resort (or arrive by private boat) to reach them.

- **Cane Garden Bay,** Tortola, British Virgin Islands. Rivaling Magens Bay for scenic beauty (see below), Cane Garden Bay is the most popular beach in the BVI. Some visitors claim its translucent waters and white sands are reason enough to visit Tortola (it is also the closest beach to the capital at Road Town).
- **Magens Bay Beach,** St. Thomas, U.S. Virgin Islands. Known for its half-mile loop of brilliant white sand and for its clear and calm waters, this public beach is the most popular in the U.S. Virgins archipelago. Two peninsulas protect the beach from erosion and strong waves, and its flat, sandy bottom makes it safe for children.
- **Trunk Bay,** St. John, U.S. Virgin Islands. Protected by the U.S. National Park Service, this beach is a favorite with cruise-ship passengers. It's known for its underwater trail, where markers guide beachcombers along the reef lying just off the white beach. Trunk Bay is consistently ranked among the top 10 beaches in the Caribbean, most recently by *Condé Nast Traveler.*
- **Sapphire Beach,** St. Thomas, U.S. Virgin Islands. Offshore of luxury hotel complexes, this beach is one of the finest on the island and a favorite with windsurfers. It's the most popular Sunday afternoon gathering place in the East End. From the beach, there is a panoramic view of St. John and other islands, some owned by the BVI.
- **Caneel Bay,** St. John, U.S. Virgin Islands. Site of a famous resort, Caneel Bay is a string of seven beaches, stretching around Durloe Point to Hawksnest Caneel. If you're not a guest of the hotel, you can reach six of these beaches only by water.

- **Sandy Point,** St. Croix, U.S. Virgin Islands. The biggest beach in the U.S. Virgin Islands, Sandy Point has shallow, calm waters. It lies in the southwestern part of St. Croix, almost like a small peninsula, directly to the west of Alexander Hamilton Airport.

## 2 The Best Honeymoon Resorts

Many hotels in the U.S. and British Virgins will help you get married, doing everything from arranging the flowers and the photographer to applying for the marriage license (see Chapter 3 for more information). Regardless of where you decide to hold your wedding, the Virgin Islands offer romantic destinations for post-wedding wind-downs and honeymoons.

- **Biras Creek Hotel,** Virgin Gorda, British Virgin Islands. Private and elegant, this hotel is perched on a narrow promontory of land with signposted nature trails cutting through its lush tropical gardens. It's a secluded 150-acre hideaway, reached only by launch. Honeymooners rinse off in the sensuous open-air walled shower discreetly located within each bathroom.
- **Little Dix Bay,** Virgin Gorda, British Virgin Islands. The elegance of this luxury resort is understated. It's popular with older couples and honeymooners alike—in fact, the powerfully amorous atmosphere makes single guests feel like wall-flowers. Spread out over 500 acres, this resort provides sporting activities galore and beaches but lets you alone if that is your desire.
- **Sapphire Beach Resort & Marina,** St. Thomas, U.S. Virgin Islands. Located on one of the island's loveliest beaches, this is a huge complex of suites and villas. You can dine out or try out your specialties on your new bride or groom in one of the condo kitchens. Honeymooners share the resort with vacationing families.
- **Hyatt Regency St. John,** St. John, U.S. Virgin Islands. A 34-acre property opening onto Great Cruz Bay, this is the perfect destination for honeymooners seeking ritz and glitz. It's more for the sybaritic honeymooner than for the weary tourist seeking tranquillity. You can choose to stay in rooms, suites, or townhouses.
- **The Buccaneer,** St. Croix, U.S. Virgin Islands. The Buccaneer boasts the most extensive facilities on the island, including an 18-hole golf course, eight highly rated tennis courts, a spa and fitness center, a two-mile jogging trail, and three beaches. You can rent beachside rooms with fieldstone terraces leading right down to the water. The 1653 sugar mill on the grounds is the most popular wedding site on St. Croix.
- **Bolongo Beach Resorts Club Everything,** St. Thomas, U.S. Virgin Islands. The most popular resort choice for honeymooners, Bolongo Beach welcomes newlyweds with a passion and plans special features for them, including a carnival night buffet, Sunday brunches, and a chilled bottle of champagne upon arrival. Lots of sporting activities are included too.

## 3 The Best Family Vacations

- **Bitter End Yacht Club,** Virgin Gorda, British Virgin Islands. Kids can be environmentally friendly here and go snorkeling at Statia Reef, explore the tidal pools and boulders of The Baths, or take an excursion to a bird sanctuary at Anegada Island. The focus for children is on watersports, snorkeling, and sailing; kids' programs entertain children six and over.

- **Sapphire Beach Resort & Marina,** St. Thomas, U.S. Virgin Islands. This is the family favorite in St. Thomas. There are supervised activities at the Little Gems Kids Klub. The hotel's toddler program caters to one- to three-year-olds. Many organized activities include the entire family. The hotel also opens onto one of the safest and best white sandy beaches on the island.
- **Bolongo Beach Resorts Club Everything,** St. Thomas, U.S. Virgin Islands. Lots of family activities are provided by the hotel staff, and there's a program for children, although it's not always divided by age. When booking, ask about the plan that allows children to stay and eat for free. Bolongo Beach is a very safe part of St. Thomas.
- **The Buccaneer,** St. Croix, U.S. Virgin Islands. This hotel is a longtime family favorite located on a 300-acre former sugar estate. It features kids' programs, including a half-day sail to Buck Island Reef, for children five through twelve. Kids trek on nature walks through tropical foliage and taste fruit in its natural state.
- **Chenay Bay Beach Resort,** St. Croix, U.S. Virgin Islands. Housed in West Indian–style cottages, families staying here can appease their three- to twelve-year-olds with organized activities. The owners of the hotel used their own children as guinea pigs to create their activity-filled program. Programs are geared to various age groups, and are active during summer and again at Christmastime.

## 4  The Best Places to Get Away from It All

Although there are tranquil retreats on St. Croix and on St. Thomas, the frenetic pace especially on St. Thomas may not be what you're after. In that case, head for St. John in the U.S. Virgin Islands, or, if even that peaceful island is too much for you, hop over to the BVI, and seek out even more tranquil oases.

- **The Sandcastle,** Jost Van Dyke, British Virgin Islands. The ultimate escapist's dream. Reached by inter-island ferry from Tortola, this little island is riddled with good hiking trails, uncrowded sandy beaches, and the ruin of an old fort. People come to the Sandcastle, a four-villa colony with octagonal-shaped cottages, in search of isolation, and that's exactly what they get. There are only a few cars on the island, and electricity is supplied by generators.
- **Anegada Reef Hotel,** Anegada, British Virgin Islands. One of the most remote, tranquil places in the entire Virgin Island chain, this hotel is not polished or refined in any way. It's loved by the yachting set cruising through these islands. Some 20 miles north of Virgin Gorda's North Sound, the hotel stands on a flat mass of coral that's about 3 miles wide. Chances are you may never meet most of the 250 local residents, although you'll occasionally see snorkelers and scuba divers. Fishermen come to this hotel for the bone fishing. The place is recommended for devotees of deserted, isolated beaches; just don't expect anything fancy anywhere on the island.
- **Guana Island,** Guana Island, British Virgin Islands. The only development on a strictly private 850-acre island, this is one of the most secluded hideaways in the Virgin Islands, maybe in the entire Caribbean Basin. Located off the coast of Tortola, the club attracts visitors who want to explore the island's nature trails and view its rare species of plant and animal life. The island, which is a virtual

wildlife sanctuary, is also known for its vacant, virgin beaches. Although it is an unspoiled outpost, Guana Island is actually the sixth largest island in the BVI.

- **Lavendar Hill Estates,** St. John, U.S. Virgin Islands. This organization offers some of the best values on the island for those who'd like to rent their own escapist villa for a week or so. More than two-thirds of St. John itself has been preserved as a national park, thanks to the generosity of Laurance Rockefeller. That means that unlike St. Thomas and St. Croix, St. John looks much like it did in the 1950s, at least in part. The day-trippers from St. Thomas come over in the morning and usually depart before 5pm. After that, you'll have St. John to yourself.

## 5 The Friendliest Islands

- **St. John.** For the most part, St. John remains an unspoiled and relatively safe destination. Its people aren't as jaded about the arrival of tourists as they are on St. Thomas, and in most places you get a genuine welcome. Crimes against tourists, especially violent crimes, are rare here. Pickpockets, however, prey on cruise-ship passengers at Trunk Bay, the island's best beach.
- **Tortola.** In many cases the managers of various hotels are the owners, and they're out to lure your business and keep it. Consequently, with a few sour exceptions, Tortola extends the proverbial welcome mat. Everything is low-key and laid-back, and the political situation is stable. There is little, if any, racial tension. There is more crime here than on Virgin Gorda (see below), but acts of violence against visitors are very rare.
- **Virgin Gorda.** People of Virgin Gorda speak of St. Thomas the way certain parts of rural America speak of New York City. Visitors are welcomed into most places with a smile. Vandalism is a very minor problem here, and home or hotel break-ins are very rare. Many locals leave their houses and cars unlocked.

## 6 The Best Restaurants

The debate over which restaurants serve the best food will rage as long as there are restaurants. Here's our list of favorites.

- **Virgilio's,** St. Thomas. An elegant hideaway serving the best Italian food on the island. Cheerful and relaxed, the place lovingly prepares all your longtime classic Italian favorites and some surprises too—especially cioppino, a kettle of savory seafood stew. The pasta dishes make you think you're on the Mediterranean. Savvy diners save room for one of the flambé desserts.
- **Eunice's Terrace,** St. Thomas. No one's ever heard of haute cuisine here, but they know how to rattle those West Indian pots and pans. After a lethal rum punch (called Queen Mary), dig into broiled fresh fish, conch fritters, savory callaloo soup, even "stew mutton." No one leaves without a slice of Eunice's sweet potato pie.
- **Provence,** St. Thomas. Patricia LeCorte brings Cordon Bleu cuisine to the island, with original interpretations of savory dishes from Provence and the Mediterranean. Open your meal with a classic such as onion soup au gratin or perhaps with salmon carpaccio accompanied by a tapenade of black olives. Like some of the great chefs of France, Le Courte has learned that to be sublime, sometimes you have to be simple. There's nothing better than her roast free-range garlic chicken with mashed potatoes, unless it's one of at least a trio of dessert soufflés.

- **Tavern on the Beach,** Marriott's Morningstar Beach Resort, St. Thomas. German-born Eddie Hale is all the rage in St. Thomas. He feeds visiting movie stars and baseball players a cuisine inspired by Spain, Provence, Thailand, Italy, even the Caribbean. His Bajan spicy butterfly prawns swimming in a bowl of gazpacho laced with saffron aïoli is the stuff of memory. Caribbean flavors surface in his mashed yams, tannia, and mango chutney.

- **Le Château de Bordeaux,** St. John. The view at this restaurant outside Cruz Bay competes with a combination of continental and Caribbean cuisine. Both the view and the cuisine are winners. The conch fritters carry pungent bits of banana and papaya; golden-yellow saffron from the fields of Spain turn pastas into sunbursts, and the West–Indian seafood chowder is a perfect blend of fish and spices. Wild game and roast rack of lamb perfumed with rosemary and with a honey-dijon nut crust also appear on the innovative, ever-changing menu.

- **Indies,** St. Croix. San Francisco-born Catherine Plav–Driggers applies everything she ever learned in California to the rich bounty of the Caribbean. The result is taste and texture unequaled on the island—spicy Caribbean chicken, spring rolls (better than you'll find in Chinatown), and grouper brought to life in coconut milk with a shrimp escort. Everything is flavored with tomato, ginger, and scallions.

- **Kendricks,** St. Croix. In a brick building crafted from 19th-century ballast, David and Jane Kendrick bring a light continental touch to dishes full of flavor. On fine china, coconut shrimp appears with a chive-studded, jalapeno-peppery aïoli. A tender pork loin encrusted in pecans makes its opening with a ginger-flavored mayonnaise. Begin with baked brie with perfectly seasoned wild mushrooms.

- **Skyworld,** Tortola (BVI). With the panoramic view, sunsets that turn the whole sky a fiery red, and one or two Pascha Coladas (passion fruit juice, rum, and cream of coconut), what does dinner matter? Here it does, and the chef cares about his guests and their palates. He takes conch fritters, french fries, and onion rings—all horrible dishes in many places of the world—and earns praise for them from the "food sharks" at *Gourmet* magazine. The cuisine's muses roam the world, although some of the chef's best ideas (such as West–Indian lobster ravioli) come from the establishment's home turf.

## 7  The Best Shopping Destinations

The U.S. Virgin Islands are the duty-free shopping bazaar of the Caribbean. The deals in St. Thomas, the major shopping destination, soak up half of its tourists' dollars.

- **St. Thomas.** In restored warehouses, the bazaars of Charlotte Amalie have been called a virtual shoppers' paradise. There are more stores and more merchandise in Charlotte Amalie than anywhere else, not only in the Virgin Islands, but in the Caribbean. Look for two local publications *This Week in St. Thomas* or *Best Buys*—either will steer you to whatever type of merchandise you're seeking. Always check out the price of comparable items in your area before leaving home. That way, you'll know if you are indeed getting a bargain in St. Thomas. Often, you're not. But if you shop well, you can sometimes purchase luxury imports from Europe (perfume, watches, or gold jewelry) at 5% to 50% off mainland prices. Sometimes, fine china and crystal will net you savings ranging from 30% to 50%. But this requires some savvy shopping and price comparisons on your part.

- **St. Croix.** Compared to St. Thomas shopping, St. Croix is a pale imitation. Nevertheless, there is much of interest to the dedicated shopper, and there is a broader range of merchandise than ever before. Even though most cruise ships call at Frederiksted, the majority of shops are found at Christiansted, the capital. You'll see many of the same shops and chains on St. Croix that you find on St. Thomas, including Little Switzerland and Java Wraps. Only here the merchandise is more limited; prices are about the same, however. Again, there are few bargains.

## 8 The Best Buys

The U.S. Virgin Islands are the shopper's mecca of the West Indies. Your best deals might be found in the following merchandise.

- **Arts & Crafts.** While arts and crafts are not the high priority items they are on such islands as Haiti and Jamaica, you can find them in the Virgin Islands. Jim Tillett at Tillett Gardens, Tutu, St. Thomas, runs the premier art gallery and craft studio in the U.S. Virgin Islands. His silk screening has been featured in fashion layouts around the world. St. John, Mongoose Junction, right at Cruz Bay, offers the best assortment of locally produced arts and crafts (all tax free for U.S. citizens) of any place on the island. Handmade pottery, sculpture, and glass are sold here, along with locally made clothing. In Christiansted on St. Croix, seek out Folk Art Traders for the largest selection of Caribbean arts and crafts. But if you want handcrafts exclusive just to the U.S. Virgin Islands, head for Many Hands, also in Christiansted.
- **Fine China and Crystal.** Sometimes (not always) you can find substantial savings—many shoppers report savings of 30% to 50%. For example, a Rosenthal place setting (the same pattern Elizabeth Taylor purchased) might go for half the price it sells for on New York's Fifth Avenue. Baccarat goblets, as we recently noted in a price comparison on St. Thomas, went for about a third of the price quoted in the U.S. catalog. You can sometimes get two Lalique plates for the price of one back in the United States. Again, know your prices before you land on St. Thomas. That way, you can wander with more knowledge through the vast field of Waterford, Orrefors, Hummel, Wedgwood, Royal Worcester, Royal Doulton, and the like.
- **Jewelry.** Watches, gold jewelry, and other such merchandise are sometimes heavily discounted in St. Thomas and St. Croix, especially during the off-season (mid-April to mid-October) and when there aren't 12 cruise ships in port at Charlotte Amalie. The sheer volume of jewelry offered in St. Thomas is stunning—diamonds, emeralds, rubies, opals, gold, platinum, both world-famous names and one-of-a-kind pieces created by local artists. But you'll want to do comparison shopping even in St. Thomas, as that Rolex watch might be selling for less at a store just around the corner. A lot of fake merchandise and discounts are touted. To play it safe, shop at stores displaying name brands.
- **Liquor.** A recent spot survey showed that prices for liquor in St. Thomas and St. Croix were 50% to 60% less than in New York City. You're allowed to bring back to the States five fifths of liquor, or six fifths if the sixth is locally produced.

Local liquor nearly always means rum in the Virgin Islands, but it could mean Southern Comfort, which is also bottled on the island (check the label). Some 90% of all rum imported into the United States comes from either Puerto Rico or the Virgin Islands. Because of the generous allowances of U.S. Customs in the Virgin Islands, St. Thomas or St. Croix might be the best places to purchase expensive French brandy, champagne, or an otherwise pricey liqueur.

- **Perfumes and Cosmetics.** Imported perfumes and beauty products such as bath gels and makeup can sometimes be real bargains, if you know what such merchandise costs at your local discount outlet. How much do you save? It depends on the product. For example, we recently did some comparison shopping between New York and Charlotte Amalie. An ounce of Yves St. Laurent's *Opium* was $40 cheaper in St. Thomas than in Manhattan. *Giorgio* was $40 cheaper in St. Thomas than in Manhattan. Since locally made fragrances are duty free (not part of your $1,200 customs allowance), you might try to find companies which distill their own fragrances. Look at the label on the bottle to see where it's produced. Tropicana Perfume Shoppes on Main Street in Charlotte Amalie has the largest selection of fragrances for both women and men in all the U.S. Virgin Islands.

## 9  The Best Nightlife

If you're a serious partier, you'll want to avoid St. John and virtually everything in the BVI and (with some exceptions) concentrate your attention on St. Thomas and, to a lesser extent, St. Croix.

- **The Top of the Reef,** Marriott's Frenchman's Reef, St. Thomas. This hot spot is for those who like their shows glitzy and in the style of Las Vegas. The island's only dinner theater the Top of the Reef presents shows, including musicals, that change every five to six weeks. Call to see what's happening—perhaps there's a Calypso Carnival, a fast-paced revue of island talent, culture, and music.
- **Turtle Rock Bar at the Sugar Bay Resort,** St. Thomas. Located near Red Hook, this place is known for burgers and bar action. Sometimes, it's karaoke, on other nights steel pan bands, or other island talent. It's the local hot spot.
- **Andiamo Ristorante/Club,** St. Thomas. A 50-minute drive west of Charlotte Amalie, this club is a longtime favorite with both visitors and locals (usually ages 18 to 30). The DJ plays rock and reggae. You can come for dinner at Andiamo, then shift your venue to Club Z later in the night when the music heats up.
- **Buccaneer Hotel,** St. Croix. This deluxe hotel has the best nightlife on the island. Call to see what's on at the time of your visit. Sometimes the hotel stages limbo shows and reggae. But in winter, it's known for booking the island's premier talent, Jimmy Hamilton. Appearing with his own quartet today, he played lead clarinet and tenor sax with Duke Ellington's orchestra for 30 years.
- **Bomba's Surfside Shack at Cappoon's Bay,** Tortola. This spot is the most interesting place to hang out on the BVI and one of the most famous bars in the West Indies. For decor, it uses junk and Day-Glo graffiti, but it's got the best electronic amplification on the island. The rum punches flow, and the hottest people visiting the BVI show up here, especially for those notorious once-a-month full moon parties, complete with "herbal tea."

## 10 The Most Intriguing Historical Sights

Most travelers in the Virgin Islands aren't terribly interested in history, at least in Caribbean history. For those who are, here are our top choices if you want to see the ruins of yesterday.

- **Fort Christian,** Charlotte Amalie, St. Thomas. Named after the Danish king, Christian V, and dating from 1672, this fort was built after the arrival of the first colonists. The oldest building on the island, it has been vastly altered over the years: bastions and masonry ramparts were added in the 1700s. Completely renovated in 1871, the form sounded a salute when Charlotte Amalie was made the capital of the island. Once, pirates were hanged in its courtyard.
- **Crown House,** Charlotte Amalie, St. Thomas. This 18th-century mansion has served as the home of two past governors. Filled with antiques, the stone-built, two-floor house has a Dutch–hipped roof and memories of Peter von Scholten, one of the island's most famous governors, who occupied the premises in 1827. A French chandelier in the mansion is said to have come from Versailles.
- **Annaberg Ruins,** St. John. The greatest reminder of the plantation heyday of this once-troubled island, the ruins of this sugar plantation lie at a point opening onto Leinster Bay. At one time, the smell of boiling molasses filled the air, as hard-working slaves—many set to rebel—turned out sugar for markets in Europe. Sugarcane once stretched over many acres, but now nature has taken over, returning the land to lush vegetation. The Annaberg estate, whose ruins have been spruced up rather than restored, dates back to 1780. Visitors can see remains of former slave quarters.
- **Fort Frederick,** Frederiksted, St. Croix. This fort, completed in 1760, is said to have been the first to salute the flag of the new United States. When an American brigantine anchored at port hoisted a homemade Old Glory, the fort returned the salute with cannon fire, violating the rules of neutrality. It was here, in 1848, that Governor Peter von Scholten read a proclamation freeing the island's slaves. A small museum is installed on the site today.
- **Fort Christiansvaern,** Christiansted, St. Croix. With a facade that hasn't changed very much since the 1820s, this fort is one of the best preserved of its type in the West Indies. Teetering at the edge of the harbor, it was constructed from ballast bricks sent over from its colonial overseer, Denmark, in battleships. The first fort on the spot was built between 1732 and 1749, and part of it remains as well. After 1878, it served for a period as the island's police headquarters.

## 11 The Best Dive Sites

Scuba diving is a year-round adventure in the Virgin Islands, both U.S. and British. The best sites include:

- **The Wreck of the RMS _Rhone,_** off Salt Island in the BVI. The wreck is the premier dive site not only in the Virgin Islands, but also in the entire Caribbean. This royal mail steamer, which went down in 1867, was featured in the murky film _The Deep._
- **Cow and Calf Rocks,** St. Thomas. Off the southeast end of the island, this site is considered the island's best dive spot. It's also a good bet if you want to snorkel. It can be reached in about 45 minutes by boat from Charlotte Amalie.

At the site, a network of coral tunnels is riddled with caves, reefs, and ancient boulders encrusted with coral.

- **Buck Island Reef.** The only underwater National Monument in the U.S., this tiny island lies 2 miles off the north coast of St. Croix. With an underwater visibility of some 100 feet, Buck Island is one of the major diving targets in the Caribbean. There are enough labyrinths and grottoes for the most experienced divers.
- **Davis Bay,** off St. Croix. Davis Bay is the site of the 12,000-foot-deep Puerto Rico Trench, the fifth-deepest body of water in the world. Other sites for deep dives include the drop-offs and coral canyons at Cane Bay and Salt River.

## 12  The Best Snorkeling Sites

A readers' poll by *Scuba Diving* magazine confirmed what Virgin Islanders knew all along: The islands of St. Croix, St. John, and St. Thomas are among the top five places to go snorkeling in the Caribbean.

- **Buck Island Reef National Monument,** St. Croix. More than 250 recorded species of fish have swum through this 850-acre island and reef system, located two miles off St. Croix's north shore. A variety of sponges, corals, and crustaceans also inhabit the monument, which is strictly protected by the National Park Service.
- **Trunk Bay,** St. John. This self-guided 225-yard-long trail has large underwater signs that identify species of coral and other items of interest. Above water, freshwater showers, changing rooms, equipment rentals, and lifeguards make snorkeling more convenient.
- **Magens Bay,** St. Thomas. On the north shore of St. Thomas, Coki Point offers year-round snorkeling. Especially enticing are the coral ledges near Coral World's underwater tower, a favorite with cruise-ship passengers.
- **Leinster Bay,** St. John. Easily accessible from land and sea, Leinster Bay offers calm, clear, and uncrowded waters teeming with an abundance of sea life.
- **Haulover Bay,** St. John. A favorite with locals, this small bay is rougher than Leinster and is often deserted. The snorkeling is dramatic, with ledges, walls, nooks, and sandy areas set close together. At this spot, only about 200 yards separate the Atlantic Ocean from the Caribbean Sea.
- **Cane Bay,** St. Croix. One of the island's best diving and snorkeling sites is off this breezy north-shore beach. On a clear day, you can swim out 150 yards to see the Cane Bay Wall that drops off dramatically to deep waters below. Multicolored fish, elkhorn, and brain coral flourish here.
- **Frederiksted Pier,** St. Croix. Conventional wisdom has designated Frederiksted Pier, located in an old ramshackle town at the west end of St. Croix, the most interesting pier dive in the Caribbean. The original pier was virtually destroyed by Hurricane Hugo of 1989, but a new pier opened in 1993. Plunge into a world of exotic creatures, including sponges, banded shrimp, plume worms, and seahorses.

## 13  The Best Golf Courses

While none of the Virgin Islands can compare with Bermuda for golf, what they do have is top-notch.

- **Carambola,** St. Croix. Known for some decades as Fountain Valley, this course at Davis Bay was designed by Robert Trent Jones, Sr., as one of the most challenging in the Caribbean. Set near the island's northwestern edge, this well-maintained course is characterized by water hazards and ravines. Measuring 6,900 yards long, it offers a renovated clubhouse and a pro shop with rental clubs and lockers. A restaurant dishing up steak sandwiches lies on the course.
- **Mahogany Run,** St. Thomas. To the north of Charlotte Amalie, this par–70, 18–hole course with its views of the British Virgin Islands is known to golfers throughout the Caribbean for its tricky "Devil's Triangle" trio of holes. The course was designed by Tom and George Fazio and is hailed by golfers as one of the most scenic in the Caribbean.

## 14  The Best Tennis Facilities

- **The Buccaneer,** St. Croix. Touted as the best tennis in the Virgin Islands, this resort is the venue of several tournaments, including the Virgin Islands Tennis Championships which take place here each July. The resort features eight all-weather Laykold courts, two of which are lit at night. There's also a pro shop. Nonresidents can play here for a fee.
- **Sugar Bay Plantation,** St. Thomas. Several tennis buffs have deserted the Buccaneer in favor of this resort at Estate Smith Bay. Sugar Bay Plantation offers the USVI's first stadium tennis court with a seating capacity of 220. In addition, it offers half a dozen Laykold courts, lit at night. Lessons are available, and there is a pro shop.

## 15  The Best Sailing Outfitters

Sailing is big in the U.S. Virgin Islands, but does not equal the British Virgins, acclaimed for having the best sailing in the Caribbean. Also see individual chapters for local outfitters. The best outfitters and suppliers include the following:

- **The Moorings,** Tortola in the BVI (☎ **809/494-2331,** 800/535-7289 in the U.S., or **813/535-1446** in south Florida). Run by Ginny and Charlie Cary, this is the finest charter service in the Virgin Islands. It has done more than any other outfitter to make the BVI the favorite destination of the world's yachters. Their fleet of sailing yachts and boats is staggering—everything from bareboat rentals to fully-crewed yachts with skipper, staff, and cook.
- **Avery's Marine, Inc.,** P.O. Box 3693, Veteran's Drive, Charlotte Amalie, St. Thomas, USVI 00803. (☎ **809/776-0113**). This organization prides itself on being one of the first yacht–chartering businesses in the Virgin Islands. It was established in 1959 by Dick Avery, who continues to maintain the organization today. It is located in the touristic heart of Charlotte Amalie, in Frenchtown, adjacent to the Chart House Restaurant. The company maintains an inventory of about a dozen sailing craft which range in size from 27 to 39 feet in length. Prospective renters fill out detailed forms describing their sailing experience and usually opt for bareboat rentals (those without crews). A skipper can be arranged as an extra option for a surcharge of around $100 a day. Depending on the season and their size, boats rent for between $1,100 and $2,000 per week, or from $160 to $290 per day.

## 16   The Best Hiking

The islands present several unusual hillclimbs and nature walks. The best of these are on St. Croix and on the less densely populated islands of Tortola and St. John. St. Thomas has simply too many cars and too many buildings to make extended treks very appealing.

- **The Annaberg Sugar Plantation Ruins Walk,** St. John. The premier route through the 10,000-acre United States Virgin Islands National Park, this paved walk is only $1/4$ mile long, and it's self-guided. Overlooking the scenic north coast, the trail traverses the ruins of what was the most important sugarcane plantation on the island. Slaves' quarters, a windmill tower, and buildings of ballast brick from Danish sailing vessels recapture a long–vanished era. Views from the ruins look toward Tortola, Great Thatch Island, and Jost Van Dyke on the opposite side of Sir Francis Drake Passage.

- **The Rain Forest Hike, St. Croix.** It takes $2^1/2$ hours one-way to hike this trail. Take Route 631 heading north of Frederiksted to the intersection of Routes 63 and 76. Continue along on Route 63 until you reach Creque Dam Road; at this point, go right, and launch your hike. After passing the 150–foot Creque Dam, you'll be deep within the rain forest in little more than a mile. Continue along the trail until you reach the Western Scenic Road. Eventually, you reach Mahogany Road (Route 76), near St. Croix Leap Project. Hikers rate this hike moderate in difficulty. For further details on the rain forest and how to explore it, see "Exploring the Rain Forest" in Chapter 6.

- **Buck Island Walk,** off St. Croix. A circumnavigation of this National Park—which is reached by boat—takes about two hours and is rated moderate by hikers. The mile-long island is an 865–acre park located off the northern coast of St. Croix. Since the island is ringed with white sandy beaches, you can interrupt your hike at any point for a refreshing swim. A trail also points into the interior. See "A Walking Tour of Buck Island" in Chapter 6 for more details.

## 17   The Best Offbeat Travel Experiences

- **The Wreck of the RMS *Rhone*.** Over drinks in any island bar frequented by scuba enthusiasts, the conversation will inevitably touch upon one of the world's most unusual dive sites, the wreck of the *Rhone*. A 310-foot steel-hulled steamship, the *Rhone* was built in Britain in 1865 and sank during a violent unexpected hurricane in 1867.

  Today, the ruined hulk rests on a steeply sloping underwater site off the western coast of Salt Island, southwest of Tortola. Scuba instructors carefully predetermine whether divers will visit either the bow of the sunken wreck (80 feet underwater) or stern (20 feet underwater). In either case, the experience is among the most eerie (and sometimes mystical) in the underwater world. Its allure was seized by Hollywood, which filmed many of the most evocative shots of Jacqueline Bissett in *The Deep* here.

- **Exploring "Treasure Island."** Norman Island, south of Tortola and east of St. John, is accessible only by boat. The island has serviced the needs of smugglers and ruffians since the 1600s, when pirates used its hillocks to spot Spanish galleons to plunder. Legend has it that this was the island that inspired

Robert Louis Stevenson's *Treasure Island,* first published in 1883. In a dinghy, you can row into the southernmost cave on the island—with bats overhead and phosphorescent patches. This is where Stevenson's Mr. Fleming, according to legend, took his precious treasure. It was reported that in 1750, treasure from the sunken *Nuestra Señora* was recovered here. The island has a series of other caves whose bottoms are filled with seawater teeming with marine life. Intrepid hikers climb through scrubland to the island's central ridge, Spy Glass Hill, to appreciate the panoramic view of the land and sea. Hiking trails are either nonexistent or poorly maintained.

- **An Expedition to Hassel Island.** The harbor at Charlotte Amalie is the temporary home of more large–scale cruise ships than virtually any other port in the Caribbean. Despite the billions of dollars worth of marine hardware floating all around it, the harbor's most visible island, Hassel Island, is almost completely deserted. The island's membership in the National Parks network prohibits most forms of development. There are no hotels or services of any kind, and swimming is limited to narrow, rock-strewn beaches with very little sand. Despite that, many visitors hire a boat to drop them off for an hour or two of relief from the congestion of Charlotte Amalie. A hike along part of the island's shoreline provides a different perspective on the bustle of Charlotte Amalie. Note that you'll need to make arrangements in advance for your return with the skipper who drops you off initially. Bring your own drinking water and food if you plan to spend more than three or so hours here.

# Introducing the Virgin Islands

Former stamping ground of some of history's most famous sea marauders, the Virgin Islands are now invaded by tourists who arrive by the thousands daily either by plane or cruise ship. Due east of what they call their "giant neighbor" (Puerto Rico, less than 30 minutes away by air), the islands lie about 1,100 miles southeast of Miami.

These green, hilly islands number about 100 in all, counting the rocks that jut out from the sea. Owned by the United States or Great Britain, most of the islands are so tiny that they are uninhabited except by a few birds or an adventurous boating party stopping off for a little skinny-dipping. For the ultimate escape, you can sometimes rent an entire island for yourself and possibly a chosen companion.

Coral reefs often shield the best beaches from the wicked surf of the Atlantic Ocean, which fronts their northern shorelines. The southern island rims open onto the usually calmer waters of the Caribbean. St. Croix, south of St. Thomas and St. John, is entirely in the Caribbean Sea.

The name "Virgins" came from that great labeler of Caribbean Islands, Columbus, who sailed by them. In 1493, impressed by their number, he named them *Las Once Mil Vírgenes* in honor of St. Ursula's 11,000 martyred maidens of Christian belief.

Part of the archipelago known as the Lesser Antilles, the Virgins are for the most part rich in vegetation, even lush, and they are of volcanic origin. The Lesser Antilles more or less mark the spot where the Atlantic Ocean ends and the calmer and more tranquil Caribbean Sea begins.

The Virgin Islands, both British and American, possess the most ideal temperatures in the West Indies, thanks to the ever-present trade winds which keep the air from getting too hot. The Virgins report lower humidity than many of the other Caribbean islands, which makes them an ideal vacation paradise, both in summer and winter. The greatest numbers of tourists visit between December and April. Summer is slower and a bit hotter, but, to compensate, all hoteliers lower their prices then.

The islands report an average annual temperature of 78°F. The welcome rain showers do come, but they pass quickly, except during hurricane season. On nearly any day of the year, you can count on sunshine, at least for part of the day. The lowest known temperature ever recorded in the Virgin Islands is 61°F.

Most of the local Virgin Islanders are descended from African slaves who worked on plantations for European owners until their emancipation in the mid-1800s after a period of great violence.

In recent years, the local population has swelled with an influx of "down island-ers," people from other islands in the Caribbean chain, which stretches to South America. Many Puerto Ricans have also moved to the U.S. islands nearby, joined by many Americans from the mainland in the north.

The old ways of the islands are all but gone in bustling St. Thomas and St. Croix, but may still be found in some pockets in the British Virgins, especially on Virgin Gorda.

## 1 Choosing the Perfect Island

Peering at the tiny Virgin Islands chain on a world map, you may find the dif-ferent islands difficult to distinguish. They vary widely, however, and so will your vacation depending on which island you choose. If you can only visit one or a few of the islands, use this section to select the islands suited to your vacation needs. For example, if you're an avid golfer, you don't want to find yourself plopped on a remote island in the British Virgins with no golf courses. Yet that same island might be ideal for a couple contemplating a long, isolated honeymoon. By pro-viding detailed information about the character of each island in both the U.S. and British Virgin Islands, we hope to guide you to your small piece of paradise.

### WHICH ISLAND CHAIN IS FOR YOU, U.S. OR BRITISH?

The American and British have left different imprints on the Virgin Islands. The USVI, except for St. John, bear traits of the mainland, including supermarkets and fast-food chains. The BVI, to the east of the U.S. Virgin Islands, are sleepy. Except for a few deluxe hotels, mostly on Virgin Gorda, they recall the way the Caribbean used to be before the advent of high-rise condos, McDonalds, and flotillas of cruise ships.

If you want shopping, a wide selection of restaurants and hotels, and the best nightlife the islands can offer, head to the U.S. Virgin Islands. St. Thomas and St. Croix in particular are jam-packed with things to do. With effort, you can find peace and quiet on St. Thomas and St. Croix, especially at the various resorts which are set apart from the action.

Only St. John among the U.S. Virgin Islands matches the British Virgins' tran-quillity. Protected by the U.S. Forest Service, it is the least developed of the U.S. Virgins. St. John is a rugged mixture of bad roads, a scattered population, and a small number of stores and services.

In total contrast to St. Thomas and St. Croix, the British Virgin Islands languish in the past, although change is in the air. Tortola is the capital and largest popu-lation center in the BVI, but its selection of shopping, nightlife, and restaurants is limited. Tortola is instead the choicest spot for boaters of all stripes and is con-sidered the cruise capital of the Caribbean. Virgin Gorda, to the east of Tortola, claims most of the British Virgins' deluxe hotels. There are accommodations and restaurants on other islands in the Virgins, such as Peter Island Resort and Yacht Club Harbor on private Peter Island.

## THE MAJOR ISLANDS IN BRIEF

**ST. THOMAS**   The most developed island in the U.S. and British Virgin chains, St. Thomas at times resembles a small city. There are peaceful retreats, but you must seek them out. The harbor at Charlotte Amalie is the cruise-ship haven of the Caribbean, and many locals and temporary residents try to avoid it when the greatest concentration of vessels is in port.

Charlotte Amalie, the capital, probably has the widest selection of duty–free shopping in the Caribbean. However, you must wander carefully through the bazaars to find the true bargains.

There are plenty of opportunities to get involved in sports, although most people come here only for swimming and sunning. Magens Bay Beach, with its tranquil surf and white sand, is considered one of the most beautiful beaches in the world, but it is likely to be over-crowded, especially on cruise-ship days. There are more secluded beaches as well.

Yachts and boats anchor at Ramada Yacht Haven Marina in St. Thomas and at Red Hook Marina on the island's somewhat isolated eastern tip. The serious yachting crowd, however, gathers at Tortola (see below).

St. Thomas has only one golf course—Mahogany Run—but it's a gem, with its celebrated "Devil's Triangle." There's even horseracing at Estate Nadir Race Track.

Sportfishermen angle from the American Yacht Harbor at Red Hook. The island also attracts snorkelers and scuba divers. Many outfitters offer equipment, diving trips, and instruction for enjoyment of the island's marine and reef life. Kayaking and parasailing also draw people away from the water's edge.

St. Thomas has the most varied and sophisticated collection of restaurants in the Virgin Islands, with special emphasis on French and continental fare. It pays more for its imported chefs (often from Europe) and secures the freshest of ingredients from the U.S. mainland or Puerto Rican markets for its tasty, flavorful cuisine. Its wide-ranging selection of eateries (which include Mexican, Chinese, Italian, American restaurants) adds an international flavor to the island's limited West Indian fare.

There's a range of accommodations on the island, from Bluebeard's Castle (a perennial favorite) to new developments in the East End, including the manicured Bolongo Elysian Beach. The island is filled with apartments and condominiums for rent and has a handful of old-fashioned Bed & Breakfast–style guesthouses at moderate prices.

If St. Thomas has a drawback, it's that the island is no longer the safe destination it once was. Crime is on the increase, and there are frequent muggings. Wandering around the island at night, especially on the back streets of Charlotte Amalie, is not recommended.

**ST. CROIX**   This island is the second major tourist destination in the Virgin Islands. Much of it, like St. Thomas, has been overdeveloped. While parts of it look like suburbia, however, true West Indian–style buildings have been preserved.

# The Virgin Islands

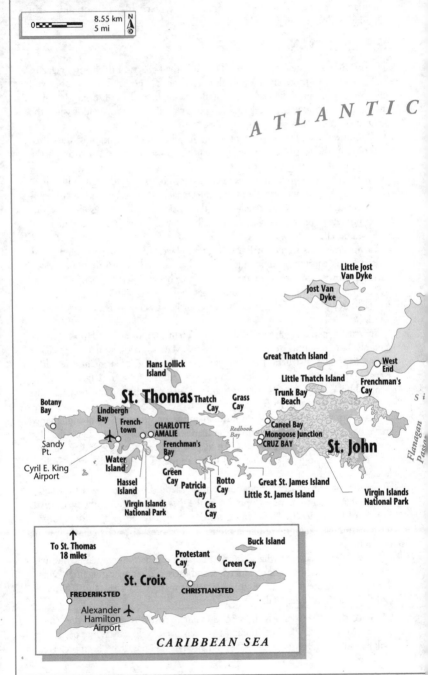

0    8.55 km
     5 mi

N

ATLANTIC

Little Jost
Van Dyke

Jost Van
Dyke

Hans Lollick
Island

Great Thatch Island

West
End

**St. Thomas** Thatch
Cay

Grass
Cay

Little Thatch Island

Frenchman's
Cay

Trunk Bay
Beach

S i

Botany
Bay

Lindbergh
Bay

French-
town

**CHARLOTTE
AMALIE**

*Redbook
Bay*

Caneel Bay

Mongoose Junction

**St. John**

Flanagan
Passa

Sandy
Pt.

Frenchman's
Bay

**CRUZ BAY**

Cyril E. King
Airport

Water
Island

Green
Cay

Patricia
Cay

Rotto
Cay

Great St. James Island

Hassel
Island

Virgin Islands
National Park

Cas
Cay

Little St. James Island

Virgin Islands
National Park

↑
To St. Thomas
18 miles

Buck Island

Protestant
Cay

Green Cay

**St. Croix**

**FREDERIKSTED**

**CHRISTIANSTED**

Alexander
Hamilton
Airport

*CARIBBEAN SEA*

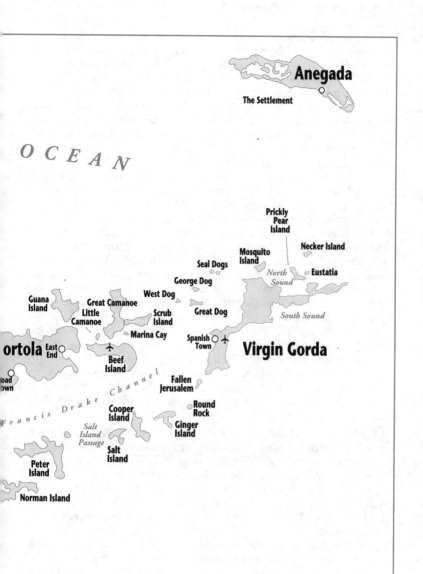

Cruise-ship passengers flood the capital, Christiansted, looking for duty-free shopping items. Nonetheless, the town has a lot of history and character, best appreciated if you can manage to visit when the throngs haven't taken over.

Golfers generally consider St. Croix their preferred destination in the Virgin Islands because of its top tee-off spot, Carambola. Designed by Robert Trent Jones, Sr., this is the most challenging course in the Virgins. It plays to a length of more than 6,900 yards. Active vacationers can also go horseback riding, parasailing, sports fishing, water skiing, snorkeling, and scuba diving. St. Croix boasts tennis courts galore. The Buccaneer Hotel, for example, has the best tennis in the Virgin Islands and is the venue of several annual tournaments.

The attraction that singlehandedly merits a trip to St. Croix is Buck Island National Park. This reef is a U.S. National Monument and draws snorkelers and certified divers from around the world. Blue signs posted along the ocean floor guide you through a woodland of staghorn coral swarming with multihued fish.

The restaurants in St. Croix are not as good as those on St. Thomas, although they claim to be. The highly touted Top Hat, for example, prides itself on its Danish dishes, but you may find split-pea soup and *Frikadeller* (ping-pong-shaped meatballs with red cabbage) not exactly to your liking on a hot Caribbean night.

Nightlife in St. Croix isn't as plentiful as on St. Thomas. It is mostly confined to a number of bars in Christiansted. One highlight is jazz at the Bombay Club, where the big treat is to hear saxophonist Jimmy Hamilton.

St. Croix has only a few real luxury hotels, not as many as on St. Thomas. But there is an abundance of small and attractive inns, including Pink Fancy. You can also easily find a condo.

Life on St. Croix is more laid–back than on St. Thomas. However, St. Croix is not without its problems. There have been racial tensions, even violence, here. Use discretion and avoid the back streets of Christiansted and especially Frederiksted at night.

**ST. JOHN**    Our personal favorite of all the U.S. Virgin Islands, St. John has only two deluxe hotels but several charming inns and plenty of campgrounds. Its primary attraction is the Virgin Islands National Park. Walks in the wild, guided tours, and safari bus tours help you navigate the park.

A third of the park is underwater. The most panoramic submerged trail is at Trunk Bay, which is the island's dream beach, in spite of the pickpockets. This beach consistently has been named one of the world's ten best by *Condé Nast Traveler* and others.

The best place to play tennis is Caneel Bay, which has 11 courts, a pro shop, and a long-standing tradition of tennis-playing guests. Snorkeling and scuba diving make St. John a top active vacation destination. It's also the preferred choice for hikers because of the extensive network of trails covering the national park.

---

### Impressions

*There could never be lands any more favorable in fertility, in mildness and pleasantness of climate, in abundance of good and pure water. A very peaceful and hopeful place that should give all adventurers great satisfaction.*
          —Captain Nathaniel Butler, HM *Frigate Nicodemus,* 1637

Although St. John has some restaurants, many residents bring supplies over on the ferryboat from St. Thomas, where prices are presumably lower and the selection broader. Nightlife usually means drinking rum in a bar at Cruz Bay and maybe listening to some local entertainment. After a day outdoors, most visitors to St. John are happy to turn in early.

**TORTOLA**   With its capital at Road Town, Tortola is the hub of the BVI, but not always the best place for tourists. Virgin Gorda has better hotels. Few visitors would want to devote more than a couple of hours to Road Town, with its minor shopping, routine restaurants, and uninspired architecture. Once you leave Road Town, you'll find Tortola more alluring. The island's best (and most unspoiled) beaches, including Smuggler's Cove with its garden of snorkeling reefs, lie at the island's western tip. The island's premier beach is Cane Garden Bay, a 1$^{1}$/2-mile stretch of white sand. Because of its gentle surf, it's one of the most secure places for families to take their children.

While tourists go fishing, hiking, horseback riding, snorkeling, and surfing, what makes Tortola exceptional is boating. The island is the boating center of the British Virgins, which are considered among the best sailing territories on earth. Tortola alone has some 100 charter yachts and 300 bareboats. Its marina and shore facilities are the most up-to-date and extensive in the Caribbean Basin. It is estimated that nearly three out of four visitors to the BVI come to the island to sail.

The waters compensate for the island's lackluster nightlife and restaurants. The food is simple and straightforward. Your best bet is locally caught fish grilled with a little lime butter.

**VIRGIN GORDA**   Our favorite island in the BVI, Virgin Gorda is the third-largest member of the archipelago, with a permanent population of about 1,000 lucky souls. Many visitors come over just for the day to see The Baths, a collection of gigantic rocks, boulders, and tide pools. Shaped by volcanic pressures millions of years ago, they have been eroded over the eons into shapes reminiscent of a Henry Moore sculpture. With 20 or so beaches (the best known of which are Spring Beach and Trunk Beach), Virgin Gorda is a beach aficionado's fantasy. Most of the beaches are likely to be uncrowded. A 1,370-foot peak in the north is ideal for hiking.

Unlike Tortola, Virgin Gorda has some of the finest hotels in the Virgin Islands, including Little Dix Bay and Biras Creek, but you must be willing to pay the high tab for the privilege of staying at these regal resorts. There are more reasonable places to stay, especially Olde Yard Inn, more of an old-fashioned retreat than a fancy resort. Outside the upscale hotels, restaurants tend to be simple places such as Teacher Ilma's.

No one takes nightlife too seriously on Virgin Gorda—a lucky thing, because there isn't very much of it.

**ANEGADA**   Isolated, sparsely inhabited, and preferred by escapists and ecologists, this island was formed by coral, while the other islands of the BVI are volcanic in origin. Flat and scrub-covered, its highest point is only 28 feet above sea level, making it difficult to spot by seaborne ships during stormy weather. Some 250 people live on this islet, along with colonies of the rare rock iguana. Many ships have been wrecked on Anegada's reefs, making them attractive to divers. Most famous of the wrecks is the sunken hulk of the *Paramatta,* which has been buried underwater for more than a century.

## 2 The Virgin Islands Past & Present

### Dateline

- **1493** Columbus sails by the Virgin Islands and is attacked by Carib Indians on St. Croix.
- **1625** Dutch and English establish frontier outposts on St. Croix.
- **1650** Spanish forces from Puerto Rico overrun English garrison on St. Croix.
- **1671** Danes take over St. Thomas.
- **1672** England adds British Virgin Islands to its empire.
- **1674** Louis XIV of France makes St. Croix part of his empire.
- **1717** Danish planters from St. Thomas cultivate plantations on St. John.
- **1724** St. Thomas is declared a free port.
- **1733** Danish West India Company purchases St. Croix from France; slaves revolt on St. John.
- **1792** Denmark announces plans to abandon the slave trade.
- **1801** England occupies the Danish Virgin Islands for 10 months.
- **1807–15** England occupies Danish Virgin Islands again.
- **1834** England frees 5,133 slaves living in BVI.
- **1848** Under pressure, the governor of St. Croix grants slaves emancipation.
- **1870** U.S. Senate rejects treaty with Denmark for sale of the Virgin Islands.
- **1902** Danish Parliament rejects U.S. offer of $5 million for sale of its islands.

*continues*

## HISTORY

### EARLY HISTORY

Christopher Columbus is credited with "discovering" the Virgin Islands in 1493, but, in fact, they had already been inhabited for 3,000 years. It is believed that the original settlers were Ciboney (or Siboney) Indians who migrated from the mainland of South America.

These Indians were nomads living off the islands's fish and vegetation. The first real homesteaders of the islands were the peaceful Arawak Indians, who arrived from Venezuela, presumably in dugout canoes with sails. Stone tools and shell jewelry have been found from these early settlers.

For about 500 years, the Arawaks occupied the Virgin Islands until the arrival of the cannibalistic Carib Indians in the 15th century. The Caribs destroyed the Arawaks, either by working them to death as slaves or by eating them. With the advent of Europeans and their diseases, these peoples were completely wiped out.

### THE AGE OF COLONIZATION

On his second voyage to the New World, Columbus spotted the Virgin Islands in November of 1493. His men were thirsty, and he was short of water, so he decided to put in at what is now Salt River on St. Croix's north shore. Instead of water, his men were greeted by a rainfall of arrows. Embittered, Columbus named the area *Cabo de Flechas* or "Cape of the Arrows." He sailed on his way, heading for Puerto Rico.

As the sponsor of Columbus's voyage, Spain laid claim to the Virgin Islands. Spain had greater goals in the Greater Antilles, however, and didn't consider the Virgin Islands worthy of colonization.

In the years to come, Spain occasionally raided the islands in search of slave labor for the Dominican gold mines, eventually causing the extermination of the native population. Lured by reports of gold, pirates circulated throughout the islands for decades.

In 1625, both the English and the Dutch established opposing frontier outposts on St. Croix. Struggles between the two powers for control of the island continued for about 20 years, until the English prevailed.

The islands soon became a virtual battleground, as the struggle among European powers widened. In 1650, Spanish forces sailing from Puerto Rico overran the British garrison on St. Croix. Soon after they were raided by the Dutch, and in 1653 the island fell into the hands of the Knights of Malta, who gave St. Croix its current name. The aristocratic French cavaliers weren't well suited to the life of West Indies plantation overseers, however, and their debts mounted. By 1674 Louis XIV of France decided to occupy St. Croix and make it part of his kingdom.

The English continued to war against Dutch settlers in Tortola, which was viewed as the most important of the British Virgin Islands. It wasn't until 1672 that England added the BVI to its ever-growing empire.

A year before, in March 1671, the Danish West India Company made an attempt to settle St. Thomas. They sent two ships, but only one arrived, the *Pharaoh*. About 90 of the original crew of 239, which included some Norwegians, were still alive. Eventually more boats arrived to reinforce the colony. By 1679, at least 156 Europeans were reported living on St. Thomas, along with their slaves who worked the fields to send indigo, cotton, tobacco, and dyewood back to Denmark. In 1724, St. Thomas was declared a free port, a position it holds today.

- **1916** Denmark signs treaty with the U.S. and sells islands for $25 million.
- **1917** U.S. Virgin Islands fall under the control of the U.S. Navy for 14 years.
- **1927** U.S. grants citizenship to island residents.
- **1936** Under FDR, the first Organic Act is passed, granting voting rights.
- **1940** Population of U.S. Virgins increases for the first time since 1860.
- **1946** First black governor of the islands is appointed.
- **1954** Revised Organic Act passed; islands under jurisdiction of Department of the Interior.
- **1966** Queen Elizabeth II visits the British Virgin Islands.
- **1967** BVI gets a new constitution.
- **1970** Officials are elected rather than appointed.

Captain Kidd, Sir Francis Drake, Blackbeard, and the other legendary pirates of the West Indies continued to use St. Thomas as their base for raids in the area. The harbor at St. Thomas also became notorious for its slave market. St. Thomas was formally declared a free port in 1724, a position it holds today.

In 1717 Danish planters sailed over to St. John from St. Thomas to begin cultivation of plantations there. The St. John planters were successful, and by 1733 an estimated 100 sugar, tobacco, and cotton plantations were operating on the island. That same year the slaves rose up and rebelled against their colonial masters, taking control of the island for about six months and killing many Europeans. It took hundreds of French troops to quell the rebellion.

In the same year, France sold St. Croix to the Danish West India Company, which divided the island into plantations and continued the flourishing slave trade. Some historians report that as many as a quarter of a million slaves were sold on the auction blocks at Charlotte Amalie before being sent elsewhere, often to the Deep South of the United States. By 1792 Denmark changed its mind and announced that it officially planned to end the slave trade. It was not until 1848, however, that they did so. The British had freed their 5,133 slaves in 1834.

Denmark was thus in complete control of what is now the U.S. Virgin Islands. In 1801 Britain occupied the islands again but left 10 months later. They returned to the Danish-held islands six years later but left for good in 1815.

---

## A Famous Virgin Islander: Dr. Frasier Crane

Born in St. Thomas, Kelsey Grammer is known to TV audiences around the world for his portrayal of Dr. Frasier Crane, the egghead at the bar in the long-running TV series *Cheers.* He appeared between 1984 and 1993, before launching his own spin-off series, *Frasier.* He studied acting at New York's Julliard School, but he was eventually kicked out. He went on to play in *Macbeth* and *Othello.*

---

The great economic boom that resulted from the plantations of the Virgin Islands began to wilt by the 1820s. The introduction of sugar beet virtually bank-rupted plantation owners, as the demand for cane sugar dropped drastically.

The latter half of the 19th century was marked by one setback after another. Cholera swept through the islands. Drought and hurricanes ravaged the islands. Workers rose up in riots. Plantations were set afire in 1878, and a rebellion broke out on St. Thomas in 1892 over the rapidly deteriorating economy.

Cuba eventually took over the sugar market in the Caribbean. By 1872 the British had so little interest in the British Virgins that they placed them in the loosely conceived and administered Federation of the Leeward Islands.

### ENTER THE U.S.

In 1867, the U.S. attempted to purchase the islands from Denmark, but the treaty was rejected by the U.S. Senate in 1870. The asking price was $7.5 million.

Following its takeover of Puerto Rico in 1902, the U.S. expressed renewed interest in acquiring the Danish islands. This time the U.S. offered to pay $5 million, but the Danish parliament spurned the offer.

Upon the eve of its entry into World War I, the U.S. Navy began to fear a possible German takeover of the islands. The U.S. was concerned that, using the islands as a base, the Kaiser's navy might prey on shipping through the Panama Canal. After renewed attempts by the U.S. to purchase the islands, Denmark agreed to sell them for $25 million, a staggering sum to pay for island real estate in those days.

By 1917, the United States was in full control of the islands, and Denmark retreated from the Caribbean after a legacy of nearly two-and-a-half centuries. The U.S. Navy looked after the islands for 14 years, and in 1954 the Virgin Islands came under the sovereignty of the Department of the Interior.

A little money was diverted to the islands during the prohibition era, as some islanders made rum and shipped it illegally to the United States, often through Freeport, Bahamas. In 1927, the United States granted citizenship to the island residents. President Hoover inspected the islands in 1931, calling them "effective poorhouses."

In 1936, under FDR, the first Organic Act was passed, giving the islanders voting rights. This act was revised in 1954, granting the islanders a greater degree of self-government.

It took the jobs generated by World War II to wake the islands from their long economic slumber. In 1940, one year before the attack on Pearl Harbor, the U.S. Virgin Islands experienced their first population increase since 1860.

After World War II tourists started to appear on the islands. In the postwar economic boom that swept across America, the Virgin Islands at long last found a replacement for sugar.

The British Virgin Islands was finally freed from the Leeward Islands Federation. In 1966 Queen Elizabeth II visited this remote colonial outpost, and in 1967 the British Virgin Islands received a new constitution. Tourism was slower in coming to the BVI than to the USVI, but it is now the mainstay of the economy.

Once the Americans took over their own islands, the big neighbor in the north dominated the Virgins more than any colonial foreign force ever did. The American way of life prevails today in the U.S. Virgins, and it has swept across to the BVI.

The region's traditional recipes and remedies, as well as the self-reliant arts of fishing, boatbuilding, farming, and even hunting, are all but gone. Today when islanders need something, they have it shipped down from Miami. In clothes, in cars, in food, in entertainment, in currency, America, not Britannia, rules the seas around both groups of islands.

## POLITICS

U.S. Virgin Islanders are not allowed to vote in national elections, a source of contention among some of the local residents. Many Virgin Islanders want to become the 51st state; others want to keep the status quo.

Since the 1936 Organic Act of the Virgin Islands, passed under the Roosevelt administration, residents 21 or over were granted suffrage and could elect two municipal councils and a Legislative Assembly for the islands.

In 1946, the first black governor of the islands, William Hastie, was appointed. In 1970 U.S. Virgin Islanders were granted the right to elect their own governor and lieutenant governor instead of having these officials appointed. Dr. Melvin Evans was elected the first governor.

Today, the U.S. Virgin Islands remain an unincorporated territory administered by the U.S. Department of the Interior. It sends a nonvoting delegate to the House of Representatives. Governors serve four years in office, and Virgin Islanders also elect 15 senators to their own legislature.

---

### Don't Let the Jumbies Get Ya!

"Don't let the jumbies get ya!" is often heard in the Virgin Islands, particularly when people are leaving their hosts and heading home in the dark. Jumbies, capable of good or bad, are supernatural beings that are believed to live around households. It is said that new settlers from the mainland of the United States never see these jumbies and therefore need not fear them. But many islanders believe in their existence, and if queried, they may enthrall you with tales of sightings.

No one seems to agree on exactly what a jumbie is. It's been suggested that it is the spirit of a dead person that didn't go where it belonged. Some islanders disagree with this assessment. "They're the souls of live people," one islander told us, "but they live in the body of the dead." The most prominent jumbies are "mocko jumbies," actually carnival stilt-walkers seen at all parades.

The British Virgin Islands remain a dependent territory of Britain. Their governor is appointed in London, and he presides over an Executive Council consisting of a chief minister, an attorney general, and a trio of other ministers. The islands, in spite of their British overseer, are largely self-governing, and they have a 12-member Legislative Council.

## 3 Island Cuisine

### DINING CUSTOMS

Just as food critics were about to publish eulogies to traditional cooking in the Virgin Islands, there was a last-minute resurgence. Many of the old island dishes have come back into vogue, and every island now has little taverns—often shanties—offering regional specialties. Therefore, for a price, you can escape from the hamburgers and the hot dogs and taste some real island flavors. Under individual island chapters, we'll recommend specific restaurants offering the best in West Indian or Virgin Island cuisine.

Still, however, a visit to the Virgin Islands is hardly an indulgence in local cuisine. The islands have some of the Caribbean's best chefs, hailing from the United States and Europe, and they prepare a sumptuous cuisine of elegant French, continental, and American dishes.

When dining in the Virgins, try fish, which is often delectable, especially dolphin (not the mammal), wahoo, yellowtail, grouper, and red snapper. These types of fish accompanied by hot lime sauce are among the tastiest island dishes. Sweet-tasting Caribbean lobster (different from the Maine variety) is likely to be the most expensive item on the menu, but in the view of many diners—especially those from Maine—it isn't worth the price. Chefs have a tendency to overcook it.

Elaborate buffets are often a feature in the major resort hotels on all the islands. Usually these buffets feature a variety of West–Indian dishes along with more standard fare, and they are almost always reasonable in price. Entertainment is most often from a West–Indian fungi band. Even if you are not staying at a particular hotel, you can partake of the buffet if you make a reservation.

Before checking into a hotel, it's a good idea to have a clear understanding of just what is included in the various plans offered. See "Tips on Accommodations" in Chapter 3.

### THE CUISINE

**APPETIZERS** The most famous soup of the islands is *kallaloo,* or callaloo, made in an infinite number of ways from a leafy green vegetable similar to spinach. This soup is flavored with salt beef, pig mouth, pig tail, hot peppers, ham bone, fresh fish, crabs, or perhaps corned conch, along with okra, onions, and spices.

Many soups are sweetened with sugar, and soups commonly contain fruit. The classic red bean soup, made with pork or ham, various spices, and tomatoes, is sugared to taste. *Tannia* soup is made from the root of the so-called "Purple Elephant Ear." Salt-fat meat and ham, along with tomatoes, onions, and spices, are added to the tannias.

*Souse* is an old-time favorite made with the feet, head, and tongue of the pig, and flavored with a lime-based sauce and various spices.

*Salt-fish salad* is traditionally served on Holy Thursday or Good Friday. It's made with boneless salt fish, potatoes, onions, boiled eggs, and an oil and vinegar dressing.

*Herring gundy* is an old-time island favorite made with salt herring, potatoes, onions, green sweet and hot peppers, olives, diced beets, raw carrots, herbs, and boiled eggs.

**SIDE DISHES**   Rice—seasoned, not plain—is popular with Virgin Islanders, who often serve several starches at one meal. Most often rice is flavored with ham or salt pork, tomatoes, garlic, onion, and shortening.

*Fungi* is a simple cornmeal dumpling that can be made more interesting with the addition of various ingredients, such as okra. Sweet fungi is served as a dessert, with sugar, milk, cinnamon, and raisins.

Okra (often spelled *ochroe* in the islands) is a mainstay vegetable, usually accompanying beef, fish, or chicken. It's fried in an iron skillet after being flavored with hot pepper, tomatoes, onions, garlic, and bacon fat or butter. *Accra,* another popular dish, is made with okra, black-eyed peas, salt, and pepper. It's dropped into boiling fat and fried until golden brown.

The classic vegetable dish—some families serve it every night—is peas and rice, made with pigeon peas flavored with ham or salt meat, onion, tomatoes, herbs, and sometimes slices of pumpkin. Pigeon peas, one of the most common vegetables in the islands because they flourish in hot, dry climates, are sometimes called congo peas or *gunga.*

**FISH & MEAT**   Locals gave colorful names to the various fish brought home for dinner, everything from "ole wife" to "doctors." "Porgies and grunts," along with yellowtail, kingfish, and *bonito,* show up on many tables. Fish is usually boiled in a lime-flavored brew seasoned with hot peppers and herbs and is commonly served with a creole sauce of peppers, tomatoes, and onions, among other ingredients. Salt fish and rice is another low-cost dish, the fish flavored with onion, tomatoes, shortening, garlic, and green pepper.

Conch creole is a tasty brew, seasoned with onions, garlic, spices, hot peppers, and salt pork. Most beef is shipped in from the mainland or from Puerto Rico. A local favorite main dish is chicken and rice, made with Spanish peppers. Curried goat, the longtime "classic" West–Indian dinner, is made with herbs, including *cardamom pods* and onions.

The famous johnnycakes that accompany many of these fish and meat dishes are made with flour, baking powder, shortening, and salt, then fried in deep hot fat or baked. Indians may have made johnnycakes with ground corn baked on hot coals.

**DESSERTS**   Sweet-potato pone is a classic, made with sugar, eggs, butter, milk, salt, cinnamon, raisins, and chopped raw almonds. The exotic fruits of the islands lend themselves to various homemade ice creams, including mango. Islanders in the old days invented many new dishes using local ingredients, such as orange-rose sherbet made with fragrant rose petal mortar pounded into a paste and flavored with sugar and orange juice. Guava ice cream is a delectable concoction, as are *soursop,* banana, and papaya. Sometimes dumplings, made with guava, peach, plum, gooseberry, cherry, and apple, are served for dessert.

# DRINK

Water is generally safe to drink on the islands. Much of the water is stored in cisterns and filtered before it's served. Delicate stomachs, however, should stick to mineral water or club soda. All the American brands of soft drinks and beer are sold in both the USVI and the BVI. Wines have to be brought in from either Europe or the United States. Most often they are quite expensive.

The *vin du pays* of the islands is Cruzan rum made with sugarcane. To help stimulate the local economy, U.S. customs allows you to bring home an extra bottle of Cruzan rum, over your usual 5-liter liquor allowance.

Long before the arrival of Coca-Cola and Pepsi, many islanders made their own drinks with whatever was available, mostly from locally grown fruits. From the guavaberry comes a liqueur rum, which is an unusual mixture whose ingredients include sorrel, fruit, ginger, prunes, raisins, cinnamon, and rum.

# 3

# Planning a Trip to the Virgin Islands

## VISITOR INFORMATION

**IN THE U.S.** Before you go to the U.S. Virgin Islands, contact the **U.S. Virgin Islands Division of Tourism,** 1270 Ave. of the Americas, New York, NY 10020 (☎ **212/332-2222**; fax 212/332-2223).

There are additional offices at the following locations: 225 Peachtree St. NE, Suite 760, Atlanta, GA 30303 (☎ **404/688-0906;** fax 404/525-1102); 500 North Michigan Ave., Suite 2030, Chicago, IL 60611 (☎ **312/670-8784;** fax 312/670-8788); 900 17th St. NW, Suite 500, Washington, DC 20006 (☎ **202/293-3707**); 2655 Le Jeune Rd. Suite 907, Coral Gables, FL 33134 (☎ **305/442-7200;** fax 305/445-9044); and 3460 Wilshire Blvd., Los Angeles, CA 90010 (☎ **213/739-0138;** fax 213/739-2005).

For data on the British Virgin Islands, get in touch with the **British Virgin Islands Tourist Board,** 370 Lexington Ave., Suite 416, New York, NY 10017 (☎ **212/696-0400,** or **800/835-8530;** fax 212/949-8254). On the West Coast, contact the **BVI Information Office,** 1686 Union St., San Francisco, CA 94123 (☎ **415/775-0344,** or **800/232-7770;** fax 415/775-2554).

You may also want to contact the State Department for background bulletins. Write to Superintendent of Documents, **U.S. Government Printing Office,** Washington, DC 20402 (☎ **202/783-3238;** fax 202/512-2250).

A good travel agent can also be a source of information. If you use one, make sure the agent is a member of the American Society of Travel Agents (ASTA). If you get poor service from an agent, you can write to **ASTA Consumer Affairs,** 1101 King St., Alexandria, VA 22314 (☎ **703/739-2851;** fax 703/684-8319).

**IN THE U.K.** Tourist information for the British Virgin Islands is available at the **BVI Information Office,** 110 St. Martin's Lane, London, England WC2N 4DY (☎ **0171/240-4259;** fax 0171/240-4270). For the U.S. Virgin Islands, information is available at

2 Cinnamon Row, Plantation Wharf, York Place, London, England SW11 3TW
(☎ **0171/978-5262;** fax 0171/924-3171).

## ENTRY REQUIREMENTS

**DOCUMENTS**    U.S. and Canadian citizens are required to present some proof
of citizenship to enter the Virgin Islands. U.S. and Canadians should have either
a voter registration card or a birth certificate to visit either the American or British chain of islands. A passport is not necessary, but carrying one is a good idea.

If you carry a passport, you can take an excursion to the nearby islands, which,
except for Puerto Rico, are foreign destinations. Entry into one of these little
island countries is always easier with a passport, even though some of them don't
absolutely require it if your other documentation is acceptable.

Visitors from Europe and other parts of the world do need a passport and a U.S.
visa to enter the U.S. Virgin Islands. Visitors who stay less than six months in the
BVI need only a passport and a return or onward ticket.

**DOCUMENT PROTECTION**    It is a good policy before leaving your country to make two copies of your most valuable documents, including your passport.
Make a photocopy of the inside page of your passport, the one with your photograph. In case you lose your passport abroad, you should also make copies of your
driver's license, a voter registration card (if you're using that instead of a license),
an airline ticket, strategic hotel vouchers, and any other sort of identity card that
might be pertinent. You should also make copies of any prescriptions you take.
Place one copy in your luggage, and carry the original with you. Leave the other
copy at home.

## CUSTOMS

American citizens clear Customs when they are leaving the U.S. Virgin Islands.
The islands are duty-free ports, and U.S. citizens are allowed to bring back $1,200
worth of merchandise duty free. Americans on a direct flight from the U.S. Virgins do not have to clear Customs when they arrive in the United States. Canadians, Australians, British, and others enter the U.S. Virgin Islands as they do the
mainland.

In the British Virgin Islands, there is a Customs review upon entry. Usually
items intended for personal use are allowed in. *No illegal drugs allowed.*

### BRINGING IT ALL HOME

**U.S. Customs**    The government generously allows $1,200 worth of duty-free
imports every 30 days, twice the amount allowed for most Caribbean Basin countries, including the British Virgin Islands, and exactly three times the $400 exemp-
tion U.S. visitors are allowed returning from most foreign countries and French
islands such as Guadeloupe or Martinique. Purchases made in the U.S. Virgin
Islands over the duty-free exemption are taxed at a flat rate of 5% (10% in the
British Virgin Islands).

Joint declarations are possible for members of a family traveling together. For
a husband and wife with two children, the exemption in the U.S. Virgins is $4,800!

Unsolicited gifts can be sent to friends and relatives at the rate of $100 a day,
and they do not have to be declared as part of your $1,200 per person exemption.
Gifts mailed from the BVI cannot exceed $50 per day.

The government allows you to bring back 5 liters of liquor duty free and an extra liter of rum if one of the bottles is produced in the Virgin Islands, including Cruzan rum. U.S. Customs exempts items made on the island, including perfume, straw hats, jewelry, and fashion. But if the value exceeds $25, you must produce a certificate of origin. Original paintings are also duty free.

Collect receipts for all purchases made abroad. If a merchant suggests giving you a false receipt, understating the value of the goods, beware: the merchant might be an informer to U.S. Customs. You must also declare all gifts received during your stay abroad.

If you purchased such an item during an earlier trip abroad, carry proof that you have already paid Customs duty on the item at the time of your previous reentry. To be extra careful, compile a list of expensive carry-on items, and ask a U.S. Customs agent to stamp your list at the airport before your departure.

If you're concerned and need more specific guidance, write to the **U.S. Customs Service,** 1301 Constitution Ave., P.O. Box 7407, Washington, DC 20044, requesting the free pamphlet, *Know Before You Go.* For information on U.S. Virgin Islands requirements, call **809/774-4554** in St. Thomas.

**Canadian Customs**   For more information, write for the booklet *I Declare,* issued by **Revenue Canada,** 875 Heron Rd., Ottawa, Canada ON K1A OL5. Canada allows its citizens a $300 exemption, and they are allowed to bring back the following items duty free: 200 cigarettes; 2.20 pounds of tobacco; 40 imperial ounces of liquor; and 50 cigars. In addition, they are allowed to mail gifts to Canada from abroad at the rate of $60 (CDN) a day, provided they are unsolicited and aren't alcohol or tobacco. On the package, mark "Unsolicited gift, under $60 value." All valuables should be declared on the Y-38 Form before departure from Canada; be sure to include serial numbers for items such as expensive foreign cameras that you already own. **Note:** The $300 exemption can be used only once a year and only after an absence of seven days.

**British Customs**   Citizens can bring in goods up to £136, and one must be 17 or older to import liquor or tobacco. Brits are allowed 200 cigarettes or 100 cigarillos, or 50 cigars, or 250 grams of tobacco. In addition, 2 liters of table wine may be brought in, as well as 1 liter of alcohol greater than 22% by volume or 2 liters of alcohol equal to or less than 22% by volume. British Customs tend to be strict and complicated in its requirements. For details get in touch with **Her Majesty's Customs and Excise Office,** New King's Beam House, 22 Upper Ground, London SE1 9PJ (☎ **0171/382-5468** for more information).

**Irish Customs**   Irish citizens may bring in 200 cigarettes or 100 cigarillos or 50 cigars or 250 grams (approximately 9 ounces) of tobacco, plus 1 liter of liquor exceeding 22% volume (such as whisky, brandy, gin, rum or vodka), or 2 liters of distilled beverages and spirits with a wine or alcoholic base of an alcoholic strength not exceeding 22% volume, plus 2 liters of other wine and 50 grams of perfume. Other allowances include duty-free goods to a value of IR £34 per person or IR £17 per person for travelers under 15 years of age.

# MONEY
## CASH & CURRENCY
Both the U.S. Virgin Islands and the British Virgin Islands use the U.S. dollar as their form of currency.

## A Note on Currency for British Travelers

British visitors will need to convert their pounds into U.S. dollars when visiting not only the U.S. Virgin Islands, but also the British Virgin Islands (unless a special dispensation is granted in the latter). Here's how pounds break down into U.S. dollars at press time (the rates are subject to market changes, of course).

**Australian Customs**   The duty-free allowance in Australia is $400 (AUS) or, for those under 18, $200 (AUS). Personal property mailed back from U.S. or British Virgins should be marked "Australian goods returned," to avoid payment of duty, providing it is what it says on the package. Upon returning to Australia, citizens can bring in 200 cigarettes or 250 grams of tobacco and 1 liter of alcohol. If you're returning with valuable goods you already own, such as expensive foreign-made cameras, you should file form B263. A helpful brochure, available from Australian consulates or Customs offices, is called *Customs Information for Travellers*.

**New Zealand Customs**   The duty-free allowance is $700 (NZ). Citizens over 17 years of age can bring in 200 cigarettes or 50 cigars or 250 grams of tobacco (or a mixture of all three if their combined weight doesn't exceed 250 grams), plus 4.5 liters of wine or beer or 1.125 liters of liquor. New Zealand currency does not carry import or export restrictions. A Certificate of Export listing valuables taken out of the country (that is, items you already owned) allows you to bring them back in without paying duty. Most questions are answered in a free pamphlet available at New Zealand consulates and Customs offices called *New Zealand Custom Guide for Travellers*.

## TRAVELER'S CHECKS

Traveler's checks are the safest way to carry cash while traveling. Most banks will give you a better rate on traveler's checks than for cash. The list of suppliers of these

## The U.S. Dollar & The British Pound

| US$ | UK£ | US$ | UK£ |
|-----|-----|-----|-----|
| 1 | .63 | 75 | 47.25 |
| 2 | 1.26 | 100 | 63.00 |
| 3 | 1.89 | 125 | 78.75 |
| 4 | 2.52 | 150 | 94.50 |
| 5 | 3.15 | 175 | 110.25 |
| 6 | 3.78 | 200 | 126.00 |
| 7 | 4.41 | 225 | 141.75 |
| 8 | 5.04 | 250 | 157.50 |
| 9 | 5.67 | 300 | 189.00 |
| 10 | 6.30 | 350 | 220.50 |
| 15 | 9.45 | 400 | 252.00 |
| 25 | 15.75 | 450 | 283.50 |
| 50 | 31.50 | 500 | 315.00 |

checks has grown somewhat shorter in recent years because of the mergers of traveler's check facilities at several major banks. Checks denominated in U.S. dollars are accepted virtually anywhere, but in some cases (perhaps for ease of conversion into local currencies), travelers might want checks denominated in other currencies.

Each of the agencies listed below will refund your checks if they are lost or stolen, provided you produce sufficient documentation. When purchasing your checks, ask about refund hotlines: American Express probably has the greatest number of offices around the world.

**American Express** (☎ **800/221-7282** in the U.S. and Canada) is one of the largest and most immediately recognized issuers of traveler's checks. No commission is charged to members of the American Automobile Association (AAA), and to holders of certain types of American Express credit cards. American Express offices charge from 1% to 5% per $100. The company issues checks denominated in U.S. dollars, Canadian dollars, British pounds sterling, Swiss francs, French francs, German marks, Japanese yen, and in Dutch guilders. The vast majority of checks sold in North America are denominated in U.S. dollars. For questions or problems which arise outside the U.S. or Canada, contact any of the company's many regional representatives.

**Citicorp** (☎ **800/645-6556** in the U.S. and Canada, or **813/623-1709** collect from other parts of the world) issues checks in U.S. dollars, British pounds sterling, German marks, Japanese yen, and Australian dollars.

**Thomas Cook** (☎ **800/223-7373** in the U.S. and Canada, or **609/987-7300** collect from other parts of the world) issues MasterCard traveler's checks denominated in U.S. dollars, Canadian dollars, French francs, British pounds sterling, German marks, Dutch guilders, Spanish pesetas, Australian dollars, and Japanese yen. Depending on individual banking laws in each of the various states, some of the above currencies might not be available at every outlet.

**Interpayment Services** (☎ **800/221-2426** in the U.S. and Canada, or **212/858-8500** collect from other parts of the world) sells VISA checks which are issued by a consortium of member banks and the Thomas Cook organization. Traveler's checks are denominated in U.S. or Canadian dollars, British pounds sterling, and German marks.

## CREDIT CARDS

Credit cards are widely accepted in both the USVI and the BVI. VISA and MasterCard are the major cards used, although American Express and, to a lesser extent, Diners Club are also popular. Credit cards can aid greatly when you travel in the Virgin Islands, sparing your valuable cash and giving you financial flexibility for large purchases or last-minute travel changes. Because the U.S. Virgin Islands are a shopping destination, being able to make purchases by credit card becomes even more important.

## AUTOMATED-TELLER MACHINES (ATMS)

You'll find automated-teller machines (ATMs) in St. Thomas, St. Croix, and Tortola. In St. Thomas, ATM outlets are at the major shopping malls, at all banks, and at the Pueblo Supermarket. These machines accept American Express, MasterCard, and Visa cards affiliated with one of the following networks: HONOR, CIRRUS, NICE, and PLUS. In St. Croix, options are more limited, with ATMs located at K-Mart, the two Pueblo Supermarkets, and all banks. The machines here accept MasterCard and Visa affiliated with the following networks: CIRRUS, NICE, and PLUS. On Tortola, there are only two ATMs, one at the Chase Manhattan Bank and the other at the Banco Popular. Machines accept MasterCard and Visa affiliated with CIRRUS, NICE, and PLUS.

## WHAT WILL IT COST?

You can live on $50 or $1,000 a day in the Virgin Islands, depending on your budget and taste. This book documents a wide range of living and eating styles to suit all but the most rock-bottom of budgets. Most of the recommendations listed are moderately priced. In the Virgin Islands, very expensive hotels in winter can command from $300 per double room (no meals); expensive places charge from $200 to $300 per double; moderately priced establishments get from $100 to $200 per double; and inexpensive hotels charge under $100 a night for a double. To these rates, a 10% hotel tax and a 10% service charge are added. Meals are extra. Hotels that offer MAP (a breakfast and dinner plan; see "Island Cuisine in Chapter 2) add a surcharge of $30 to $55 per day to your tab. Of course, this is only a general rule of thumb for the archipelago as a whole. Each island has different rate structures. The good news is that from mid-April to mid-December hotel prices are slashed 25% to 50%.

An expensive dinner in the islands costs from $50 for one, including tip, but not wine; moderate restaurants charge from $25 to $35 for dinner; and inexpensive places ask under $25 for dinner.

| What Things Cost in St. Thomas | U.S.$ |
| --- | --- |
| Taxi from airport to an East End hotel | 9.00 |
| Local bus from Charlotte Amalie to Red Hook ferry | 3.00 |
| Local telephone call | .25 |
| Double at Marriott's Frenchman's Reef (deluxe) | 260.00 |
| Double at Blackbeard's Castle (moderate) | 140.00 |
| Double at Bunkers' Hill Hotel (budget) | 80.00 |
| Lunch for one at Bravo Café (moderate)* | 18.00 |
| Lunch for one at Eunice's (budget)* | 8.00 |
| Dinner for one at Hotel 1829 (deluxe)* | 50.00 |
| Dinner for one at Alexander's (moderate)* | 35.00 |
| Dinner for one at East Coast (budget)* | 15.00 |
| Pint of beer in a bar | 3.50 |
| Coca-Cola in a café | 1.25 |
| Cup of coffee in a café | 1.00 |
| Glass of wine in a restaurant | 3.75 |
| Roll of ASA 100 color film, 36 exposures | 10.00 |
| Admission to Magens Bay Beach | 1.00 |
| Movie ticket | 5.00 |
| *Includes tax and tip but not wine | |

There are fewer than 100 guesthouses and hotels in the British Virgin Islands and some of the smaller islands have only one hotel. Price differences among these establishments are enormous. The BVI has several posh pockets that command and easily get the highest prices in the Virgin Island chain in the winter months, when guests are often asked to take half or full board when making reservations.

## 2 When to Go

With each passing year, the Virgin Islands become more of a vacation spot for all seasons. Although they receive more rain in the late spring and summer, the islands have so little variation in temperature that you can enjoy a visit there at any time. Most accommodations have air conditioning and ceiling fans. Sunshine is practically an everyday affair, even between the rain showers.

**High season** in the Virgin Islands, when hotels charge their highest prices, runs roughly from mid-December to mid-April. Winter is generally the dry season in the islands, but there can be heavy rainfall at any time of year.

During the winter months, make reservations as far in advance as possible, and, if you rely on the mail, take into account that it sometimes takes a long time. Instead of writing to reserve your own room, make reservations through the Stateside representatives all major and many minor hotels use, or else deal directly with a travel agent. If you choose to contact hotels directly, you should telephone the hotel of your choice, agree on terms, and rush a deposit to hold the room. A few of the big hotels have toll-free numbers. More and more travelers, of course, are handling reservations by direct faxes to the hotel.

The Virgin Islands' **off-season** is when North America warms up and most vacationers head for Cape Cod or the Jersey shore, thinking, perhaps, that the Virgin Islands are a caldron at this time. This is not the case. The fabled weather is balmy all year, with temperatures varying little more than 5° between winter and summer. Air conditioned by the trade winds, the temperature varies between 75° and 85°F all year.

Dollar for dollar, you'll save more money by renting a house or self-sufficient unit in the Virgin Islands than you will on Cape Cod, Fire Island, Laguna Beach, or the coast of Maine.

The off-season in the Virgin Islands—roughly from mid-April to mid-December—amounts to an 8-month long summer sale. In most cases, hotel rates are slashed a startling 20% to 50%. It's a bonanza for cost-conscious travelers, especially families.

There are other reasons besides slashed prices to visit the Virgin Islands off-season. In spring, summer, and autumn a less hurried way of life prevails, and you will have a better chance to appreciate the food, culture, and local customs. And finally, everything is less crowded off-season—swimming pools, beaches, resorts, restaurants, golf courses, tennis courts, and stores.

## CLIMATE

All the islands in both BVI and USVI enjoy balmy climates all year. Temperatures go up in the 80°s during the day and drop more comfortably into the 70°s at night. Don't worry about too much rain—most of the islands rarely get enough. Sometimes a tropical shower comes and goes so quickly you don't have time to get off the beach.

## Average Temperatures and Rainfall in the U.S. Virgin Islands

|            |          | Jan  | Feb  | Mar  | Apr  | May  | June | July | Aug  | Sept | Oct  | Nov  | Dec  |
|------------|----------|------|------|------|------|------|------|------|------|------|------|------|------|
| St. Croix  | Temp. °F | 75.9 | 75.8 | 77.5 | 78.7 | 79.3 | 81.9 | 83   | 83.3 | 82.6 | 82   | 79.8 | 78.3 |
|            | Precip. "| 2.72 | .46  | 1.44 | 4.25 | 7.19 | 2.35 | 1.20 | 4.07 | 2.11 | 3.08 | 7.64 | 2.77 |
| St. John   | Temp. °F | 75.4 | 75.1 | 77.3 | 78.1 | 77.8 | 79.7 | 80.3 | 82.6 | 81.7 | 80.4 | 78.3 | 76.4 |
|            | Precip. "| 2.08 | 1.03 | .81  | 8.02 | 10.6 | 1.92 | 2.55 | 4.61 | 1.86 | 4.02 | 8.42 | 3.44 |
| St. Thomas | Temp. °F | 76.8 | 76.7 | 77.3 | 79   | 78.5 | 81.6 | 82.2 | 82.6 | 81.7 | 82.6 | 80.5 | 76.9 |
|            | Precip. "| 1.86 | .95  | .97  | 8.32 | 9.25 | 1.62 | 2.25 | 3.6  | 2.04 | 4.43 | 7.77 | 2.46 |

You can obtain current weather information on many destinations, including the Virgin Islands, by calling **Weather Trak** (☎ 900/370-8725). A taped message gives you a three-digit access code to call for the place you're interested in—in this case, the 809 area code. The cost is 75¢ for the first minute and 50¢ for each additional minute.

### THE HURRICANE SEASON

The curse of Caribbean weather, the hurricane season, officially lasts June through November. But there is no cause for panic. More tropical cyclones pound the U.S. mainland than hurricanes devastate the Virgin Islands. Hurricane Hugo in 1989 was exceptional, causing the most widespread damage in years, especially on St. Croix.

Islanders hardly stand around waiting for a hurricane to strike. Satellite forecasts in general give adequate warning so that precautions can be taken in time. And of course, there is always prayer: Islanders have a legal holiday in the third week of July called Supplication Day, when prayers are said so that the Virgin Islands may be spared another hurricane. In late October, at the end of the season of danger, a supplemental Thanksgiving Day is celebrated.

If you're heading for the Virgin Islands during hurricane season, call the nearest branch of the National Weather Service. In your phone directory, look under the U.S. Department of Commerce. Radio and TV weather reports keep you posted from the National Hurricane Center in Coral Gables, Florida.

## HOLIDAYS

In addition to the standard legal holidays observed in the United States, the U.S. Virgin Islanders also observe the following: January 6 (Three Kings' Day); March 31 (Transfer Day, commemorating the transfer of the Danish Virgin Islands to the Americans); June 20 (Organic Act Day—in lieu of a constitution, the USVI have an Organic Act); July 3 (Emancipation Day, commemorating the freeing of the slaves by the Danes in 1848); July 25 (Hurricane Supplication Day); October 17 (Hurricane Thanksgiving Day); November 1 (Liberty Day); and December 26 (Christmas Second Day). The islands also celebrate two carnival days on the last Friday and Saturday in April: Children's Carnival Parade and Grand Carnival (adults') Parade.

In the British Virgin Islands, public holidays include the following: New Year's Day; March 12 (Commonwealth Day); Good Friday; Easter Monday; Whitmonday (sometime in July); July 1 (Territory Day Sunday; date can vary); Festival Monday and Tuesday (sometime during the first week of August); October 21 (St. Ursula's Day); November 14 (Birthday of the Heir to the Throne); Christmas Day; and December 26 (Boxing Day).

# U.S. VIRGIN ISLANDS CALENDAR OF EVENTS

## April

✪ **St. Thomas Carnival**    The most spectacular carnival in all the Virgin Islands, this annual celebration has roots in Africa. Over the years, the festivities have become Christianized, but the fun and gaiety remain. Mocko Jumbies, people dressed as spirits, parade through the streets on stilts nearly 20 feet high. Steel and fungi bands, "jump-ups," and parades mark the event.

**Where:** Islandwide but best on the streets of Charlotte Amalie. **When:** After Easter, sometime in April. **How:** Obtain a schedule of events from the tourist office in St. Thomas.

## July

• **Carnival of St. John.** Parades, bands, and colorful costumes lead up to the selection of Ms. St. John and King of Carnival. First week of July.

## August

• **Virgin Islands Open Atlantic Blue Marlin Tournament.** Sports fishermen from all over the world, some from as far as Australia, flock to this annual competition. Several marlin catches have set world records. Weekend closest to the full moon.

## December

✪ **Christmas in St. Croix**    This is a major event on the calendar, as it launches the beginning of a 12-day celebration and festival that includes Christmas, the legal holiday on December 26, New Year's Eve—called "Old Year's Day"—and New Year's Day. It ends January 6 at the observation of the Feast of the Three Kings, sometimes called Little Christmas, with a parade of flamboyantly attired merrymakers.

**Where:** Christiansted and other venues. **When:** December 25 to January 6.

# BRITISH VIRGIN ISLANDS CALENDAR OF EVENTS

## April

✪ **BVI Spring Regatta**    When the islands are at their best in spring, they host this regatta, the second leg of the Caribbean Ocean Racing Triangles events. A range of talents, from the most dedicated racers to bareboat crews out for "rum and reggae" join in the three-day race. For the Caribbean boat crowd, it's a major event.

**Where:** Tortola. **When:** Mid-April. **How:** For more information, write BVI Spring Regatta Committee. P.O. Box 200, Road Town, Tortola, BVI (☎ **809/494-3286**).

## August

✪ **BVI Summer Festival**    Many visitors from the other islands flock to the BVI at carnival time. Dancing to fungi and reggae bands, a Unity Day Parade, and general festivities sweep up the locals in their three-day big blast of the year.

**Where:** Mainly the fairgrounds in Road Town. **When:** First week in August. **How:** Just join the fun at the fairgrounds, with nightly rides, games, and dancing.

## 3 The Active Vacation Planner

The Virgin Islands vacationer does not need to be pegged to the pool and bar. While you will have endless opportunities to sit mindlessly by the crashing surf, use this section to plan activities that will help you actively enjoy the islands.

### SPORTS A TO Z

The Virgin Islands are increasingly accommodating to sports-minded tourists. While the Virgins' coral reefs and stunning beaches provide a scenic backdrop for a variety of watersports, landlubbers can also be active. Golfers, tennis players, and horseback riders need not forgo their respective sports while vacationing in the Virgin Islands. Of course, if you do tire of the active life, the beach is never far away. The section below presents an overview of the opportunities to get involved in different sports; see the sports sections of individual chapters for more specific information.

**CAMPING**   The best campsites are on St. John. The campgrounds at **Maho Bay** and **Cinnamon Bay** are considered the finest in the entire Caribbean.

In the BVI, the best campsite is **Brewers Bay Campground** on Tortola, which rents tents and basic equipment and is open year-round.

**GOLF**   The major golf course in the Virgin Islands is the 18-hole **Carambola Golf Course** (☎ 778-0747), designed by Robert Trent Jones, Sr. It took a beating from the 1989 Hurricane Hugo that devastated St. Croix, but it has been restored. Originally called Fountain Valley, this golf course is open to the general public.

On St. Thomas, the 18-hole **Mahogany Run** (☎ 775-5000), lies on the north shore, and is known for its scenery. This 6,350-yard, par-70 course was designed by Tom and George Fazio, and its special hazard is the "Devil's Triangle," the 13th, 14th, and 15th holes that border a cliffside.

**HORSEBACK RIDING**   If you want to include this sport in your Virgin Islands holiday, visit St. Croix. There, Jill's Equestrian Stables at Sprat Hall Plantation (see "Sports A to Z" in Chapter 6) is the premier equestrian stable not only in the Virgin Islands, but also in the Caribbean. The stables are known throughout the islands for the quality of the horses and the trail rides through forests. Both neophytes and experienced riders can participate.

**SAILING & YACHTING**   The Virgin Islands are a yachting paradise, offering smooth sailing through turquoise waters. There are seemingly endless coves and inlets, along with protected harbors, for anchoring for the day.

If you're qualified, it's possible to sail your own craft. If you're well heeled, or you join with a number of others to form a party, you can charter a vessel with a full crew. Most visitors are content to go on day sails, which are easy to organize, especially in St. Thomas. See individual chapters for more information. In St. Croix, the most popular day sail is to the natural paradise of Buck Island.

The most popular cruising area in the Virgin Islands, both U.S. and British, is quite small, encompassing the 45 miles or so between St. Thomas and North Sound (Virgin Gorda). Although the appeal of St. Croix is great, the island lies relatively far from the more interesting sailing within the deep and scenic Sir Francis Drake Channel. Named after the 16th-century English explorer and rake, it's surrounded by mountainous islands on all sides, with crisp sailing breezes year-round. In heavy weather, the surrounding network of islands shelters yachties from the force of the open sea, and the views are incomparably beautiful.

Waters in the Sir Francis Drake Channel are usually very deep and are therefore likely to be used by large cruise ships. Outside the Channel, however, the archipelago contains reefy areas which separate many of the islands from their neighbors. To navigate such areas, you need to use a depth chart and have some nautical knowledge of the area. (Free advice, often more than you'll be able to assimilate easily over one drink, is usually willingly offered at any of the Virgin Island marinas. Navigation, however, is relatively easy once you're armed with the proper depth charts and a bit of experience.)

Except for Anegada, which is a low-lying atoll of coral limestone and sandstone set off to the archipelago's northeast, all the Virgin Islands are high and easily spotted. The clearness of the water is another advantage for sailors. Specific distances between each of the islands of the chain can be misleading because of the circuitous route you might need to follow to navigate from one point to another, but the shortest distance between St. Thomas and St. Croix is 35 nautical miles; from St. John to St. Croix, 35 nautical miles; from St. Thomas to St. John, 2 miles; from Tortola to St. Thomas, 10 nautical miles; from Virgin Gorda to Anegada, 13 nautical miles, and from St. John to Anegada, 30 miles. It's a relatively long run of 45 nautical miles between Virgin Gorda and St. Croix.

If you don't know how to sail but would like to learn, that too is possible. Sailing schools exist on St. Croix. Service is provided by **Annapolis Sailing School,** 1215 King Cross St., Christiansted, St. Croix, USVI 00820 (☎ **809/773-4709,** or **800/638-9192**). Using three 24-foot day sailers, they charge $195 for a two-day lesson, per person, and $310 for a three-day lesson. However, if you take lessons with someone else, the extra person is charged only $180 for the two-day lesson or $250 for the three-day lesson. No class or sailing excursion has more than four students.

A nonprofit organization, **Virgin Island Charter Yacht League,** Flagship, 5100 Long Bay Rd., St. Thomas, USVI 00802 (☎ **809/774-3944,** or **800/524-2061**), provides prospective yachters with information on how to set sail.

The possibilities for yachting on Tortola in the USVI are endless. The major center for this activity is **The Moorings,** Road Harbour, Wickhams Cay

## A Program for Women Sailors

A program for women of all ages and levels of nautical expertise is offered by **Womanship, Inc.,** The Boat House, 410 Severn Ave., Annapolis, MD 21403 (☎ **410/267-6661,** or **800/342-9295** in the U.S.). Established in 1984 as the first organization of its kind, Womanship offers expert sailing instruction by women for all-women groups, up to a maximum of six "students" with two instructors. Participants sleep aboard the sailing vessel in accommodations containing 8 to 10 berths. Tortola is the primary port of departure for the Caribbean division of this company, and sailing instruction is taught in the many cays and estuaries, as well as the open waters, of the British Virgin Islands. Most courses last a full week. At the end of the course, participants are presented with "Cruising Certificates" that can be used as evidence of expertise for future bareboat charters. A week-long program costs $1,350 from December through April; off-season, the cost is $1,196.

(☎ **809/494-2332**) in Tortola. This 100-slip marina has complete facilities and yachting services and also arranges rentals.

The BVI is also the headquarters of the **Offshore Sailing School,** Treasure Isle Jetty, Road Town (☎ **809/494-2501**). The school offers sailing instruction year-round. For information before you go, write Offshore Sailing School, 16731 McGregor Blvd., Ft. Myers, FL 33908 (☎ **813/454-1700,** or **800/221-4326** in the U.S.).

*The Yachtsman's Guide to the Virgin Islands,* for more than a quarter of a century the classic cruising guide to this area, is annually updated. The detailed 240-page text is supplemented by 22 sketch charts, more than a hundred photographs and illustrations, and numerous landfall sketches showing harbors, channels, landmarks, and such. Subjects covered include piloting, anchoring, communication, weather, fishing, and more. Copies of the guide are available at major marine outlets, bookstores, and direct from Tropic Isle Publishers, Inc., P.O. Box 610938, North Miami, FL 33261-0938 (☎ **305/893-4277**), for $15.95 postpaid.

**SEA KAYAKING/ISLAND CAMPING TOURS** **Arawak Expeditions,** Cruz Bay, St. John (☎ **809/693-8312,** or **800/238-8687** in the U.S.), is the only outfitter in the Virgin Islands offering multiple day sea-kayaking/island-camping excursions. Full-day and half-day trips are also available. You cruise through the islands much like the Arawaks did—except that they used dugout canoes. Today's vessels are two-person fiberglass kayaks, complete with foot-controlled rudders. The outfit provides all the kayaking gear, healthful meals, camping equipment, and two experienced guides. The cost of a full-day trip is $55, while a half-day excursion is $30; multiple day excursions range in price from $750 to $1,195.

**SNORKELING & SCUBA DIVING** The warm waters of St. Croix are perfect for these sports. The most popular site is the underwater trails off Buck Island, reachable by day sails from the harbor in Christiansted. St. Croix is also known for its "dropoffs," including the famous Puerto Rico Trench. At 12,000 feet, the trench is the fifth-deepest body of water on earth. You can easily arrange scuba instruction, day and night dives, and equipment rental.

On St. Thomas, all major hotels rent fins and masks for snorkelers, and all the day-sail charters feature this type of equipment on board. Many firms on St. Thomas, such as the St. Thomas Diving Club, feature scuba programs.

The best snorkeling on Virgin Gorda is around its major attraction, The Baths. Lying off Anegada Island, Anegada Reef has been the "burial ground" for ships for centuries, an estimated 300 wrecks, including many pirate ships. The wreckage of the RMS *Rhone,* in the vicinity of the westerly tip of Salt Island, is the most celebrated dive spot in the BVI. This vessel went under in 1867 in one of the most disastrous hurricanes ever to hit the Virgin Islands.

**SPORTFISHING** In the last 25 years or so, about 20 world records have been set in the waters off the U.S. Virgin Islands. Many of these records were for the capture of the blue marlin. Other abundant fish include bonito, tuna, sailfish, and skipjack. But you needn't go to sea to fish. On both St. Thomas and St. John, the U.S. government posts lists where shoreline fishing is possible. Local tourist offices will advise you.

In St. Croix, grouper, wahoo, snapper, mahi-mahi, and the blue dolphin (not the mammal) are major prizes from the sea. Cruzans claim the world billfishing record. Many places arrange fishing trips.

**TENNIS**   Tennis is a major sport in the Virgin Islands, and most courts are all-weather or Laykold. Because the heat at midday is intense, many courts are lit for night games. Pro instruction and pro shops are found on all the major islands, especially St. Croix and St. Thomas.

St. Thomas offers six free courts, on a first-come, first-served basis. If the courts at the major hotels aren't occupied by resident guests, most hotels will allow you to play for a fee. Bolongo Bay and Marriott's Frenchman's Reef Beach Resort have four courts each.

On St. Croix, the Buccaneer Hotel has the best courts, eight in all, maintained in perfect condition. Its pro shop is state-of-the-art. The island also has seven public courts.

On Tortola, most of the tennis action centers along Prospect Reef with six courts, available at times for a fee to the general public. If you're a serious tennis buff and are contemplating staying on Virgin Gorda, make your hotel selection Little Dix Bay, which has seven courts—the best on the island—reserved for guests only.

## 4 Educational Travel & Homestays

Offbeat, alternative modes of travel often cost less, and can be a far more enriching way to travel and really get to know a place. Some of the organizations which arrange such travel are listed below.

### EDUCATIONAL TRAVEL

The best information is available at the **Council on International Educational Exchange (CIEE),** 205 E. 42nd St., New York, NY 10017 (☎ **212/661-1414**). This outfit not only arranges low-cost travel opportunities, through its travel subsidiary, Council Travel (see below), but it also offers information about working and studying abroad. Request a copy of the 606-page *Work, Study, Travel Abroad: The Whole World Handbook* ($14.45 by mail), listing more than 1,000 study opportunities abroad.

One of the most dynamic organizations of postretirement studies for senior citizens is **Elderhostel,** 75 Federal St., Boston, MA 02110 (☎ **617/426-7788**), established in 1975. Elderhostel maintains an array of programs throughout Europe as well as several programs in the Caribbean. Its Europe programs include airfare; its Caribbean programs do not. Most courses last two or three weeks and are a good value, considering that hotel accommodations in student dormitories or modest inns, all meals, and tuition are included. Courses involve no homework, are ungraded, and center mostly on the liberal arts. This is not a luxury vacation but rather an academic experience not available to senior citizens until several years ago. Participants must be age 60 or older. However, if two members go as a couple, only one member needs to be 60 or over. Write for their free newsletter and a list of upcoming courses and destinations. See "Tips for Special Travelers" later in this chapter for organizations catering to seniors.

### HOMESTAYS OR VISITS

**Servas,** 11 John St., Suite 407, New York, NY 10038 (☎ **212/267-0252**), is a nonprofit, nongovernmental, international, interfaith network of travelers and hosts whose goal is to help build world peace, goodwill, and understanding. They provide opportunities for deeper, more personal contacts among people of different cultural and political backgrounds. Servas travelers are invited to share living space in a privately owned home with a community, normally staying for visits lasting a maximum of two days. Visitors pay a $55 annual fee, fill out an application, and are interviewed for suitability by one of more than 200 Servas interviewers throughout the country. They then receive a Servas directory listing the names and addresses of Servas hosts who want visitors in their homes. This program embraces 130 countries, including the Virgin Islands.

A series of international programs for persons over 50 years of age who are interested in combining travel and learning is offered by **Interhostel.** Each program lasts two weeks and is led by a university faculty or staff members and is arranged in conjunction with a host college, university, or cultural institution. Participants can extend a stay beyond two weeks if they wish. Interhostel offers programs that consist of cultural affairs and intellectual activities, with field trips to museums and other centers of interest. For information, get in touch with the University of New Hampshire, Division of Continuing Education, 6 Garrison Ave., Durham, NH 03824 (☎ **603/862-1147,** or **800/733-9753**).

**Friendship Force,** 57 Forsyth St. NW, Suite 900, Atlanta, GA 30303 (☎ **404/ 522-9490**), is a nonprofit organization existing for the sole purpose of fostering and encouraging friendship worldwide. Dozens of branch offices throughout North America arrange visits *en masse,* usually once a year. Because of group bookings, the airfare to the host country is usually less than you'd pay if you bought an individual APEX ticket. Each participant is required to spend two weeks in the host country, one week of which is as a guest in the home of a family. Most volunteers spend the second week traveling in the host country.

## HOME EXCHANGES

If you don't mind staying put and having a stranger living in your home, you can avail yourself of a "house swap," which certainly keeps costs low. Sometimes the exchange includes use of the family car.

Many directories are published detailing the possibilities of using this type of service. Sometimes it's a straight house exchange for vacation purposes; other times it's more complicated. For example, your teenage child might be housed free in exchange for free room and board when the host child visits your hometown. Sometimes the deal is for a housesitter.

**The Invented City,** 41 Sutter St., Suite 1090, San Francisco, CA 94104 (☎ **415/673-0347**), is an international home-exchange agency. Home-exchange listings are published three times a year, in February, May, and November. A membership fee of $50 allows you to list your home, and you can also give your preferred time to travel, your occupation, and your hobbies.

**Intervac U.S.,** P.O. Box 590504, San Francisco, CA 94119 (☎ **415/ 435-3497,** or **800/756-HOME** in the U.S.), is part of the largest worldwide home-exchange network. It annually publishes four catalogs containing more than 9,400 homes in more than 36 countries. Members contact each other directly. The $65 fee, plus postage, covers the purchase of three of the company's catalogs (which will be mailed to you) and the inclusion of your own listing in the catalog you select. If you want to publish a photograph of your home, there is an additional $11 fee. Hospitality and rentals are also available.

## 5 Health & Insurance

# HEALTH

Traveling to the U.S. or British Virgin Islands need not impair your health. Finding a good doctor in the Virgin Islands is not a problem, and all of them speak English. See "Fast Facts" later in this chapter and individual island chapters for specific names and addresses.

If your medical condition is chronic, talk to your doctor before leaving home. He or she may have specific advice to give you, depending on your condition. For conditions such as epilepsy, a heart condition, or diabetes, wear Medic Alert's Identification Tag, which will immediately inform any doctor about your problem and also provide Medic Alert's 24-hour hotline, so a foreign doctor can obtain your medical records. The cost of a lifetime membership is a well-spent $35 for a stainless-steel ID bracelet. In addition, there is a $15 annual fee. Contact the **Medic Alert Foundation,** P.O. Box 1009, Turlock, CA 95381 (☎ **800/ 432-5378**).

Of course, take all your vital medicine and drugs with you in your carry-on luggage, in case your checked luggage is lost.

Although tap water is generally considered safe to drink, if you have a delicate stomach it is better to avoid it and drink mineral water instead. This applies even to iced drinks. Stick to beer, hot tea, or soft drinks.

At some point in a vacation, most visitors experience some diarrhea, even those who follow the usual precautions. This is often the result of a change in diet and eating habits, not usually from bad or contaminated food and water. Mild forms of diarrhea usually pass quickly without medication. As a precaution, take along some antidiarrhea medicine, moderate your eating habits, and drink only mineral water until you recover. Always drink plenty of fluids during the course of your disturbance to prevent dehydration. Consuming more than your usual intake of salt will help your body retain water. Eat only simply prepared foods at such times, such as plain bread (no butter) and boiled vegetables or some broth. Avoid dairy products at the time, except yogurt.

If symptoms persist, you may have dysentery, especially if you notice blood or mucus in your stool. At this point you should consult a doctor.

Sometimes travelers find that a change in diet will lead to constipation. If this occurs, eat a high-fiber diet and drink plenty of mineral water. Avoid large meals and don't drink wine.

**SUNBURN**    One of the most dangerous elements in the Virgin Islands and the Caribbean in general is the very thing you might have gone there to enjoy: the sun. It can be brutal, especially if you're coming from a winter climate and haven't been exposed to it in some time.

Wear sunglasses to protect yourself from the glare. When walking, wear a hat, wide brimmed if possible, and a coverup for your shoulders. In selecting a sunscreen lotion, seek one, as doctors advise you, with a high sun protection factor.

Experts also advise that you should limit your time on the beach, especially at first. If you forget and do get burned, try an aloe plant medication or a first-aid spray. Stay out of the sun until you recover. If your exposure is followed by fever, chills, a headache, or a feeling of nausea or dizziness, go to a doctor.

**INSECTS & PESTS** Mosquitoes exist, but they are not the dangerous malaria-carrying kind that you might find elsewhere in the Caribbean. Nevertheless, they are still a nuisance. One of the biggest menaces is the "no-see-ums." These biting little insects appear mainly in the early evening. Even screens can't keep these critters out. You'll have to spray yourself with your favorite bug repellent.

**VACCINATIONS** Vaccinations aren't needed to enter either the U.S. or British Virgin Islands if you're coming from the United States, Canada, Australia, New Zealand, or one of the countries of Western Europe such as Great Britain and Ireland.

**MEDICINES** Take along an adequate supply of any prescription drugs that you need and a written prescription that uses the generic name of the drug as well—not the brand name. Consult your pharmacist about taking such over-the-counter drugs as Colace, a stool softener, or Metamucil. Other items to take include first-aid cream, insect repellent, aspirin, nose drops, Band-Aids, and hydrogen peroxide. If you're subject to motion sickness on a plane or train, remember to bring along motion-sickness medicine as well.

## INSURANCE

Insurance needs for the traveler abroad fall into three categories:

1. Health and accident.
2. Trip cancellation.
3. Lost luggage.

First, review your present policies before traveling internationally—you may already have adequate coverage with your existing policies and what is offered by credit-card companies.

Many credit-card companies insure their users in case of a travel accident, providing a ticket was purchased with their card. Sometimes fraternal organizations have policies that protect members in case of sickness or accidents abroad.

Many homeowners' insurance policies cover theft of luggage during foreign travel and loss of documents—your airline ticket, for instance. Coverage is usually limited to about U.S. $500. To submit a claim on your insurance, remember that you'll need police reports or a statement from a medical authority that you did in fact suffer the loss or experience the illness for which you are seeking compensation. Such claims, by their very nature, can be filed only when you return from the Virgin Islands.

Some policies (and this is the type you should have) provide advances in cash or transferrals of funds so that you won't have to dip into your precious travel funds to settle medical bills.

If you've booked a charter fare, you will probably have to pay a cancellation fee if you cancel a trip suddenly, even if it is due to an unforeseen crisis. It's possible to get insurance against such a possibility. Some travel agencies provide such coverage, and often flight insurance against a cancelled trip is written into tickets paid for by credit cards from such companies as VISA or American Express. Many tour operators or insurance agents provide this type of insurance.

Among the companies offering such policies are:

**Travel Guard International,** 1145 Clark St., Stevens Point, WI 54481 (☎ **715/345-0505** in Wisconsin, **800/826-1300** outside Wisconsin), offers a comprehensive seven-day policy that covers basically everything, including lost luggage. The cost of the package is $62, including emergency assistance, accidental death, trip cancellation and interruption, medical coverage abroad, and lost luggage. There are restrictions, however, that you should understand before you accept the coverage.

**Travelers Insurance PAK,** Travel Insured International, Inc., P.O. Box 280568, East Hartford, CT 06128 (☎ **203/528-7663,** or **800/243-3174**), offers illness and accident coverage starting at $10 for 6 to 10 days. For lost or damaged luggage, $500 worth of coverage costs $20 for 6 to 10 days. You can also purchase trip-cancellation insurance for $5.50 per $100 of coverage to a limit of $10,000 per person.

**Mutual of Omaha (Tele-Trip),** Mutual of Omaha Plaza, Omaha, NE 68175 (☎ **800/228-9792**), offers insurance packages priced from $115 per couple for a three-week trip. Included in the standard package are travel-assistance services; and financial protection against trip cancellation, trip interruption, flight and baggage delays, accident-related medical costs, accidental death and dismemberment, and medical evacuation coverages. A deluxe package costing $213 per couple offers double the coverage of the standard policy. Applications for insurance can be made over the phone for major credit card holders.

**HealthCare Abroad (MEDEX),** 107 W. Federal St., Suite 13, P.O. Box 480, Middleburg, VA 22117 (☎ **703/687-3166,** or **800/237-6615**), offers coverage for between 10 and 120 days at $3 per day; this policy includes accident and sickness coverage to the tune of $100,000. Medical evacuation is also included, along with a $25,000 accidental death and dismemberment compensation. Provisions for trip cancellation can also be written into this policy at a nominal cost.

**Access America,** 6600 West Broad St., P.O. Box 11188, Richmond, VA 23230 (☎ **800/284-8300**), offers travel insurance and 24-hour emergency travel, medical, and legal assistance. One call to their hotline center, staffed by multilingual coordinators, connects travelers to a worldwide network of professionals able to offer specialized help in reaching the nearest physician, hospital, or legal advisor and in obtaining emergency cash or the replacement of lost travel documents. Varying coverage levels are available.

**Insurance for British Travelers**   Most big travel agents offer their own insurance and will probably try to sell you their package when you book a holiday. Think before you sign. Britain's Consumers' Association recommends that you insist on seeing the policy and reading the fine print before buying travel insurance.

You should also shop around for deals. You might contact **Columbus Travel Insurance Ltd.** (☎ **0171/375-0011** in London), or, for students, **Campus Travel** (☎ **0171/730-3402** in London). Columbus Travel will sell travel insurance only to people who have been official residents of Britain for at least a year.

## 6  Tips for Travelers with Disabilities, Seniors, Singles, Students & Families

### FOR TRAVELERS WITH DISABILITIES

Travelers with disabilities should make as many advance preparations as possible before embarking upon a trip. Hotels rarely advertise which facilities, if any, they offer the handicapped, so it's always best to contact the hotel directly. Tourist offices don't tend to keep very good data about such matters either.

There are a number of agencies that can provide information to help you plan your trip. A good source is the **Travel Information Service,** MossRehab Hospital, 1200 W. Tabor Rd., Philadelphia, PA 19141-3099 (☎ **215/456-9600**), which provides information to telephone callers only.

You can also obtain a copy of *Air Transportation of Handicapped Persons,* published by the U.S. Department of Transportation. You can obtain a free copy by writing for Free Advisory Circular No. AC12032, Distribution Unit, U.S. Department of Transportation, Publications Division, M-4332, Washington, DC 20590.

You may also want to consider joining a tour specifically for travelers with disabilities. Names and addresses of such tour operators can be obtained by writing to the **Society for the Advancement of Travel for the Handicapped,** 347 Fifth Ave., Suite 610, New York, NY 10016 (☎ 212/447-7284; fax 212/725-8253). Yearly membership dues in this society are $45 ($25 for senior citizens and students). Send a stamped self-addressed envelope for information.

You might also consider the **Federation of the Handicapped** (FEDCAP), 154 W. 14th St., New York, NY 10011 (☎ 212/727-4200; fax 212/727/4374), which offers summer tours for its members, who pay a yearly membership fee of $4.
**The Information Center for Individuals with Disabilities,** Fort Point Place, 27-43 Wormwood St., Boston, MA 02210 (☎ **617/727-5540**), is another good source. It has lists of travel agents who specialize in tours for travelers with disabilities.

For the blind or visually impaired, the best reference is the **American Foundation for the Blind,** 15 W. 16th St., New York, NY 10011 (☎ **212/620-2147,** or **800/232-5463** for ordering of information kits and supplies; fax 212/502-7777). It offers information on traveling with seeing-eye dogs, including details on transport and border formalities. It also issues identification cards to those who are legally blind.

For a $20 annual fee, consider joining **Mobility International USA,** P.O. Box 10767, Eugene, OR 97440 (☎ **503/343-1284;** fax 503/343-6812). With over 150 branch offices worldwide, this organization dispenses information about the accessibility of transportation, hotels, restaurants, and sightseeing destinations for the handicapped. It also provides referral numbers for legal advice for any discrimination problems with airlines or other organizations; an international educational exchange program specifically designed for the disabled; and a variety of workshops that focus on discrimination awareness, cross-cultural employment, and the Americans with Disabilities Act (ADA).

Finally, a bimonthly publication, *Handicapped Travel Newsletter* (☎ **903/667-1260**), keeps you current on worldwide sights accessible to travelers with disabilities. A subscription costs $15 per year.

**TIPS FOR BRITISH TRAVELERS WITH DISABILITIES    RADAR (Royal Association for Disability and Rehabilitation),** Unit 12, City Forum, 250 City Rd., London EC1V 8AF (☎ **0171/250-3222;** fax 0171/250-0212), publishes two annual holiday guides for travelers with disabilities. *Holidays and Travel Abroad,* costs £5, while *Holidays in the British Isles* is £7. RADAR (whose patroness is Elizabeth, the Queen Mother), also provides a number of holiday fact sheets on subjects like sports and outdoor holidays, insurance, financial arrangements for people with disabilities, and accommodations within nursing care units for groups or for the elderly. Each of these fact sheets is available for 75p. Fact sheets and holiday guides can be mailed outside the U.K. for a nominal mailing fee.

Another helpful organization is the **Holiday Care Service,** 2 Old Bank Chambers, Station Road, Horley, Surrey RH6 9HW (☎ **01293/774-535;** fax 01293/784-647), a national charity that advises the elderly and people with disabilities on accessible accommodations. An annual membership costs £25. Members receive a newsletter and access to a free reservation network for hotels throughout Britain and—to a lesser degree—Europe and the rest of the world. The organization's Holiday Care Awards recognize people, hotels, and travel wholesalers in the tourism industry who provide excellent service for people with disabilities.

If you're flying around the world, the airlines and ground staff will help you on and off planes and reserve seats for you with sufficient leg room, but it is essential to arrange for assistance *in advance* by contacting your airline.

## FOR SENIORS

Many discounts are available for seniors. Be advised, however, that you have to be a member of an association in order to obtain certain discounts.

Write for a free booklet called *101 Tips for the Mature Traveler,* available from **Grand Circle Travel,** 347 Congress St., Boston, MA 02210 (☎ **617/350-7500,** or **800/221-2610**). This tour operator offers extended vacations, escorted programs, and cruises that feature unique learning experiences for seniors at competitive prices.

**Mature Outlook,** 6001 N. Clark St., Chicago, IL 60660 (☎ **800/336-6330**), is a travel organization for people over 50 years of age. Members receive discounts at International Travel Card (ITC) member hotels and a bimonthly magazine. Annual membership costs $9.95 and entitles members to discounts, and in some cases free coupons, for merchandise from Sears Roebuck Co. Savings are also available on selected auto rentals and restaurants.

**SAGA International Holidays** is well known for its all-inclusive tours for seniors, preferably those 60 and over. Both medical and trip-cancellation insurance are included in the net price of any of their tours, except cruises. Contact SAGA International Holidays, 222 Berkeley St., Boston, MA 02115 (☎ **800/343-0273**).

The **AARP Travel Experience from American Express,** 400 Pinnacle Way, Suite 450, Norcross, GA 30071 (☎ **800/927-0111** for tours and cruises, or **800/424-3410** for car and hotel reservations), provides travel arrangements for members of the American Association of Retired Persons (AARP). Travel Experience offers a wide variety of escorted, hosted, go-any-day packages. Discounts on car rentals, hotels, and other services are offered through AARP's Purchase Privilege Program, a separate program from Travel Experience.

Information is also available from the **National Council of Senior Citizens,** 1331 F St. NW, Washington, DC 20004 (☎ **202/347-8800**). A nonprofit organization, the council charges $12 per person or couple. Members receive a monthly newsletter with travel tips; as well as discounts on hotels, motels, and auto rentals; and supplemental medical insurance.

## FOR SINGLES

A recent American census showed that 77 million Americans over 15 years of age are single. Unfortunately for them, the travel industry is geared toward couples. In the Caribbean, most resorts charge the same rate regardless of whether there are one or two travelers in a room, so sharing an accommodation with a travel companion can save a lot of money. One company has made heroic efforts to match single travelers with like-minded companions and is now the largest and best-listed company of its kind in the United States. Jens Jurgen, the German-born founder, charges $99 for a six-month listing in his well-publicized records. New applicants desiring a travel companion fill out a form stating their preferences and needs. They then receive a listing of potential travel partners. A bimonthly newsletter gives numerous money-saving travel tips for singles. A sample issue is available for $5. For an application and more information, write to Jens Jurgen, **Travel Companion,** P.O. Box P-833, Amityville, NY 11701 (☎ **516/454-0880**).

**Singleworld,** 401 Theodore Fremd Ave., Rye, NY 10580 (☎ **914/967-3334,** or **800/223-6490**), offers a selection of cruises and tours for single travelers. Tours and cruises are grouped by age (20s to 30s, 40s plus, and all ages). Annual dues are $25.

Another agency to check is Grand Circle Travel, which offers escorted tours and cruises for retired people, including singles. Once you book one of their trips, membership is included, and you get vouchers providing discounts for future trips. Grand Circle Travel is located at 347 Congress St., Boston, MA 02210 (☎ **617/350-7500,** or **800/221-2610**).

## FOR STUDENTS

The most wide-ranging travel service for students is **Council Travel,** 205 E. 42nd St., New York, NY 10017 (☎ **212/661-1414**). In addition to its New York office, Council Travel has 37 other offices located throughout the United States. This outfit provides details about budget travel, study abroad, working permits, and insurance. It also compiles a number of helpful publications, including *Student Travels,* which describes information on study and work opportunities abroad. It's distributed free, plus $1 postage. Council Travel also issues a useful International Student Identity Card (ISIC) for $15 that entitles holders to discounts on plane travel, hotels, and attractions around the world.

## FOR FAMILIES

The Virgin Islands is a contender for the number-one family vacation destination. The smallest toddlers can spend blissful hours on beaches and in shallow seawater or pools. Older children can amuse themselves with boat rides, horseback riding, hiking, and snorkeling. Most resort hotels have organized activities for children of different age groups; see Chapter 1 for a list of the best family resorts.

Before you go, arrange for such necessities as a crib, bottle warmer, and car seat (if you're driving anywhere) for the very young, as well as for cots in your room for older children. Find out if the place where you're staying stocks baby food, and if not, take it with you.

Babysitters can be hired through most hotels, and nearly all of them speak English. Talk with the sitter yourself, and introduce her or him to those to be cared for before you leave the hotel room or nursery.

*Family Travel Times* is published quarterly by **TWYCH (Travel With Your Children),** and includes a weekly call-in service for subscribers. Subscriptions cost $55 a year and can be ordered by writing to TWYCH, 45 W. 18th St., 7th Floor, New York, NY 10011 (☎ **212/206-0688**). To receive an information packet describing TWYCH's publications with a recent sample issue send $3.50 to the above address. TWYCH also publishes two detailed informational guides, *Skiing with Children* ($29) and *Cruising with Children* ($22), which are discounted to newsletter subscribers.

**Families Welcome!,** 21 West Colony Place, Suite 140, Durham, NC 27705 (☎ **919/489-2555,** or **800/326-0724**), specializes in worry-free vacations for families to destinations in Europe, the United States, and the Caribbean. The company organizes children's programs, children-only activities, and adventures for parents and kids.

# 7 Getting There

## BY PLANE

The biggest islands have regularly scheduled air service to the North American continent. The smaller islands are tied into this vast network through their own carriers. For example, to reach Tortola, capital of the BVI, you might fly from Chicago to Puerto Rico, where a smaller plane will take you the rest of the way.

Ask travel agents about special stopover privileges, since "island-hopping" is becoming an increasingly popular diversion for both summer and winter holidays.

For information on how to reach a specific island by plane, refer to the "Getting There" section in the specific chapter.

### REGULAR FARES

The best strategy for securing the lowest airfare is to shop around. Sometimes cheaper tickets are sold at the last minute if the flight is not fully booked.

For those who can't leave everything to the last minute, there are certain things to keep in mind. Most airlines charge different fares according to seasons. Peak season, which means the mainland winter in the Virgin Islands, is most expensive; basic season, during the summer months, offers the least expensive fares. Shoulder season refers to the spring and fall months.

Most airlines also offer an assortment of fares from first class to economy which is the lowest-priced regular airfare carrying no special restrictions or requirements. Most airlines also offer promotional fares, which carry stringent requirements like advance purchase, minimum stay, and cancellation penalty. The most common such fare is the APEX (Advance Purchase Excursion). Land arrangements (that is, prebooking of hotel rooms) are often tied in with promotional fares offered by airlines.

### OTHER GOOD-VALUE CHOICES

Bear in mind that in the airline industry what constitutes good value is always changing. What was the lowest possible fare one day can change the next day when a new promotional fare is offered.

**BUCKET SHOPS**   A bucket shop (or consolidator) acts as a clearinghouse for blocks of tickets that airlines discount and consign during normally slow periods of air travel. In the case of the Virgin Islands, that usually means mid-April to mid-December.

Charter operators (see below) and bucket shops used to perform separate functions, but their services in many cases have been blurred in recent times, and many outfits now perform both functions.

Tickets are sometimes—but not always—priced at up to 35% less than full fare. Terms of payment can vary from 45 days prior to departure to the last minute. Tickets can be purchased through regular travel agents, who usually mark up the ticket by least 8% to 10%, which obviously reduces your discount. Many users of consolidators complain that since they do not qualify for advance seat assignment, they are likely to be assigned a "poor seat" on the plane at the last minute.

In a recent survey, most users of consolidators estimated their savings at around $200 per ticket, and nearly one-third reported savings of up to $300. Many, however, reported no savings at all, as the airlines sometimes match the consolidator ticket by announcing a promotional fare. The situation is a bit tricky and calls for some careful investigation on your part to determine just how much you are saving.

Bucket shops abound from coast to coast, but just to get you started, here are some recommendations. Look also for their ads in your local newspaper's travel section.

One of the biggest U.S. consolidators is **Travac,** 989 Sixth Ave., New York, NY 10018 (☎ **212/563-3303,** or **800/TRAV-800** in the U.S.), which offers discounted seats throughout the U.S. to most cities in Europe on airlines such as TWA, United, and Delta. Another Travac office is at 2601 East Jefferson St., Orlando, FL 32803 (☎ **407/896-0014**).

In New York try **TFI Tours International,** 34 W. 32nd St., 12th Floor, New York, NY 10001 (☎ **212/736-1140** in New York State, or **800/745-8000** from other parts of the U.S.). This tour company offers services to 177 cities worldwide.

If you live in the Midwest, explore the possibilities of **Travel Avenue,** 10 S. Riverside Plaza, Suite 1404, Chicago, IL 60606 (☎ **800/333-3335** in the U.S.), a national agency with headquarters in Chicago. The tickets offered by Travel Avenue are often cheaper than most shops, and the organization charges the customer only a $25 fee on international tickets, rather than taking the usual 10% commission from an airline. Travel Avenue rebates most of that back to the customers—hence, the lower fares.

For New Englanders, a well-known bucket shop is **TMI (Travel Management International),** 39 JFK St. (Harvard Square), 3rd Floor, Cambridge, MA 02138 (☎ **800/245-3672** in the U.S.), which discounts on youth fares and student fares.

**CHARTER FLIGHTS**    Charter flights allow you to save money on regularly scheduled flights. Many of the major carriers offer charter flights at rates that are sometimes 30% (or more) off the regular airfare.

There are some drawbacks to charter flights, however. Advance booking of up to 45 days or more may be required. You could lose most of the money you've advanced if you cancel a flight. (It is now possible to take out cancellation insurance against such an eventuality; see the section on insurance above.) You must depart and return on a scheduled date.

Charter flights are complicated, and it's best to ask a good travel agent to explain the pros and cons.

One reliable charter-flight operator is **Council Charter,** run by the Council on International Educational Exchange, 205 E. 42nd St., New York, NY 10017 (☎ **212/661-0311,** or **800/800-8222**), which arranges charter seats on regularly scheduled flights.

**REBATORS**    Rebators are outfits that pass along to the passenger part of their commission, although many of them assess a fee for their services. Although they are not the same as travel agents, they sometimes offer roughly similar services. Sometimes a rebator will sell a discounted travel ticket and offer discounted land arrangements, including hotels and car rentals. Most rebators offer discounts averaging anywhere from 10% to 25% with a $25 handling charge.

Specializing in clients within the Midwest, **Travel Avenue,** 10 S. Riverside Plaza, Suite 1404, Chicago, IL 60606 (☎ 312/876-1116, or 800/333-3335), is reputedly one of the oldest agencies of its kind. It offers up-front cash rebates on every airfare over $300 it sells. In a style similar to a discount brokerage firm, they pride themselves on *not* offering travel counseling. Instead, they sell airline tickets to independent travelers who have already worked out their travel plans. Also available are tour and cruise fares, plus hotel reservations, usually at prices lower than if you had pre-reserved them on your own.

Another major rebator is **The Smart Traveller,** 3111 SW 27th Ave., P.O. Box 330010, Miami, FL 33133 (☎ **305/448-3338, or 800/448-3338**). The agency offers discounts on packaged tours.

**PROMOTIONAL FARES**   To take advantage of promotional fares you'll have to have a good travel agent or do a lot of shopping or calling around yourself to learn what's currently available at the time of your intended trip. Be sure to browse national newspapers for special deals.

**TRAVEL CLUBS**   Travel Clubs regularly offer discounts to the Caribbean. To receive discounts, join a club that supplies an unsold inventory of tickets offering discounts in the range of 20% to 60%. Some of the deals involve cruise-ship and complete tour packages.

After you pay an annual fee, you are given a hotline that you call when you're planning to go somewhere. Many of these discounts become available several days before departure, and sometimes you might have as much as a month. You're limited to what's available, so you have to be fairly flexible.

Some of the best of these clubs include the following:

**Moment's Notice,** 425 Madison Ave., New York, NY 10017 (☎ **212/ 486-0500**), charges around $25 per year for membership which allows spur-of-the-moment participation in dozens of tours. Each is geared for impulse purchases and last-minute getaways, and each features air-and-land packages which sometimes represent substantial savings over what you'd have paid through more conventional channels. Although membership is required for participation in the tours, anyone can call the company's hotline (☎ **212/750-9111**) to learn what options are available. Most of the company's bargain tours depart from New Jersey's Newark airport.

**Sears Discount Travel Club,** 3033 S. Parker Rd., Suite 900, Aurora, CO 80014 (☎ **800/255-1487** in the U.S.), offers members a catalog (issued four times a year), maps, discounts at select hotels, and a limited guarantee that equivalent packages will not be undersold by any other travel organization. Membership costs $50. The club also offers a 5% rebate on the value of all airline tickets, tours, hotel rooms, and car rentals which are purchased through them. (To collect this rebate, participants are required to fill out some forms and photocopy their receipts and itineraries.)

## FLIGHTS FROM THE U.K.

Though there are no direct flights from the U.K. to either the U.S. Virgin Islands or the British Virgin Islands, **British Airways** (☎ **0181/897-4000** in London) flies directly to San Juan, Puerto Rico. There are two flights a week (December through April) and once a week the rest of the year. In San Juan, several airlines make the final connection to either St. Thomas, St. Croix in the USVI, Tortola and Virgin Gorda in the BVI.

## 8　Cruises

If you'd like to sail the Caribbean, a cruise ship might be for you. It's slow and easy, and it's no longer enjoyed only by the idle rich who have months to spend away from home. Most cruises today appeal to the middle-income voyager who probably has no more than one or two weeks to spend cruising the Caribbean. Some 300 passenger ships sail the Caribbean each month, and in January and February that figure may go up another hundred or so. St. Thomas is one of the major ports of call. Pick up a copy of *Frommer's Cruises* for more detailed information.

Most cruise-ship operators suggest the concept of a total vacation. Some promote constant activities, while others suggest the possibility of doing nothing but relaxing. Cruise ships are self-contained resorts, offering a range of activities on board and sightseeing once you arrive in a port of call.

For those who don't want to spend all their time at sea, some lines offer a fly-and-cruise vacation. You spend a week cruising the Caribbean and another week staying at a hotel at reduced prices. These total packages generally cost less than purchasing the cruise and air portions separately.

Another version of fly-and-cruise is to fly to and from the cruise. Most plans offer a package deal from the principal airport closest to your residence to the major airport nearest to the cruise-departure point. It's possible to purchase your air ticket on your own and book your cruise ticket separately, but you'll save money by combining the fares in a package deal.

Miami is the cruise capital of the world, but vessels also leave from San Juan, New York, Port Everglades, Los Angeles, and other points of embarkation.

Most of the cruise ships travel at night, arriving the next morning at the day's port of call. In port, passengers can go ashore for sightseeing, shopping, and the odd meal. Cruise prices vary widely. Sometimes the same route with the same ports of call carries different fares.

Consult a good travel agent for the latest offerings.

**Vacations to Go,** 2411 Fountain View, Houston, TX 77057 (☎ **800/ 338-4962**), established in 1984, specializes in establishing contacts between cruise lines and cruise participants at discounted prices. Annual membership costs $19.95 per family and provides access to catalogs and newsbriefs about cost-conscious cruises through the Atlantic, Caribbean, and Mediterranean.

What follows is a rundown of various cruise ships cruising the Virgin Islands.

**Carnival Cruise Lines** (☎ **305/599-2600,** or **800/327-9501**) operates from such ports as Miami, San Juan, St. Thomas, and Grand Cayman. This enormous company operates seven relatively youthful ships, ranging from medium-sized (37,000 tons) to gargantuan (70,000 tons). Although the oldest of the ships entered service in 1982 (and was renovated in 1989), four of the newest were launched since 1990. Cruises range from three to seven nights and feature non-stop activities, lots of glitter, and the hustle and bustle of armies of clients and crew members embarking and disembarking at every port. Specific ships include the *Tropicale,* the *Festivale,* and the *Celebration* (all midsized). Much larger are the company's quartet of 70,000-ton superships, which include the *Ecstacy,* the *Fantasy,* the *Fascination,* and the *Sensation.* Their overall atmosphere is comparable to floating theme parks, loaded with whimsy and with lots of emphasis on partying in a style you might have expected in Atlantic City. Lots of single passengers opt for this line, where the average on-board age is a relatively youthful 42.

**Celebrity Cruises** (☎ **305/262-6677,** or **800/437-3111**) maintains three newly built, medium-sized ships ranging in size from 30,000 tons to 47,000 tons, each offering cruises of between 5 and 11 nights. (Each of the three ships, *Horizon, Meridian,* and *Zenith,* entered service between 1990 and 1992). Ports of call usually include Key West, San Juan, Grand Cayman, Ocho Rios, St. Thomas, Antigua, and St. Barts, among others. Accommodations are roomy and well-equipped, and many passengers compare their vessels to all-inclusive resorts.

**Commodore Cruise Line** (☎ **305/444-4600,** or **800/227-4759**) makes no apologies for its ships' ages. They bear the names *Enchanted Seas* and *Enchanted Isles,* each sized rather modestly at around 23,000 tons. Launched under the auspices of other companies in 1958, they've both been refurbished several times since then. Although some of the accoutrements might be a bit old-fashioned and the ship's brass or painted surfaces have begun to pit and crack, many clients like this company's cruises because of their reasonable prices. Cruises range from 7 to 14 days and visit Grand Cayman, the largest ports of Puerto Rico, St. Croix, Antigua, Martinique, and ports along the Mexican coast. There's a good share of families on board, as well as lots of couples who don't particularly care about the ships' relative lack of state-of-the-art facilities.

**Costa Cruise Lines** (☎ **305/358-7325,** or **800/462-6782**) has relatively large (around 54,000 tons each) and new (built since 1991) ships that hold around 1,300 passengers each. Ports of call include Nassau, San Juan, St. Thomas, St. Martin, and Key West. Days at sea range from 7 to 11 nights. There's an Italian flavor and lots of Italian design on board here. The atmosphere is one of relaxed indulgence. The ships are named the *Costa Classica* and the *Costa Romantica.* Entertainment themes are generally Mediterranean—Roman Bacchanalia, Carnival in Venice, and foccacia and pizza parties by the pool.

**Cunard** (☎ **800/221-4770**) is one of the premier cruise lines in the world, with an undeniable flair that extends even into its relatively inexpensive vessels. Some visitors remember Cunard fondly from transatlantic journeys they've taken in the past on the line's very British flagship, the *QE2.* Cunard ships which sail in Caribbean waters include the *Cunard Countess* (the least expensive of the lot), the *Crown Dynasty,* the *Crown Jewel,* the *Sagafjord,* and the *Sea Goddess I,* all small and elegant. The ships call on San Juan, St. Thomas, St. Kitts, Barbados and, in some cases, isolated ports in the southern Caribbean. With the exception of the 67,000-ton *QE2,* all the ships weigh in at less than 20,000 tons; the *Sea Goddess I* carries only 116 passengers in yacht-like (and very expensive) intimacy.

**Diamond Cruise Lines** (☎ **305/776-6123,** or **800/333-3333**) has only one ship. The *Radisson Diamond* is small (only 20,000 tons), engineered with twin hulls like a catamaran (for improved speed and stability), and doesn't make a fuss about table seatings (its small size permits open seating at every meal). Cruises last from four to seven nights and often originate in St. Thomas, Barbados, or San Juan. En route, the ship stops at such off-the-beaten-track places as Jost Van Dyke and islands in the Grenadines. The ship was originally designed for oceangoing conferences and conventions and in some ways seems a lot like a large floating hotel.

(This vision is encouraged by Radisson, the hotel giant that helps manage it.) Its wide berth (made possible by its catamaran design) and relatively short length contribute to a design that's unique in the cruise industry. The ship tends to remain relatively stable even in rough seas, a blessing for anyone prone to seasickness.

**Norwegian Cruise Line** (☎ 305/447-9660, or 800/327-7030) appeals to all ages and income levels, with Scandinavian officers, an international staff, and a pervasive modern-Viking theme. The company's five ships (*Dreamward, Norway, Seaward, Starward,* and *Windward*) usually cruise for between three and seven days, stopping at Nassau, Key West, the beaches of Mexico, St. Thomas, Aruba, Tortola, and a Bahamian island which is wholly owned by Norwegian Cruise Line called Great Stirrup Key. The company's largest ship and corporate symbol, *The Norway,* weighs in at a massive 76,000 tons and offers what's usually considered the best amenities and services; its smallest ship, *The Starward,* weighs only 16,000 tons and cruises to relatively exotic destinations in the southern Caribbean. In terms of size, all of the other ships fall somewhere in between. Each features a snappy array of on-board activities and, in many cases, a revolving array of international sports figures for game tips and lectures.

**Renaissance Cruises** (☎ 305/463-0982, or 800/525-5350) has eight vessels that sail the world, including the waters of Asia. The only ship that makes regularly scheduled stops in the Caribbean is the small and discreetly elegant *Renaissance III.* The 100 passengers the ship can carry tend to be prosperous, cultivated, and relaxed, often seeking out unusual destinations and faithfully attending the on-board lectures and cultural events. Cruises usually last about a week. Meals are served with an open seating plan, and the ship's small size provides for a close-knit environment.

Ports of call include St. Croix and Virgin Gorda.

**Royal Caribbean Cruise Line** (☎ 305/539-6000) leads the industry in the development of mega-ships. Three of this company's six vessels weigh in at 73,000 tons and are among the largest of any line. They include *Majesty of the Seas, Monarch of the Seas,* and *Sovereign of the Seas.* The remaining three are *Nordic Empress, Song of America,* and *Sun Viking.* A house-party theme tends to permeate the on-board ambience of these ships, although it's a bit less frenetic than that found aboard the mega-ships of other cruise lines. The company is well-run, and there are enough on-board activities to suit virtually any taste and age level. Though accommodations and accoutrements are more than adequate, they are not upscale. The line regularly calls on St. John, St. Thomas, and St. Croix.

**Royal Viking Cruise Line** (☎ 305/447-9660, or 800/327-7030) owns only two ships, a 10,000-ton, yacht-like vessel with room for only around 200 passengers (the *Royal Viking Queen*), and the much larger *Royal Viking Sun* (38,000 tons). The company is a well-managed, hardworking chain with appealing itineraries, excellent service, and some of the best on-board cuisine of any cruise line in the world. Clients tend to be a bit more sedate and well-mannered than on many other cruises, and much emphasis is placed on neat attire. Itineraries include Barbados, St. Barts, Key West, Virgin Gorda, San Juan, and selected ports within the Virgin Islands.

**Seabourn Cruise Line** (☎ 415/391-7444) is considered a desirable, upscale, and expensive outfit whose *Seabourne Pride* offers cruises of from 10 to 14 days in unabashed luxury. Stops include the islands of St. Thomas, Jost Van Dyke,

## Chartering a Boat

There may be no better way to have a vacation in the Virgin Islands than on the deck of your own yacht. Impossible? Not really. No one said you had to own the yacht.

Experienced sailors and navigators with a sea-wise crew can charter a "bareboat," that is, a rented fully equipped boat with no captain or crew. You're on your own, and you'll have to prove you can handle it before you're allowed to go on such a craft. Even if you're your own skipper, you may want to take along an experienced sailor familiar with the sometimes tricky local waters.

If you can afford it, the ideal is to charter a boat with a skilled skipper and a competent crew. Four to six people, maybe more, often charter yachts measuring from 50 to more than 100 feet.

Most yachts are rented on a weekly basis and come with a fully stocked bar and equipment for fishing and water sports. More and more bareboat charters are learning that they can save money and select menus more suited to their tastes by doing their own provisioning, rather than relying on the yacht company that rented them the vessel.

The best outfitter for this is **The Moorings,** P.O. Box 139, Wickhams Cay, Road Town, Tortola, BVI (☎ **809/494-2331**). Arrangements can be made for bareboating with a skipper or fully crewed with both a skipper and cook. Boats come equipped with barbecue, snorkeling gear, dinghy, and linens. A Windsurfer comes with crewed boats but costs extra for boats not crewed. The Moorings has an experienced staff of mechanics, electricians, riggers, and cleaners. If you're going out on your own, you'll get a thorough briefing session about Virgin Island waters and anchorages. To make reservations in the U.S. or Canada, call **800/535-7289.** You can also write for information to The Moorings Ltd., 19345 U.S. 19 North, Suite 402, Clearwater, FL 34624 (☎ **813/530-5424**). Bareboat rentals, without a crew or skipper, cost $1,190 to $3,185 per week in the summer (suitable for from 2 to 10 passengers). In the high season (winter), weekly rentals for bareboat cruises range from $2,163 to $6,020 per week (for between 2 and 10 persons). Rentals for ships with crews, obviously, are more expensive and vary with the number and the nature of the crew members.

Virgin Gorda, and the French part of St. Martin. There is a great array of activities, a surprising amount of on-board space per passenger, and nouvelle cuisine. The dining room is unapologetically formal, and the emphasis is on good service and luxury.

**Silversea Cruises** (☎ **305/522-4477**) has Caribbean itineraries for the most part aboard the *Silver Cloud,* which weighs in at a modest 17,000 tons and carries around 300 passengers to Caribbean ports such as La Romana, Antigua, Barbados, and Virgin Gorda. Most cruises begin in Fort Lauderdale. The ship was launched in 1994 and was designed to be midway between a very large yacht and a very small ocean liner. Many visitors prefer it to the very small ships from other lines which also offer extra amenities and facilities. The ship's appeal is its added stability during rough seas and the on-board sense of luxury and attentive service. There's a heavy emphasis on water sports during port stops.

**Sun Line Cruises** (☎ **212/397-6400,** or **800/872-6400**) has one ship, the *Stella Solaris,* built in 1953, rebuilt in 1973, and refurbished in 1993. It's small (18,000 tons), can carry only 620 passengers, and usually makes runs of between 10 and 12 days from ports which include Galveston and Fort Lauderdale. Ports of call include Nassau; Grand Cayman; St. Lucia; St. Martin; St. Thomas; Puerto Limón, Costa Rica; and the beaches on the Mexican coasts.

# 9 Package Tours

Package tours are peddled through every travel agency in the world, and many of them offer reduced prices for predefined blocks of hotel space and airfare to the Caribbean. The different options are daunting in their variety and scope; there are more permutations than grains of sand on a tropical beach. What's especially confusing is the tendency for what appears to be roughly equivalent packages priced at widely differing prices. (Stopovers at the same hotel during the same season for the same number of nights can vary by several hundred dollars per person per week.)

Of course, you can devote lots of time and labor to researching the various price options yourself, but to save time, consider hiring the services of TourScan, Inc., P.O. Box 2367, Darien, CT 06820 (☎ **203/655-8091,** or **800/962-2080**). Widely considered a pioneer in the simplification of the package tour industry, the company has been referred to by travel authority Arthur Frommer himself as "the most systematic, scientific exposure of travel marketing practices in the [travel] industry."

Every season, the company gathers and computerizes the contents of most of the travel brochures to the Caribbean, the Bahamas, and Bermuda—a total of about 200 brochures and flyers containing 10,000 different vacations at 1,600 hotels on 56 different islands. (In some cases, up to 80 packages are available which feature overnights at the same hotel.) TourScan selects the best value at each hotel and condo, and the results are made available to travelers.

TourScan prints two catalogs each year listing a wide choice of hotels on most of the islands of the Caribbean in all price ranges. (The sheer scope of the islands and resort hotels which are included is amazing.) Catalogs cost $4, which is credited to any TourScan vacation. Prices are based on travel from New York, Newark, Baltimore, Philadelphia, and Washington, D.C., although the company will arrange trips originating from any location in the U.S. or abroad on request. Included in the reports is most of the information needed to intelligently evaluate a proposed vacation, including hotel class, room count, availability, and price of meal plans.

Other tour operators include the following:

**Caribbean Concepts Corp.,** 575 Underhill Blvd., Syosset, NY 11791 (☎ **516/496-9800,** or **800/423-4433** in the U.S.), offers low-cost air-and-land packages to the islands, including apartments, hotels, villas, or condo rentals. Car rentals and local sightseeing can also be arranged.

**Adventure Tours,** 7677 Dr. Phillips Blvd., Orlando, FL 32819 (☎ **800/ 241-1700**), has some interesting land-and-air packages to St. Thomas. This company is a wholesaler; you can use its services through your travel agent.

The major U.S. air carriers offer combined land-and-air packages. For more information, contact the following: **American Airlines Fly-Away Vacations**

(☎ 800/321-2121); **Delta's Dream Vacations** (☎ 800/872-7786); **TWA Getaway Vacations** (☎ 800/GETAWAY); and **United Airlines Vacations** (☎ 800/328-6877).

If you're seeking general independent packages, consider **Domenico Tours,** 751 Broadway, Bayonne, NJ 07002 (☎ 800/554-8687), which offers packages to Puerto Rico, St. Maarten, St. Thomas, Aruba, and Jamaica. Prices include airfare, airport transfers, accommodations, and car rentals. **Sunbrella Vacations,** 2655 Lejeune Rd., Suite 400, Coral Gables, FL 33134 (☎ 800/874-0027), part of Renaissance Vacations, offers deals to Ocho Rios, Jamaica, St. Thomas, and Grenada.

**FOR BRITISH TRAVELERS**    Package tours can be booked through **British Virgin Islands Holidays,** a division of Wingjet Travel Ltd., 11-13 Hockerill St., Bishop's Stortford, Herts. CM23 2DW (☎ 01279/656111). This company is the major booking agent for all the important hotels in the BVI. Stays can be arranged in more than one hotel if you'd like to visit more than one island. The company also offers staffed yacht charters and bareboat charters.

**Caribbean Connection,** Concorde House, Forest St., Chester CH1 1QR (☎ 01244/341131), offers all-inclusive packages (airfare and hotel) to both the U.S. Virgin Islands and the British Virgin Islands. If you desire a villa instead of a hotel, that too can arranged.

Other Caribbean specialists operating out of England include **Tradewinds Faraway Holidays,** Station House, 81-83 Fulham High St., London SW6 3 JP (☎ 0171/7318000); **Kuoni House,** Kuoni Travel, Dorking, Surrey RH5 4AZ (☎ 01306/7422220); and **Caribtours,** 161 Fulham Rd., London SW3 6SN (☎ 0171/5813517).

# 10  Getting Around

Once you arrive, getting around the island you're on or doing some island-hopping becomes important. There are several methods outlined below.

## BY PLANE

Airplanes provide the best link between St. Thomas and St. Croix and between St. Thomas and Tortola's airport at Beef Island. To reach St. John by air, passengers usually land first at St. Thomas, then travel to St. John by boat. **American Airlines** (☎ 800/433-7300) is one of the airlines that provides the most frequent daily service from the U.S. mainland to St. Thomas, with continuing service to St. Croix.

No nonstop air service is available between the U.S. mainland and the BVI. Consequently, most visitors fly either to St. Thomas or to Puerto Rico, where air links to either Tortola/Beef Island or Virgin Gorda (and sometimes both) are provided by **American Eagle** (☎ 800/433-7300), **St. Thomas Air** (☎ 800/ 522-3084), or **LIAT** (☎ 800/468-0482).

## BY TRAIN OR BUS

There are no **rail** connections on any of the islands.

The only island that has a really recommendable **bus** service is St. Thomas. Buses leave from Charlotte Amalie and circle the island in each direction. See "Getting Around," in Chapter 4, for details. On the other islands, bus service is highly erratic and is used mainly by workers going to and from their jobs. In the BVI,

Virgin Gorda offers safaris, brightly painted open-air buses, and a more economical minibus service operated by Scato's. (See Chapter 7 for more details).

## BY TAXI

Taxi is the main method of transportation for getting around all the islands. On St. Thomas taxi vans carry up to a dozen passengers going to multiple destinations. Private taxis are also available. Rates are regulated and posted at the airport, where taxi vans meet all arriving planes. On St. John, both private taxis and shuttles that carry three or more passengers are available.

On St. Croix taxis are available at both the airport and in Christiansted. Even if your hotel is remotely anchored in St. Croix, your hotel desk can generally summon a cab for you in about 30 minutes, often much less. Taxis are unmetered, and you should always settle the rate before setting out.

Taxis are one of the best ways—practically the only way at times—for getting around the BVI. In the BVI, taxis service the islands of Tortola, Virgin Gorda, and Anegada, and rates are fixed by the government.

## BY CAR

If you can afford it and don't mind driving on the left, a rented car is the best way to get around the Virgin Islands. Count on paying at least $50 a day for the rental, which includes unlimited mileage. If you book a car for a week, you get a slight reduction on this rate.

All the major car-rental companies are represented in the islands, including **Avis, Budget,** and **Hertz.** (For detailed information, refer to "Getting Around" in specific island chapters.) Many local agencies also compete in these markets. Most cars are picked up at the airport on both St. Thomas and St. Croix. On St. John there are car-rental stands at the dock where the boat arrives from St. Thomas.

If you want a car for only part of your stay, you can call from your hotel, and a car will be delivered, usually with no more than a two-hour wait. The papers are filled out on the spot. You must have a valid credit card and driver's license. In winter, cars might be in short supply, so you should reserve as far in advance as possible.

In the BVI, many visitors have a successful holiday without ever bothering to rent a car. Some of the roads, like those on Tortola, have been compared to roller-coaster rides. Driving on the left and many, many hairpin curves don't add to the pleasure of driving.

Vehicles come in a wide range of styles and prices, including Jeeps, Land Rovers, mini-mokes, and even six- to eight-passenger Suzukis. Weekly rates are slightly cheaper. You must purchase a local driver's license for $10 from police headquarters or at the car-rental desk. The minimum age limit for renting a car in the BVI is 25. Major U.S. companies, such as **Budget,** are represented in the islands, and there are many local companies as well.

Parking lots are found in Charlotte Amalie, in St. Thomas, and in Christiansted on St. Croix. In Frederiksted, you can generally park on the street. Most hotels, except those in the congested center of Charlotte Amalie, have extensive parking lots, especially the resort hotels. Parking is free on hotel grounds.

**GASOLINE**    This is usually in plentiful supply on St. Thomas and St. Croix, with plenty of service stations such as Mobil on the outskirts of Charlotte Amalie. Gasoline stations are also found at strategic points along the island, especially in the north and in the more congested East End.

On St. Croix, most of the gasoline stations are in Christiansted, but they are also found along major highways and at Frederiksted. On St. John, make sure your tank is filled up at Cruz Bay, the capital, before striking out on a motor tour of the island.

Gasoline stations are not as plentiful, but they are adequate in the BVI. Road Town, the capital of Tortola, has the most gas stations, at both the western and eastern approaches to town. Fill up here before embarking on extensive island touring in the hills. Virgin Gorda has a limited but sufficient number of gas stations. Chances are you won't be using a car on any other island in the BVI.

**DRIVING RULES**   *Drive on the left.* This rule seems logical for the British Virgin Islands, whose parent country has long had a tradition of driving on the left. It is less understandable in the U.S. islands, and it causes endless confusion and a somewhat higher rate of accidents than on the U.S. mainland. Drive extra carefully, especially when merging into lanes of traffic.

Highway codes and signs are generally the same as those used throughout the U.S. mainland.

Canadians and Americans do not need to obtain an international driver's license.

**ROAD MAPS**   Adequate maps are available for free on the islands at the individual tourist offices. If you arrive by plane, go to the tourist information office at the airport and request a map. If you plan to drive in a rented car to your hotel, have the tourist staff member trace the best route for you.

**BREAKDOWNS & ASSISTANCE**   All the major islands, including St. Thomas, St. John, St. Croix, Tortola, and Virgin Gorda, have garages that will come to your assistance and tow your vehicle if necessary. In the likely case that the car is rented, call the rental company first. Usually someone there will bring motor assistance to you. If your car requires extensive repairs because of a mechanical failure, a new one will be sent to replace it.

## BY BOAT

There is no ferry service between St. Thomas and St. Croix (it's better to fly), but ferry service forms the vital link between St. Thomas and St. John. Private water taxis also operate between St. Thomas and St. John. Launch services link Red Hook (in the east of St. Thomas) with both Charlotte Amalie and St. John.

On St. Croix, the major boat link is to Buck Island, the big offshore attraction.

In the BVI getting around by ferry and private boat is the major means of travel. Many ferries link Road Town (the capital of Tortola) with the island's West End. Service to Virgin Gorda (the second major island) is also provided. Even some of the smaller islands, such as Anegada and Jost Van Dyke, have ferry connections, often about two per day. On some of the really remote islands in the chain, boat service may be only once a week. Many of the private islands, such as Peter Island, provide launches from Tortola.

For details on these transportation connections, with sample prices, see the "Getting Around" sections of the individual island chapters.

## BY BICYCLE

Much of the hilly terrain of St. Thomas and Tortola does not lend itself to extensive bicycling. A lot of St. John can, however, be covered by bicycle, and St. Croix, which is flatter, is ideal for bicycle rides. For specific information on bicycle or motor-scooter rental, see the "Getting Around" sections of the individual island chapters.

## SUGGESTED ITINERARIES

### If You Have 1 Week

**Day 1**   Fly to St. Thomas and give yourself absolutely nothing to do the first day. Rest, relax, recuperate, have a rum punch, and listen to some Caribbean music. Enjoy a typical West–Indian dinner.

**Day 2**   After a long, leisurely morning and a late breakfast, drive or take a taxi or bus into Charlotte Amalie for a day of lunching, shopping, and taking my guided walking tour (see Chapter 4).

**Day 3**   Spend most of the day at Magens Bay on St. Thomas.

**Day 4**   Take the short boat ride from Red Hook to St. John and take a whirl-wind tour of the island. Spend the remaining time at Trunk Bay, the small island's biggest attraction and a beach lover's find.

**Day 5**   Spend the day exploring the attractions of the capital, Charlotte Amalie.

**Day 6**   Spend the morning driving around the island. Take a dive on the *Atlantis* submarine.

**Day 7**   Set off on one of the many boat trips offered on St. Thomas for a day on the sea with sun, snorkeling, and an open bar.

### If You Have 2 Weeks

**Days 1–7**   See above.

**Day 8**   Fly to St. Croix and relax at your hotel the first day; have a quiet dinner after putting in some beach time.

**Day 9**   Explore the old city of Christiansted. Check out the shops in town, which have the same duty-free arrangement as St. Thomas.

**Day 10**   Take an all-day excursion to the white coral sands of Buck Island, which has an underwater snorkeling trail.

**Day 11**   Journey to Frederiksted to see the second city of St. Croix.

**Day 12**   Check out the beaches, especially Buccaneer and Cormorant.

**Day 13**   Devote yourself to a day of your favorite sport: snorkeling, waterskiing, golf at the Carambola Golf Course, tennis on one of the courts of the Buccaneer Hotel, fishing, windsurfing, or horseback riding at Jill's Equestrian Stables.

**Day 14**   After a leisurely morning in bed, and a late breakfast with tropical fruit, stroll to the beach and later have a light lunch before heading for Christiansted for a final look at the town and its shops. If they're appearing on the island, go to hear Jimmy Hamilton ("Mr. Sax"), or attend a performance of the Quadrille Dancers.

### If You Have 3 Weeks

**Days 1–14**   See above.

**Day 15**   Fly to Beef Island and transfer by taxi to Road Town, capital of Tortola and the British Virgin Islands. Spend the afternoon at the beach and enjoy a dinner at your hotel or attend a West–Indian buffet nearby.

**Day 16**   Book one of the sightseeing tours of the island.

**Day 17**   Spend a day devoted to the beaches or sporting attractions, either tak-ing one of the boat trips offering snorkeling or scuba, or else enjoying a day on the sands. Have a final dinner at Mrs. Scatliffe's Restaurant and enjoy a good-bye toast at the Moorings on the waterfront.

**Day 18**   Fly or take a boat to Virgin Gorda, the second-largest cluster of the British Virgins, lying 12 miles east of Road Town. Spend the remaining time enjoying a good beach and have dinner at your hotel.

**Day 19**   Explore the attractions of Virgin Gorda by taking one of the escorted tours, which will take you to The Baths, a phenomenon of tranquil pools and caves formed by gigantic house-size boulders. Enjoy some beach life.

**Day 20**   Check out some of the sporting possibilities on the island, including Kilbride's Underwater Tours, or else do some boating or snorkeling.

**Day 21**   This day regrettably might be spent in transit, as you will have to get back from Virgin Gorda to Tortola en route to St. Thomas or Puerto Rico to make your connection back to the mainland.

## 11  Getting Married in the Virgin Islands

In recent years, the high cost of traditional weddings and the greater incidence of second or third weddings has led to an increased demand for less showy (and less expensive) weddings in warm-weather settings. If you yearn to tie the knot with your beloved on a sun-dappled island far from the prying eyes of everyone you've ever known, here are some basics for planning a wedding on the different islands in the Virgins. See "The Best Honeymoon Resorts" in Chapter 1 for our favorite places for post–nuptial getaways.

**BRITISH VIRGIN ISLANDS**   You need not reside here to get married, but the paperwork (whether you mail it yourself from off-island or whether you apply in person) usually takes about three days to process. Present a passport or birth certificate, plus certified proof of your marital status and any divorce or death certificates which apply to former spouse(s). The fee ranges from $35 to $110, depending on the site you select for your marriage ceremony. Marriages can be performed by the local registrar or by the officiant of your choice. Write to **Registrar's Office,** P.O. Box 418, Road Town, Tortola, BVI. (☎ **809/494-3701,** or **809/494-3492**).

**U.S. VIRGIN ISLANDS**   No blood tests or physical examinations are necessary, but there is a required $25 license fee, a notarized application, and an eight-day waiting period which is sometimes waived, depending on circumstances. A civil ceremony before a judge of the territorial court costs $200; a religious ceremony by a qualified clergyperson is equally valid. Fees and schedules for church weddings must be negotiated directly with the officiant.

Your wedding in the Virgin Islands can be planned by any number of ser-vices, including **Virgin Island Wedding Consultants,** P.O. Box 1192, St. Thomas, USVI 00801 (☎ **809/775-9203** or **800/843-3566**). You can also contact **Weddings the Island Way,** P.O. Box 11694, St. Thomas, USVI 00801 (☎ **809/776-4455**). Weddings for cruise passengers and hotel guests in St. Thomas or St. John can also be arranged by **Weddings by IPS,** Dept. MB, P.O. Box 9979, St. Thomas, USVI (☎ **800/937-1346**).

The guide, *Getting Married in the U.S. Virgin Islands,* is distributed by USVI tourism offices and gives background information on all three islands, as well as information about wedding planners, places of worship, florists, and limousine services. The guide also provides a listing of island accommodations that offer in-house wedding services.

Couples can begin their nuptial arrangements by first applying for a marriage license for weddings on St. Thomas and St. John by writing to the **Territorial Court of the Virgin Islands,** P.O. Box 70, St. Thomas, USVI 00804 (☎ **809/ 774-6680**). For weddings on St. Croix, applications are available by writing the

**Territorial Court of the Virgin Islands,** Family Division, P.O. Box 929, Christiansted, St. Croix, USVI 00821 (☎ **809/774-6680**).

# 12  Tips on Accommodations

The Virgin Islands offer a bewildering choice of accommodations, ranging from cottages to condos, from West–Indian guesthouses to plush resort hotels, from self-catering facilities to home exchanges. For information on home exchanges and homestays, see "Educational Travel and Homestays" earlier in this chapter.

## THE MEAL PLAN ABBREVIATIONS USED IN THIS GUIDE

If, like most guests, you plan to stay at a hotel or resort, you'll have to determine beforehand the type of arrangement you want, including the various meal plans offered. It is generally cheaper to take the half-board rate (MAP or Modified American Plan) or the full-board plan (AP or American Plan). You'll save more money on these plans than if you stay at a hotel or resort and order all your meals à la carte. In winter, some hotels may request that you book at the MAP rate. EP means European Plan, offering a room but not meals, and CP means Continental Plan, providing a room and a continental breakfast only.

## HOTELS & RESORTS

It's particularly galling to learn that the couple next door who is staying in a similar room to yours perhaps even enjoying an ocean view as opposed to your "mountain view," is paying some $200 to $300 less per week. That happens more often than you'd imagine, especially during slow months when Caribbean hoteliers want to promote business.

Resorts and hotels offer package deals galore, and though they have many disadvantages, the deals are always cheaper than rack rates (what an individual who literally walks in from the street pays). Therefore it's always good to go to a reliable travel agent to find out what is available in the way of land-and-air packages before booking into a particular hold.

There is no rigid classification of Caribbean hotels. The word "deluxe" is often used—or misused—when first class might be more appropriate. First class itself often isn't what it claims to be. For that and other reasons, we've presented fairly detailed descriptions of the properties, so that you'll get an idea of what to expect. However, even in the deluxe and first-class properties, don't expect top-rate service and efficiency. Life in the tropics has a slower pace. When you go to turn on the shower, sometimes you get water and sometimes you don't. You may even experience island power failures. To prepare yourself, read the Herman Wouk novel *Don't Stop the Carnival,* and go to the Virgin Islands prepared.

## THE WEST INDIAN GUESTHOUSE

Most of the Antilleans stay in guesthouses when they travel to the Virgin Islands. Some of these are surprisingly comfortable, and many have private baths in each room, air conditioning, and swimming pools. The rooms are sometimes cooled by ceiling fans or trade winds blowing through open windows at night. Of course, don't expect the luxuries of a fabulous resort, but for value the guesthouse can't be topped. Staying in a guesthouse, you can journey over to a big beach resort, using its seaside facilities. This, however, must be cleared with the reception desk.

If you use any of the hotel's equipment or services, you'll be asked to pay for what you use. Sometimes the hotels, thinking you'll patronize their drinking and eating facilities, encourage "drop-in" business.

Although free of frills, the guesthouses we've recommended are clean, decent, and they are considered safe for families and single women. Many of the cheapest ones are not places in which you'd like to spend 24 hours a day, but who wants to do that in the Virgin Islands anyway?

## SELF-CATERING HOLIDAYS

Particularly if you're a family or friendly group, a housekeeping holiday can be one of the least expensive ways to vacation in the Virgin Islands. This type of accommodation is now available on nearly all the islands reviewed. Some are individual cottage; others are housed in one building. Some are private homes rented when the owners are away. All have small kitchens or kitchenettes where you can do your own cooking.

A housekeeping holiday, however, doesn't always mean you'll have to work. Most of the self-catering places have chamber service included in the rental, and you're given fresh linen as well.

Cooking most of your meals yourself and dining out on occasion (such as when a neighboring big hotel has a beachside barbecue with entertainment) is the surest way of keeping holiday costs at a minimum.

## RENTAL VILLAS & VACATION HOMES

Even Princess Margaret rents out her private villa on Mustique in the Grenadines. Of course, she asks thousands of dollars per week, but throughout the Caribbean, including the Virgin Islands, you can often secure good deals by renting privately owned villas, apartments, condos, or cottages.

Private apartments are rented with or without chamber service. This is more of a no-frills option than the villas and condos. The apartment might not be in a building with a swimming pool, and it might not have a front desk to help you. Cottages are the most freewheeling of the four major categories of vacation homes. Most cottages are fairly simple, and many open onto a beach. Others are clustered around a communal swimming pool. Many contain no more than a simple bedroom with a small kitchen and bath. In the peak winter season, reservations should be made at least five to six months in advance.

Dozens of agents throughout the United States and Canada offer rentals. Try one of the following.

**At Home Abroad,** Suite 6-H, 405 E. 56th St., New York, NY 10022-2466 (☎ 212/421-9165), has a roster of private homes for rent in St. Thomas and St. John, each with maid service included. They rent out villas and condos.

**Caribbean Connection +,** P.O. Box 261, Trumbull, CT 06611 (☎ 203/261-8603), offers island-hopping itineraries and accommodations of all kinds (inns, condos, villas, hotels) in the Caribbean. Golf vacations in the islands are their specialty. "Caribbean Essence" vacations customize itineraries to a client's interest by local experts. This agency is the only one that offers itineraries that include from one to six islands. Caribbean Connection + caters to four different budgets—shoestring, comfortable, deluxe, and fantasy.

**Hideaways International,** 767 Islington St., Portsmouth, NH 03801 (☎ 603/430-4433, or 800/843-4433 in the U.S.), publishes *Hideaways Guide,* a 140-page pictorial directory fully describing home rentals throughout the Caribbean. Rentals range from cottages to staffed villas to whole islands! On most rentals, you deal directly with the owners. Hideaways offers member discounts at condos and small resorts. Other services include yacht charters, airline ticketing, car rentals, and hotel reservations. Annual membership is $99; a four-month trial membership is $39.

Sometimes local tourist offices also advise you on vacation home rentals if you write or call them directly.

For diverse rentals in the U.S. Virgin Islands, make inquiries from **Property Management Caribbean, Inc.,** Route 6, Cowpet Bay, St. Thomas, USVI 00802 (**☎ 809/775-6220,** or **800/524-2038**). Rentals range from studio apartments to four-bedroom villas suitable for up to eight people. Each has a fully equipped kitchen. No food is provided, but there's a coffee starter set. A minimum stay of three days is required in any season; the minimum stay is seven nights around Christmas.

**Island Villas, Property Management Rentals,** 14A Caravelle Arcade, Christiansted, St. Croix, USVI 00820 (**☎ 809/773-8821,** or **800/626-4512**), offers some of the best properties on St. Croix. The outfit specializes in villa and condo rentals, very private residences with pools; many are on the beach. The range goes from one-bedroom units to six-bedroom villas, with prices from $1,200 to $5,000 per week.

**Villas of Distinction,** P.O. Box 55, Armonk, NY 10504 (**☎ 914/273-3331,** or **800/289-0900** in the U.S.), is one of the best agencies, offering "complete vacations," including airfare, rental car, and domestic help. Some private villas have two to five bedrooms, and almost every villa has a swimming pool. You can rent villas on St. Martin, Mustique, Barbados, the U.S. Virgins, the Cayman Islands, St. Lucia, St. Barts, Jamaica, and Antigua, among others.

**Ocean Property Management, Inc.,** P.O. Box 8529, St. Thomas, USVI 00801 (**☎ 809/775-5901,** or **800/775-5901**), rents accommodations at Secret Harbourview Villas, on a garden set on a hillside in St. Thomas. Condo suites with private balconies and ocean views, the rentals lie only a short walk from the beach. The company rents out condo suites on other parts of St. Thomas as well.

## 13  Renting Your Own Island

For extremely well-heeled escapists, the British Virgin Islands rents private islands. If you're not that rich, you can ask friends to join you and share the cost. Even splitting the bills, it'll still be costly. Here's what's up for grabs:

- **Guana Island** (see Chapter 7 for more details). Some 30 or so guests can take over this privately owned island, the sixth largest of the British Virgin Islands, for a negotiable fee. The 850–acre island is a nature sanctuary with seven virgin beaches and a network of trails, and a visit here is a total retreat from the world.

- **Mosquito Island (North Sound)** (see Chapter 7 for more details). This is a sandy 125–acre island just north of Virgin Gorda. Guests sail in on yachts and take over the entire 12–unit Drake's Anchorage Resort Inn. The island, which has four beaches, is the perfect hideaway without TV, phones, or other modern amenities. Only five minutes by boat from Virgin Gorda, the resort has solar panels for heating water. Yachties gather offshore. See Chapter 7 for room prices.

- **Necker Island** (**☎ 800/231-1445,** or **212/696-4566** in New York City). This island is a 74-acre hideaway enveloped by its own unpolluted coral reef. It's owned by Richard Branson, of Virgin Records and Virgin Atlantic Airways, who is well acquainted with its trio of white sandy beaches. When he's not around, he leases the entire island to such personages as Eddie Murphy and Princess Di. At the core of the island is a 10–bedroom villa built in Bali style. Sun pours into the villa's lush tropical garden, and there are a private freshwater pool and two Jacuzzis. Two one–bedroom guesthouses can accommodate your friends. The daily rate is $10,900, including food and drink for up to 20 members of your entourage. Guests are ferried over from the Beef Island airport on Tortola.

## 14  Tips on Dining

Dining in the Virgin Islands is generally more expensive than it is in either the United States or Canada since, except for locally caught fish, virtually everything is imported. Service (10%–15%) is automatically added to most restaurant tabs, and if the service has been good, it is customary to tip extra.

If you're booked into a hotel on MAP (half board), which some hotels require in peak season, get out and sample some of the local restaurants at lunch.

In some of the posh resorts such as Caneel Bay on St. John, it is customary for men to wear a jacket, but in summer, virtually no establishment requires it. If in doubt, always ask the restaurant, or check the policy of the hotel before going to a particular establishment.

At the better places, women's evening attire is casual chic. During the day it is proper everywhere to wear a cover up over your bathing suit if you're in a restaurant.

Whenever possible, stick to regional food, which is fresher. For a main dish, that usually means Caribbean lobster or fish caught in the deep sea. Many world-class chefs cook in the Virgin Islands, but they are only as good as their ingredients, which are not always the freshest.

Nevertheless, the food is better than ever in the islands, and many fine talents, including many top-notch female chefs from California, now cook there. Many have adapted Stateside recipes with the local ingredients available to come up with Caribbean/California cuisine.

Check to see if reservations are required before going to a place. In summer, you can almost always get in, but in winter, all the tables may be taken at some of the famous but small places.

If you're going out in the evening, especially if you drink, it is a good idea to go by taxi and arrange for the taxi to pick you up or have the restaurant call a cab for you. It generally arrives in no more than 30 minutes.

Whatever you do, try to get out and eat at some of the local places. The prices are more reasonable, and the fare is more adventurous and interesting.

## 15  Tips on Shopping

The surprise is that the island's best buys are not necessarily products made within the Virgin Islands (although some local wares are also good values). Many visitors end up buying items that are available at home but that are *sometimes* cheaper because they are duty free. With discount stores mushrooming in Canada and the United States, your hometown might offer better bargains. Don't expect the fabled bargains in the Virgin Islands so highly touted even as recently as the 1970s.

U.S. residents are entitled to $1,200 worth of duty-free exports from the American islands (not Puerto Rico) every 30 days. That is three times the exemption allowed from most foreign destinations. For more information see the "Information" section earlier in this chapter.

You can protect your duty-free allowance by sending home unsolicited gifts not totaling more than $100 per day. You pay no duty, and you don't have to declare such gifts on your Customs form when leaving. Many shoppers pick up island-made, duty-free items like leather sandals, paintings, island dolls, locally made clothing, pottery, boutique canvas bags, locally recorded music, straw products, batiks, and unusual handmade jewelry.

If you're visiting only the British Virgin Islands and make purchases there, you will be taxed at the same rate as any foreign destination. Besides, selections pale in the BVI compared to the shopping malls of St. Croix and especially St. Thomas, which is the best shopping center in all of the Caribbean.

The smart shopper will still find some good buys in Road Town (Tortola), because even though the capital is not a duty-free port, there is no duty on goods imported from Britain. You might find some good buys on English fabrics, china, and some other items—certainly they will be cheaper than in London. You will have to pay duty when you bring them back into the United States if their value exceeds the limit imposed by U.S. Customs.

St. Thomas has far more shops and far more merchandise than St. Croix and certainly more than little St. John, which has only a few shops in its capital, Cruz Bay, most at Mongoose Junction. Shopkeepers often falsely claim that prices are generally 20% to 50% lower in the U.S. Virgins than Stateside, but don't count on it. It is wise to know the Stateside price if you're in the market for a particular item. Don't rely on the merchant to tell you the price.

In general, the best buys are liquor (because of the generous U.S. allowance—see "Information" earlier in this chapter), jewelry, and china. You might get bargains on crystal, certain clothing, porcelain, and leather goods, watches, and even furs, if you know what you're looking for.

Cigarettes are marked down, and imported beauty products such as perfume are generally excellent buys.

In clothing, the best buys are woolen items, such as sweaters. Cashmere sweaters are sometimes good values. Fashions from the Far East, especially China, are usually cheap, and European and U.S. designer labels are often discounted, but perhaps you'll find the same discounts back in your hometown shopping mall.

Jewelry is the most common item for sale in St. Thomas. Look over the selections of gold and gem stones (emeralds are traditionally considered the finest savings). Gold that is marked 24K in the U.S. and Canada is marked 999 (99.9% pure gold) on European items. Gold marked 18K in the U.S. and Canada has a European marking of 750 (or 75% pure), and 14K gold is marked 585 (or 58.5% pure).

In porcelain and crystal, you'll find the best selections from Europe at prices sometimes lower than Stateside. It is easy to be taken unless you know current prices in your home country. Most stores will arrange shipment. Name-brand watches are sold throughout Charlotte Amalie and, to a lesser degree, St. Croix.

Theoretically, bargaining is not the rule, but over the years we have found merchant after merchant willing to do so, particularly on expensive items such as jewelry and perfume. Obviously, the slow summer, late spring, and fall seasons are the best times to try to make deals.

Take caution when souvenir shopping, and follow guidelines issued by the World Wildlife Fund. Some souvenirs made have been made from endangered species. When in doubt, the agency advises to grill the vendor. If answers are not forthcoming or if the vendor seems uninformed, then don't buy.

Endangered species include black coral, which in some cases can take decades to grow one inch. Many wild birds, especially parrots, are threatened. The sea turtle, especially the hawksbill turtle, is also under threat of extinction.

Sometimes you'll see *Buyer Beware* brochures at airports. Customs officials are also informed. For more information, send a stamped, self-addressed envelope to the **World Wildlife Fund** 1250 24th St. NW, Washington, DC 20037.

## FAST FACTS: The U.S. Virgin Islands

**American Express**   In St. Thomas, service is provided by Caribbean Travel Agency, Inc./Tropic Tours, 9716 Estate Thomas (☎ **774-1855**). Visitors to St. John should use the services provided by the St. Thomas agency. On St. Croix, the American Express Travel Service representative is Southerland, Chandler's Wharf, Gallows Bay (☎ **773-9500**).

**Area Code**   The area code for all the U.S. Virgin Islands is **809,** which you can dial directly from the mainland of the United States.

**Banks**   Several major banks are represented in the U.S. Virgins. While hours vary, many are open Monday through Thursday from 9am to 2:30pm and Friday from 9am to 2pm and 3:30 to 5pm.

**Business Hours**   Typical business hours are Monday through Friday from 9am to 5pm and Saturday from 9am to 1pm.

**Camera and Film**   Most well-known brands of film, such as Kodak, are sold in the Virgin Islands. Film isn't cheap here, nor is the cost of getting your film processed locally. It might be cheaper to send your film home for processing. Protect your camera in the Virgin Islands, not only from theft, but also from saltwater and sand. It can also overheat if left in the sun or locked in the trunk of a car. For the best commercial camera stores in the U.S. Virgins, see the individual island chapters.

**Climate**   See "When to Go," in Chapter 3.

**Currency**   U.S. currency is used on the U.S. Virgin Islands.

**Customs**   See "Visitor Information, Entry Requirements & Money," in Chapter 3.

**Documents Required**   See "Visitor Information, Entry Requirements & Money," in Chapter 3.

**Driving Rules**   Remember to drive on the left. Obey speed limits, which are 20 m.p.h. in town, 35 m.p.h. outside.

**Drugs**   A branch of the federal narcotics strike force is permanently stationed in the U.S. Virgin Islands. If convicted of possession of marijuana, severe penalties are imposed, ranging from 2 to 10 years. Possession of hard drugs such as cocaine can lead to 15 years in prison.

**Drugstores**   Carry all prescription medicine with you, enough for the duration of your stay. If you need any other medications, such as in case of sunburn, or a prescription filled, you'll find many drugstore outlets in St. Thomas and St. Croix, with limited offerings on St. John. See specific island "Fast Facts" for drugstore recommendations.

**Electricity**　The electrical current in the Virgin Islands is the same as on the mainland: 110 volts AC, 60 cycles.

**Embassies and Consulates**　There are no embassies or consulates here.

**Emergencies**　Police, **915;** fire, **921;** ambulance, **922;** Coast Guard, **774-1911.**

**Etiquette**　Proper etiquette in the U.S. Virgins concerns dress. Cover up in restaurants or when walking along the streets of the main towns.

**Hitchhiking**　It isn't illegal, but it isn't widely practiced. It might be more practical on St. Croix, because of the distances involved, than on the other islands, but we don't recommend it anywhere.

**Holidays**　See "When to Go," in Chapter 3.

**Hospitals**　See "Fast Facts" for the individual islands.

**Information**　See "Visitor Information, Entry Requirements & Money," in Chapter 3.

**Laundry**　Often your hotel will arrange to have your clothing laundered for you, but you pay a surcharge above what it would cost in a laundromat. See "Fast Facts" under the individual island listings for the names of laundromats.

**Liquor Laws**　You must be 21 years of age or older to purchase liquor in stores or buy drinks in hotels, bars, and restaurants.

**Mail**　Postage rates are the same as on the U.S. mainland.

**Maps**　Tourist offices provide free maps of all three islands. If you plan extensive touring, purchase a copy of the *Official Road Map of the United States Virgin Islands,* available in most bookstores. This map has detailed routes of all three islands and city maps of Christiansted, Frederiksted, Cruz Bay, and Charlotte Amalie.

**Newspapers and Magazines**　Daily newspapers from the mainland are flown in to St. Thomas and St. Croix every day, and local papers, such as the *Virgin Island Daily News,* available on St. Thomas and St. Croix, also carry the latest news. St. Croix has its own daily newspaper, the *St. Croix Avis.*

**Passports**　See "Visitor Information, Entry Requirements & Money," in Chapter 3.

**Pets**　To bring your pet to the USVI, you must produce a health certificate from a mainland veterinarian. You will also be required to show proof of vaccination against rabies. Very few hotels allow animals, so check in advance. Both St. Croix and St. Thomas have veterinarians listed on the yellow pages. If you're strolling with your dog through the national park on St. John, the dog must be on a leash. Pets are not allowed at campgrounds, picnic areas, or on public beaches.

**Police**　Call **915.** For local stations see "Police" under "Fast Facts" for the individual islands.

**Radio and TV**　All three islands receive both cable and commercial TV stations. Radio weather reports can be heard at 7:30pm and 8:30am on 99.5 FM.

**Restrooms**　These exist at public beaches and at airport terminals, with limited public facilities available in towns. Usually toilets are found at the main squares. Many visitors use the facilities of a bar or restaurant, but it is considered polite to order something, if only a mineral water, as in theory these facilities are restricted to patrons.

**Safety**   There have been recent reports that the crime rate of the U.S. Virgin Islands is increasing. Exercise caution and stay alert. Be aware of your immediate surroundings. Avoid wandering the back streets of Charlotte Amalie, Frederiksted, or Christiansted at night. Be particularly careful with cameras, purses, and wallets, all favorite targets of thieves and pickpockets.

**Taxes**   There is no departure tax for the U.S. Virgin Islands. Hotels add a 7.5% tax to rates that is not always included in the rate quoted to you. Always ask just to be sure.

**Telephone, Telex, and Fax**   Local calls at a telephone booth cost 25¢. From all points on the mainland you can dial direct to the Virgin Islands using the area code **809.** Cable service is available as well. Most hotels are equipped to send telex and fax. You can also do so at local post offices on the islands. See "Telephone, Telex, and Fax" under "Fast Facts" under individual island listings for specific addresses.

**Time**   The U.S. Virgins are on Atlantic time, which places the islands one hour ahead of eastern standard time. However, during daylight saving time, the Virgin Islands and the East Coast are on the same time. So when it's 6am in Charlotte Amalie, it's 5am in Miami; during daylight saving time it's 6am in both places.

**Tipping**   As a general rule tip 15%. Some hotels add a 10% to 15% surcharge to cover service. When in doubt, ask.

**Tourist Offices**   See "Visitor Information, Entry Requirements & Money," in Chapter 3. In St. Thomas, the Visitors Center is at Emancipation Square (☎ 774-8784); in St. Croix at the Old Scalehouse (☎ 773-0495) on the waterfront at Christiansted, and also in the Customs House Building, Strand Street, Frederiksted (☎ 772-0357); and in St. John at Cruz Bay (☎ 776-6450).

**Visas**   U.S. and Canadian citizens do not need a visa to enter the U.S. Virgin Islands. Visitors from other nations should have a passport and a U.S. visa. Those visitors may also be asked to produce an onward ticket. See "Entry Requirements" in Chapter 3.

**Water**   There is ample water for showers and bathing in the Virgin Islands, but you are asked to conserve. Many visitors drink the local tap water with no harmful after effects. Others, more prudent or with more delicate stomach should stick to bottled water.

**Yellow Pages**   The telephone company of the U.S. Virgin Islands publishes an annual directory with extensive listings of services and establishments. All three islands are condensed into one book.

## FAST FACTS: The British Virgin Islands

**American Express**   Local representatives include Travel Plan, Ltd., Waterfront Drive (☎ 494-2347), in Tortola; and Travel Plan, Ltd., Virgin Gorda Yacht Harbour (☎ 495-5586), in Virgin Gorda.

**Area Code**   The area code is **809.** When calling from outside the islands, you must then dial **49** before all BVI numbers.

**Banks**   Banks are generally open Monday through Thursday from 9am to 3pm, Friday from 9am to 5pm. To cash traveler's checks, try Bank of Nova Scotia, Wickhams Cay (☎ **494-2526**) or Barclays Bank, Wickhams Cay (☎ **494-2171**), both near Road Town.

**Bookstores**   The best bookstore on the island is the National Educational Services Bookstore, Wickhams Cay in Road Town (☎ **494-3921**). In spite of its name, it is a privately owned and funded bookstore.

**Business Hours**   Most offices are open Monday through Friday from 9am to 5pm. Government offices are open Monday through Friday from 8:30am to 4:30pm. Shops are generally open Monday through Friday from 9am to 5pm and Saturday from 9am to 1pm.

**Camera and Film**   The best place for supplies and developing on Tortola is Bolo's Brothers, Wickhams Cay (☎ **494-2867**).

**Climate**   See "When to Go," in Chapter 3.

**Crime**   See "Safety," below.

**Currency**   The U.S. dollar is the legal currency, much to the surprise of arriving British who find no one willing to accept their pounds.

**Customs**   You can generally bring into the BVI items intended for your personal use. But if you make purchases here, U.S. Customs allows only a $400 duty-free exemption, providing you have been out of the United States for 48 hours. You can mail back home unsolicited gifts providing they don't exceed $50 per day in value to any single address. You don't pay duty on items classified as handcrafts, art, or antiques.

**Dentist**   In Tortola call the Department of Health (☎ **494-3474**) for a referral.

**Doctor**   See "Hospitals," below.

**Documents Required**   See "Visitor Information, Entry Requirements & Money," in Chapter 3.

**Driving Rules**   Driving in the BVI is only for those who like hairpin turns and terrain like a Coney Island Cyclone. You need a valid Canadian or American driver's license and must pay $10 at police headquarters for a three-month British Virgin Islands driving permit. Some of the larger car-rental companies keep a supply of these forms. Remember to drive on the left.

**Drug Laws**   Drugs, their use, possession, or sale, are strictly prohibited. Penalties are stiff.

**Drugstores**   The best place to go is J.R. O'Neal, Ltd., Main Street, Road Town (☎ **494-2292**), in Tortola. It is closed on Sunday. Stock up here on any prescribed medicines or other supplies you'll need if you're planning visits to the other islands.

**Electricity**   The electrical current is 110 volts, AC, 60 cycles, as in the U.S.

**Embassies and Consulates**   There are none.

**Emergencies**   Thirteen doctors practice in Tortola, and there is a hospital, Peebles Hospital, Porter Road, Road Town (☎ **494-3497**), with X-ray and laboratory facilities. One doctor practices on Virgin Gorda. Your hotel can put you in touch with the island's medical staff.

**Etiquette**   Unlike in some parts of the Caribbean, nudity is an offense punishable by law in the BVI.

**Hairdresser**   The best place for men and women is Scissors, Prospect Reef (☎ **494-3221**), in Road Town.

**Hitchhiking**   Travel by thumb is illegal.

**Holidays**   See "When to Go," in Chapter 3.

**Hospitals**   In Road Town, you can go to Peebles Hospital, Porter Road (☎ **494-3497**).

**Information**   See "Visitor Information, Entry Requirements & Money," in Chapter 3.

**Laundry and Dry Cleaning**   In Tortola, one of the best places is Freeman's Laundry & Dry Cleaning, Purcell Estate (☎ **494-2285**).

**Library**   The public library, Main Street (☎ **494-3428**), is in Road Town.

**Liquor Laws**   The legal minimum age for purchasing liquor or drinking alcohol in bars is 21.

**Lost Property**   Go to the police station. Sometimes they'll broadcast notice of your lost property on the local radio station.

**Mail**   Most hotels will mail letters for you, or you can go directly to the post office. Allow four days to one week for letters to reach the North American mainland. Postal rates in the BVI have been raised now to 30¢ for a postcard (airmail) to the U.S. or Canada, and 45¢ for a first-class airmail letter ($^1/_2$ ounce) to the U.S. or Canada, or 35¢ for a second-class letter ($^1/_2$ ounce) to the U.S. or Canada.

**Maps**   The best map of the British Virgin Islands is published by Vigilate and is sold at most bookstores in Road Town.

**Newspapers and Magazines**   Papers from the mainland, such as *The Miami Herald,* are flown into Tortola and Virgin Gorda daily, and copies of the latest issues of *Time* and *Newsweek* are sold at hotel newsstands and at various outlets in Road Town. The BVI has no daily newspaper, but *The Island Sun,* published Wednesday and Friday, is a good source of information on local entertainment.

**Passports**   See "Visitor Information, Entry Requirements & Money," in Chapter 3.

**Pets**   To bring in a pet, you'll need proof of vaccination against rabies and a health certificate from your veterinarian. You need clearance far in advance. Write to the Chief Agricultural Officer, Road Town, Tortola, BVI, or call **495-2451.**

**Police**   The main police headquarters is on Station Street (☎ **494-3822**) in Tortola. There is also a police station on Virgin Gorda (☎ **495-5222**) and another police station at Jost Van Dyke (☎ **495-9345**).

**Radio & TV**   Hotels subscribe to cable TV and get such broadcasts as CNN. The BVI has two local FM stations with nonstop music, including Z-HIT (94.3) and Z-WAVE (97.3).

**Religious Services**   In Tortola, there are several small churches, including Church of Christ, Main Street (☎ **494-4233**) in Road Town; in Virgin Gorda there is the Church of God Holiness, Manse (☎ **495-5248**). For information about Baptist services, call **494-4104;** for information about Catholic services, call **494-2690.**

**Restrooms**   Available at airports and ferry terminals, restrooms are hard to find elsewhere, and visitors must rely on those at commercial establishments, such as restaurants and hotels.

**Safety**   The BVI is one of the safest places in the Caribbean. But crime does exist, and you should take all the usual precautions. Don't leave items unattended on the beach. See "Safety," in "Fast Facts: U.S. Virgin Islands," earlier in this chapter.

**Shoe Repair**   Try Bolo's Brothers, Wickhams Cay (☎ **494-2867**), in Road Town.

**Taxes**   There is no sales tax. A government tax of 7% is imposed on all hotel rooms. A $7 departure tax is collected from everyone leaving by air, $5 for those departing by sea.

**Telephone, Telex, and Fax**   You can call the British Virgins from the continental U.S. by dialing area code **809,** followed by **49,** and then five digits. Once here, omit both the 809 and the 49 to make local calls. Most hotels (not the small guesthouses) will send a fax or telex for you.

**Time**   See "Fast Facts: The U.S. Virgin Islands," earlier in this chapter.

**Tipping**   See "Fast Facts: The U.S. Virgin Islands," earlier in this chapter.

**Tourist Offices**   The headquarters of the BVI Tourist Board is in the center of Road Town, close to the ferry dock, south of Wickhams Cay (☎ **494-3134**).

**Visas**   Visitors who stay for fewer than six months don't need a visa if they possess a return or onward ticket.

**Water**   See "Fast Facts: The U.S. Virgin Islands," earlier in this chapter.

**Yellow Pages**   All of the island phone numbers are contained in one volume, the British Virgin Islands telephone book, issued annually. In the back of the book is a helpful yellow pages section of goods and services available on the island.

# The U.S. Virgin Islands: St. Thomas

# 4

The busiest cruise-ship harbor in the West Indies, St. Thomas is about 12 miles long and three miles wide. It is the second largest of the U.S. Virgins and lies about 40 miles north of St. Croix, which is the largest Virgin. The U.S. Virgins' capital is Charlotte Amalie, which is also the shopping center of the Caribbean. Due to the great commercial activity and the island's drug and crime problem, St. Thomas has been called the most "un-virgin" of the Virgin Islands.

Vacationers discovered St. Thomas right after World War II, and they've been flocking here ever since in increasing numbers. Tourism has raised the standard of living here to one of the highest in the Caribbean. Condominium apartments and expensive villas have sprouted up over the debris of bulldozed shacks.

St. Thomas is a boon for cruise-ship shoppers, who flood Main Street, the three- to four-block-long shopping center in the heart of town. While this area gets very crowded, it's away from all beaches, major hotels, most restaurants, and entertainment facilities.

You can still find seclusion at a hotel in more remote sections of the island. Hotels on the north side of St. Thomas look out at the Atlantic, while those on the south side front the calmer Caribbean. Because of the steep hills which divide the islands and provide sweeping views, it's possible for the sun to be shining in the south while the north experiences showers.

St. Thomas is the most cosmopolitan of all the Virgin Islands, either U.S. or British. It is a port not only for cruise ships but for privately owned million-dollar yachts. It is especially known for its string of beautiful beaches, including the very best, Magens Bay. St. Thomas and the Virgin Islands have been rated by *National Geographic* as among the top destinations in the world for sailing, scuba diving, and fishing.

Charlotte Amalie, with its white houses and bright red roofs glistening in the sun, is one of the most beautiful towns in the Caribbean. Parts of it, however, are less than picturesque. While the town is famous for its shopping, it is also filled with historic sights. Attractions include Fort Christian, the oldest building in St. Thomas, built by the Danes in the 17th century. The town's architecture reflects the cultural diversity of St. Thomas. In Charlotte Amalie, the doors are Dutch, the red tile roofs Danish, the iron grillwork French, and the Andalusian-style patios Spanish.

---

## What's Special About St. Thomas

Beaches
- Magens Bay, 3 miles north of Charlotte Amalie, one of the most beautiful beaches in the world.
- Stouffer Grand Beach, one of the island's most stunning, with many water sports.
- Sapphire Beach, with its luxury hotel complexes in the background, one of the finest on the island, and a favorite with windsurfers. The most popular Sunday-afternoon gathering place on the East End.

Discoveries
- Coral World, a marine complex featuring a three-story underwater observation tower 100 feet offshore.
- Jim Tillett's Art Gallery and Boutique, built around an old plantation-era sugar mill.

Great Towns/Villages
- Charlotte Amalie, the capital of St. Thomas, one of the most beautiful port cities in the Caribbean.
- Frenchtown, settled by the descendants of immigrants from the French islands, famous for its "cha-chas," or straw hats.

Historic Buildings
- The St. Thomas Synagogue, second oldest in America built by Sephardic Jews in 1833.
- Government House, at Government Hill in Charlotte Amalie, the official residence of the U.S. Virgin Islands governor.
- Fort Christian, constructed by the Danes in 1671 and named for King Christian V.

---

St. Thomas is known for its excellent climate and enjoys sunshine all year round, with temperatures generally in the 80°s during the day, dropping into the 70°s at night.

# 1  Orientation

## ARRIVING
### BY PLANE

Nonstop flights to the U.S. Virgin Islands from New York and Atlanta take $3^3/_4$ and $3^1/_2$ hours, respectively. Flight time between St. Thomas and St. Croix is only 20 minutes. Flying to San Juan from mainland cities and changing planes may save you money over the APEX nonstop fare (see "Getting There" in Chapter 3).

**American Airlines** (☎ **800/433-7300**) offers one of the easiest and most comprehensive routes into St. Thomas and St. Croix from the U.S. mainland. A daily nonstop flight departs from New York at 9:15am every day and arrives on St. Thomas at 2pm. Passengers originating in other parts of the world are usually routed into St. Thomas through American's hubs in Miami, San Juan, and Raleigh-Durham, all of which offer nonstop service (often several times a day) into

St. Thomas. Connections from Los Angeles or San Francisco to either St. Thomas or St. Croix are usually made through either New York, San Juan, or Miami. American's tour desk can arrange discount air passage if a hotel reservation is made through American at the same time. American's lowest fare to St. Thomas requires a 14-day advance payment and a delay of between 3 to 30 days before activating the return portion. A penalty will be imposed if you make any changes before departure from North America. APEX fares vary with the season, and traveling in either direction on Monday through Thursday usually saves money. Requesting a change of planes at American's hub in Puerto Rico, or opting for an early-morning or late-night flight might also save you money. Flights from Puerto Rico to the U.S. Virgin Islands are usually on American's partner, **American Eagle** (☎ 800/433-7300).

**Delta** (☎ 800/221-1212) offers two daily nonstop flights between New York's Kennedy International Airport and St. Thomas and a third nonstop flight from Atlanta to St. Thomas. Additionally, one of the New York flights provides connections to St. Croix.

**TWA** (☎ 800/221-2000) does not fly nonstop into any of the Virgin Islands but offers connections on other carriers through San Juan, Puerto Rico. TWA flies into San Juan twice daily nonstop from New York's JFK, once daily nonstop from Miami, and once daily with a touchdown in Miami from St. Louis.

Travelers from the South and Midwest have better access to St. Thomas and St. Croix since **United Airlines** (☎ 800/241-6522) formed an alliance with **Sunaire Express Airlines** (☎ 800/495-2840). Sunaire Express is a St. Croix–based commuter airline. The two companies agreed to a code-share that lists Sunaire flights from Puerto Rico to the U.S. Virgin Islands as connecting United Airlines flights. Passengers flying from Chicago, Miami, and other United Airlines points of origin to Puerto Rico are able to board any of 18 flights to St. Croix and St. Thomas via Sunaire. Under the agreement, the carriers coordinate their schedules and provide quick transfers of passengers and luggage.

**Virgin Islands Paradise Airways** (☎ 800/299-USVI) flies daily to St. Thomas and St. Croix, with nonstop flights originating in Miami and Newark. A professional crew clad in island-style clothing serves local Virgin Islands cuisine, including pâtés and Cruzan rum, to guests aboard the 727-200s. Caribbean music serenades passengers, while a TV screen provides previews of places to see and things to do in St. Thomas, St. John, and St. Croix. *Black Enterprise* magazine listed the airline's parent company, NavCom Systems, Inc., 59th on their list of 100 top black-owned companies.

*A final hint:* Bargain-seeking passengers should ask their airline to connect them with the tour desk. Someone there can usually arrange discounted hotel rates if a hotel reservation is arranged simultaneously with air passage. The options are so varied and complicated that only an airline staff member or a travel agent can describe them in detail.

## BY BOAT

St. Thomas's capital, Charlotte Amalie, is the busiest cruise-ship port in the Caribbean. For details on cruise-ship travel, see "Getting There," Chapter 3. St. Thomas maintains no ferry connections to St. Croix, some 40 miles to the south. The best way to get there is to fly.

If you are already in the British Virgin Islands and want to visit St. Thomas, there is a well-traveled route by boat between Charlotte Amalie and Tortola, the capital of the BVI. Trip time is only 45 minutes between these two capitals, and the one-way cost is $35. The principal carriers based in Tortola making the run to St. Thomas include **Smith's Ferry** (☎ 775-7292) and **Native Son** (☎ 774-8685).

St. Thomas is also linked by boat to St. John, its neighbor island, some three to five miles away (depending from where you measure). Ferries depart from Red Hook on the East End of St. Thomas and reach St. John (or rather its capital of Cruz Bay) in about 20 minutes; the cost is $3 one-way. For complete ferry schedules, telephone **776-6282.**

## VISITOR INFORMATION

In St. Thomas, the Visitors Center is at Emancipation Square (☎ 774-8784). They dispense helpful advice. You can also pick up a copy of *St. Thomas This Week,* which includes maps of St. Thomas and St. John.

## CITY LAYOUT
### MAIN STREETS & ARTERIES

The capital, Charlotte Amalie, is the only town on St. Thomas. It borders the waterfront, and its seaside promenade is called **Waterfront Highway** or just the Waterfront. Its old Danish name is Kyst Vejen. From the waterfront, you can take any number of streets or alleyways leading back into town to the **Main Street** or Dronningens Gade. Principal links between Main Street and the Waterfront include **Raadets Gade, Tolbod Gade, Store Tvaer Gade,** and **Strand Gade.**

Main Street is aptly named, as it is the center of the capital and the location of the major shops. The western part of Main Street is **Market Square,** which was once the site of the biggest slave market auctions in the Caribbean Basin. It lies near the intersection with Strand Gade. Today, it is an open-air block of stalls where farmers and gardeners on the island peddle their produce daily except Sunday and particularly on Saturday. Go early in the morning to see the market at its best.

Running parallel to Main Street and lying north of it is **Back Street** or Vimmelskaft Gade, which has many stores, including some of the less expensive ones. *Note:* It's quite dangerous to walk along Back Street at night, but it's reasonably safe for daytime shopping.

In the eastern part of town, midway between Tolbod Gade and Fort Pladsen, lies **Emancipation Park,** northwest of Fort Christian, commemorating the liberation of the slaves in 1848. Most of the major historical buildings, including the Legislature, Fort Christian, and Government House, lie within a short walk of this park.

Southeast of the park looms **Fort Christian,** crowned by a clock tower and painted a rusty red, constructed by the Danes in 1671. The Legislative Building, seat of the elected government of the U.S. Virgin Islands, lies on the harbor side of the fort.

**Kongens Gade** (or King's Street) leads to **Government Hill,** which overlooks the town and the harbor. **Government House,** a white brick building dating from 1867, stands atop the hill.

Between **Hotel 1829,** a former mansion constructed in that year by a French sea captain, and Government House is a staircase known as the **Street of 99 Steps.** Actually, someone miscounted: It should be called the Street of 103 Steps. The steps lead to the summit of Government Hill.

Near here are the remains of the 17th-century **Fort Skytsborg** or Blackbeard's Tower, a reference to the notorious pirate Edward Teach, who is said to have spied on treasure galleons entering the harbor in the 1700s. Today a 22-room hotel, **Blackbeard's Castle,** stands here.

This should not be confused with **Bluebeard's Tower,** which crowns a 300-foot hill at the eastern edge of town. This is the site of what is perhaps the best known (but not the best) hotel in the Virgin Islands. It's called Bluebeard's Castle.

Finding an address in Charlotte Amalie is relatively easy, even though many stores don't advertise or even display their street numbers. Even numbers run up one side of the street and odd numbers up the other. No. 25 might be across the street from No. 14.

*St. Thomas This Week,* distributed free by the tourist office and handed out to cruise-ship passengers, contains a two-page map in its center, including not only a clear, easy-to-follow street plan of Charlotte Amalie, but also all the important landmark buildings. It pinpoints all the leading shops of Charlotte Amalie, giving the name of the shop in an index which corresponds with an easy-to-find number on the map. Pick up a copy of this map if you're going on a walking tour of Charlotte Amalie or a shopping spree.

## Neighborhoods in Brief

Charlotte Amalie is too small to be divided into neighborhoods. A highly navigable little town by foot, it forms its own closely knit geographical unit.

Its only neighborhood of any significance is **Frenchtown,** which for years was called *Cha-Cha Town,* now considered pejorative, after the straw hats worn by the original settlers of the town. Some of the older generation still speak a distinctive Norman-French dialect.

Since the heart of Charlotte Amalie is considered a dangerous place to go wandering at night, Frenchtown, with its many fine restaurants and interesting bars, has now become the center of nightlife and is a much safer place to be after dark. To reach Frenchtown, take Veterans Drive west of town along the waterfront, turning left shortly after you pass the Windward Passage Hotel on your right at the sign pointing to the Villa Olga.

The only other neighborhood is **Frenchman's Hill,** site of the famous Harbor View Hotel and restaurant. The Huguenots built many old stone villas here, which open onto panoramic views of the town and its harbor.

# 2  Getting Around

If you arrive by cruise ship, you will be deposited right in the heart of Charlotte Amalie, where you can begin your shopping adventures. Should you arrive by air, you will land at the Cyril E. King Airport to the west of Charlotte Amalie along Route 30. A plentiful supply of taxis always meets every arriving plane. Chances are you will be staying at a hotel east of Charlotte Amalie. Getting there can involve long delays and traffic jams on any day when a lot of cruise ships happen to visit the port.

## BY BUS

St. Thomas has the best public transportation of any island in the U.S. chain. Buses (called Vitrans) leave from the center of Charlotte Amalie, fanning out east and west along all the most important highways on the island. Vitran stops are found beside the roads. You rarely have to wait more than 30 minutes during the day, and they run between 6am and 9pm daily, charging 75¢ for rides within Charlotte Amalie and $1 for rides anywhere else on the island. This is an excellent and comfortable form of public transportation. You may not be delivered to your door, however. For information about Vitran buses, their stops, and schedules, call **774-5678.**

## BY TAXI

In St. Thomas taxis are plentiful and are the chief means of transport. The cabs are unmetered, and fares are controlled and widely posted; however, it is still important to agree with the driver on a rate before you get into the car. Surcharges, ranging from $1.50 to $2, are added after midnight. If you rent a taxi and a driver (who just may serve as guide) for a day, the cost is about $30 for two passengers for two hours of sightseeing; each additional passenger pays $12. For 24-hour radio dispatch taxi service, call **774-7457.**

Many taxis transport 8 to 12 passengers in vans to multiple destinations. Of course, it's cheaper to travel in one of these—say, if you're going from your hotel to the airport instead of renting the taxi all to yourself. For example a taxi from the airport to the Stouffer Grand Beach Resort costs $9 individually, but only $6 per person if others are going in the same direction.

## BY CAR

**RENTING A CAR**   Partly because of its status as a U.S. territory, St. Thomas has many leading North American car-rental firms at the airport, and competition is stiff. The big companies, however, tend to be easier to deal with in cases of billing errors. Before you go, compare the rates of the "big three": **Avis** (☎ **800/ 331-2112**), **Budget** (☎ **800/626-4516**), and **Hertz** (☎ **800/654-3001**). There is no tax on car rentals in the Virgin Islands.

St. Thomas has a high accident rate: Many visitors are not used to driving on the left, the hilly terrain shelters blind curves and entrance ramps, and some drivers unwisely drive after too many drinks. In many cases, the roads are narrow and the lighting is poor.

Because of these factors, collision-damage insurance is strongly recommended. It costs from $10 to $13 per day extra, depending on the fine print, but even if you purchase insurance, you still might be responsible for a whopping deductible if you have an accident. The company with the least-attractive insurance policies, at press time, was Hertz. Even if you bought the insurance, priced at $13 a day, you'd still be liable for the first $3,000 worth of damage to your rented vehicle in the event of an accident. Personal accident insurance, available only at Avis and Hertz but not at Budget, costs $3 extra per day. Obviously, it pays to ask questions about insurance coverage and your financial responsibilities before you rent. The minimum age requirement for drivers at all three companies is 25.

At press time, the least expensive cars at Avis, Budget, and Hertz cost $193, $199, and $177, respectively, for week-long rentals with unlimited mileage. The lowest-rate cars at Avis and Hertz came with automatic transmission and air

# The U.S. Virgin Islands

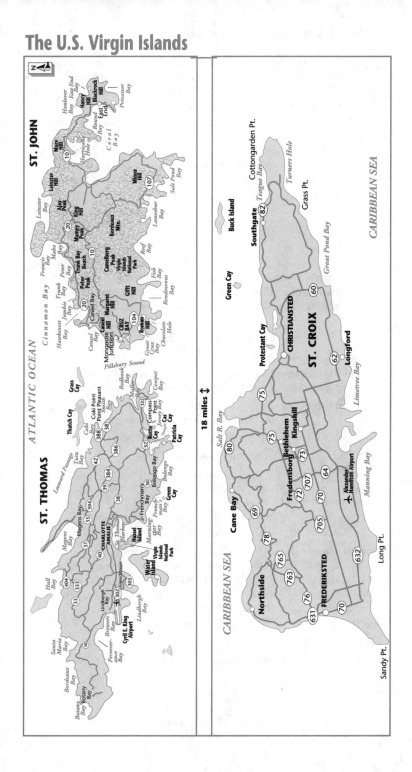

conditioning; the least costly car at Budget had automatic transmission but no air conditioning. Budget's cars with automatic transmission, air conditioning, and un-limited mileage rented for a minimum of $219 per week. Each of the companies also offered larger cars, usually Mazdas, Suzukis, and Mitsubishis.

**PARKING**   If you can't find a place to park along the waterfront (free), go to the large, sprawling lot to the east of Fort Christian, across from the Legislature. Charges are nominal here, and you can park your car and walk northwest toward Emancipation Park or else along the waterfront until you reach the shops and attractions. Because of congested and one-way streets, don't try to drive within the town.

**DRIVING RULES**   Always drive on the left. The speed limit is 20 m.p.h. in town, 35 m.p.h. outside town. Be especially careful driving since roads are dangerous and poorly lit.

## ON FOOT

This is the only way to explore the heart of Charlotte Amalie. All the major attractions and the principal stores are close enough to walk to. However, the other major attractions of the island, such as Coral World or the beach at Magens Bay, are long, hot hauls from the center, and it's better to go by bus or taxi.

## FAST FACTS: St. Thomas

**Airport**   Directly west of Charlotte Amalie, Cyril E. King Airport, Airport Road (☎ 774-5100), is a modern terminal, with 11 major gates and 5 commuter gates. A line of taxis meets all arriving flights to take you to your hotel.

**American Express**   In St. Thomas, service is provided by the Caribbean Travel Agency, Inc./Tropic Tours, 9716 Estate Thomas, Havensight (☎ 774-1855).

**Area Code**   The area code is **809.** You can dial direct from North America.

**Babysitters**   Make arrangements through your hotel.

**Banks**   Several major banks are represented in the U.S. Virgins. While the hours vary, many are open Monday through Thursday from 9am to 2:30pm, Friday from 9am to 2pm and 3:30 to 5pm.

**Bookstores**   Dockside Bookshop, Havensight Mall (☎ 774-4937), where the cruise ships dock, has a selection of books, cards, and maps.

**Business Hours**   Typical business hours are Monday through Friday from 9am to 5pm, Saturday from 9am to 1pm. Store hours are generally 9am to 5pm Monday through Friday and 9am to 1pm Saturday. Some open Sunday for cruise-ship arrivals. Usual hours for bars are daily 11am to midnight or 1am, although some hot spots stay open much later.

**Car Rentals**   See "Getting Around," above.

**Climate**   See "When to Go," in Chapter 3.

**Currency**   See "Visitor Information, Entry Requirements & Money," in Chapter 3.

**Currency Exchange**   Most major hotels will cash your traveler's checks. You can also go to any of the major banks in Charlotte Amalie, including Chase Manhattan Bank, Veterans Drive (☎ 776-2222) and Citibank, Veterans Drive (☎ 774-4800). Citibank issues Citicorp Traveler's Checks.

**Dentist**   The Virgin Island Dental Association, Raphunne Hill (☎ **775-9110**), is a member of the American Dental Association and has the largest number of members practicing throughout the island. It is also linked with various specialists.

**Doctor**   Doctors-on-Duty, Vitraco Park (☎ **776-7966**) in Charlotte Amalie, is a medical facility.

**Documents Required**   See "Visitor Information, Entry Requirements & Money," in Chapter 3.

**Driving Rules**   In St. Thomas motorists drive on the left. Speed limits and road signs are similar to those on the U.S. mainland.

**Drugstores**   Cathedral Pharmacy, 22 Kronprindsens Gade (☎ **776-4080**), sells over-the-counter medications, but to fill prescriptions, visitors go to Apothecary, 19 Droningensgade (☎ **774-1341**).

**Electricity**   110 to 115 volts, 60 cycles, as on the U.S. mainland.

**Embassies and Consulates**   St. Thomas has no embassies or consulates. Go to one of the various U.S. government agencies if you have a problem.

**Emergencies**   Police, **911;** ambulance, **922;** fire, **921.**

**Etiquette**   U.S. Virgin Islanders tend to be a bit conservative. Save the skimpy swimwear for the beach, and cover up when patronizing public places.

**Eyeglasses**   Vision Center, 14B Norre Gade (☎ **774-2020**), has the fullest optical care and services on the islands. They specialize in contact lenses and offer immediate prescription and repair services.

**Hairdressers and Barbers**   Many hotels have a beauty shop on the premises. If not, women can go to Nora's Beauty Palace, 8 First St. Estate (☎ **776-5992**), in Charlotte Amalie. Celsa's House of Beauty, Windward Passage (☎ **776-3094**), has a wide range of unisex services, including facial treatments, coloring, manicures, pedicures, and permanent waves and relaxers. Call either of these places for an appointment.

**Holidays**   See "When to Go," in Chapter 3.

**Hospitals**   The St. Thomas Hospital is at 48 Sugar Estate (☎ **776-8311**), Charlotte Amalie.

**Hotlines**   Call the police at **911** in an emergency. In case of a boating mishap, call the U.S. Coast Guard Rescue at **809/729-6800,** ext. **140,** which operates out of San Juan, Puerto Rico but handles rescue calls for the U.S. Virgin Islands, including St. Thomas. Scuba divers should have the number of a Recompression Chamber (☎ **776-2686**).

**Laundry and Dry Cleaning**   Many of the major hotels arrange this service, but it's also more expensive, of course, than independent establishments on the island. For dry cleaning go to One-Hour Martinizing, Barbel Plaza (☎ **774-5452**), in Charlotte Amalie. The island also has a few Laundromats, including Lemon Fresh Laundry, at the Yacht Haven Marina, 4 Long Bay Rd. (☎ **774-0250**), in Charlotte Amalie. A good full-service laundry is 4-Star Laundromat, 68 Kronprindsens Gade (☎ **774-8689**), in Charlotte Amalie.

**Library**   Go to the Enid M. Baa Library, Main Street at Gutters Gade (☎ **774-0630**), in Charlotte Amalie.

**Liquor Laws**    Persons must be at least 21 years of age to patronize bars or purchase liquor in St. Thomas.

**Lost Property**    There is no office for recovering lost property. You can call the police at **911** to report a lost item. Leave a description of the item, your name, and your mailing address, should the item ever be turned in to the police.

**Luggage Storage and Lockers**    Check with Native Son, Inc. on Veterans Drive (☎ 774-8685). They will store suitcases for one full day or less for passengers eventually headed to the airport. Storage is free.

**Mail**    Postal rates are the same as on the U.S. mainland.

**Maps**    See "Orientation," earlier in this chapter.

**Money**    See "Visitor Information, Entry Requirements & Money," in Chapter 3.

**Newspapers and Magazines**    Copies of U.S. mainland newspapers, such as *The New York Times, USA Today,* and *The Miami Herald,* arrive daily in St. Thomas and are sold at hotels and newsstands around the island. The latest copies of *Time* and *Newsweek* are also for sale. *St. Thomas Daily News* covers local, national, and international events. Pick up a free copy of *Virgin Islands Playground,* with much tourist-related data, and definitely get *St. Thomas This Week,* which is packed with information and distributed free all over the island.

**Photographic Needs**    Try Blazing Photos, Inc., Veterans Drive (☎ 774-5547), in Charlotte Amalie, with a branch office at Havensight Mall (☎ 776-5547), where cruise-ship passengers arrive.

**Police**    Dial **911** in an emergency.

**Post Office**    The main post office is at 9846 Estate Thomas (☎ 774-1950), Charlotte Amalie, open Monday through Friday from 7:30am to 5:30pm and Saturday from 7:30am to 2:30pm.

**Radio**    St. Thomas has several radio stations which broadcast news and music, including WIYC FM-104 and WVGN-V105 FM.

**Religious Services**    St. Thomas has a number of churches and synagogues, including St. Peter's and Paul's Roman Catholic Church, 22-AB Kronprindsens Gade (☎ 774-0201); Hebrew Congregation of St. Thomas, Crystal Gade (☎ 774-4312); Calvary Baptist Church, 200 Altona (☎ 774-1759); and Christchurch Methodist, Market Square (☎ 774-0797).

**Restrooms**    See "Fast Facts: The U.S. Virgin Islands," in Chapter 3.

**Safety**    St. Thomas has an unusually high crime rate, particularly in Charlotte Amalie. It is reasonably safe during the day, but don't wander around town at night, particularly on Back Street. Guard your valuables. Store them in hotel safes if possible, and make sure you keep your doors and windows shut at night.

**Shoe Repairs**    Go to Zora's of St. Thomas Shoe Repair, 34 Norre Gade (☎ 774-2559), Charlotte Amalie. The shop also does handbag and luggage repair. It has been in business since 1962 doing custom and ready-made sandals. It also makes high-quality canvas bags and luggage, its primary business. Hours are Monday through Friday from 8am to 5pm and Saturday from 8:30am to 4pm.

**Taxes**    The only local taxes are an 8% surcharge added to all hotel tariffs.

**Taxis**    See "Getting Around," earlier in this chapter.

**Telephone, Telex, and Fax**   Pay phones operate as they do in the United States. All island phone numbers have seven digits. It is not necessary to use the 809 area code when dialing within St. Thomas. Numbers for all three islands, including St. John and St. Croix, are found in the U.S. Virgin Islands phone book. Hotels will send fax and telexes for you, often for cost plus a small service charge. Long-distance, international, and collect calls are made the same way they are on the U.S. mainland.

**Television**   Many of the major resort hotels subscribe to cable TV, including CNN. Local TV stations include WSVI-TV Channel 8 and WTJX-TV Channel 12.

**Time**   See "Fast Facts: The U.S. Virgin Islands," in Chapter 3.

**Tipping**   See "Fast Facts: The U.S. Virgin Islands," in Chapter 3.

**Transit Information**   Call **524-2017** to order a taxi 24 hours a day. Call for airport information at **774-5100,** and dial **776-6282** for information about ferry departures for St. John.

**Water**   See "Fast Facts: The U.S. Virgin Islands," in Chapter 3.

**Weather**   Call the U.S. Weather Service at **791-3490.**

**Yellow Pages**   See "Fast Facts: The U.S. Virgin Islands," in Chapter 3.

## 3  Accommodations

Nearly every beach has its own hostelry, and St. Thomas just might have more inns of character than any other place in the Caribbean. You're faced with the choice of whether to stay in the capital, Charlotte Amalie, or at any of the far points of the island, including the unusual Bolongo Bay and Sapphire Beach resorts.

If you want to stay in St. Thomas on the cheap, you'll have to select one of the guesthouses or motels in the Charlotte Amalie area. All the glittering, very expensive properties lie in the East End. Hotels slash their prices in summer by 20% to 60%. What follows is a breakdown of daily winter rates in double rooms with private baths. "Very Expensive" indicates rooms charging upwards of $195 for a double room. "Expensive" is a double renting for between $170 and $195; "Moderate" is a double for $135 to $170; and "Inexpensive" is a double under $135. In this category, double rates can drop to as little as $65 per night for two people. The prices quoted above are only guidelines; it is also possible to book a "moderate" room in an "expensive" hotel because of the sometimes wide differences in the quality and size of the rooms themselves. Unless otherwise noted, the rates listed do *not* include the 8% government tax.

## CHARLOTTE AMALIE
### VERY EXPENSIVE

#### Bluebeard's Castle
Bluebeard's Hill, P.O. Box 7480, Charlotte Amalie, St. Thomas, USVI 00801. ☎ **809/774-1600,** or 800/524-6599. Fax 809/744-5134. 170 rms (all with bath). A/C TV TEL Winter, $195–$235 single or double. Summer, $150–$185 single or double. Extra person $30. Breakfast $10 extra. MAP $50 per person. AE, DC, MC, V. Parking: Free.

Almost a monument in St. Thomas, this popular, all-around resort lies on the bay overlooking Charlotte Amalie. In the 1930s, the U.S. government turned what had been a private home dating from 1665 into a hotel. Over the years, Bluebeard's has had many additions and extensions to accommodate the ever-increasing throng of vacationers. The hill surrounding the hotel is now heavily built-up with everything from offices to time shares. Many guests prefer rooms in the old tower, especially room 139 or 140. Some 50 rooms in the newer unit, which also includes meeting rooms, have less charm. If you want a place on the beach, look elsewhere, although transportation to the beach is provided by the hotel. You may find the best way to stay here is on a package deal (ask your travel agent for details).

**Dining/Entertainment:** The Terrace Restaurant commands a panoramic view and offers many American and Caribbean specialties, open-air brunch, lunch, and late-night dining. The hotel also has another open-air restaurant, Entre Nous, which serves international cuisine (see separate recommendations under "Dining," below).

**Services:** Free transportation to Magens Bay Beach.

**Facilities:** Freshwater swimming pool, two whirlpools, two lit tennis courts, physical fitness center, tour desk, car-rental facility, on-site free-port shopping.

## MODERATE

### ⑤ Blackbeard's Castle

Blackbeard's Hill, P.O. Box 6041, Charlotte Amalie, St. Thomas, USVI 00801. ☎ **809/776-1234,** or 800/344-5771 in the U.S. Fax 809/776-4321. 18 rms (all with bath), 3 junior suites, 3 apt suites. A/C TV TEL Transportation: Taxi. Rates (including continental breakfast): Winter, $110 single; $140 double; $170 junior suite for two; $190 apt suite for two. Summer, $75 single; $95 double; $120 junior suite for two; $145 apt suite for two. AE, MC, V. Parking: Free.

Blackbeard's Castle was the inspiration of Illinois businessman Bob Harrington and his Brazilian partner, Henrique Konzen, that transformed what had been a private residence into a genuinely charming inn. It enjoys one of the finest views of Charlotte Amalie and its harbor, thanks to its perch high on a hillside above town. The owners weren't alone in their appreciation of this location; in 1679, the Danish governor erected a soaring tower of chiseled stone here as a lookout for unfriendly ships. Legend has it that Blackbeard himself lived in the tower half a century later.

Each of the bedrooms has a lattice-enclosed veranda, a flat-weave Turkish kilim, tile floors and eclectic furnishings. Some of the suites are in the Southern-plantation style with white shutters. Guests enjoy two swimming pools and the establishment's social center, which is within the stylish bar and restaurant (see "Dining," below). In winter there's live jazz in the lounge Tuesday through Sunday—no cover, no minimum.

### ✪ Hotel 1829

Kongens Gade, P.O. Box 1567, Charlotte Amalie, St. Thomas, USVI 00804. ☎ **809/776-1829,** or 800/524-2002. Fax 809/776-4313. 13 rms (all with bath), 2 suites. A/C TV TEL Rates (including continental breakfast): $70–$160 single; $80–$170 double; from $220 suite. Summer, $50–$110 single; $60–$120 double; from $155 suite. AE, MC, V. Parking: Free.

After a major restoration, this once-decaying historical site has become one of the leading small hotels of character in the Caribbean. Right in the heart of town, it stands about three minutes from Government House, built on a hillside with many levels and steps (no elevator). The 1829 has been a hotel since the 19th century and has entertained such guests as King Carol of Romania, Edna St. Vincent

Millay, and Mikhail Baryshnikov. Today it's not likely to draw such an illustrious roster, catering instead to business people.

The upper rooms, which overlook a central courtyard with a miniature swimming pool, lie amid a cascade of flowering bougainvillea. The hotel has a Spanish-style design. The units, some of which are small and boxy, are well designed, comfortable, and attractive; most face the sea. During the restoration, the old parts of the hotel were preserved wherever possible, and some rooms have antiques. The hotel is a 15-minute ride from the beach.

### Villa Santana

Denmark Hill, St. Thomas, USVI 00802. ☎ **and fax 809/776-1311**. 7 rms (all with bath). TV TEL Rates: Winter, $100–$195 single or double; off-season, $75–$135 single or double. AE.

This all-suite property was built by General Antonio López de Santa Ana of Mexico in the 1850s and offers a panoramic view of Charlotte Amalie and the St. Thomas Harbor. All rooms have fully equipped kitchens, TVs, telephones, private baths, and ceiling fans. The decor is Mexican with clay tiles, rattan furniture, and stonework. The property includes a pool, sundeck, and small garden with hibiscus and bouganvillea. The property is a 5-minute walk from the shopping district in Charlotte Amalie and a 10-minute drive to several beaches.

### ⑤ Windward Passage Hotel

Veterans Dr., P.O. Box 640, St. Thomas, USVI 00804. ☎ **809/774-5200,** or 800/524-7389 in the U.S. Fax 809/774-1231. 151 rms (all with bath), 11 junior suites. A/C TV TEL Transportation: Vitran bus. Rates (including continental breakfast): Winter, $125–$150 single; $135–$160 double; $180–$230 suite. Summer, $90–$125 single; $100–$135 double; $140–$180 suite. AE, DC, MC, V. Parking: Free.

Even though its charm is not immediately visible, this modern, many-balconied hotel enjoys one of the consistently highest rates of return bookings of any hotel on the island. Everything about it meets the needs of businesspeople and sports teams arriving for short-term stays.

Built in 1968 and last renovated in 1992, the hotel's rooms are arranged around a massive central atrium which contains a soaring concrete fountain; a restaurant, "On the Bay," serving an Italian cuisine; a bar with a devoted local clientele; a rectangular swimming pool; and a variety of facilities for children. There is no beach nearby, but there are frequent shuttle buses to and from Magens Bay, Morningstar Beach, and Sapphire Beach. The 54 harborfront rooms have views of some of the world's largest cruise ships and are subject to street noise. Many frequent visitors request a bedroom overlooking the adjacent Emile Griffith Park, where baseball games provide the entertainment. Bedrooms are pastel colored and comfortably modern, with marble-trimmed bathrooms.

## INEXPENSIVE

### ⑤ The Admiral's Inn

Villa Olga, P.O. Box 6162, Frenchtown, Charlotte Amalie, St. Thomas 00802. ☎ **809/774-1376,** or 800/544-0493 in the U.S. 16 rms (all with bath). A/C TV TEL Transportation: Vitran bus line. Rates (including continental breakfast): Winter, $99–$149 single or double. Summer, $79–$109 single or double. Children under 12 stay free in parents' room. AE, MC, V.

Set on a peninsula in Frenchtown, near the western entrance to Charlotte Amalie's harbor, this waterfront hotel attracts yachtspeople and divers. Modern lodging is provided in a relaxed setting with both harbor and oceanfront views. The secluded yet central location is just a short walk to town. Units, which were refurbished in 1992, lie upon a landscaped hillside. The freshwater pool was terraced into the slope and has a large sun deck and flowering borders. The saltwater beach and sea pool lie a few paces from the lanai-style oceanview units. The poolside bar remains open for hotel guests throughout the morning and afternoon. Dinner is served in the on-site Chart House Restaurant (see "Dining," below).

### Bunkers' Hill Hotel

7 Commandant Gade, Charlotte Amalie, St. Thomas, USVI 00802. ☎ **809/774-8056.** Fax 809/774-3172. 11 rms (all with bath), 4 suites. A/C TV TEL Rates (including continental breakfast): Winter, $70 single; $80 double; $90 suite. Summer, $59 single; $69 double; $79 suite. MC, V. Parking: Free.

This clean and centrally located guest lodge is suitable for anyone who's on a tight budget but who doesn't want to sacrifice comfort and safety and doesn't mind putting up with some street noise. Some of the rooms share a small kitchenette. Ten rooms have balconies, some of which offer a view of the city and sea. In 1990, the hotel was upgraded with a new lobby and improved furnishings. The management prepares meals for guests with advance notice.

### ⑤ Danish Chalet Inn

9E-9J Nordsidevej (Solberg Rd.), P.O. Box 4319, St. Thomas, USVI 00803. ☎ **809/774-5764,** or 800/635-1531 in the U.S. and Canada. Fax 809/777-4886. 15 rms (5 with bath). TEL Rates (including continental breakfast): Winter, $75 single or double without bath; $85–$95 single or double with bath. Summer, $60 single or double without bath; $70–$80 single or double with bath. MC, V. Parking: Free.

Set high above Charlotte Amalie on the western edge of the cruise-ship harbor, this inn is a five-minute walk to the harborfront. A trio of buildings sits on a steeply inclined acre of land dotted with tropical shrubs and bougainvillea behind a façade of lattices and modern verandas. The heart and soul of the place is the panoramic terrace, which has a 180-degree view over the cruise ships and an honor bar. Bedrooms are neat, clean, and colorful; all but the cheapest contain air conditioning and refrigerators. The others have ceiling fans.

Much of this hotel's business stems from its willingness to accept one-night guests (many other small island hotels insist on bookings of several nights), making it popular with cruise-ship passengers.

The establishment has no swimming pool, but it does have a semisecluded Jacuzzi spa for the relaxation of its guests. No meals other than breakfast are served.

### ⑤ Galleon House

Government Hill, P.O. Box 6577, Charlotte Amalie, St. Thomas, USVI 00804. ☎ **809/774-6952,** or 800/524-2052. Fax 809/774-6952. 14 rms (13 with bath). A/C TV TEL Rates (including continental breakfast): Winter, $59 single without bath, $109 single with bath; $69 double without bath, $119 double with bath. Summer, $49 single without bath, $69 single with bath; $59 double without bath, $79 double with bath. AE, MC, V. Parking: Free.

The main attraction of this pleasant little guesthouse is its location, set next to the Hotel 1829 on Government Hill about one block from the main shopping section of St. Thomas. To get to the establishment, walk up a long flight of stairs past a neighboring restaurant's veranda to the concrete terrace that doubles as this hotel's reception area. Rooms are scattered in several hillside buildings, and each contains a ceiling fan and air conditioning, phones, and a cable TV with HBO. Some rooms have private balconies and refrigerators. There's also a small freshwater pool and sundeck. Breakfast consists of a variety of freshly prepared items such as waffles and assorted muffins and is served on a veranda overlooking the harbor.

# St. Thomas Accommodations/Sports

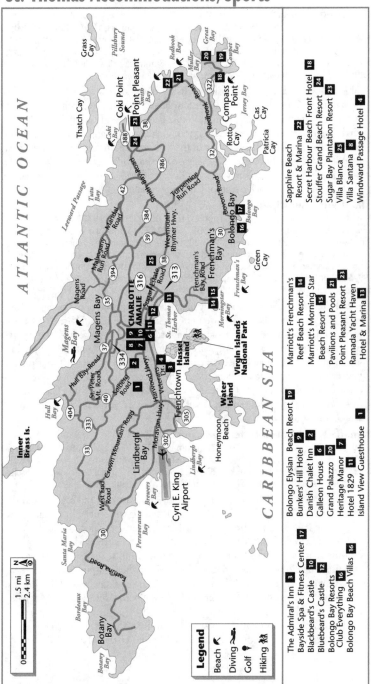

**Legend**

Beach ⚓
Diving 🤿
Golf ⛳
Hiking 🥾

The Admiral's Inn 3
Bayside Spa & Fitness Center 17
Blackbeard's Castle 10
Bluebeard's Castle 12
Bolongo Bay Resorts 16
Club Everything 16
Bolongo Bay Beach Villas 16

Bolongo Elysian Beach Resort 19
Bunkers' Hill Hotel 9
Danish Chalet Inn 2
Galleon House 6
Grand Palazzo 20
Heritage Manor 7
Hotel 1829 11
Island View Guesthouse 1

Marriott's Frenchman's Reef Beach Resort 14
Marriott's Morning Star Beach Resort 15
Pavilions and Pools 21
Point Pleasant Resort 23
Ramada Yacht Haven Hotel & Marina 13

Sapphire Beach Resort & Marina 22
Secret Harbour Beach Front Hotel 18
Stouffer Grand Beach Resort 24
Sugar Bay Plantation Resort 23
Villa Blanca 25
Villa Santana 8
Windward Passage Hotel 4

### ⑤ Heritage Manor
1A Snegie Gade, P.O. Box 90, Charlotte Amalie, St. Thomas, USVI 00804. ☎ **809/ 774-3003,** or 800/828-0757 in the U.S. Fax 809/776-9585. 8 rms (4 with bath), 2 apts. A/C Rates (including continental breakfast in winter only): Winter, $70 single or double without bath; $95 double with bath; $115–$130 apt. Summer, $50 single or double without bath; $75 double with bath; $85–$95 apt. AE, MC, V. Parking: Free.

This 150-year-old restored Danish merchant's town house is located in the historical district of Charlotte Amalie, about four blocks from the sea. Intimate and personal, it offers well-furnished, comfortable bedrooms and two apartments with kitchens. The rooms contain many extras, including fans and refrigerators. Most of the accommodations have a view of the harbor. The small inn has a freshwater pool installed in a former Danish bakery complete with chimney. A taxi, van, or bus will take you to the nearest beaches. Be careful walking back to the guesthouse at night through the back streets of Charlotte Amalie.

### Island View Guesthouse
11-C Contant, P.O. Box 1903, St. Thomas, USVI 00803. ☎ **809/774-4270,** or 800/ 524- 2023 for reservations only. Fax 809/774-6167. 15 rms (13 with bath). TV TEL Directions: From the airport, turn right onto Rte. 30. Then cut left, and continue to the unmarked Scott Free Road, where you go left. Look for the sign. Rates (including continental breakfast): Winter, $60 single without bath; $94 single with bath; $65 double without bath, $99–$119 double with bath. Summer, $40 single without bath, $68 single with bath; $45 double without bath, $73–$93 double with bath. AE, DC, MC, V. Parking: Free.

Island View is located within a steeply inclined neighborhood of private homes and villas about a seven-minute drive west of Charlotte Amalie. Set 545 feet up Crown Mountain, it has sweeping views of Charlotte Amalie and the harbor. Family-owned and managed, it was originally built in the 1960s as a private home. Enlarged in 1989, the guesthouse contains main-floor rooms (two without private baths), some poolside rooms, and six units in a recent addition (three with kitchens and all with balconies). The bedrooms are cooled by breezes and fans, and the newer ones have air conditioning. A self-service, open-air bar on the gallery operates on the honor system.

### Ramada Yacht Haven Hotel & Marina
5400 Long Bay Rd., P.O. Box 7970, St. Thomas, USVI 00802. ☎ **809/774-9700,** or 800/524-7877 in the U.S. Fax 809/776-3410. 151 units (all with bath), 3 suites. A/C TV TEL Rates: Winter, $125 single or double; $225 suite. Summer, $90 single or double; $180 suite. Tax and service extra. Breakfast $8 extra. AE, DC, MC, V. Parking: Free.

Centrally located at the mouth of the cruise-ship port near the beaches and the shops on the Vitran route heading east, this hotel is adjacent both to one of the largest and best-equipped private marinas in the Caribbean and and to the West Indies Cruise-Ship Dock. Charter yacht packages can be arranged from its private 200-slip marina. Although some rooms are priced in the inexpensive range, the amenities suit a moderate accommodation. Behind the shell-pink façade, the spacious units contain extra-large double or king-size beds, radios, and VCRs. Rooms, which have recently drawn fire from readers, have been refurbished and the bathrooms remodeled.

**Dining/Entertainment:** Castaways Bar and Restaurant, above the marina, serves three meals a day in a relaxed, nautical atmosphere. The Pool Bar, which

| Hotels of St. Thomas at a Glance | Access for Disabled | A/C in Bedrooms | Childcare Facilities | Children are Welcome | Convention Facilities | Credit Cards Accepted | Directly Beside Beach | Fitness Facility | Golf Course Nearby | Live Entertainment | Marina Facilities | Restaurant & Bar | Spa Facilities | Swimming Pool | Tennis Courts | TV in Bedroom | Watersports |
|---|---|---|---|---|---|---|---|---|---|---|---|---|---|---|---|---|---|
| Admiral's Inn | | ✓ | | ✓ | | ✓ | | | | ✓ | | ✓ | | ✓ | | ✓ | |
| Bayside Spa/Fitness | | ✓ | | ✓ | | ✓ | ✓ | ✓ | | | | | ✓ | ✓ | | ✓ | ✓ |
| Blackbeard's Castle | | ✓ | | ✓ | | ✓ | | | | ✓ | | ✓ | | ✓ | | ✓ | |
| Bluebeard's Castle | ✓ | ✓ | | ✓ | ✓ | ✓ | | ✓ | | ✓ | | ✓ | | ✓ | ✓ | ✓ | ✓ |
| Bolongo Club | ✓ | ✓ | ✓ | ✓ | ✓ | ✓ | ✓ | ✓ | | ✓ | | ✓ | | ✓ | ✓ | ✓ | ✓ |
| Bolongo Beach Villas | | ✓ | ✓ | ✓ | ✓ | ✓ | ✓ | ✓ | | ✓ | | ✓ | | ✓ | ✓ | ✓ | ✓ |
| Bolongo Elysian | ✓ | ✓ | ✓ | ✓ | ✓ | ✓ | ✓ | ✓ | | ✓ | ✓ | ✓ | | ✓ | ✓ | ✓ | ✓ |
| Bunkers' Hill Hotel | | ✓ | | ✓ | | ✓ | | | | | | | | | | ✓ | |
| Danish Chalet Inn | | | | ✓ | | ✓ | | | | | | | | | | | |
| Galleon House | | | | ✓ | | ✓ | | | | | | | | ✓ | | ✓ | |
| Grand Palazzo | ✓ | ✓ | | | ✓ | ✓ | ✓ | ✓ | | ✓ | ✓ | ✓ | | ✓ | ✓ | ✓ | ✓ |
| Heritage Manor | | ✓ | | ✓ | | | | | | | | | | ✓ | | | |
| Hotel 1829 | | ✓ | | ✓ | | ✓ | | | | ✓ | | ✓ | | ✓ | | ✓ | |
| Island View Guesthouse | | | | ✓ | | ✓ | | | | | | | | | | ✓ | |
| Marriott's Frenchman's Reef | ✓ | ✓ | ✓ | ✓ | ✓ | ✓ | ✓ | ✓ | | ✓ | | ✓ | | ✓ | ✓ | ✓ | ✓ |
| Marriott's Morningstar | ✓ | ✓ | ✓ | ✓ | ✓ | ✓ | ✓ | ✓ | | ✓ | | ✓ | | ✓ | ✓ | ✓ | ✓ |
| Pavilions & Pools | ✓ | ✓ | | ✓ | | ✓ | ✓ | | | | | | | ✓ | | ✓ | ✓ |
| Point Pleasant Resort | ✓ | ✓ | | ✓ | | ✓ | ✓ | | | ✓ | | ✓ | | ✓ | ✓ | ✓ | ✓ |
| Ramada Yacht Haven | ✓ | ✓ | | ✓ | ✓ | ✓ | ✓ | | | ✓ | ✓ | ✓ | | ✓ | | ✓ | ✓ |
| Sapphire Beach Resort | ✓ | ✓ | ✓ | ✓ | ✓ | ✓ | ✓ | ✓ | | ✓ | ✓ | ✓ | | ✓ | ✓ | ✓ | ✓ |
| Secret Harbour | ✓ | ✓ | ✓ | ✓ | | ✓ | ✓ | ✓ | | | | ✓ | | ✓ | ✓ | ✓ | ✓ |
| Stouffer Grand | ✓ | ✓ | ✓ | ✓ | ✓ | ✓ | ✓ | ✓ | | | ✓ | ✓ | ✓ | ✓ | ✓ | | ✓ |
| Sugar Bay Plantation | ✓ | ✓ | | ✓ | ✓ | ✓ | ✓ | ✓ | | | | ✓ | | ✓ | ✓ | ✓ | ✓ |
| Villa Blanca | | | | ✓ | | ✓ | | | | | | | | ✓ | | ✓ | |
| Villa Santana | | | | ✓ | | ✓ | | | | | | | | ✓ | | ✓ | |
| Windward Passage | ✓ | ✓ | ✓ | ✓ | ✓ | ✓ | | | | ✓ | | ✓ | | ✓ | | ✓ | |

has seating in the water, is a favorite for a light lunch while guests sunbathe by the pool. If you're rushed, you can stop by the Wok on the Water Express for Chinese fare. Deli sandwiches are available at Gourmet Gallery, and La Crêperie is a French-style open-air café open for breakfast daily. The newest eatery is St. Clair's overlooking the harbor and the marina and offering continental and West Indian cuisine for lunch and dinner.

**Services:** Daily shuttle service to beach, valet laundry, guest services desk.

**Facilities:** Florist, beauty salon, water sports, Laundromat.

### § Villa Blanca

4 Raphune Hill, Rte. 38, Charlotte Amalie, St. Thomas, USVI 00801. ☎ **809/776-0749.** Fax 809/779-2661. 12 rms (all with bath and kitchenette). TV Rates (without breakfast): Winter, $105–$125 single; $115–$135 double. Summer, $75–$85 single, $85–$95 double. AE, DC, MC, V. Parking: Free.

Small and intimate, this small-scale hotel lies on three secluded acres of hilltop land that connoisseurs claim is among the most panoramic on the island. Originally built in 1953 as the private home of Christine Cromwell, heiress to the Dodge fortune, the hotel's main building served as the private home of its present owner, Blanca Terrasa Smith, between 1973 and 1985. After the death of her husband, Mrs. Smith added a 12-room annex in her garden and opened her grounds to paying guests.

Each of the rooms contains a ceiling fan, a well-equipped kitchenette, and a private balcony or terrace with 360° views either eastward to St. John or westward to Puerto Rico and the harbor of Charlotte Amalie. Although no meals of any kind are served on the premises, a homelike ambience prevails. The villa has a freshwater swimming pool and a large, covered patio suitable for quiet reading or socializing. The hotel is 1¹/₂ miles east of Charlotte Amalie.

## FLAMBOYANT POINT
### VERY EXPENSIVE

#### Marriott's Frenchman's Reef Beach Resort

Flamboyant Point, Charlotte Amalie, St. Thomas, USVI 00801. ☎ **809/776-8500,** or 800/524-2000 in the U.S. Fax 809/776-3054. 421 rms (all with bath). 18 suites. A/C MINIBAR TV TEL Transportation: Water or land taxi from Charlotte Amalie. Rates: Winter, $260–$295 single or double; from $428 suite. Summer, $165–$190 single or double; from $248 suite. MAP $52 per person extra. AE, DC, MC, V. Parking: Free.

The Frenchmen's Reef, lying 3 miles east of Charlotte Amalie, has a winning southern position on a projection of land overlooking both the harbor at Charlotte Amalie and the sea. The hotel stands in such a conspicuous position that it's impossible to miss. Whatever your vacation needs, chances are they'll be met at The Reef. To reach the private beach, you take a glass-enclosed elevator. The bedrooms vary greatly, but most are traditionally furnished.

**Dining/Entertainment:** Seafood with a continental flair is served in Windows on the Harbour, which resembles the inside of a cruise ship and has a view of the harbor. You can also get meals at the Lighthouse Bar, once an actual lighthouse. In the evening, the Top of the Reef, a supper club, offers entertainment, or you can go to La Terrazza lounge. In addition, Caesar's offers an Italian cuisine at surfside.

The Oriental Terrace features Japanese exhibition cooking on the Teppanyaki Grill. The Raw Bar offers fresh seafood appetizers and light meals daily from 11am to 11pm.

**Services:** Room service, full-service beauty salon, unisex hair salon, drugstore, valet, babysitters, travel and tour desks.

**Facilities:** Two giant swimming pools, suntanning areas, poolside bar, four tennis courts, water sports (snorkeling, scuba diving, sailing, deep-sea fishing), private beach.

### ✪ Marriott's Morning Star Beach Resort

Frenchman's Reef Beach Resort, Flamboyant Point, Charlotte Amalie, St. Thomas, USVI 00802. ☎ **809/776-8500,** or 800/BEACH CLUB in the U.S. Fax 809/776-8500. 96 rms (all with bath). A/C MINIBAR TV TEL Transportation: Water or land taxi from Charlotte Amalie. Rates: Winter, $315–$395 single or double. Summer, $195–$270 single or double. AE, DC, MC, V. MAP $52 per person extra. Parking: Free.

Both the public areas and the plushly outfitted accommodations here are among the most desirable on the island. They were built on the landscaped flatlands near the beach of the well-known Frenchman's Reef Beach Resort as the elegant twin neighbor of the older hotel. The resort has five cruciform buildings, each containing between 16 to 24 units. Guests have the amenities and attractions of a large hotel nearby yet maintain the privacy of an exclusive enclave. Each accommodation has rattan furniture; a color scheme of lilac, plum, and red mahogany; and views of the garden or beach. Swimming can be supplemented with a wide array of water sports.

**Dining/Entertainment:** Tavern on the Beach, the hotel's premier restaurant, is one of the most outstanding on the island (see separate recommendation under "Dining," below). Caesar's Ristorante, located at the water's edge on Morning Star Beach, serves lunch, pizza, and snacks daily from 11am to 5pm. Dinner is served from 6 to 10pm under the stars with a southern Italian menu of light tomato sauces and grilled main dishes brushed with olive oils. The Oriental Terrace offers Japanese cuisine and is studded with Hibachi paraphernalia. The Sand Bar is an ideal spot for sunset cocktails. There's also a variety of restaurants and bars at the adjoining Marriott's Frenchman's Reef Beach Resort.

**Services:** Room service, babysitting, valet, and all the services provided by Frenchman's Reef next door.

**Facilities:** Frenchman's Reef has two giant swimming pools; four tennis courts; a water-sports program, including parasailing; diveshop; a Jacuzzi; and a private beach, all shared by Morning Star.

## EAST END

### VERY EXPENSIVE

### ✪ Bolongo Elysian Beach Resort

50 Estate Bolongo, Cowpet Bay, P.O. Box 7337, St. Thomas, USVI 00801. ☎ **809/ 779-2844,** or 800/524-4746. Fax 809/775-3208. 120 rms, two-bedroom loft suite. A/C MINIBAR TV TEL Transportation: Hotel-owned open-air shuttle. Rates (including continental breakfast): Winter, $285–$425 single or double; $690 two-bedroom loft suite for six. Summer, $205–$275 single or double; $475 two-bedroom loft suite for six. AE, DC, MC, V. Parking: Free.

This elegant resort opened in 1989 on Cowpet Bay between a pair of upscale condo complexes in the East End. The resort has a European kind of glamour, and it's a 20-minute drive from Charlotte Amalie. The thoughtfully planned bedrooms have kitchens and large balconies, and some offer sleeping lofts reached by a spiral staircase. The decor is tropical, with white ceramic-tile floors, rattan and bamboo furnishings, and natural-wood ceilings. Rooms are in a bevy of four-story buildings connected to landscaped gardens.

**Dining/Entertainment:** A member of the Bolongo Bay Beach Resorts, the hotel offers elegant international dining in its Royal Palm Court Restaurant and also has weekly barbecues on the terrace. Other dining choices include the Oasis right on the beach, serving light fare. Drinks are enjoyed either at the pool bar or in the Royal Palm Court Lounge. In season, live entertainment is offered, as well as theme nights such as West Indian Carnival night.

**Services:** Open-air shuttle to town, room service, masseur, babysitting.

**Facilities:** Fitness center, sauna, scuba, aerobics classes, yoga classes, swimming pool, snorkel gear, canoes, Sunfish sailboats, tennis court.

### ✪ Grand Palazzo

Great Bay, St. Thomas, USVI 00802. ☎ **809/775-3333**, or 800/545-0509. Fax 809/775-5635. 150 oceanview suites. A/C MINIBAR TV TEL Rates: Winter, $475–$865 suite for two; Apr 3–May 31 and Nov 21–Nov 30, $350–$650 suite for two; June 1–Nov 20 and Dec 1–Dec 19, $250–$475 suite for two. MAP $65 per person extra. AE, DC, MC, V. Parking: Free.

The recent purchase of one of the last large tracts of seafront land on the island (15 acres) was viewed as a minor triumph. Shortly after its acquisition, the developers of this luxury hotel immediately hired top-notch architects, decorators, and landscape experts to create what is today probably the most desirable hotel in St. Thomas. The hotel is near Red Hook, about $4^1/_2$ miles southeast of Charlotte Amalie.

Opened in August of 1992, its accommodations lie within a half-dozen three-story villas designed with Italian Renaissance motifs and pastel versions of Mediterranean colors like yellow ocher and burnt sienna. These encircle a freshwater pond, home to a colony of Bahamian ducks. Guests register in the "reception palazzo," whose arches and accessories were inspired by a palace in Venice, before heading to bedrooms whose themes are unabashedly European. These contain all the electronic amenities you'd expect (including a digital safe), marble bathrooms, and many thoughtful touches. Public rooms carry nautical themes of navy blue and white, interspersed with themes from the surrounding gardens. The swimming pool is designed such that it appears to stretch into the sea.

**Dining/Entertainment:** The Palm Terrace, set beneath soaring rows of rhythmically graceful arcades, is the more formal of the hotel's two restaurants. Equally appealing is the Café Vecchio, whose lavish murals depict the botanical diversity of a latter-day garden of Babylon. On the premises is a trio of bars, one of which has a pianist.

**Services:** 24-hour room service, beauty salon, laundry and valet service, top-notch tennis instructors, massage, concierge.

**Facilities:** Air-conditioned health club/gym, free use of Hobie Cats and Sunfish sailboats, a 53-foot catamaran (*The Lady Lynsey*) for cocktail sails, four tennis courts, swimming pool.

### Pavilions & Pools

6400 Estate Smith Bay, St. Thomas, USVI 00802. ☎ **809/775-6110**, or 800/524-2001. Fax 809/775-6110. 25 units (all with bath). A/C TV TEL. Transportation: Taxi. Rates (including continental breakfast in winter only): Winter, $235–$255 single or double. Summer, $175–$195 single or double. AE, DC, MC, V. Parking: Free.

Ideal for a honeymoon, this is the ultimate in small-scale luxury—you have your own villa with floor-to-ceiling glass doors opening directly onto your own private

swimming pool. The resort, 7 miles east of Charlotte Amalie, is a string of condominium units, tastefully built and furnished. After checking in and following
a wooden pathway to your attached villa, you don't have to see another soul
until you check out, if that is your desire. The fence and gate are high, and your
space opens into tropical greenery. Around your own swimming pool is an encir-
cling deck. Inside, a high room divider screens a full, well-equipped kitchen. Each
bedroom has its own style, with plenty of closets behind louvered doors. The bath
has a garden shower where you can rinse off surrounded by greenery and protected
from Peeping Toms. The resort adjoins Sapphire Bay, which has an excellent
beach. Honeymooners should inquire about packages.

**Dining/Entertainment:** A small bar and barbecue area is set against a wall on
the reception terrace, where rum parties and cookouts are held. Informal, simple
meals are served nightly. Occasionally a musician or singer entertains.

**Services:** Helpful front desk, day sails, restaurant reservations.

**Facilities:** Free snorkeling gear.

## Point Pleasant Resort

Estate Smith Bay No. 4, St. Thomas, USVI 00802. ☎ **809/775-7200,** or 800/524-2300. Fax
809/776-5694. 134 rms (all with bath). A/C MINIBAR TV TEL Transportation: Taxi. Rates:
Winter, $275–$295 double. Summer, $200–$265 double. Breakfast $10 extra. AE, MC, V.
Parking: Free.

This is a very private, unique resort on Water Bay, on the northeastern tip of St.
Thomas. It's a series of condo units rented when the owners are not in residence.
From your living-room gallery, you look out on a collection of islands—Tortola,
St. John, and Jost Van Dyke. The complex is set on a 15-acre bluff with flowering
shrubbery, century plants, frangipani trees, secluded nature trails, old rock
formations, and lookout points. Some of the villa-style accommodations have kitchens, and the furnishings are light and airy, mostly with rattan and floral fabrics.

**Dining/Entertainment:** The restaurant, Agave Terrace, is one of the finest on
the island and offers three meals a day. The cuisine, featuring seafood, is a blend
of nouvelle American dishes with Caribbean specialties. Local entertainment is
provided several nights a week.

**Services:** Complimentary use of a car four hours per day, shopping and dinner
shuttle.

**Facilities:** Three freshwater swimming pools, lit tennis courts, snorkeling equipment, Sunfish sailboats.

## ✪ Sapphire Beach Resort & Marina

Rte. 6, Smith Bay Rd., P.O. Box 8088, St. Thomas, USVI 00801. ☎ **809/775-6100,** or 800/
524-2090. Fax 809/775-4024. 171 suites and villas (all with bath). A/C TV TEL Transportation: Taxi. Rates: Winter, $295–$335 suite for two; $355–$395 villa for two. Summer, $190–
$225 suite for two; $235–$265 villa for two. Extra person $35. Children 12 and under eat
free if staying in parents' room. MAP $60 per person extra. AE, MC, V. Parking: Free.

One of the finest modern luxury resorts in the Caribbean, this secluded retreat in
the East End merits an extended stay. Guests can arrive by yacht and occupy a
berth in the 67-slip marina or else take a superb suite or villa.

The accommodations exude casual elegance and open onto a horseshoe bay,
with one of St. Thomas's most spectacular beaches. The beaches are actually two
ivory sand crescents broken by the coral-reef peninsula of Prettyklip Point. The
suites have fully equipped kitchens with microwaves; bedroom areas; living/
dining rooms with queen-size sofa beds; and large, fully tiled outdoor galleries
with lounge furniture. Villas are on two levels; the main level contains the same

amenities as the suites, while the upper level includes a second full bath, a bedroom and sitting area with a queen-size sofa bed, and a sundeck with outdoor furniture. Suites accommodate one to four guests, whereas villas are suitable for up to six guests.

**Dining/Entertainment:** Meals are served at the beach bar, and at night you can dine at the Seagrape, along the seashore, one of the island's finest eating places. Sometimes a five-piece band is brought in for dancing under the stars. See separate recommendation under "Dining," below. For casual dining, the Sailfish Café features standard fare such as hamburgers and Mexican dishes.

**Services:** Daily chamber service, guest-services desk, babysitting.

**Facilities:** Snorkeling equipment, Sunfish sailboats, windsurfing boards, all-weather tennis court, quarter-acre freshwater pool, diving center.

### Secret Harbour Beach Front Hotel

2H25 Estate Nazareth, Nazareth Bay, P.O. Box 7576, St. Thomas, USVI 00802. ☎ **809/ 775-6550,** or 800/524-2250. Fax 809/775-1501. 60 suites (all with bath). A/C TV TEL Transportation: Vitran bus. Rates (including continental breakfast): Winter, $265 studio double; $310 one-bedroom suite; $480 two-bedroom suite for up to four people. Summer, $169 studio double; $199 one-bedroom suite; $290 two-bedroom suite for up to four people. AE, MC, V. Parking: Free.

This all-suite resort is on the beach at Nazareth Bay, right outside Red Hook. The four contemporary buildings have a southwestern exposure and is only a 20-minute ride from Charlotte Amalie. Each unit has a private deck or patio and a full kitchen. There are three kinds of accommodations: studio apartments with a bed-sitting-room area, patio, and dressing-room area; one-bedroom suites with a living/dining area, a separate bedroom, and a sundeck; and the most luxurious, a two-bedroom suite with two baths and a private living room.

**Dining/Entertainment:** Tamarind by the Sea, on the beach, offers open-air dining, serving dinner daily from 6:30 to 10pm. The Secret Harbour Beach Café offers breakfast and lunch on an outdoor terrace or in the gazebo. Both restaurants

---

### ℹ️ Family-Friendly Hotels

**Sapphire Beach Resort** *(see p. 91)* The resort does more for kids than most hotels on the island, and the sweeping expanses of one of the finest beaches on the island gives them plenty of room to play. Children under 12 stay and eat free when accompanied by their parents. There are even supervised activities at the Little Gems Kids Klub.

**Secret Harbour** *(see p. 92)* Children under 12 stay free at this hotel, which opens onto Nazareth Bay. Many units have kitchenettes where families can prepare light meals. Beach facilities are at the doorstep.

**Stouffer Grand Beach Resort** *(see p. 93)* This big resort offers a daily year-round children's program free for guests. Children aged 3 to 14 are invited to join in the fun, directed by counselor-supervised trained personnel. There's also a kiddie pool.

**Bolongo Beach Resorts Club Everything** *(see p. 94)* Ideal for families, these villas have programs designed to give parents some time off. The Kid's Korner Center provides planned day activities and lunches and dinners when children are not with their parents.

have bars for drinks. A weekly manager's cocktail party for guests features local music, rum punches, and hors d'oeuvres.

**Services:** Babysitting, daily maid service.

**Facilities:** Five-star PADI dive center and water-sports facility on the beach, catamaran for sail charters, two all-weather tennis courts, fitness center, fresh-water pool, and Jacuzzi.

### ✪ Stouffer Grand Beach Resort

Smith Bay Rd., Rte. 38, P.O. Box 8267, St. Thomas, USVI 00801. ☎ **809/775-1510,** or 800/ 468-3571 in the U.S. Fax 809/775-3757. 254 rms, 36 suites. A/C MINIBAR TV TEL Transportation: Taxi. Rates: Winter, $315–$435 single or double; from $895 suite for six. Summer, $215–$355 single or double; from $550 suite for six. MAP $55 per person extra. AE, DC, MC, V. Parking: Free.

Seven miles northeast of Charlotte Amalie, perched on a steep hillside, above a 1,000-foot white sandy beach, this resort occupies 34 acres on the northeast shore of St. Thomas. Accommodations are in two separate areas—poolside and hillside. The two-story town-house suites and one-bedroom suites have whirlpool spas, and all units are stylishly outfitted. Each accommodation has an open balcony or patio.

**Dining/Entertainment:** You can enjoy beachfront breakfast, lunch, and dinner at Baywinds, featuring continental and Caribbean cuisine. Dinner and an award-winning Sunday brunch are served in Smugglers Bar and Grill. Lighter fare is offered at the poolside snack bar at lunch. For cocktails, live entertainment, and dancing, there's the Baywinds Lounge.

**Services:** Daily children's program, babysitting, laundry, tropical garden tour, 24-hour room service, twice-daily chamber service, concierge, newspaper and coffee with wake-up call.

**Facilities:** Two swimming pools, free daily scuba and snorkel lessons, free Sunfish sailboats, kayaks, Windsurfers, snorkel equipment, on-site full-service dive shop, water-sports center (where you can arrange for day sails, deep-sea fishing and other excursions), six lit tennis courts, exercise facility, nearby 18-hole golf course, newsstand, gift shop, boutique, beauty salon.

### ✪ Sugar Bay Plantation Resort

6500 Estate Smith Bay, St. Thomas, USVI 00802. ☎ **809/777-7100,** or 800/927-7100 in the U.S. Fax 809/777-3269. 294 rms, 6 suites. A/C TV TEL Rates: Winter, $270–$370 single or double; from $550–$795 suite. Summer, $180–$280 single or double; $450–$595 suite. MAP $35 per person extra. AE, DC, MC, V. Parking: Free.

This hotel, a five-minute ride from Red Hook, lies on the East End adjacent to the Stouffer Grand Beach Resort. It was built in 1992 as an upscale branch of the Holiday Inn chain and hosts conventions. It contains a central core where visitors register and six pale-green and white-sided outbuildings that contain the accommodations. About 90% of the rooms have balconies and ocean views. Decors feature rattan furniture and pastel color schemes inspired by the tropics.

**Dining/Entertainment:** The resort has several eateries, the most glamorous of which is the Manor House, serving international food in a recreated plantation house. Other choices include the Ocean Club, near the hotel lobby (no food); its bar evokes a cruise-ship lounge complete with big windows and a sweeping view of the sea. There are also a poolside bar and snack bar.

**Services:** Room service, babysitting, tour desk.

**Facilities:** Three swimming pools, sandy beach, health club, snorkeling equipment. The tennis facilities are the finest on the island; they contain the first stadium tennis court (seating 220) six additional Laykold courts lit at night, and a pro shop.

## EXPENSIVE

### Bolongo Bay Beach Villas

50 Estate Bolongo, P.O. Box 7337, St. Thomas, USVI 00801. ☎ **809/779-2844,** or 800/ 524-4746. Fax 809/775-3208. 39 suites. A/C TV TEL Transportation: Taxi. Rates: Winter, $290–$475 single or double. Summer, $210–$355 single or double AE, DC, MC, V. Parking: Free.

Bolongo Bay Beach Villas is a good value for families. Located steps from the beach and pool, each seaside one-, two-, or three-bedroom villa is beautifully furnished and completely equipped to provide a retreat with the comforts of home, including a full kitchen. It is located right next to the Bolongo Beach Resorts Club Everything facilities, including water sports, a beginner's scuba lesson, tennis, volleyball, basketball, a deluxe fitness center, a kid's center with planned youth activities and supervised child care, session shuttle service to Limetree Beach, and Bolongo's five restaurants. Kids 16 and under stay free and get three free boat cruises when accompanied by a paying parent. Kids 12 and under eat free. Special children's menus are available at each of Bolongo's restaurants.

**Dining/Entertainment:** There's nightly entertainment at Bolongo Beach Resorts Club Everything. Restaurants such as Lord Rumbottoms, Caribbean Lobster House, and Iggie's are accessible by complimentary shuttle.

**Services:** Kids Korner Recreation Center with supervised child care and planned youth activities.

**Facilities:** Fitness center, swimming pool, water sports, windsurfing, Sunfish sailboats, tennis courts, St. Thomas Diving Club, gift shop.

### Bolongo Beach Resorts Club Everything

50 Bolongo Estate, St. Thomas, USVI 00802. ☎ **809/779-2844,** or 800/524-4746 in the U.S. Fax 809/775-3208. 161 rms, 40 suites. A/C MINIBAR TV TEL Transportation: Vitran bus. Rates (including all meals): Winter, $235–$245 double; $260 suite for two. Summer, $190–$205 double; $215 suite. AE, DC, MC, V. Parking: Free.

This well-established Bolongo Beach Resort has combined three of its four widely scattered properties into one sprawling complex that has welcomed more honeymooners than any other place on the island. It also operates the Bolongo Elysian Beach Resort (see above). This resort complex with its beachside location is called "Club Everything" because of the wide range of activities it offers, from scuba lessons to fitness centers to sports, especially tennis. The original Bolongo Villas and Bolongo Bay Beach are side by side on the same beach, and a section originally known as "Limetree" is farther along the shoreline and connected to the other sections by minivan shuttles. This resort is a family affair, run by Dick and Joyce Doumeng, aided by their children. Club Everything offers handsomely furnished rooms and villa suites, set either beside beaches or in gardens, all with beachfront or ocean views along two palm-lined beaches.

**Dining/Entertainment:** The five restaurants include Viola's Calypso Kitchen, with West Indian food; Lord Rumbottom's, serving giant-cut prime ribs with a large salad bar; the Caribbean Lobster House, with fresh fish and a local lobster and raw bar; Coconut Henry's Family Restaurant, for lunch and dinner with a sundae bar; and Iggie's Sing-along and Sports Bar, for light meals at lunch and dinner.

**Services:** Open-air shuttle to town, babysitting, "Kid's Korner" program with a full range of challenging recreational activities for children 3 to 21.

**Facilities:** Six tennis courts; three swimming pools with swim-up bars; scuba-diving club; a fleet of private boats (Bolongo offers more boat trips than many excursion companies); Bayside Spa and Fitness Center.

## INEXPENSIVE

### Bayside Spa & Fitness Center

7140 Bolongo, St. Thomas, USVI 00802. ☎ **809/779-2844,** or 800/524-4746. Fax 809/775-3298. 4 rms. A/C TV TEL Transportation: Taxi. Rates: Winter, $95 single or double. Summer, $80 single or double. AE, MC, V. Parking: Free.

Bayside Inn is a West Indian manor that was completely renovated and converted into a deluxe spa and fitness center in early 1993. Guests staying in Bayside Inn's quiet, comfortable rooms are just steps away from Bolongo Beach Resorts Club Everything and are welcome to the use of the beach facilities and water sports. Bayside Inn is the ideal way to combine relaxation, fitness, and fun into one vacation.

**Services:** Hair salon, massage therapist, complete facial and body treatment services, hydroaerobics.

**Facilities:** Swimming pool, scuba lesson, water sports, sauna.

# 4  Dining

The cuisine in St. Thomas is among the best in the entire West Indies. Unfortunately, prices are high, and many of the best spots can be reached only by taxi. With a few exceptions, the finest restaurants aren't in Charlotte Amalie but are out on the island.

St. Thomas has a wide range of cuisines, including American, Mexican, and Chinese. Try some of the local dishes, especially the fish, including "ole wife" and yellowtail. Cooked native style, the fish is served with a creole mixture of peppers, onions, and tomatoes. The best side dish is *fungi* (pronounced *foon*-gee), made with okra and cornmeal.

The best local soups are *bullfoot,* made with meat and vegetables and seasoned with herbs and spices, and *callaloo,* made with ham hock, crab, and greens. Most main dishes consist of either fish, goat, pork, chicken, or conch. Local restaurants serve the most popular bread, johnnycake, a fried unleavened bread. Fried plantain is also a popular dish.

Restaurants rated "expensive" charge from $35 to $60 per person for dinner, plus wine. Those rated "moderate" can charge up to $30 or more for dinner, but the smart diner can also eat in most of them for only $25, plus wine, which places them in the budget category, at least for St. Thomas. For inexpensive meals under $25, refer to "Local Favorites," below.

# CHARLOTTE AMALIE
## EXPENSIVE

### ✪ Blackbeard's Castle

Blackbeard's Hill. ☎ **776-1234.** Reservations recommended for dinner. Transportation: Taxi. Appetizers $5–$10.75; main dishes $17.50–$27; Sunday brunch from $12. AE, MC, V.  Lunch

Mon–Fri 11:30am–2:30pm; dinner daily 6–10pm; Sun brunch 11am–3pm. Closed Mon for dinner in summer. AMERICAN/SEAFOOD.

This elegant dining room in the hotel of the same name (see "Accommodations," above) serves seafood and new American cuisine. Awarded a trio of gold medals for ambience, Caribbean dishes, and overall food in local culinary contests, owners Bob Harrington and Henrique Konzen serve lunch and Sunday brunch with the *New York Times* and board games. In winter, live jazz is enjoyed from Tuesday to Saturday, 8pm to midnight. Don't miss the elaborately ornate cast-iron chandelier hanging in the anteroom of the bar. The chandelier was once owned by the Delano-Roosevelt family. The laughing cherubs were found in a Danish manor house and given a new home overlooking one of the best harbor views on the island.

Specials include toasted ravioli, pistachio fried oysters, grilled tournedos, and a macadamia-nut-crusted mahi mahi. Lunches, slightly less elaborate and about one-third the price, feature salads, delicately seasoned platters, and frothy rum-based drinks.

### Entre Nous

Bluebeard's Castle, Bluebeard's Hill. ☎ **776-4050.** Reservations recommended. Appetizers $7–$15; main dishes $19–$38. AE, MC, V. Dinner Mon–Sat 6–9:30pm. Closed Sept. FRENCH/ITALIAN.

This established restaurant in the most famous hotel of St. Thomas (see "Accommodations," above) serves some of the island's finest cuisine. An open-air restaurant with a panoramic view, it offers candlelight dinners and a view of the harbor. Caesar salad will be prepared at your table, followed by such classic dishes as seafood málange, jerk-spiced duck breast, rack of lamb, or filet mignon Entre Nous. Seafood specialties are heavily featured as well, especially North Atlantic sea scallops. The menu has changed with the times, and you can also order dishes low in fat. Of course, all that dieting is tossed aside when the dessert trolley arrives. Baked Alaska is a specialty. The hotel also has a good wine list, with vintages from Italy to California.

### Hotel 1829

Kongens Gade. ☎ **776-1829.** Reservations recommended, but not accepted more than one day in advance. Appetizers $7.50–$11.50; main dishes $21–$40. AE, DC, MC, V. Dinner Mon–Sat 6–10pm. CONTINENTAL.

Hotel 1829 (see "Accommodations," above) has some of the finest food in St. Thomas. Diners walk up the hill east of the post office and climb the stairs of this old structure and then head for the attractive bar for a before-dinner drink. Dining is on a terrace or in the main room, whose walls are made from ships' ballast and which is cooled by ceiling fans. The floor is made of 18th-century Moroccan tiles.

The cuisine has a distinctively European twist, with many dishes prepared and served from trolleys beside your table. For an appetizer, try assorted seafood cocktails or one of the velvety-smooth soups such as lobster bisque. Fish and meat dishes are usually excellent and include choices such as Anguillan rock lobster in a garlic scallion blanc sauce, rack of lamb, filet mignon in a pepper sauce, or medallions of veal layered with Gruyère and prosciutto with wild mushrooms and a flavoring of Marsala. The chateaubriand for two is a house specialty. Dessert might include an array of soufflés, including chocolate, amaretto, and raspberry.

## MODERATE

### Virgilio's

18 Dronningens Gade. ☎ 776-4920. Reservations recommended. Appetizers $8.95–$11.95; main dishes $12–$25. AE, MC, V. Lunch daily 11:30am–4:30pm; dinner daily 4:30–10:30pm. ITALIAN.

Virgilio's is considered one of the best Italian restaurants in the Virgin Islands. Sheltered beneath heavy ceiling beams and brick vaulting, the restaurant remains the way it was originally designed 200 years ago. Its entrance is off a narrow alleyway running between Main Street and Back Street. A well-trained staff attends to only 12 tables at one of the smallest and most intimate restaurants on St. Thomas. The menu includes a full complement of northern Italian cuisine, including homemade pastas, elegant salads, seafood dishes such as red snapper l'amatriciana and cioppino (a savory seafood stew), veal chop celestino (stuffed with prosciutto, mozzarella, and mushrooms), and an extensive array of desserts, many of them flambéed.

## INEXPENSIVE

### Greenhouse

Veterans Dr. ☎ 774-7998. Reservations not required. Transportation: Vitran bus. Appetizers $4–$6.75; main dishes $4.50–$16.95. AE, MC, V. Breakfast daily 7–11am; lunch daily 11am–5pm; dinner daily 5–9:30pm. AMERICAN.

Fronted with big windows which flood the plant-filled interior with sun, this all-purpose waterfront restaurant has a menu which changes throughout the day. A breakfast menu of eggs, sausages, and bacon will cost from around $2.95. This segues into daily specialties, many of which borrow from Jamaican cuisine. Happy hour, from 4:30 to 7pm every day but Sunday, includes half-priced tropical libations. After 10pm the place devotes its energies to a nightlife venue (see "St. Thomas After Dark," below).

### Hard Rock Café

In International Plaza, The Waterfront, Queen's Quarter. ☎ 777-5555. Reservations not accepted. Appetizers $5.95–$7.95; main dishes $8.95–$13. AE, MC, V. Tues–Thurs and Sun 11am–10pm Fri–Sat 11am–midnight. AMERICAN.

Occupying the second floor of a pink-sided mall whose big windows overlook the ships moored in Charlotte Amalie's harbor, this restaurant is a member of the international chain that defines itself as the Smithsonian of rock 'n' roll. Entire walls are devoted to the memorabilia of such artists as John Lennon, Eric Clapton, and Bob Marley. Throughout most of the day, the place functions as a restaurant, serving barbecued meats, salads, sandwiches, burgers (including a well-flavored veggie burger), fresh fish, steaks, and probably the best fajitas in the Virgin Islands. On Friday and Saturday nights when a live band performs, the small dance floor gets busy and the bar trade picks up considerably.

# FRENCHTOWN
## MODERATE

### Alexander's

Rue de St. Barthélemy, Frenchtown. ☎ 776-4211. Reservations recommended. Transportation: Vitran bus. Appetizers $5.25–$8.50; main dishes $12–$20. AE, MC, V. Lunch Mon–Fri 11am–5pm, Sat 11am–3pm; dinner daily 5:30–10pm. AUSTRIAN/GERMAN.

Alexander's accommodates you in air-conditioned comfort with picture windows overlooking the harbor. Named for its Austrian-born owner, Alexander Treml, the small restaurant offers Austrian specialties with flair. There's a heavy emphasis on seafood dishes, including conch schnitzel. Other dishes from the Middle European kitchen include mouth-watering Wiener Schnitzel, Nürnberger Rostbraten, goulash, and homemade pâté. For dessert, you might try the homemade apple strudel or the richly caloric Schwarzwald torte. Midday meals consist of a variety of crêpes, quiches, and a daily chef's special. The wine list frequently changes and is the best value on St. Thomas.

At both lunch and dinner, the menu offers a selection of at least 15 different pasta dishes. The establishment's sports bar keeps the same hours as the restaurant.

### Bravo Café

17 Crown Bay. ☎ **776-4466.** Reservations not required. Appetizers $4.50–$9.50; main dishes $10–$22; gourmet pizzas $8. AE, MC, V. Lunch daily 11:30am–3pm; dinner daily 6–11pm. MEDITERRANEAN.

Opening onto the East Gregerie Channel just west of Frenchtown, this restaurant is a good choice for a quiet afternoon of boat watching. Guests anchor at the mahogany bar beneath ceiling beams and swirling fans in a breezy open-sided pavilion. Drinks are served here all day and night. Lunch is likely to include a choice of deli sandwiches, a West Indian specialty of the day, and omelets. The dinner menu features Caribbean lobster, swordfish, and pastas. The chef bakes his own bread fresh daily in the café's kitchen.

### ⊙ Café Normandie

Rue de St. Barthélemy, Frenchtown. ☎ **774-1622.** Reservations recommended. Transportation: Taxi. Appetizers $5.50–$14.50; fixed-price dinner $28.50–$38.50. AE, MC, V. Dinner daily 6–10pm. FRENCH.

The fixed-price meal offered here is one of the best dining values on the island. It begins with soup, although you have a choice of ordering an à la carte appetizer. Then you're served a salad and sorbet before your main-course, which you select from specialties ranging from lobster Mornay to the poached catch of the day in white wine. The dessert special (not featured on the fixed-price meal) is their original chocolate fudge pie, and the chef definitely will not divulge the recipe. The restaurant is air-conditioned, and the glow of candlelight makes it elegant. The service is excellent. There is a relaxed informality about the dress code, but you shouldn't show up in a bathing suit.

### Chart House Restaurant

At the Admiral's Inn, Villa Olga, Frenchtown. ☎ **774-4262.** Reservations not required. Transportation: Taxi. Appetizers $4.95–$8.95; main dishes $16.95–$29.95; fixed-price dinner (until 6:30pm) $14.95. AE, DC, MC, V. Dinner Sun–Thurs 5–10pm, Fri 5–11pm. STEAKS.

The stripped-down 19th-century villa that contains the Chart House was the Russian consulate during the island's Danish administration. It lies a short distance beyond the most densely populated area of Frenchtown village, but it has a completely separate management from the Admiral's Inn. The dining gallery is a spacious open terrace fronting the sea.

Cocktails start daily at 5pm, when the bartender breaks out the ingredients for his special drink known as a Bailey's banana colada.

The Chart House features the best salad bar on the island, with a choice of 30 to 40 items, and comes with dinner. Menu choices range from chicken to

Australian lobster tail. This chain is known for serving the finest cut of prime rib anywhere. For dessert, order the famous Chart House "mud pie."

## ✪ Provence

rue de St. Barthélemy, Frenchtown. ☎ **777-5600.** Reservations recommended. Appetizers $4.50–$12; main dishes $13–$18.50. AE, MC, V. Dinner daily 6–10:30pm. Closed Sun off-season. PROVENÇAL/MEDITERRANEAN.

Established in 1993, this well-managed French bistro is owned by Patricia LeCorte, a Paris-trained Cordon Bleu chef who works hard to keep the quality high and the prices moderate. Set on the second floor of a clapboard-sided building in Frenchtown, the restaurant is decorated with murals of agricultural scenes in Provence and a donkey cart loaded with fresh flowers, vegetables, and loaves of bread. A wine bar in the corner dispenses 20 kinds of French and Italian wines by the glass, priced at $4 to $7 each depending on the vintage. Ms. LeCorte's dishes might include salmon carpaccio with a tapenade of black olives, romaine salad with roasted anchovies and garlic dressing, roast goat cheese salad, braised lamb shank with al dente vegetables and orzo pasta, roast free-range garlic chicken with mashed potatoes, a traditional steak au poivre, a selection of fresh seafood which arrives according to market conditions, and at least three kinds of dessert soufflés. Many guests appreciate the elegant array of Mediterranean antipasti which are displayed as a before-dinner temptation.

# SUB BASE
## INEXPENSIVE

### Barnacle Bill's

At the Crown Bay Marina, in the Sub Base. ☎ **774-7444.** Reservations not required. Appetizers $3–$6; main dishes $13.75–$24.50; lunch sandwiches and platters $5–$9. AE, DC, MC, V. Mon–Sat 11:30am–11pm, Sun 5–11pm. Bar (with live music) till at least 1am (see "St. Thomas After Dark," below). INTERNATIONAL.

Established by hardworking entrepreneur Bill Grogan, this restaurant is best known as a bar with live music. Its fans, however, also enjoy its view of one of the island's most prestigious marinas (Crown Point) and its food. Portions, large and well-prepared, include everything from steaks to lobsters, with lots of burgers, sandwiches, pastas, and salads as well. The setting is a pastel-colored clapboard-sided house with lots of outdoor terraces and decks overlooking the yachts moored in the nearby marina.

# COMPASS POINT
## MODERATE

### For the Birds

Scott Beach, near Compass Point, off Rte. 32. ☎ **775-6431.** Reservations not required. Transportation: Taxi. Appetizers $3.50–$12; main dishes $10.50–$20. AE, MC, V. Lunch daily 11am–3pm; dinner daily 6–10:30pm. MEXICAN/SEAFOOD/BARBECUE.

Set in a green-roofed bungalow, this pleasant restaurant offers reasonably priced, well-prepared food in gargantuan helpings. A few steps from the restaurant's big windows, the surf and a sandy beach beckon. Spicy temptations include a dinner platter smothered with heaps of nachos or onion rings, a plate of the best baby back ribs on the island, filet mignon, and fresh fish. There's also a selection of Mexican specialties such as beef or chicken enchiladas and burritos. Margaritas are huge, 46 ounces, and beer comes in mason jars. A disc jockey plays music nightly.

### Raffles

41 Frydenhoj, Compass Point, off Rte. 32. ☎ **775-6004.** Reservations recommended. Transportation: Taxi. Appetizers $5–$8; main dishes $12–$25. AE, MC, V. Dinner Tues–Sun 6:30–10:30pm. CONTINENTAL/SEAFOOD.

Named after the legendary hotel in Singapore, this establishment is filled with tropical accents more evocative of the South Pacific than of the Caribbean. The furnishings include peacock chairs, wicker, and ceiling fans. A pianist plays Gershwin and Porter during dinner, and show time is 10:30pm. Dishes are organized on the menu into categories; you can choose from fresh seafood, beef, veal, lamb, chicken, and live Maine lobster. The fresh fish of the day is well prepared with various tasty sauces. The chef's specialty is duck marinated for two days then steamed and crisped before serving. The kitchen is also known for its curry and chutney dressing. Raffles nestles beside the lagoon at Compass Point, one mile west of Red Hook.

### WindJammer Restaurant

41 Frydenhoj, Compass Point, off Rte. 32. ☎ **775-6194.** Reservations recommended. Transportation: Taxi. Appetizers $3.75–$7.75; main dishes $7.75–$18.75. MC, V. Lunch Mon–Sat 11:30am–5pm; dinner Mon–Sat 5–10pm. Closed Sept. SEAFOOD/GERMAN.

The paneling and smoothly finished bar of this cozy place are crafted largely from thick slabs of island mahogany and illuminated by light streaming in from the open windows. After dark, the soft glow of oil lamps adds a nautically romantic glow to a relaxed atmosphere with traces of tropical *Gemütlichkeit*. The restaurant lies within a seaport village one mile west of Red Hook, near the easternmost tip of the island.

The extensive menu features more than 40 main dishes, many reflecting the restaurant's German heritage. These might include red snapper Adlon (boneless filet of snapper topped with shrimp and mushrooms) or lots of schnitzels. Appetizers include escargots in garlic butter and veal soup. The classic desserts—key lime pie, a light and creamy cheesecake, and chocolate rum cake (made with aged local rum)—are all homemade.

# IN & AROUND RED HOOK
## EXPENSIVE

### Palm Court

Bolongo Elysian Beach Resort, 50 Estate Bolongo, Cowpet Bay. ☎ **775-1000.** Reservations recommended. Transportation: Taxi. Lunch appetizers $2.95–$8.95, lunch main dishes $6.95–$10.95; dinner appetizers $5.50–$9.50, dinner main dishes $14.50–$29. AE, DC, MC, V. Lunch daily 11:30am–3pm; dinner daily 6:30–9:30pm. INTERNATIONAL.

On the premises of a luxury resort (see "Accommodations," above), the cuisine, decor, and service of this restaurant achieve a subtle, European-style glamor better than any other in St. Thomas.

The lunch menu lists salads, soups, sandwiches, burgers, and brochettes of chicken. Dinner is more of a culinary showcase for the talents of the chef and might include a spinach-and-oyster chowder; a vegetarian mousse of the day; fricassée of monkfish garnished with scallops, crayfish, and Armagnac sauce; and medallions of veal with lobster, white asparagus, and Pernod.

# FLAMBOYANT POINT
## EXPENSIVE

### ✪ Tavern on the Beach

Marriott's Morning Star Beach Resort, Flamboyant Point. ☎ **776-8500.** Reservations recommended in winter. Transportation: Water or land taxi from Charlotte Amalie. Appetizers $5.25–$11.95; main dishes $17.95–$34.50. AE, DC, MC, V. INTERNATIONAL/CARIBBEAN.

One of Florida's best known chefs, German-born Eddie Hale now runs this oceanside hot spot (see "Accommodations," above, for hotel review). Most recently Hale worked at the Heritage Grille in St. Petersburg, where a local food writer said he was "not only a master of exotic flavors and textures, but his fabulous food appeals to a spectrum of customers." The same applies to his operation in St. Thomas.

His courses, divided into first, second, and third "plates," reflect both Caribbean and international influences. Sample "first plate" dishes include Thai-flavored pork satay with crispy noodle salad and lemongrass/coconut dipping sauce; Bajan-spiced butterfly prawn adrift on gazpacho with saffron aioli; warm, cracked conch sumo maki roll with tea-smoked macadamia dipping sauce. "Second plate" dishes may include annatto seared, jumbo sea scallops with chardonnay fruit "paints" and red beet spaghetti; sautéed local snapper with a Cruzan rum/brown butter, sweet potato salad, and braised endives; jerk marinated roasted rack of lamb with mashed yams, tannia, and mango chutney. "Third Plate" includes cashew caramel tart with a vanilla bean and banana sundae or lemon-drop flan with ginger and herb-flavored exotic fruit salsa.

## MODERATE

### Piccola Marina Ristorante

6300 Smith Bay, Red Hook, Rte. 38. ☎ **775-6250.** Reservations required for dinner. Transportation: Red Hook bus. Appetizers $5–$8.25; main dishes $13–$24; lunch platters $4.50–$13.50; pizzas $9.50–$12.50. AE, MC, V. Lunch Mon–Sat 11am–3pm; dinner Sun–Thurs 6–10pm, Fri–Sat 5:30–11pm; brunch Sun 11am–3pm. ITALIAN.

Built on stilts over the water within touching distance of one of the Caribbean's most varied assortment of yachts, this popular eatery has an open veranda, a bar, and enough business to fill every table on weekends. The menu includes various salads, from Caesar to Greek to a fresh antipasto primavera, and an assortment of sandwiches, not to mention charcoal-broiled hamburgers. Sunday brunch offers everything from the traditional eggs Benedict to flaky croissants filled with Canadian bacon. Fresh pasta dishes, such as carbonara, are on the menu, as are fresh fish, steak, chicken, and shrimp. Desserts include a homemade brownie special on Sunday and cheesecakes. All the food is homemade from only fresh ingredients whenever possible. The kitchen doesn't turn out magic, but the fare is acceptable.

## INEXPENSIVE

### East Coast

Red Hook Plaza, Rte. 38. ☎ **775-1919.** Reservations not required. Transportation: Red Hook bus. Appetizers $2.50–$4.75; main dishes $6.75–$18.75. AE, MC, V. Dinner daily 5:30–11pm; brunch Sun noon–4pm. Bar daily 4:30pm–4am. CARIBBEAN.

Across the street from Red Hook Plaza, East Coast nightly packs a tourist and local crowd of sports fans into its pine-sheathed interior to cheer their favorites on TV.

Though you might not expect it, the adjacent restaurant serves very good meals. You can dine in a denlike room or on an outdoor terrace in back. Each day, a different fish is prepared according to the way you like it—grilled, baked, or broiled. The selections might include tuna, wahoo, dolphin, swordfish, or snapper (best in a garlic cream sauce). The kitchen also turns out Cajun shrimp and their famous "Coast burgers." Live bands sometimes entertain in the Shark Room from 8:30pm to 2am, but call before and by the schedule.

## SAPPHIRE BEACH
### EXPENSIVE

#### Seagrape
Sapphire Beach Resort & Marina, Rte. 6, Smith Bay Rd. ☎ **775-6100.** Reservations recommended. Transportation: Taxi. Appetizers $4.95–$12.50; main dishes $18.50–$24.50. AE, MC, V. Lunch daily 11am–3pm; dinner daily 6–10pm; brunch Sun 11am–3pm. CONTINENTAL/AMERICAN.

Counted among the finest dining rooms along the east coast of St. Thomas, Seagrape is open to the sea breezes of one of the most famous beaches in the Virgin Islands: Sapphire Beach. The restaurant's attractions are the accompanying sounds of the waves, a well-trained staff, and fine-quality food. The lunch menu includes the grilled catch of the day and freshly made salads; a children's menu is also available. Abel Anaya Lucca, the Puerto Rican chef, developed his own eclectic style with French, Creole, Italian, and continental cuisines. His innovative new dishes include a salad of wild mushrooms sautéed in garlic and olive oil and served over mixed baby greens with blue cheese crumbs and roasted walnuts, freshly caught mahi mahi with a Chinese barbecue sauce, and grilled shrimp and scallops with Jamaican jerk seasoning.

For a separate recommendation of the hotel's Sunday brunch, see below.

## NORTH COAST
### EXPENSIVE

#### ✪ Romano's Restaurant
97 Smith Bay Rd. ☎ **775-0045.** Reservations recommended. Transportation: Vitran bus. Appetizers $7.95–$10.95; main dishes $22.95–$26.95; pastas $15.95–$18.95. AE, MC, V. Dinner Mon–Sat 6:30–10:30pm. Closed a week in April for Carnival. ITALIAN.

Located on the flatlands near Coral World, this restaurant is skillfully decorated with exposed brick and well-stocked wine racks like you'd find in a *trattoria* in northern Italy. The creation of New Jersey–born Tony Romano, the chef-owner, Romano's is considered the best Italian restaurant in St. Thomas and offers the flavorful and herb-laden cuisine that diners yearn for after a constant diet of Caribbean cooking. Specialties include linguine con pesto; four-cheese lasagne; penne pianello with mushrooms, prosciutto, and pine nuts; osso buco; scaloppine marsala; and broiled salmon. Another specialty is veal sweetbread with mushrooms, brandy peppercorns, and cream. All desserts are made on the premises. Although Tony doesn't advertise, his place is always full.

## DINING WITH A VIEW

#### Agave Terrace
Point Pleasant Resort, Estate Smith Bay No. 4. ☎ **775-4142.** Reservations recommended. Transportation: Taxi. Appetizers $6–$10; main dishes $17.50–$38. AE, MC, V. Dinner daily 6–10pm. CARIBBEAN.

Perched high above a steeply inclined and heavily forested hillside on the eastern tip of St. Thomas, this restaurant offers a sweeping panorama and matchless romantic atmosphere.

The house drink, created by the bartender, is Desmond Delight, a combination of Midori, rum, pineapple juice, and a secret ingredient.

Following one or more Delights, you might opt for dinner. The house appetizer is an Agave sampler prepared for two, which includes portions of crabmeat, conch fritters, and chicken pinwheel. For a main course, the preferred the chef's specialty is lobster cardinale, served with a lobster-flavored cream and fresh tomato sauce on a bed of angelhair pasta. Many diners opt for the catch of the day, which the chef can prepare seven different ways. There is an extensive wine list. A live steel drum band draws listeners Tuesday and Thursday nights.

## LOCAL FAVORITES

### Ⓢ Eunice's

66-67 Smith Bay, Rte. 38. ☎ **775-3975.** Reservations recommended at dinner. Transportation: Red Hook bus. Lunch appetizers $2.50–$7.95, lunch main dishes $4–$7.95; dinner appetizers $7–$11, dinner main dishes $9.95–$26. AE, MC, V. Lunch Mon–Sat 11am–3:30pm; dinner Mon–Sat 6–10pm. WEST INDIAN/AMERICAN.

Eunice's, one of the best known West Indian restaurants on St. Thomas, has evolved over the years from a simple shack into a modern building. A mix of construction workers, locals, and tourists from nearby Stouffer's Grand Beach Hotel crowd into its confines for generous platters of island food.

A concoction called a Queen Mary (a combination of tropical fruits laced with dark rum) is a favorite throughout the late morning and afternoon. Dinner specialties include conch fritters, broiled or fried fish, sweet potato pie, and a number of chalkboard specials that are usually served with *fungi,* rice, or fried plantain. Local lobster, when available is considered a delicacy; *callaloo* soup, "stew mutton," and *souse* are also featured. For lunch, try a fishburger, a sandwich, or one of the daily specials, such as Virgin Islands pork or mutton. Key lime pie is a choice dessert.

### Victor's Hide Out

32A Sub Base, off Rte. 30. ☎ **776-9379.** Reservations recommended. Transportation: Call for directions or take a taxi. It's a bit tricky to find at night. Appetizers $5–$7.95; main dishes $9.95–$50. AE, MC, V. Lunch Mon–Sat 11:30am–3:30pm; dinner daily 5:30–10pm. WEST INDIAN/AMERICAN.

Victor Sydney's restaurant has some of the strongest West Indian flavor and best seafood and local dishes on the island. First you must find it, though—it truly is a hideout. Perched on a hilltop the large, airy restaurant affords panoramic views. The menu features conch chowder, fresh lobster Montserrat style (in a garlicky creamy sauce) or grilled in the shell, and juicy barbecued ribs. Most dishes are served with rice and beans or *fungi* (made with cornmeal and okra). Try the coconut, custard, or apple pie.

## SUNDAY BRUNCH

### Palm Court

Bolongo Elysian Beach Resort, 50 Estate Bolongo, Cowpet Bay. ☎ **775-1000.** Reservations recommended. Transportation: Taxi. Buffet, $16.95 adults; $10.95 children under 12. AE, DC, MC, V. Sun 11am–3pm. INTERNATIONAL.

---

### 🍊 Family-Friendly Restaurants

**Seagrape** *(see p. 104)* Kids delight in being taken to Sapphire Beach, where they eat off a special menu while enjoying the wide sands and palm trees of the beach. If they're guests of the hotel and are 12 or under, they dine free.

**Eunice's** *(see p. 103)* Eunice's likes children, and everybody seems to have a good time here. This place offers a tasty introduction to West Indian cooking. Kids like the fishburgers, the conch fritters, the sweet potato pie, and everybody's favorite, key lime pie.

**Iggie's** *(see p. 104)* If there is one place on the island where kids like to go, it's this spot at Limetree Beach (see Bolongo Beach Resorts Club Everything in "Accommodations" above). Here they munch on Iggie's wings (spicy Buffalo wings). Iggie's nachos, and many types of burgers (garnished with everything from Monterey Jack cheese to guacamole), along with a "basket o' fries."

---

An exquisite Sunday brunch buffet is offered at this deluxe hotel (see "Accommodations," above). Items include roast meats, omelets, smoked fish, soups, fresh vegetables, eggs Benedict, freshly prepared seafood dishes, European-style pâtés, a sumptuous salad bar, tropical fruits, imported cheeses, and a delectable dessert table. You dine to keyboard music.

**Seagrape**

Rte. 6, Smith Bay Rd. ☎ **775-6100.** Reservations recommended. Transportation: Taxi. Sun brunch $6.95–$12.95. AE, MC, V. Sun 11am–3pm. INTERNATIONAL.

Acclaimed as one of the finest Sunday brunches in St. Thomas, Seagrape's fare affords a chance to enjoy good food and the sea. Various egg dishes are offered, including the eternal Sunday brunch favorite, eggs Benedict with zesty hollandaise. You can also order a number of the chef's "Sunday favorites," including Grand Marnier french toast, Belgian waffles topped with fresh fruit, even tortellini Alfredo. A live band entertains from 2 to 5pm.

## LIGHT & CASUAL FOOD

**Iggie's Restaurant**

Bolongo Limetree Beach Hotel, Frenchman's Cove, Frenchman's Bay Rd. (Rte. 30). ☎ **779-2844.** Reservations not required. Transportation: Taxi. Appetizers $3.50–$8.95; burgers and sandwiches $7.95–$9.95; main dishes $9.95–$15.95. AE, DC, MC, V. Lunch daily noon–3pm; dinner daily 6:30–10pm. AMERICAN.

Set beneath an enormous white gazebo, with giant TV screens showing sports or great moments from the history of rock 'n' roll, this place has indestructible furniture, lots of electronic action, and a crowd of aggressively informal clients who don't mind if children are present. The menu is geared to the kinds of hands-on food that kids like (burgers, oversize sandwiches, pastas). Adults order such sudsy tropical drinks as an Iggie's Queen (coconut cream, crème de Noya, and rum) or the "Ultimate Kamikazi."

For more on this restaurant, see "St. Thomas After Dark," below.

## PICNIC FARE AND WHERE TO EAT IT

Because there are dozens of restaurants and beachside cabanas selling hamburgers and beer, many would-be picnickers tend to forgo advance picnic arrangements

# St. Thomas Dining

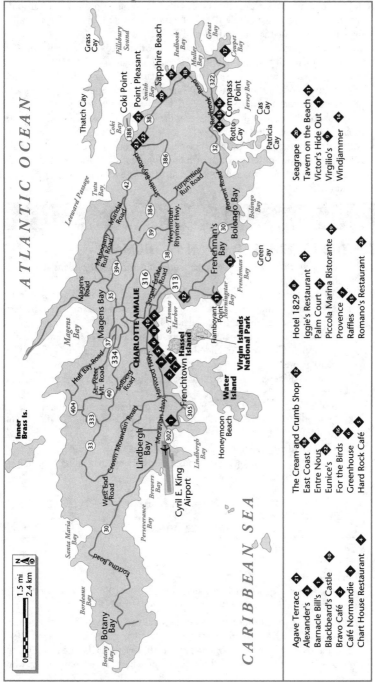

Agave Terrace 21
Alexander's 3
Barnacle Bill's 1
Blackbeard's Castle 10
Bravo Café 2
Café Normandie 3
Chart House Restaurant 4

The Cream and Crumb Shop 12
East Coast 18
Entre Nous 9
Eunice's 22
For the Birds 16
Greenhouse 6
Hard Rock Café 5

Hotel 1829 8
Iggie's Restaurant 13
Palm Court 17
Piccola Marina Ristorante 9
Provence 7
Raffles 15
Romano's Restaurant 23

Seagrape 20
Tavern on the Beach 11
Victor's Hide Out 8
Virgilio's 9
Windjammer 14

in favor of a quick beachside bite followed by a snooze on the sands. Ideal spots are the sands of Magens Bay Beach, Drake's Seat, and any of the secluded high-altitude panoramas along the island's western end.

You can, however, create a successful picnic with the culinary expertise of **The Cream and Crumb Shop,** Building 6, Havensight Mall (☎ **774-2499**). Located at the point where most cruise ships dock for daytime excursions into St. Thomas, this cheerful, modern shop is easy to miss amid the crush of tax-free jewelers and perfume shops that surround it.

The shop sells some of the best pizza on the island ($2.50 a slice), although the thickly layered deli sandwiches ($4.75 to $6.75) or salads (shrimp, chicken, potato, or crabmeat) might be more practical for take-out. You can also get freshly baked pastries, four different kinds of yogurt (piña colada is perfect), and 18 different kinds of deliciously fattening ice cream. Hours are Monday to Saturday from 6:30am to 6pm.

# 5 Attractions

## THE TOP 10 THINGS TO DO ON ST. THOMAS

1. Coral World: See the underwater world of natural coral gardens and colorful tropical fish.
2. Atlantis Submarine: Take a two-hour underwater tour to depths of 90 feet.
3. A Visit to Mountaintop: Trek up to the highest point on the island. Be sure to try the world-famous banana daiquiri.
4. Vendors Plaza: Outdoor shopping bargains in the heart of Charlotte Amalie.
5. Shopping: Charlotte Amalie, Tillett Gardens, Mountaintop—duty-free items galore.
6. Gondola Ride: Take the St. Thomas Tramway up to a 697-foot peak at Paradise Point.
7. Beach Life at Magens Bay: Named one of the best beaches in the world.
8. Exploring Fort Christian: The oldest structure still in use in the Virgin Islands.
9. Tillet Gardens: Music, art, shopping, and food.
10. Water sports: Sailing, jet skis, windsurfing, boating, parasailing, swimming, scuba, snorkeling, and more.

## WALKING TOUR
### Charlotte Amalie

**Start:** King's Wharf.
**Finish:** Waterfront.
**Time:** 2¹/₂ hours.
**Best Times:** Any day between 10am and 5pm.
**Worst Times:** When a cruise ship is in port.

The color and charm of the Caribbean come vividly to life in the waterfront town of **Charlotte Amalie,** capital of St. Thomas, where most visitors begin their sightseeing of the small island. Seafarers from all over the globe used to flock to this old-world Danish town, as did pirates and members of the Confederacy, who used the port during the American Civil War. St. Thomas was at one time the biggest slave market in the world.

The old warehouses once used for storing pirate goods still stand. Nowadays they mostly house shops. In fact, the main streets called "Gade" here (a reflection of their Danish heritage) now coalesce into a virtual shopping mall and are usually packed. Sandwiched among these shops are a few historic buildings, most of which can be covered on foot in about two hours.

All of the historic buildings of interest can easily be covered on a walking tour of Charlotte Amalie (see below). Before starting your tour, stop off in the so-called **Grand Hotel,** near Emancipation Park. No longer a hotel, it contains shops and a visitor's center (☎ **774-8784**).

Begin your tour along the eastern harborfront at:

**1.** **King's Wharf,** site of the Virgin Islands Legislature, which are housed in the apple green military barracks dating from 1874. From here walk away from the harbor up Fort Pladsen to:

**2.** ✪ **Fort Christian,** dating from 1672. Named after the Danish king Christian V, the structure has been everything from a governor's residence to a jail. Many pirates were hanged in the courtyard of the fort. Some of the cells have been turned into the Virgin Islands Museum, which displays some minor Native American artifacts. It's open Monday through Friday from 8am to 5pm and from 1 to 5pm on Saturday. Admission is free. Continue walking up Fort Pladsen to:

**3.** **Emancipation Park,** where a proclamation freeing African slaves and indentured European servants was read on July 3, 1848. Facing the west side of the park is the:

**4.** **Grand Hotel,** where a visitor's center dispenses information. When this hotel was launched in 1837, it was considered a rather grand address, but it later fell into decay, finally closing in 1975. Its former guest rooms upstairs have been turned into offices and a restaurant. Northwest of the park, at Main Street and Tolbod Gade, stands the:

**5.** **Central Post Office,** displaying murals by Stephen Dohanos, who became famous as a *Saturday Evening Post* cover artist. From the post office, walk east along Norre Gade to Fort Pladsen, to the:

**6.** **Frederik Lutheran Church,** built between 1780 and 1793. The original Georgian-style building, financed by a free black parishioner, Jean Reeneaus, was rebuilt in 1825 after a fire and rebuilt again in 1870 after it was damaged in a hurricane. Exiting the church, walk east along Norre Gade to Lille Taarne Gade. Turn left (north) and climb to Kongens Gade (King Street), passing through a neighborhood of law firms, to:

**7.** ✪ **Government House,** the administrative headquarters for all the Virgin Islands. It's been the center of official life in the islands since it was built—around the time of the American Civil War. Visitors are allowed on the first two floors, Monday through Saturday from 8am to noon and 1 to 5pm. Some paintings by former resident Camille Pissarro are on display, as are works by other St. Thomian artists. Turn left on Kongens Gade. After leaving Government House, turn immediately to your left and look for the sign for:

**8.** **Seven Arches Museum,** Government Hill, a two-century-old Danish house completely restored to its original condition and furnished with antiques. You can walk through the yellow ballast arches into the Great Room with its view of the busiest harbor in the Caribbean. You can also view the original separate stone Danish kitchen above the cistern. The admission of $7.50 includes a cold tropical drink served in a walled garden filled with flowers. Hours are Tuesday through Sunday from 10am to 3pm.

After visiting the museum, return to Government House. Directly to your left, as you face the building, is

**9. Frederik Church Parsonage,** dating from 1725, and one of the oldest houses on the island. It is the only structure in the Government Hill district to retain its simple 18th-century lines.

Continue to walk west along Kongens Gade until you reach:

**10. Hotel 1829.** The former Lavalette House, it was designed by one of the leading merchants of Charlotte Amalie. This is a landmark building and a hotel of great charm and character that has attracted many of the island's most famous guests over the years.

☕ **TAKE A BREAK    Hotel 1829,** Kongens Gade, provides the perfect veranda with a view, ideal for a drink at midday but perfect for a sundowner. You may fall in love with the place, abandon the walking tour, and stick around for a dinner—it's that special. Its bar is open daily from 10am to midnight, serving drinks for $3 and up. (See "Dining," above.)

Next door (still on the same side of the street), observe the:

**11. Yellow-Brick Building** from 1854. It was built in what local architects called "the style of Copenhagen." You can go inside the building, as part of it is filled with shops.

At this point, you can double back slightly on Kongens Gade if you'd like to climb the famous:

**12. 99 Steps.** The steps, which were erected in the early 1700s, take you to the summit of Government Hill, from where you'll see the 18th-century:

**13. Crown House,** immediately to your right on the south side of the street. This was a stately home that was the residence of two of the past governors of the Virgin Islands. The rich and privileged lived here in the 1700s, surrounded

---

### ❓ Did You Know?

- In 1825, the last pirate was hanged at St. Thomas.
- St. Thomas was a base for blockade runners and privateers sympathetic to the Confederate cause in the Civil War.
- The U.S. Senate in 1870 rejected a treaty signed with Denmark agreeing to pay $7.5 million for the U.S. Virgins.
- The U.S. Virgin Islanders celebrate more holidays than anywhere else in the U.S.—23.
- Charlotte Amalie was named after a queen of Denmark.
- A Jewish synagogue in Charlotte Amalie is the oldest in the U.S., and still maintains its sand floors.
- Locally made products from St. Thomas are not taxable.
- For centuries, St. Thomas had the largest slave auctions in the Caribbean Basin.

# Walking Tour—Charlotte Amalie

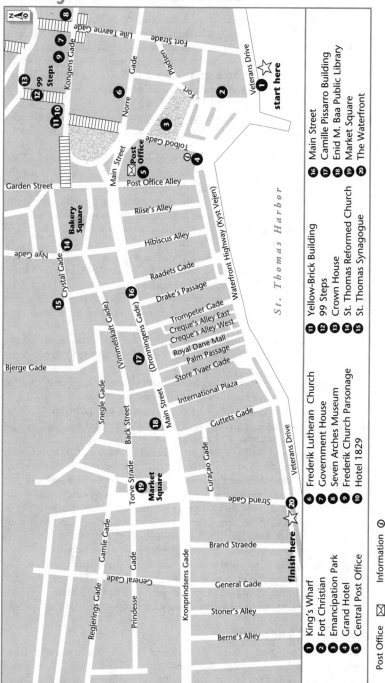

1. King's Wharf
2. Fort Christian
3. Emancipation Park
4. Grand Hotel
5. Central Post Office
6. Frederik Lutheran Church
7. Government House
8. Seven Arches Museum
9. Frederik Church Parsonage
10. Hotel 1829
11. Yellow-Brick Building
12. 99 Steps
13. Crown House
14. St. Thomas Reformed Church
15. St. Thomas Synagogue
16. Main Street
17. Camille Pissarro Building
18. Enid M. Baa Public Library
19. Market Square
20. The Waterfront

Post Office ⊠    Information ⊘

9862

by Chinese wall hangings, a crystal chandelier from Versailles, and carved West Indian furniture. It was also the home of von Scholten, the Danish ruler who issued a proclamation of emancipation in 1848 (see Emancipation Park, above).

Walk back down the steps and continue right (west) along Kongens Gade, then down a pair of old brick steps until you reach Garden Street. Go right (north) on Garden Street and take a left onto Crystal Gade. On your left, at the corner of Nye Gade and Crystal Gade you'll see:

**14. St. Thomas Reformed Church,** formerly Dutch and dating from 1844. Designed like a Greek temple, much of its original structure has been preserved intact.

Continue up Crystal Gade. On your right (north side), you'll come to:

**15. St. Thomas Synagogue,** the oldest synagogue in continuous use under the American flag and the second oldest in the Western Hemisphere. It still maintains the tradition of sand on the floor, commemorating the exodus from Egypt. Erected in 1833 by Sephardic Jews, it was built of local stone along with ballast brick from Denmark and mortar made of molasses and sand. It is open to visitors from 9am to 4pm, Monday through Friday.

Retrace your steps (east) to Raadets Gade and turn south toward the water, crossing the famous Vimmelskaft Gade or "Back Street" of Charlotte Amalie. Continue along Raadets Gade until you reach:

**16. Main Street** (Dronningens Gade), the most famous shopping street of St. Thomas and its major artery. Turn right (west) and walk along Main Street until you come to the mid-19th-century:

**17. Camille Pissarro Building,** on your right, at the Amsterdam Sauer Jewelry Store. Pissarro, a Spanish Jew who became one of the founders of French Impressionism, was born in this building as Jacob Pizarro in 1830. Before moving to Paris and becoming involved with some of the greatest artists of his day, he worked for his father in a store along Main Street.

Continuing west along Main Street, you will pass on your right:

**18. Enid M. Baa Public Library,** the former von Bretton House, dating from 1818. Keep heading west until you reach:

**19. Market Square,** officially known as Rothschild Francis Square, at the point where Main Street intersects Strand Gade. This was the center of a large slave-trading market before the emancipation was proclaimed in 1848. It is an open-air fruit and vegetable market today, selling, among other items, *genips* (break open the skin and suck the pulp off a pit). The wrought-iron roof came from Europe, and at the turn of the century covered a railway station. It's open Monday through Saturday, with Saturday its busiest day.

If the *genip* doesn't satisfy you, take Strand Gade down (south) to:

**20. The Waterfront** (Kyst Vejen), where you can purchase a fresh coconut. The vendor will whack off the top with a machete, so you can drink the sweet milk from its hull. Here you'll have an up-close preview of one of the most scenic harbors in the West Indies, though it's usually filled with cruise ships.

## NEARBY ATTRACTIONS

West of Charlotte Amalie, Route 30 (Veterans Drive) will take you to **Frenchtown.** (Turn left at the sign to The Admiral's Inn.) The town was settled by a French-speaking people who were uprooted when the Swedes invaded and took over their homeland in St. Barts. They were known for wearing *cha-chas* or straw hats. Many of the people who live here today are the direct descendants of those long-ago immigrants, who were known for speaking a distinctive patois.

This colorful village, inhabited by many fishers, contains a bevy of restaurants and taverns. Now that Charlotte Amalie can be a dangerous place at night, Frenchtown has picked up the business and is the best choice for nighttime dancing, entertainment, and drinking.

West of Charlotte Amalie, Harwood Highway (Route 308) will lead you to **Crown Mountain Road,** a scenic drive opening onto the best views of the hills, beaches, and clear seas around St. Thomas. Eventually, you arrive at a former hotel which is a traditional stopping-off point. Mountain Top, Crown Mountain (☎ 777-4707), is a modern building with a restaurant and bar, plus some two dozen shops. Most people come here to enjoy the view and sip the world-famous banana daiquiris. The bar here is said to have invented them! It is generally considered one of the most scenic perches in St. Thomas, as it opens onto a view of Sir Francis Drake Channel, which separates the U.S. Virgin Islands from the British Virgin Islands.

Farther down the road, you'll usually see tour buses filled with cruise-ship passengers converging on another scenic mountain lookout spot. This will be **Drake's Seat,** which locals claim offers the best view on the island. According to local legend, Sir Francis Drake sat there and charted the channels and passages of the Virgin Islands. You'll have spread at your feet the entire sweep of almost all the Virgin Islands, both U.S. and British.

## DRIVING TOUR
### St. Thomas

**Start:** Fort Christian.
**Finish:** Magens Bay Beach.
**Time:** 2¹/₂ hours.
**Best Times:** Sunday, when traffic is lightest.
**Worst Times:** Wednesday and Saturday, when traffic is heaviest.

Begin at Fort Christian in the eastern part of Charlotte Amalie and head west along the waterfront. To your left you'll see cruise ships anchored offshore and on your right all the stores that make Charlotte Amalie the shopping hub of the Caribbean. Continue west on Route 30 and pass the Cyril E. King Airport on your left. As the road forks toward the airport, keep right along Route 30, which runs parallel to the airport where you'll have a very close view of jumbo jets from the United States landing.

At about 2.4 miles from Fort Christian on your right will be:

1. **The University of the Virgin Islands,** which is the major university in the Virgin Islands. It is a modern complex with landscaped campus grounds. Continue west on Route 30 until you reach:

2. **Brewers Bay** on your left, with its good sand beach. You may want to park near here and go for a swim, as this is considered one of the more desirable beaches on the island.

    Continue 3.8 miles west, climbing uphill through scrub country along a hilly drive past the junction with Route 301. This far west Route 30 is called:

3. **Fortuna Road,** considered one of the most scenic areas of St. Thomas, with panoramic views of the water and offshore islands on your left. Along the way you'll come across parking areas where you can pull off and enjoy the view. The one on Bethesda Hill is particularly panoramic. The names of the districts you pass through—Bonne Esperance and Perseverance—come from the old plantations that used to stand here. The area is now primarily residential. At Bordeaux Hill you descend sharply, and the road narrows until you come to a dead end.

   At this point, turn around and head back east along Route 30. The road is badly marked at this point, and you'll probably need the *Official Road Map of the United States Virgin Islands,* available at bookstores in the USVI. Turn left and head northeast at the junction with Route 301. You will come to the junction of:

4. **Crown Mountain Road,** the most scenic road in the Virgin Islands. Turn left at this junction onto Route 33. The road will sweep northward before it makes an abrupt switch to the east. You will be traversing the most mountainous heartland of St. Thomas. Expect hairpin turns during your descent. You'll often have to reduce your speed to 10 miles an hour, especially in the Mafolie district. The road will eventually lead to the junction with Route 37, where you should go left, but only for a short distance, until you reach the junction with Route 40. At one point Routes 37 and 40 become the same highway. When they separate, turn right and stay on Route 40 to:

5. **Drake's Seat,** the legendary perch where Sir Francis Drake is said to have figured out the best routes for the colonial European powers to take their ships from the Atlantic into the Caribbean Sea. Continue left onto Route 35. The road will veer northwest. Follow it all the way to:

6. **Magens Bay Beach,** hailed as one of the most beautiful beaches in the world. Here you can arrange Sunfish, glass-bottom paddleboat, and windsurf rentals. There is a full array of lounge chairs, changing facilities, showers, and lockers. There are also picnic tables.

   ☕ **TAKE A BREAK**   **Magens Bay Bar & Grill,** Magens Bay Beach (☎ 775-4669), is an ideal place for light meals on this heart-shaped beach. The snack bar overlooks the beach. You can order sandwiches from $3.75, salads from $3.95, and soft drinks from $1.50. Pizza is sold by the slice.

## ESPECIALLY FOR KIDS

**Coral World**   *(see p. 114)* This is *the* place on St. Thomas to take your children. It's a hands-on experience—children can even shake hands with a starfish at the Touch Pond. Later they can discover exotic Marine Gardens, where 20 aquariums showcase the Caribbean's incredible natural treasures.

**Magens Bay Beach**   *(see p. 115)* If you can introduce your children to only one beach in the entire Caribbean, make it this one. It's one of the finest in the world, with white sand and lots of facilities, including picnic tables.

***Atlantis* Submarine**   *(see p. 117)* Children thrill to this unique underwater adventure in "space age air." They dive to depths of up to 150 feet to see exotic fish, colorful sea gardens, coral formations, and unusual marine creatures. Children must be at least 4 years old.

# Driving Tour—St. Thomas

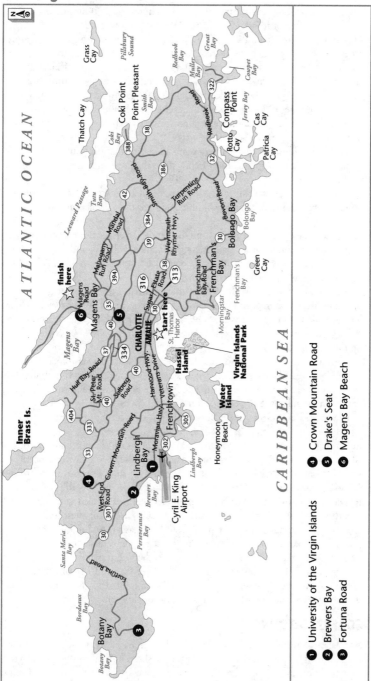

1 University of the Virgin Islands   4 Crown Mountain Road

2 Brewers Bay   5 Drake's Seat

3 Fortuna Road   6 Magens Bay Beach

The number-one tourist attraction of St. Thomas is a 20-minute drive from downtown off Route 38. The **Coral World Marine Park & Underwater Observatory,** 6450 Coki Point (☎ 775-1555), is a marine complex that features a three-story underwater observation tower 100 feet offshore. Separated only by windows from underwater be in its natural state, you'll see sponges, fish, and coral. In the Marine Gardens Aquarium saltwater tanks display everything from sea horses to urchins. Another attraction is an 80,000-gallon reef tank teeming with exotic marine life of the Caribbean; another tank is home to sea predators, with circling sharks and giant moray eels, among other creatures. You enter the complex through a waterfall of cascading water.

The latest addition to the park is a semi-submarine that lets you enjoy the panoramic view and the "down under" feeling of a submarine without ever leaving the ocean's surface.

Coral World's guests can take advantage of adjacent Coki Beach for snorkel rental, scuba lessons, or simply swimming and relaxing. Lockers and showers are available.

Also included in the marine park are the Tropical Terrace Restaurant, duty-free shops, and a tropical nature trail. Activities include daily fish and shark feedings and exotic bird shows. The complex is open daily from 9am to 6pm. Admission is $16 for adults and $10 for children.

A popular attraction in the 1970s, the **Paradise Point Tramway** resumed operation in the summer of 1994. Taking visitors up to a dramatic view of Charlotte Amalie harbor, a ride ascens a 697-foot peak. Paradise Point Tramway operates six cars, each with a 12-person capacity, and carries up to 600 people an hour on the $3^1/_2$-minute ride.

The gondolas, similar to those used at ski resorts, will carry customers from the Havensight area to Paradise Point, where riders may disembark to visit retail shops and the popular restaurant and bar. The Paradise Point Gondolas run daily from 9am to 9pm and cost $10 per person round-trip.

**Estate St. Peter Greathouse Botanical Gardens,** corner of Route 40 (St. Peter Mountain Road) and Barrett Hill Road (☎ 774-4999), spreads across 11 lushly planted acres of grounds at the volcanic peaks on the northern rim of the island. It's the creation of Howard Lawson DeWolfe, a Mayflower descendant who, with his wife Sylvie, bought the estate in 1987 and set about transforming it into a tropical paradise. Damaged by Hurricane Hugo in 1989, the property was reopened again in 1992. A virtual Garden of Eden, it is riddled with self-guided nature walks that will acquaint you with some 200 varieties of West Indian plants and trees, including an umbrella plant from Madagascar. A rain forest, an orchid jungle, a monkey habitat, waterfalls, and reflecting ponds make the estate Edenic. From a panoramic deck, you can see some 20 of the Virgin Islands, including Hans Lollick, an uninhabited island between Thatched Cay and Madahl Point. The house itself is worth a visit; its interior filled with local art. It is open daily from 9am to 5pm; admissions $8 for adults and $4 for children.

## ORGANIZED TOURS

An **"Island Safari"** is conducted Monday through Saturday. Reservations can be made through hotel activities or reception desks. Though no one outfit has a monopoly on these tours, Tropic Tours is a good choice. A van is sent to pick you up (usually around 9am), and you're taken on a tour of Charlotte Amalie with stopovers at Drake's Seat and Mountain Top, with its banana daiquiris and panoramic view of the Virgin Islands. The tour usually lasts until 12:30pm. Guests are then dropped off in the center of Charlotte Amalie for shopping and can be brought back to their hotels around 3:30pm. The regular cost is $20, except on Monday when Coral World is included and the price rises to $36 per person.

## 6  Sports A to Z

Chances are, your hotel will be right on the beach, or very close to one, and this is where you'll anchor for most of your stay, perhaps occasionally going out in a Sailfish or Hobie Cat. Incidentally, all beaches in the Virgin Islands are public.

In addition to beaches, St. Thomas offers one of the biggest sporting programs in the West Indies, everything from golf to boating, from scuba diving to deep-sea fishing.

## BEACHES

Most of the beaches of St. Thomas lie from 2 to 5 miles from Charlotte Amalie.

### NORTH SIDE

**Magens Bay**   Located 3 miles north of the capital, Magens Bay is one of the world's most beautiful beaches. Admission is $1 for adults and 25¢ for children under 12. The carpark costs $1. There are changing facilities, snorkeling gear, and lounge chairs for rent. This white sand beach, administered by the government, is half a mile long and lies between two mountains. There is no public transportation to reach it. From Charlotte Amalie, take Route 35 north all the way. The gates to the beach are open daily from 6am to 6pm. After 4pm, you should use insect repellent to protect yourself from mosquitoes and sand flies.

**Coki Beach**   Located in the northeast near Coral World, Coki Beach tends to be overcrowded whenever cruise ships are in port. Snorkelers and scuba divers are attracted to this popular beach, with its abundance of reef fish. So are pickpockets so protect your valuables. You can rent lockers at Coral World next door. It is absolutely forbidden to remove coral or marine life from the water. Most people take a taxi from the center of Charlotte Amalie. The East End Vitro runs to Smith Bay, letting you off at the gate to Coral World and Coki Beach.

**Stouffer Grand Beach**   On the north side of the island is one of its most beautiful beaches, with a luxury hotel in the background. You can try out many water sports at this palm-lined beach of white sand, opening onto Smith Bay in the vicinity of Coral World. The beach lies right off Smith Bay Road (Route 38) east of Charlotte Amalie. It's reached by taxi from Charlotte Amalie.

### SOUTH SIDE

**Morningstar**   At this beach near Frenchman's Reef Hotel, about 2 miles east of Charlotte Amalie, you can appear in your most daring swimwear, as this is the premier gathering spot on the island for bikini wearers (and watchers). You can also rent sailboards, sailboats, snorkeling equipment, and lounge chairs. The beach is reached by a cliff-front elevator at Marriott's Frenchman's Reef Beach Resort, which also owns the adjoining Marriott's Morning Star Resort. Because of its proximity to town, many residents of Charlotte Amalie use this beach, and the east side of the beach is often filled with young people who work in the hotels and restaurants of St. Thomas at night, occupying their day on the beaches. There is no public transportation to the beach, but it's only a short taxi ride from Charlotte Amalie.

**Limetree Beach**   Set against a backdrop of sea grape trees and shady palms, Limetree lures those who want a serene spread of sand where they can mix suntanning with feeding hibiscus blossoms to iguanas. You can rent snorkeling gear, lounge and beach chairs, and towels. Cool drinks are served, including a Limetree green piña colada. There is no public transportation, but the beach can easily be reached by taxi from Charlotte Amalie.

**Brewers Bay**   One of the island's most popular beaches, Brewers Bay lies in the southwest part of the island, near the University of the Virgin Islands. This beach of white coral sand is almost as long as the beach at Magens Bay. Students from the nearby university often come here for a swim between classes. Light meals and drinks are served along the beach. It's not good for snorkeling, however. From Charlotte Amalie, take the Fortuna bus heading west. Get off at the edge of Brewers Bay, across from the Reichhold Center, the cultural center of St. Thomas.

**Lindbergh Beach**   With lifeguard, toilet facilities, and a bathhouse, Lindbergh is used extensively by the locals, who sometimes stage political rallies here as well as carnival parties. It lies at the Island Beachcomber Hotel. Drinks, such as piña coladas, are served on the beach. It is not good for snorkeling. Take the Fortuna bus route west from Charlotte Amalie.

## EAST END

**Secret Harbour**   Small and special, Secret Harbour lies near a number of condos whose owners frequent the beach. With its white sand, coconut palms, and tranquil waters, it is a cliché of Caribbean charm. Many residents of St. Charlotte Amalie visit on the weekends because of its proximity to town, so it is at its most crowded then. No public transportation stops here, but it's an easy taxi ride east of Charlotte Amalie in the direction of Red Hook.

**Sapphire Beach**   One of the finest beaches in St. Thomas is Sapphire Beach, popular with windsurfers. A large reef is located close to the fine, white-coral-sand shore, and there are good views of offshore cays and St. John. It is set against the backdrop of one of the most desirable hotels and condominiums in St. Thomas, Sapphire Beach Hotel, where you can lunch or order drinks if you wish. You can rent snorkeling gear and lounge chairs. To reach Sapphire Beach, take the East End bus from Charlotte Amalie via Red Hook. Get off at the entrance to Sapphire Bay.

# SPORTS

## BOATING

The biggest charter-boat business in the Caribbean is conducted by Virgin Islanders. In St. Thomas, most of the business centers around the Red Hook and Yacht Haven marinas.

Perhaps the easiest way to go out to sea is to charter your own yacht for the day from *Yacht Nightwind,* Red Hook (☎ **775-4110** 24 hours a day), for only $85 per person. You're granted a full-day sail with champagne buffet lunch and open bar aboard this 50-foot yawl. You're also given free snorkeling equipment and instruction. Operators Stephen and June Marsh have taken visitors out since 1977. If you're interested, ask them about two- or three-bedroom villas for rent on the beach.

*New Horizons,* 6501 Red Hook Plaza, Suite 16, Red Hook (☎ **775-1171**), offers wind-borne excursions amid the cays and reefs of the Virgin Islands. This two-masted 60-foot ketch was built in 1969 in Vancouver. It has circumnavigated the globe and has been used as a design prototype for other boats.

Owned and operated by Canadian Tim Krygsveld, it contains a hot-water shower, serves a specialty drink called a New Horizons Nooner (its melon-liqueur base seems color-coordinated with the sea), and carries a complete line of snorkeling equipment for adults and children. A full-day excursion, with a "hot buffet Italian al fresco" and an open bar, costs $85 per person. Excursions depart every day, weather permitting, from the Sapphire Beach Club Marina. Call ahead for reservations and information. Children aged 2 to 12, who must be accompanied by an adult, pay $42.50.

*True Love,* P.O. Box 7595 (☎ 775-6547), is a sleek 54-foot Malabar schooner used during the filming of *High Society* starring Bing Crosby, Frank Sinatra, and Grace Kelly. It sails daily at 9:30am from Sapphire Beach Club Marina and costs $85 per person. Bill and Sue Beer have sailed it since 1965. You can join one of the captain's snorkeling classes and later enjoy one of Sue's gourmet lunches with champagne.

If you want something more elaborate, you can go bareboating—that is, rent a craft of which you're the captain. You must first prove that you can handle the craft. If you'd like everything done for you, you can charter a fully crewed yacht with a captain at your service. Either type of charter rental is available through **Avery's Marina,** P.O. Box 5248, Veterans Drive Station, St. Thomas, USVI 00803 (☎ 776-0113 during the day, 775-2773 at night).

If you want to get to the bottom of it all, go on the *Atlantis* **submarine,** which takes you on a one-hour voyage to depths of 150 feet, unfolding a world of exotic marine life. You'll gaze on coral reefs and sponge gardens through 2-foot windows on the air-conditioned 65-foot-long sub, which carries 46 passengers. You take a surface boat from the West Indies Dock, right outside Charlotte Amalie, to the submarine, which lies near Buck Island (the St. Thomas version, not the more famous Buck Island near St. Croix). Divers swim with the fish and bring them close to the windows for photos. The fare is $68 per person; children 4 to 12 pay $25 (ages under 4 not permitted). The *Atlantis* operates daily from November through April and only Tuesday through Saturday from May through October. Reservations are imperative. For tickets, go to the Havensight Shopping Mall, Building 6, or call 776-5650 for reservations.

## DEEP-SEA FISHING

The U.S. Virgins have very good deep-sea fishing—some 19 world records have been set in recent years (eight for blue marlin). Sportfishers can angle off the *Fish Hawk* (☎ 775-9058). Capt. Al Petrosky of New Jersey sails from Fish Hawk Marina Lagoon at the East End on his 43-foot diesel-powered craft fully equipped with rods and reels. All equipment (but not lunch) is included in the rate of $400 per half day for up to six passengers. A full-day excursion, depending on how far the boat goes out, ranges from $700 to $800.

## GOLF

On the north shore, **Mahogany Run,** at the Mahogany Run Golf & Tennis Resort, Mahogany Run Road (☎ 775-5000, or 800/253-7103), is an 18-hole, par-70 course. Designed by Tom and George Fazio, this is considered one of the most beautiful courses in the West Indies. The course rises and drops like a roller coaster on its journey to the sea, where cliffs and crashing sea waves are the ultimate hazards at the 13th and 14th holes. Greens fees from December through April are $70 for 18 holes or $35 for 9 holes. After 2pm, you get the twilight rate of $55 for 18 holes. Off-season greens fees are $50 for 18 holes or $25 for 9 holes, reduced to $35 for 18 holes after 2pm. A cart is mandatory, costing $15 for 18 holes or $10 for 9 holes.

## SCUBA DIVING & SNORKELING

With 30 spectacular reefs just off St. Thomas, the U.S. Virgins are rated as one of the "most beautiful areas in the world" by *Skin Diver* magazine.

**St. Thomas Diving Club,** Bolongo Beach Resorts, 7147 Bolongo Bay (☎ 776-2381), or **800/538-7348**), is a full-service PADI five-star IDC center and is considered the best on the island. If you're a guest at this resort, you get such extras as a sail to St. John and a harbor cruise on the resort's 52-foot *Heavenly Daze.* An open-water certification course, including four scuba dives, costs $330. An advanced open-water certification course, including five dives that can be accomplished in two days, goes for $275. Every Thursday, participants are taken on an all-day scuba excursion that includes a two-tank dive off the wreck of the RMS *Rhone* in the British Virgin Islands; the cost is $110. You can also enjoy local snorkeling for $22 per day.

**Dive In,** Sapphire Beach Resort & Marina, Smith Bay Road, Route 6 (☎ 775-6100), is a recommended and complete diving center, offering some of the finest diving services in the U.S. Virgin Islands. Services include professional instruction for all levels, daily beach and boat dives, custom dive packages, underwater photography and videotapes, snorkeling trips, and a full-service PADI dive center. An introductory course costs $55; a one-boat dive costs $50, and two-boat dives cost $140. An open-water certification course with four dives over a period of three days costs $350, and a six-dive pass is $185. The center is especially convenient for guests of hotels on the east side.

## TENNIS

St. Thomas has many courts lit for night play. The **Bolongo Bay Beach and Tennis Club,** Bolongo Bay (☎ 779-2844), has four outstanding courts, two of which are lit until 10pm. It is free to members and hotel guests only; lessons cost $18 per hour and are available to everyone.

Your best bet for great tennis on the island is **Sugar Bay Plantation Resort,** 6500 Estate Smith Bay (☎ 777-7100), which has the Virgin Island's first stadium tennis court, seating 220, plus six additional Laykold courts lit at night. There's also a pro shop.

At **Marriott's Frenchman's Reef Tennis Courts** (☎ 776-8500, ext. 444), there are four courts lit until 10pm. Nonguests pay $8 per half hour per court.

At the famous **Bluebeard's Castle,** Bluebeard's Hill (☎ 774-1600), nonguests are charged $4 per hour for a court.

## WINDSURFING

You can easily jump on a Windsurfer at the major resort hotels and at some public beaches, including Brewers Bay, Morningstar Beach, and Limetree Beach. Stouffer Grand Beach Resort (☎ 775-1510), Smith Bay Road, Route 38, is the major hotel hot spot for windsurfing. Stouffer guests are granted a lesson for $25 and use of the equipment for free. If you're a nonresident, the cost goes up to $35 per hour for a lesson and rental of equipment.

# 7  Shopping

The $1,200 duty-free allowance in the Virgin Islands (see "Entry Requirements," Chapter 3) makes every purchase a double bargain. If you go over the limit, duty is charged at a flat rate of 5% up to $1,000 rather than at the 10% imposed on goods from other countries. You can send as many gifts as you want to family or friends duty free—but not more than one per day to $100. These items do not have to be declared on your exemption.

You can find some well-known brand names at savings of up to 60% off mainland prices. You often however, have to plow through a lot of junk to find the savings. You need to know the price back home of the item to determine if you are in fact saving money. Having sounded that warning, we'll mention some St. Thomas shops where we have found good buys.

Most of the shops, some of which occupy former pirate warehouses, are open Monday to Saturday from 9am to 5pm. Some stores open Sunday and holidays if a cruise ship is in port. *Note:* Friday is the biggest cruise-ship visiting day at Charlotte Amalie (we once counted eight at once), so try to avoid shopping then.

Recently, town leaders ordained that it was illegal for most street vendors to ply their trades outside of a designated area called Vendors Plaza, at the corner of Veterans Drive and Tolbod Gade. Hundreds of vendors converge at 7:30am, remaining there usually no later than 5:30pm, Monday through Saturday. (Very few hawk their wares on Sunday, unless a cruise ship is scheduled to arrive.) The only exception to this strictly maintained ordinance are the food vendors, who are permitted to sell on sidewalks outside of Vendors Plaza.

## BEST BUYS & WHERE TO FIND THEM

Nearly all the major shopping in St. Thomas goes on along the harbor of Charlotte Amalie. Cruise-ship passengers mainly shop at the **Havensight Mall** where they disembark at the eastern edge of Charlotte Amalie. The principal shopping street is called **Main Street** or Dronningens Gade (its old Danish name). North of this street is another merchandise-loaded street called **Back Street** or Vimmelskaft.

Many shops are also spread along the **Waterfront Highway** (also called Kyst Vejen). Between these major streets or boulevards are a series of side streets, walkways, and alleys, all filled with shops. Major shopping streets are Tolbod Gade, Raadets Gade, Royal Dane Mall, Palm Passage, Storetvaer Gade, and Strand Gade.

All the major stores in St. Thomas are located by number on an excellent map in the center of the publication *St. Thomas This Week,* distributed free to all arriving plane and boat passengers.

If you want to combine a little history with shopping, enter the courtyard of the old Pissarro Building through the archway off Main Street. The Impressionist painter lived here as a child, and the old apartments have been turned into a warren of interesting shops.

The **best buys** on St. Thomas include china, crystal, perfumes, jewelry (especially emeralds), Haitian art, fashions, and items made of wood. Cameras and electronic items, based on our experience, are not the good buys they're reputed to be.

St. Thomas is perhaps the finest place in all the Caribbean for discounts in porcelain. Look for the imported patterns for the biggest savings, but even U.S. brands may be purchased for 25% off the retail price of the mainland. There are also good deals on brand-name watches.

All of the stores recommended below can be reached on foot along the streets directly in the center of Charlotte Amalie.

A lot of the stores don't have street numbers, or don't display them, so look for their signs instead.

# SHOPPING A TO Z
## ART

### Camille Pissarro Art Gallery
14 Dronningens Gade. ☎ **777-5511.**

Located on the second floor of the Camille Pissarro building overlooking the court-yard, this art gallery honors the so-called dean of French Impressionists, who was born at this address on July 10, 1830. Two high-ceilinged, airy rooms display a variety of original and fine art from local and regional artists.

## BOOKSTORES

### Dockside Bookshop
Havensight Mall. ☎ **774-4937.**

If you need a beach read, head for this well-stacked store near the cruise-ships dock, east of Charlotte Amalie. The shop has the best selection of books on island lore as well as a variety of general reading selections.

## CAMERAS & ELECTRONICS

### Royal Caribbean
33 Main St. ☎ **776-4110.** Additional branches at 23 Main Street (☎ **776-5449**) and Havensight Mall (☎ **776-8890**).

Since 1977, Royal Caribbean has been the largest camera and electronics store in the Caribbean. The outlets carry Nikon, Minolta, Pentax, Canon, Olympus, Samsung, Aiwa, Sony, and Panasonic products. They also sell watches, including such brand names as Seiko, Movado, Baume & Mercier, Corum, Fendi, Tissot, Paolo Gucci, Concord, and Swatch. They have a complete collection of Philippe Charriol watches, jewelry, and leather bags. In addition, there is a wide selection of Mikimoto pearls, 14K and 18K jewelry, and Lladró figurines.

## CHINA, CRYSTAL & WATCHES

### A. H. Riise Gift & Liquor Stores
37 Main St. at A. H. Riise Gift & Liquor Mall. ☎ **776-2303,** or 800/524-2037.

Displayed in a beautifully restored 18th-century Danish warehouse that extends from Main Street to the waterfront, this store's selection of quality imported merchandise is unusually wide. The store boasts a collection of fine jewelry and watches from Europe's leading craftspeople, including Patek Philippe, Vacheron Constantin, Hublot, Gucci, Movado, Omega, and Tag-Heuer. Featured among the many internationally known name brands in the china and crystal department are Waterford, Lalique, Daum, Baccarat, Wedgwood, Royal Crown Derby, Royal Doulton, Royal Copenhagen, and Lladró figurines. Also available are Crabtree & Evelyn and Scarborough products, liquor, tobacco, and duty-free art including a wide selection of Caribbean prints and note cards. A. H. Riise Gift & Liquor Stores also has a vast selection of fragrances for men and women, as well as cosmetics. Every purchase is backed by a 60-day unconditional guarantee. For brochure and shop-by-phone service, call **800/524-2037** from 9am to 5pm Atlantic standard time, Monday through Saturday except major holidays. Phone lines are open on Sunday from 9am to 1pm.

### Little Switzerland
5 Main St. ☎ **776-2010.**

With stores in downtown Charlotte Amalie and one on the dock at Havensight Mall, Little Switzerland is known as the premier watch retailer in the Caribbean. They are the exclusive agent for many famous brands, including Audemars Piguet, Bertolucci, Eterria, Kreiger, Memosail, Rado, Rolex, Sector, Swiss Army, Tiffany, Zodiac, and the famous Little Switzerland line of high-fashion watches. You will also find Baume & Mercier, Omega, Raymond Weil, and Tag-Heuer. The shop carries only Swiss-made watches. There's also an extensive selection of 14K and 18K gold, colored stone, and diamond jewelry from Europe and Asia, as well as a beautiful collection of "private label" Little Switzerland jewelry.

Little Switzerland stocks the finest names in china and crystal, including Ansley, Atlantis, Baccarat, Caithness, Christofle, Daum, Gallo, Herend, Hutschenreuther, Kosta Boda, Lalique, Marcolinh, Orrefors, Rosenthal, Royal Albert, Royal Crown Derby, Royal Doulton, Villeroy & Boch, Waterford, and Wedgwood; figurines from D'Argenta, David Winter, Goebel-Hummel, Lladró, and Swarovski; and flatware by Christofle, Jean Couzon, Retroneu, Rosenthal, and WMF. Little Switzerland has branched out elsewhere in the Caribbean, with locations in St. Croix, St. Martin, St. Barthélemy, Antigua, Aruba, and Curaçao, as well as St. Kitts and Nevis.

## CLOTHING

### Coki
Compass Point. ☎ **775-6560.**

Coki stands 1½ miles from Red Hook in the East End amidst a little restaurant row, so you might want to combine a gastronomic tour with a shopping expedition.

---

⭐ **Frommer's Favorite St. Thomas Experiences**

**A Day at Magens Beach.** In the north of the island, Magens Bay Beach is a glistening loop of white sand, stretching about half a mile along calm waters with two peninsulas to protect it. It has a flat, sandy bottom, and for sunning and swimming it alone is worth the trip to St. Thomas.

**Shopping in Charlotte Amalie.** To this little island in the West Indies cargo ships from all over the world bring an array of merchandise to dazzle and delight the shopper. The merchandise looks even more tempting to U.S. residents who are allowed $1,200 worth of purchases duty free.

**Sunset at Drake's Seat.** Few views in all the West Indies equal the panoramic vista from this point, where the old English pirate himself is said to have sat, plotting a safe passage for his ships coming in from the Atlantic. It's a wide-angle view of Charlotte Amalie with the entire Virgin Island chain spread before you.

**Sailing on Your "Yacht for a Day."** Virgin Islanders run the biggest charter business in the Caribbean, taking visitors out for a day on the high seas, with snorkeling, picnics, and swimming adding to the fun.

From the store's expansive cutting boards come some of the most easy-to-wear cotton clothes in the Virgin Islands. You'll see pieces of canvas or handwoven Madras cotton being turned into the kind of chic resortwear suitable for yachting, beaching, or hanging out. Throughout the year the shop is open Wednesday through Monday from 9am to 9pm.

### Cosmopolitan, Inc.
Drakes Passage and the waterfront. ☎ **776-2040.**

Since 1973, this store has drawn a lot of repeat business. In the shoe salon, you can find Bally of Switzerland and handmade A. Testoni of Italy. The swimwear department offers one of the best selections of Gottex of Israel for women and Gottex, Hom, Lahco of Switzerland, and Fila for men. In the men's wear section, the brands include Paul & Shark from Italy, Metzger shirts from Switzerland, and Burma Bibas sports shirts. You can also find a selection of tennis wear. The outlet also stocks ties by Gianni Versace and Pencaldi of Italy (both brands are at least 30% less than you'd find in the U.S.). There's also an array of Nautica sportswear for men.

### Java Wraps
American Yacht Harbot, Red Hook. ☎ **777-3450.**

From the East Indies to the West Indies, Java Wraps are known for hand-batiked women's, men's, and children's resortwear. A kaleidoscope of colors and prints dazzle the eye. The store evokes the celluloid image of Dorothy Lamour as local salespeople demonstrate the wrapping and tying of Java Wraps' beach pareos and sarongs. The men's shirts come in a wide array of tropical and flamboyant prints, and there's also a collection of clothing for children.

### Lion in the Sun
A. H. Riise Alley. ☎ **766-4203.**

This is one of the most upscale sportswear outlet stores on the island. Patrons shop here for the collection of designer casual apparel and accessories. Whether it's tanks, T's, shorts, pants, or skirts, this store is likely to have what you're looking for. It has a men's department as well. The owner is firm about prices as marked—no bargaining here.

### Polo/Ralph Lauren Factory Store
2 Garden St./2A-2C Commandant Gade. ☎ **774-3806.**

The sportswear at this factory outlet is discounted by about 30% from what you'd have paid at a retail outlet in the mainland U.S. The store stocks a full range of the designer's most popular items for both men and women.

## GIFTS & CRAFTS

### Caribbean Marketplace
Havensight Mall (Building III). ☎ **776-5400.**

Shop here for one of the best selections of Caribbean handcrafts, including Sunny Caribbee products—a vast array of condiments ranging from spicy peppercorns to nutmeg mustard. There's also a wide selection of Sunny Caribbee's botanical products from foaming rosemary bath gel to natural beauty soaps made from chamomile and coconut. Take back island treasures like steel-pan drums from Trinidad, wooden Jamaican jigsaw puzzles, Indonesian batiks, and local fragrances made upstairs.

> **In Their Footsteps**
>
> **Camille Pissarro** (1830–1903) Known as the dean of the French Impressionist painters, Pissarro was one of the most famous natives of St. Thomas. Attracted by the work of Camille Corot and, later, Gustave Courbet, Pissarro moved in a lofty artistic circle of friends that included Monet, Cézanne, and Renoir. He painted landscapes and scenes of rural life and some portraits.
>
> **Birthplace:** Danish St. Thomas, July 10, 1830, son of Jewish parents of French/Spanish extraction. **Residences:** The Pissarro Building, off Main Street in Charlotte Amalie; Paris. **Resting Place:** Paris.

## Down Island Traders
At the Waterfront. ☎ **776-4641.**

A spicy aroma will lead you to this authentic native market, which has an attractive array of spices, teas, seasonings, candies, jellies, jams, and condiments, most of which are made from natural Caribbean products. The owner carries a line of local cookbooks, as well as silk-screened T-shirts and bags, Haitian metal sculpture, handmade jewelry, Caribbean folk art, and children's gifts.

## Java Wraps Home Store
American Yacht Harbor, Red Hook. ☎ **775-6407.**

In the world of Java Wraps, textiles for the home cascade from antique Dutch colonial chests, and old teak tables are laden with hand-drawn batik tablecloths, napkins, and card placements. The store also sells intricately patterned hand-batik quilted bedcovers and elegant mahogany hand-carved desk accessories. To add tropical flavor to your tablewear, check out the collection of island-inspired, hand-painted fish plates, large banana leaf trays, and coral reef salad bowls.

## Mountain Top
Route 33. ☎ **774-2400.**

Set near the center of the island, this modern shopping mall contains only about a dozen shops, but many clients are lured here for the view as well as for the merchandise. The boutiques sell everything from beachwear to island-inspired prints and engravings to jams, jellies, and local crafts. There are an aquarium and aviary, a snack bar, and an observation platform with a view of the rest of the island.

## JEWELRY

### Blue Carib Gems and Rocks
2 Back St. ☎ **774-8525.**

For a decade the owners prospected for gemstones all over the world, and the stones have been brought directly from the mine to you. The raw stones are cut and polished and then fashioned into jewelry by the lost-wax process. On one side of the store you can see the craftspeople at work and on the other side, you can examine their finished products, including handsomely set stones such as larimar—the sea/sky-blue-patterned variety of pectolite found only in the Caribbean. A lifetime guarantee is given on all handcrafted jewelry. Since the items are locally made, they are duty free and are not included in the $1,200 Customs exemption. Incidentally, this establishment also provides emergency eyeglass repair.

### Cardow Jewelers
39 Main St. ☎ **776-1140.**

Often called the Tiffany's of the Caribbean, Cardow Jewelers boasts the largest selection of fine jewelry in the world. This shop, where more than 20,000 rings are displayed, offers savings because of its worldwide direct buying, large turnover, and duty-free prices. Unusual and traditional designs are offered in diamonds, emeralds, rubies, sapphires, and Brazilian stones, as well as pearls and coral. Cardow has a whole wall of Italian gold chains, and antique coin jewelry and Piaget watches are also for sale.

### Colombian Emeralds International
Havensight Mall. ☎ **774-2442.**

The Colombian Emerald stores are renowned throughout the Caribbean for offering the finest collection of Colombian emeralds, both set and unset. In addition to jewelry, the shop stocks some of the world's finest watches, including Raymond Weil and Seiko. There's another outlet on Main Street.

### H. Stern Jewellers
Havensight Mall. ☎ **776-1939,** or 800-524-2024.

Stern's sells colorful gem and jewel creations. Locations in St. Thomas include three on Main Street, one at the Havensight Mall above, and branches at Stouffer Grand Beach Resort and Marriott's Frenchman's Reef. Stern gives worldwide guaranteed service, including a one-year exchange privilege.

### Irmela's Jewel Studio
In the Old Grand Hotel, Main St. ☎ **774-5875,** or 800/524-2047.

Irmela's has made a name for itself in the highly competitive jewelry business in St. Thomas. Here the jewelry is unique, custom-designed by Irmela and handmade by her studio or imported from around the world. Irmela has the largest selection of cultured pearls in the Caribbean, including freshwater Biwa and South Sea pearls. Choose from hundreds of clasps and pearl necklaces. Irmela has a large selection of unset stones, such as rubies, sapphires, emeralds, and the unusual tanzanite and alexandrite. The diamond collection includes every shape and size. The studio has designed and produced a Virgin Islands Gold Piece, a commemorative coin minted in pure gold with the American eagle and the inscription of the Virgin Islands on it.

## LEATHER GOODS

### The Leather Shop, Inc.
1 Main St. ☎ **776-0290.**

Here you'll find a good selection from Italian designers, including Fendi, Moschino, Bottega Veneta, De Vecchi, Prima Classe, Furla, and Il Bisonte. There are many styles of handbags, belts, wallets, briefcases, and attaché cases, as well as all-leather luggage from Land. The traditional Indian molas of Colombia and Panama, which are still stitched entirely by hand, have been incorporated into sophisticated leather handbags. There's also a branch at the Havensight Mall.

### Louis Vuitton
24 Main St., at Palm Passage. ☎ **774-3644.**

For fine leather goods, you can't beat Louis Vuitton, where the complete line by the world-famous French designer is available, including suitcases, handbags, wallets, and other accessories.

# Shopping In Charlotte Amalie

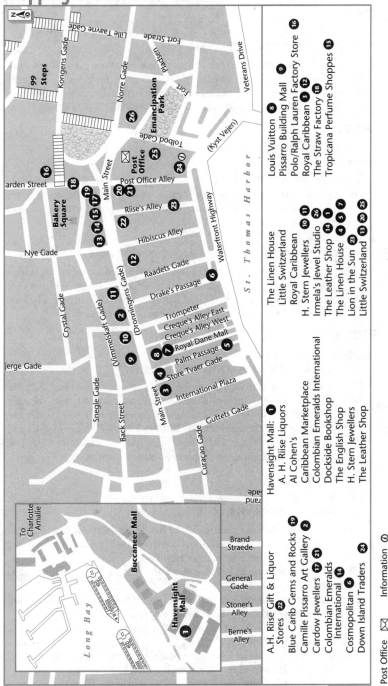

**Havensight Mall:**
- A. H. Riise Liquors **1**
- Al Cohen's
- Caribbean Marketplace
- Colombian Emeralds International
- Dockside Bookshop
- The English Shop
- H. Stern Jewellers
- The Leather Shop

The Linen House
Little Switzerland
Royal Caribbean **10 11**
H. Stern Jewellers **3**
Irmela's Jewel Studio **25**
The Leather Shop **14**
The Linen House **4 5 7**
Lion in the Sun **23**
Little Switzerland **13 20 25**

Louis Vuitton **8**
Pissarro Building Mall **9**
Polo/Ralph Lauren Factory Store **16**
Royal Caribbean **3**
The Straw Factory **18**
Tropicana Perfume Shoppes **15**

A.H. Riise Gift & Liquor Stores **22**
Blue Carib Gems and Rocks **19**
Camille Pissarro Art Gallery **2**
Cardow Jewellers **17 21**
Colombian Emeralds International **14**
Cosmopolitan **6**
Down Island Traders **24**

Post Office ⊠    Information ⓘ

## LINENS

### The Linen House
7A Royal Dane Mall. ☎ **774-8117.**

The Linen House is considered one of the best stores for linen in the West Indies. You'll find a wide selection of place mats, decorative tablecloths, and many hand-embroidered goods. There are many high-fashion styles. Other branches are at A. H. Riise Mall (☎ **774-0469**) and Havensight Mall (☎ **774-0868**).

## LIQUOR

### Al Cohen's
Long Bay Rd. ☎ **774-3690.**

In Al Cohen's big warehouse at Havensight, across from the West Indies Company dock where cruise-ship passengers come in, you can purchase discount liquor, fragrances, T-shirts, and souvenirs. Your liquor can be delivered free to the airport or your ship.

### A. H. Riise Liquors
37 Main St. (☎ **774-2303**) and Havensight Mall (☎ **774-6900**).

This store has almost every brand of liquor worth mentioning, along with a well-stocked supply of cigarettes and cigars. Fine ports, vintage Madeiras, rare cognacs and Armagnacs, and even "island flavor" favorites are sold here. The store will package your purchases for delivery to the airport or cruise ship.

## PERFUMES

### Tropicana Perfume Shoppes
2 and 14 Main St. ☎ **774-0010,** or 800/233-7948.

The two shops are near the Emancipation Park post office. The first is billed as the largest parfumerie in the world. Behind the rose-colored façade, the shop offers famous names in perfumes and cosmetics, including Pierre Cardin and Chanel for women and men. Men will also find Europe's best colognes and aftershave lotions here. When you return home, you can mail-order these same fragrances by taking advantage of Tropicana's toll-free number.

## SILK SCREENING

### Jim Tillett
Tillett Gardens, Tutu. ☎ **775-1929.**

A visit to the art gallery and craft studios of Jim Tillett combines shopping with sightseeing. The Tillett compound was converted from a Danish farm called "Tutu." The Tillett name is famous for high-fashion silk-screen printing by the Tillett brothers, who for years had their exquisite fabrics used by top designers and featured in magazines like *Vogue* and *Harper's Bazaar*. After creating a big splash in Mexico, Jim Tillett settled in St. Thomas. At his nearby compound, you can visit the adjoining workshop to see silk screening in progress.

The complex also has an art gallery, with an abundance of maps, paintings, sculpture, and graphics made by local artists. Mr. Tillett created a series of maps on fine cotton canvas that have become a best-selling item. Buy a square of florid Tillett fabric and frame it when you return; it will make a vivid wall hanging.

Arts Alive Arts and Crafts weekend festivals are held in the Tillett Gardens three times a year—in March, August, and November. These fairs provide local artists with a showcase for their work. Other events include crafts demonstrations, puppet shows for children, steel bands, calypso music, and dancing—folk, tap, ballet, and modern.

To reach Jim Tillett, take Route 38 east from Charlotte Amalie.

# 8  St. Thomas After Dark

St. Thomas has more nightlife than any other island in the Virgins, U.S. and British, but it's not as extensive as you might think. The big hotels, such as Marriott's Frenchman's Reef Beach Resort and Bluebeard's, have the most evening goings-on.

After a day of sightseeing and shopping in the hot West Indies sun, sometimes your best bet is to stay at your hotel in the evening, perhaps listening to a local fungi band. Big-time, big-name entertainment doesn't exist here.

Charlotte Amalie is no longer the rocking, swinging town it used to be at night. Many of the dark streets are considered dangerous, and muggings are frequent—so visitors have relatively abandoned it, except for a few places, such as the Greenhouse. Much of the action has shifted to Frenchtown, which is not big on nightclubs but which does have some of the best restaurants and bars; however, some of these little hot spots are along dark, badly lit roads.

There are infrequent cultural performances (see below), but most of the action revolves around listening to a local band at your hotel.

## THE PERFORMING ARTS

### Reichhold Center for the Arts

University of the Virgin Islands, Brewers Beach. ☎ **774-8475.** Admission $8–$35. Performances begin at 8 or 8:30pm (call the theater to check). Transportation: Taxi or Vitran bus.

This artistic center, considered the premier venue in the Caribbean, lies west of Charlotte Amalie. Call the theater or check with the tourist office to see if one of the frequent performances is offered at the time of your visit.

Its lobby displays a frequently changing exhibition (free admission) of paintings and sculptures by Caribbean artists.

The theater itself is a Japanese-inspired amphitheater set into a natural valley, with seating space for 1,196. The smell of gardenias adds to the beauty of the performances. The stage is used for presentations by several different repertory theaters of music, dance, and drama.

## THE CLUB & MUSIC SCENE

### Iggie's Bolongo

Limetree Beach Hotel, Frenchman's Bay Rd., Frenchman's Bay. ☎ **779-2844.** Admission free. Drinks $4. Open Mon–Tues and Thurs 8am–midnight; Fri–Sat 8am–1am.

During the day, Iggie's gazebolike premises function as an informal open-air restaurant serving hamburgers, sandwiches, and salads (see "Dining," above). After dark, however, it turns into one of a trio of clubs that make Bolongo one of the leading nightlife complexes on the island. An area of tropical drinks lubricate the vocal chords of karaoke singers.

### Paradise Club Disco & Caribbean Lobster House

Bolongo's Limetree Beach Resort, Frenchman's Bay Road, Frenchman's Bay. ☎ **776-4470.** Admission $12. Drinks from $4. Open Tues and Fri–Sat 10pm–2am.

Located on an elevated terrace near the lobby of the Bolongo Beach Resort Hotel, the restaurant and nightclub, are separated by a quasi-sound-proof glass wall. Guests move freely from one area to another. The Paradise Club features live, local bands playing a combination of reggae, socca, calypso, and contemporary sounds and a DJ. The Caribbean Lobster House is a full-service restaurant offering fresh local seafood. Enjoy drinks as you are cooled by breezes wafting in from the patio.

## Barnacle Bill's

At the Crown Bay Marina, in the Sub Base. ☎ **774-7444.** Admission free except on "Limelight Mondays" when several different bands from local amateurs to imported pros perform one after the other. The cover charge for this event is $3 per person. Beer from $2.25 to $2.75. Open daily 11:30am–midnight or later.

The enormous plastic lobster which perches on Bill's roof was originally designed as part of a float in a local parade. Today, the pastel-colored building functions as a restaurant during the day and as one of the liveliest nightclubs on St. Thomas in the evening. Beginning around 9pm, a parade of local and imported musical talent plays to full houses till at least 1am. The bar is open nightly; live music is presented every night except Tuesday and Sunday.

## The Top of the Reef

Marriott's Frenchman's Reef Beach Resort, Flamboyant Point. ☎ **776-8500.** Admission $20 adults, $10 children 10 and under. Open Mon–Sat 6–10:30pm.

Set in a dining room with a professional stage, this is the island's only dinner theater (see "Dining," above for a review of the restaurant). The revivals of comedies, dramas, and musicals change every five to six weeks and include performances by local and visiting theatrical troupes. Performances begin at 8pm, with restaurant service from 6pm. Main courses on an à la carte menu in the restaurant range from $13 to $25.

## Bluebeard's Castle Hotel

Bluebeard's Hill. ☎ **774-1600.** Admission free. Drinks from $4. Open Sun–Fri 11am–midnight, Sat 11am–1am.

Overlooking the pool and yacht harbor, the Dungeon Bar at Bluebeard's offers piano-bar entertainment nightly and is a popular gathering spot for both residents and visitors. You can dance from 8pm to midnight on Thursday and from 8pm to 1am on Saturday. On Monday there's a steel band. Other nights a piano player entertains. Drink specialties are named after Bluebeard himself—Bluebeard's wench, cooler, and ghost.

## Epernay

rue de St. Barthélemy, Frenchtown. ☎ **774-5348.** Admission free. Open Mon–Sat 4:30pm–1am. Transportation: Taxi.

Located adjacent to Alexander's Restaurant, this watering hole adds a European touch to the neighborhood. You can order glasses of at least six different brands of champagne and vintage wines by the glass ($4 to $10). No main courses are served, but the list of appetizers ($6 to $10) is a perfect accompaniment to the wines and includes sushi, fresh oysters, caviar, and a tempting array of desserts.

## Fat Tuesday

26A Royal Dane Mall. ☎ **777-8676.** Admission free. Drinks $2 to $9.25. Open daily 10am–midnight or 1am (later on Fri–Sat if crowd warrants it).

Located on the waterfront in downtown Charlotte Amalie, this nightspot serves up frozen concoctions from a bank of slurpee machines. In the party-like atmosphere of Fat Tuesday, patrons enjoy specialties like the Tropical Itch (a frozen punch made with bourbon and 151 rum) or the Moko Jumbi Juice (made with vodka, bourbon, 151 rum, and banana and cocoa liqueurs). There's also a wide variety of beer, highballs, and shooters, including the "Head Butt," which contains Jagermeister, Bailey's, and amaretto. Each night the bar has special events like Monday night football or T.G.I.F. night. A light lunch is served from 11am to 4pm daily.

### Turtle Rock Bar (Mangrove Restaurant)
At the Sugar Bay Resort, 6500 Estate Smith Bay. ☎ **777-7100.** Admission free. Drinks $4. Open daily 2pm–midnight.

A few minutes' drive west of Red Hook, this popular bar features live music, steel bands, and karaoke as diversions from the nearby beach life. Although there's lots of space on the premises should anyone get the urge to dance, very few clients ever get off their feet and prefer instead to listen to the steel bands which play from 2pm to closing every night. More elaborate bands play on Tuesday, Sunday, and other nights, depending on availability. On Thursday night patrons sing along to karaoke. If you're hungry, you can get burgers, salads, steaks, and grilled fish at the Mangrove Restaurant a few steps away. Entrance to the complex is free, and every night there's happy hour (when most drinks are half-price) from 4 to 6pm.

### Courtyard Bar
Windward Passage Hotel, Veterans Dr. ☎ **774-5200.** Admission free. Drinks $3.50. Open daily 11am–10:30 or 11pm.

You'd never know that the roar of Charlotte Amalie's coastal boulevard lies just outside the Courtyard Bar. Sheltered in semi-secluded cabaña, you can enjoy drinks like a "Paradise" (rum with cream of coconut, grenadine, and three kinds of fruit juice).

### Greenhouse
Veterans Dr. ☎ **774-7998.** Admission $5 Wed including first drink; other nights free. Beer $2.50; meals from $15. Open daily 7am–2am.

Set directly on the waterfront, this bar and restaurant is one of the few choice nightlife venues in Charlotte Amalie. Each night a different entertainment is featured, ranging from oldies night to rock 'n' roll. Wednesday night is a big blast.

### Andiamo Ristorante/Club Z
41 Contant Rd., Rte. 33. ☎ **776-4655.** Admission free, but every Friday, from 6 to 8pm, a $10 admission charge provides a limitless array of bar drinks and access to a buffet of hors d'oeuvres. Appetizers $4.50–$9; main courses $12–$19; drinks from $3.

This famous nightspot is a five-minute drive west of Charlotte Amalie. Offering a panoramic view of the capital, the former Great House on Contant Hill attracts a young crowd. Patrons come here to dine or to enjoy after-dinner dancing. An Italian-American cuisine featuring pizzas, pastas, veal, chicken, and beef dishes is served in either the bistro or the main dining room. Dinner is served on Monday through Saturday from 6:30 to 11pm.

Club Z is open Monday through Saturday from 9pm to 3:30am, attracting a crowd generally aged 18 to 30. The DJ changes the focus of the music from reggae to Latin to rock 'n' roll, depending on the tastes of the crowd.

**Walter's**

3 Trompeter Gade. ☎ **774-5025.** Admission Fri–Sat $3; free at all other times. Open daily 5pm–4am.

Walter's is the choicest nightspot in Charlotte Amalie after Adiamo, but if you go, be careful outside the club at night. Located about a hundred yards from the island's famous synagogue in a clapboard town house built around 1935, Walter's was established by Nevis-born Walter Springette. The cellar bar features an intimate atmosphere with music from the '50s, '60s, and '70s.

## 9  Networks & Resources

Most of the networks and resources that exist in larger places, such as Los Angeles, London, or Paris simply aren't available on St. Thomas. There are no rape crisis centers, counseling for gay men or lesbians, or even many student services.

**FOR STUDENTS**    St. Thomas is generally considered an expensive destination for students and doesn't offer discounts for them. Students tend to pass through St. Thomas en route to St. John's famous campsites or the campsite on Tortola in the British Virgin Islands.

Students seeking economical lodgings for one night or longer in Charlotte Amalie should try **Bunkers' Hill,** 7 Commandant Gade (☎ **774-8056**). You'll be in the center of town, near the bars and nightlife of Frenchtown, and you'll avoid expensive taxi rides to the island's East End.

Other than at the Greenhouse, the most reasonably priced food in Charlotte Amalie is served at that familiar chain favorite, **Arby's Bar and Restaurant,** 29-30 Main St. (☎ **776-5150**).

**FOR GAY MEN & LESBIANS**    St. Thomas might be the most cosmopolitan of the Virgin Islands, but it is no longer the "gay paradise" it was in the 1960s and 1970s. The Caribbean action has shifted now mainly to San Juan. The major gay scene in the U.S. Virgins is in Frederiksted on St. Croix (see Chapter 7).

That doesn't mean that gay men and lesbians aren't attracted to St. Thomas. They are, but many of the clubs that used to cater exclusively to them are gone. What is available today are pockets of gay men and women who attend predominantly straight establishments.

These places include Blackbeard's Castle, Hotel 1829, and even the Greenhouse on Veterans Drive (see "St. Thomas After Dark," above).

**FOR WOMEN**    St. Thomas is not an ideal place for single women travelers. Sexual harassment can be a problem in certain bars in Charlotte Amalie, where few single women would want to be alone at night anyway. Any of the major resort hotels are generally safe.

Women might enjoy participating in one of the all-women sailing groups that use St. Thomas as a port of departure (see "The Active Vacation Planner," Chapter 2).

**Jane's International,** 2603 Bath Ave., Brooklyn, NY 11214 (☎ **718/266-2045**), links potential travel companions with each other, has no age limit, and charges no fees for its service. Jane La Corte also functions as a full-service travel agent and a part-time "matchmaker."

Many women traveling alone prefer to go on an organized tour arranged by **Singleworld,** 402 Theodore Fremd Ave., Rye, NY 10580 (☎ **914/967-3334,** or

**800/223-6490**). About half its clients are women, and shared accommodations can be arranged through its travel packages, which greatly cuts down on expenses.

## 10  An Excursion to Water Island

The fourth-largest of the U.S. Virgins with 500 acres of land, **Water Island** is only one-half mile long and about one-half to 1-mile wide. Its nearest point is about ³/₈ mile from St. Thomas.

Visitors head for Water Island to spend the day on Honeymoon Beach, where they swim, snorkel, sail, waterski, or just sunbathe on the palm-shaded beach and order lunch or a drink from the beach bar. The highest elevation is only 300 feet above sea level.

Originally inhabited by the Arawaks, the island was later a stopover for sailing vessels which used its freshwater ponds to replenish their casks. During World War I, the U.S. Army used Fort Segarra as a base.

Virgin Islanders seeking an escapist holiday often visit Water Island via private boat from St. Thomas. If you're not lucky enough to have access to a private yacht, you can take one of the public ferryboats maintained by Launch with Larry. Priced at $3 per person each way ($5 each way for evening passages), it runs from the Crown Bay Marina (part of St. Thomas' submarine base) to a pier opposite Tickles Restaurant. It departs from St. Thomas every day at 7, 8, 11am, and noon and at 2, 4, 5, and 6pm, with a return to St. Thomas scheduled for approximately 30 minutes later. On Tuesday, Friday, and Saturday nights, there are additional departures from St. Thomas at 9 and 10pm, with a return from Water Island to St. Thomas 30 minutes later.

If you happen to miss any of these departures, the ferryboat operator will sometimes schedule private departures for a minimum price of $20 for up to four passengers. Getting information about departure times of the individual boats is somewhat awkward; you must leave a beeper message for Launch with Larry by calling either **775-8071** or **779-6807** and hope for a return call. Although not associated with the ferryboat, the reception staff at Water Island's only hotel (the Limestone Reef; ☎ **800/872-8784**) can also provide data and information about ferryboat transit to and from Water Island from St. Thomas.

# 5

# The U.S. Virgin Islands: St. John

About 3 to 5 miles east of St. Thomas, across a glistening and turquoise-colored channel known as Pillsbury Sound, St. John rises out of the waters of the Atlantic. Only 7 miles long and 3 miles wide, it has a total landmass of some 20 square miles, making it the smallest of the three main U.S. Virgins. It is also the least densely populated.

Under the Danish regime, the island's surface was subdivided into parcels for development by plantation owners. A number of slave rebellions and the decline of sugar production ended that plan forever.

In 1917, the U.S. Government purchased St. John from the Danes. In the 1940s, word of the island's rare beauty circulated widely through yachting circles and among developers in the U.S.

Today St. John (unlike some other U.S. Virgins) is truly pristine, its preservation rigidly enforced by the U.S. Park Service. Thanks to the efforts of Laurance Rockefeller, who purchased large tracts of its acreage and donated them as a gift to the American people, the island's shoreline waters, as well as more than half of its landmass, comprise the Virgin Islands National Park.

St. John is ringed with a rocky coastline that forms crescent-shaped bays and white sand beaches; the island array of bird and wildlife is the envy of ornithologists and zoologists around the world. The island contains miles of serpentine hiking trails, whose edges are dotted with panoramic views and the ruins of 18th-century Danish plantations. At scattered intervals along the trails, there are mysteriously geometric petroglyphs incised into boulders and cliffs. Of unknown age and origin, they have never been deciphered.

The pleasures and beauties of St. John are not limited to its land. Sailors and boaters seek out its dozens of sheltered coves for anchorages, swimming, and extended vacations. The hundreds of coral gardens that surround St. John's perimeter are protected as rigorously as its land by the National Park Service. Any attempt to damage or remove coral from these waters is punishable with large and strictly enforced fines.

The island's status as a national park does not preclude the presence of well-maintained roads, a scattering of hotels and restaurants, and a small commercial center (Cruz Bay) on the island's western

## What's Special About St. John

Beaches

- Trunk Bay—wide and long—one of the most beautiful beaches in the West Indies.
- Caneel Bay, site of the famous resort, with its string of seven beaches that stretch around Durloe Point to Hawksnest Caneel.
- Cinnamon Bay, site of one of the best campsites in the Caribbean.
- Maho Bay, largest beach on the north shore, once the site of an old sugar plantation.
- Hawksnest Bay—ideal for a beach party, with its white sand, picnic tables, and charcoal grills.

Discoveries

- Cruz Bay, the capital, a stage-set version of a little West Indian village, with pastel-painted houses.
- Annaberg Ruins, site of a Danish sugar mill and plantation from the early 1700s.

National Parks

- The Virgin Islands National Park—9,500 acres of land filled with historical sites.
- National Park trails, including a $2^{1}/_{2}$-mile section that passes by petroglyphs carved into boulders by mysterious people of the past.

tip. Growth and commercial development on the island are limited to the parcels of privately owned land that are not part of the National Park.

Despite the unspoiled beauty of much of St. John, the island does contain most of the services that are necessary for modern tourism, including a sampling of restaurants, car-rental kiosks, yacht-supply facilities, hotels, and campgrounds. Cinnamon Bay, founded by the National Park Service in 1964 is the most famous campsite in the Caribbean.

One of the most exciting ways to see St. John is to rent an open-sided car to drive around its tortuous perimeter. The panoramas are endlessly variable, dramatically steep, richly tinted with tones of forest green and turquoise, and liberally accented with flashes of silver and gold from the strong and clear sunshine. Snorkelers, scuba divers, hikers, sailing enthusiasts, and underwater photographers alike benefit from the island's unique status as one of the National Park Service's greatest treasures.

# 1  Orientation

## ARRIVING
### BY BOAT

The easiest and most common way to get to St. John is by **ferryboat** (☎ **776-6282**), which leaves from the Red Hook landing pier on St. Thomas is eastern tip and goes to Cruz Bay or St. John; the trip takes about 20 minutes each way. Beginning at 6:30am, boats depart more or less every hour, with minor exceptions throughout the day. The last ferry back to Red Hook departs from St. John's Cruz Bay at 11:15pm. Because of such frequent departures, even cruise-ship passengers temporarily anchored in Charlotte Amalie for a short visit can visit St. John for a quick island tour. The one-way fare is $3 for adults, $1 for children under 11. Schedules can change without notice, so call in advance before your intended departure.

To reach the ferry on St. Thomas, take the Vitran bus from a point near Market Square in Charlotte Amalie directly to Red Hook. The cost is $3 per person one-way. In addition, you can negotiate a price to Red Hook with privately owned taxis.

It's also possible to board a boat for St. John directly at the Charlotte Amalie waterfront for a cost of $7 one-way. The ride takes 45 minutes. The ferryboat departs from Charlotte Amalie at 9am and continues at intervals of between one and two hours until the last boat at around 7pm. (The last boat departing St. John's Cruz Bay for Charlotte Amalie is at 5:15pm.)

There's also a launch service which departs once daily from the dock at Caneel Bay on St. John and heads for the National Park dock at Red Hook on St. Thomas. The departure time from Caneel Bay is 10:30am, with a return at 11:10am. The one-way fare is $9 per person. In some instances, the National Park boat will continue from Red Hook to Charlotte Amalie, in which event the one-way fare from Caneel Bay to Charlotte Amalie is $12. For more information, call **776-6111**.

Should you ever get stranded, you can call a privately operated launch service, whose hours and priorities are less rigid than those of the publicly operated ferryboats. (Because of their expense, these services are usually an option only if all else fails.) Suitable for up to four passengers, the private launches cost $56 per trip until midnight, when it goes up to $95.

## VISITOR INFORMATION

The **St. John Tourist Office** (☎ **776-6450**) is located near the Battery, a 1735 fort which is a short walk from where the ferry from St. Thomas docks. Get whatever information you are seeking about St. John here, and pick up a free map of the island, which colorfully illustrates where everything is located inside Cruz Bay. On the back is a map of the entire island, illustrating the major roads and the location of all the main attractions, including restaurants, beaches, and campsites.

## 2 Getting Around

The 20-minute ferry ride from St. Thomas will take you to Cruz Bay, the capital of St. John, which seems a century removed from the life you left behind. There are no cruise ships here, no array of milling shoppers—St. John is definitely sleepy, and that's why many people like it. Don't come here looking for street addresses, as they don't exist. In fact, Cruz Bay is so small its streets are without names. It is sufficient to write Cruz Bay, St. John, U.S. Virgin Islands on any mail to St. John.

Cruz Bay has a few shops—the Mongoose Junction shopping center (definitely worth a visit), a scattering of restaurants, and a small park. After a stroll around the shops, seek out the natural attractions of the island.

## BY BUS OR TAXI

The **bus** service runs from Cruz Bay to Maho Bay and stops at Caneel and Cinnamon bays. The one-way bus fare is $4.

The most popular way to get around St. John is by **surrey-style taxi.** If you want to go from the ferry-landing dock to Trunk Bay, the cost is about $7.50 for two passengers. Between midnight and 6am fares are increased by 40%.

## BY CAR OR JEEP

The extensive stretches of St. John's national park have kept the edges of the island's roads undeveloped and uncluttered, with some of the most panoramic vistas anywhere. Because of these views, many visitors opt to rent a vehicle (sometimes with four-wheel drive) to tour the island. Unless you have luggage which should probably be locked away in a trunk, you might consider one of the open-sided, Jeep-like vehicles which allow a maximum view of the surroundings and a minimum of plush accessories. Sturdy, informal, and endlessly ventilated with manual transmissions, they are the most fun way to tour St. John. Because of the island's relatively limited facilities, most tourists need a car for only a day or two.

**Avis Rent-a-Car** (☎ 809/776-6374, or 800/331-2112) has a branch at Cruz Bay. Avis charges between $45 and $75 per day, depending on the model. In winter, Avis tends to be fully booked for many weeks in advance. Drivers must be 25 or older and must present a valid credit or charge card at the time of rental. A collision-damage waiver costs $11.95 per day.

**Hertz** (☎ 809/776-6412, or 800/654-3001) rents four types of vehicles, some of which have four-wheel drive. Depending on the model, the cost ranges from $65 to $80 per day; a collision-damage waiver is around $10 extra per day. Use of certain credit or charge cards sometimes eliminates the need for extra insurance, but the fine print of every card issuer varies widely from card to card. Drivers must be at least 25 years old and must present a valid credit or charge card at the time of rental.

If you want a local firm, try **St. John Car Rental, Inc.,** across from the post office in Cruz Bay (☎ 809/776-6103). It offers daily or weekly rentals in air-conditioned four-door sedans, Suzuki jeepsters, eight-passenger safaris, and seven-passenger minivans. Sedans cost $50 to $60 per day.

**PARKING** No problem on St. John. Parking is available in abundance in most places. Hotels don't charge for parking.

**DRIVING RULES** *Remember to drive on the left!* Otherwise, follow posted speed limits, which are generally very low, and traffic signs, which are the same as on the U.S. mainland.

## BY SCOOTER

At press time, no business offered scooter rentals. They are legal, however, and if you ask at the ferry dock, you may be directed to one of the locals who will rent

### Impressions

*[St. John has] the most superb beaches and view of any place I've seen, and [is] the most beautiful island in the Caribbean.*

—Laurence Rockefeller

you one for the day. Expect to spend $30 to $40 a day in summer and $40 to $50 a day in winter, with the payment of a $300 cash deposit required. Note, again, that there is no one to call or no office to go to.

## ON FOOT

Walking is the only way to explore Cruz Bay and Mongoose Junction, but you'll need a taxi, scooter, motorcycle, or rented car to go to some of the faraway beaches or hidden pockets of beauty on the island. The national park has countless hiking trails, and most of its more interesting sections can be explored on foot.

## FAST FACTS: St. John

**American Express**   See "Fast Facts: St. Thomas," in Chapter 4.

**Area Code**   The area code is 809. You can dial direct from the U.S.

**Babysitting**   There is no central agency. Make arrangements through your hotel.

**Business Hours**   Banking hours are Monday through Thursday 9am to 2:30pm, Friday 9am to 2pm and 3:30 to 5pm. Typical business hours are Monday through Friday from 9am to 5pm, Saturday from 9am to 1pm. Stores are open Monday through Friday from 9am to 5pm, Saturday from 9am to 1pm.

**Car Rentals**   See "Getting Around," earlier in this chapter.

**Climate**   See "When to Go," in Chapter 3.

**Currency**   See "Visitor Information, Entry Requirements & Money," in Chapter 3.

**Currency Exchange**   Go to a branch of Chase Manhattan Bank, Cruz Bay (☎ **776-6881**).

**Dentists**   See "Fast Facts: St. Thomas," in Chapter 4.

**Doctor**   Call **922** for a medical emergency. Otherwise, go to St. John Myrah Keating Smith Community Health Clinic, 3B Sussanaberg (☎ **693-8900**).

**Drugstores**   Go to St. John Drugcenter Inc., Boulon Shopping Center, Cruz Bay (☎ **776-6353**). The staff here not only fills prescriptions, but also sells film. Hours are Monday through Saturday from 9am to 6pm and Sunday from 10am to 2pm.

**Electricity**   110 to 115V, 60 cycles, as in the mainland U.S.

**Emergencies**   Police, **915**; ambulance, **922**; fire, **921.**

**Etiquette**   St. Johnians tend to be a bit conservative. Save the skimpy swimwear for the beach, and cover up when patronizing public places, such as restaurants, hotel lobbies, or when shopping at Mongoose Junction.

**Holidays**   See "When to Go," in Chapter 3.

**Hairdresser**   Try Grapevine, Mongoose Junction (☎ **776-6962**).

**Laundry**   Try Inn Town Laundromat, Cruz Bay (☎ **693-8590**), open Monday through Friday from 8:30am to 5pm; Saturday from 8am to 4pm. It shuts down for lunch from noon to 1pm. It's drop-off service only.

**Liquor Laws**   Persons must be at least 21 years of age to patronize bars or purchase liquor in St. John.

**Mail**   Postage rates are the same as on the U.S. mainland.

**Maps**   See "Visitor Information," earlier in this chapter.

**Newspapers and Magazines**   Copies of U.S. mainland newspapers, such as *The New York Times* and *The Miami Herald* arrive daily and are for sale at Mongoose Junction, Caneel Bay, and Hyatt. The latest copies of *Time* and *Newsweek* are also for sale. Complimentary copies of *Here's How: St. Thomas & St. John* contain many helpful hints. It is the official guidebook of the St. Thomas and St. John Hotel Association and is available at the tourist office (see "Tourist Information," below) and at various hotels.

**Photographic Needs**   To purchase film on St. John, go to the St. John Drugcenter Inc. (see "Drugstores," above). However, to have film developed, you'll have to take it to St. Thomas (see "Fast Facts: St. Thomas," in Chapter 4).

**Tourist Information**   See "Visitor Information," earlier in this chapter.

## 3  Accommodations

The number of accommodations on St. John is limited, and that's how most die-hard St. John fans would like to keep it. Your choices range from an elegant tropical haven to a no-frills campsite.

Prices are often slashed in summer by 30% to 60%. But in winter, expect to spend from $320 to $645 for a double room rated "very expensive." House-keeping units are considered "expensive" if they ask more than $200 per night, but "moderate" if the going price for two persons is between $95 and $200 a night. (See "Tips on Accommodations," Chapter 3, for an explanation of the abbreviations AP, CP, EP, and MAP). Inns around Cruz Bay are considered "inexpensive" if they offer either standard rooms or efficiencies (with small kitchens) for $50 to $95 per day. Campgrounds (see below) are the most economical way to stay on St. John, not to mention a great way to appreciate its natural wonders.

## LUXURY RESORTS
### VERY EXPENSIVE

✪ **Caneel Bay, Inc.**
Virgin Islands National Park, St. John, USVI 00831. ☎ **809/776-6111,** or 800/928-8889. Fax 809/693-8280. 171 rms (all with bath). A/C MINIBAR TV Transportation: Taxi. Rates: Dec 20–Mar 31, $335–$695 single or double; off-season, $225–$450 single or double. MAP $65 per person extra. AE, DC, MC, V.

The style of this resort isn't flashy—its beauty is subtle and conservative, appreciated by a discerning (and usually wealthy) clientele. Caneel Bay itself is the first to admit that for a certain kind of client, the resort is a dream come true; for others, it simply isn't appropriate. The resort was established upon the rolling seaside acreage of a sugar plantation with stone-sided mills and towers that today are heavily weighted with cascading bougainvillea. The site was deliberately and personally selected by Laurance Rockefeller for its seven beaches, its array of convenient yacht anchorages, and its 170-acre location next to land that he eventually donated to the U.S. Government for use as a national park.

The resort was conscientiously designed as an environment where families could fraternize in elegant but uncluttered settings. Tennis courts are deliberately not illuminated for nighttime play, accommodations contain no telephones, and bungalows lie far from their neighbors.

**Dining/Entertainment:** See "Dining," below, for descriptions of the Caneel Bay Beach Terrace Dining Room and Equators. Nightly entertainment is offered in the Caneel Bay Bar beneath the soaring ceiling of a stone-and-timber pavilion.

**Services:** Scheduled garden tours, fishing expeditions, diving excursions to offshore wrecks, deep-sea fishing, free snorkeling lessons, tennis lessons, valet, laundry.

**Facilities:** Full-service dive shop and water-sports activities desk, 11 tennis courts, free use of Sunfish sailboats and Windsurfers, swimming pools, seven beaches.

### Hyatt Regency St. John

Great Cruz Bay, St. John, USVI 00831. ☎ **809/693-8000,** or 800/233-1234. Fax 809/ 693-8888. 285 rms (all with bath). A/C MINIBAR TV TEL Transportation: Taxi. Rates: Winter, $330–$515 single or double; summer, $195–$295 single or double. MAP $62 per person extra. AE, DC, MC, V. Parking: Free.

The Hyatt, the splashiest hotel on St. John, sits on 34 acres of what used to be scrub forest on the southeast side of the island. It's a favorite with the convention crowd. The 13 cedar-roofed postmodern buildings have ziggurat-shaped angles, soaring ceilings, large windows, and an overall style that seems inspired by Aztec, Egyptian, or neocolonial models. Herringbone-patterned brick walkways connect the gardens (where 400 palms were imported from Puerto Rico) with the beach and the most unusual swimming pool in the Virgin Islands.

Each of the stylish accommodations contains fan-shaped windows, curved ceilings, unusual but pleasing dimensions, and a softly vibrant color scheme of rose and mauve.

**Dining/Entertainment:** One of the leading dining choices is Ciao Mein (see "Dining," below). The Café Grand serves breakfast and dinner, featuring a buffet at both meals. The Splash Grill draws the lunch crowd with its barbecues and island drinks. The Splash Bar is open daily from 11am to midnight, and entertainment is often presented in season.

**Services:** Round-trip transfers from St. Thomas airport, supervised activities program for children.

**Facilities:** 11,000-square-foot swimming pool, six lit tennis courts, 1,200-foot beach, water sports, spa and health club.

## VILLAS & CONDOS

Villa vacations are on the rise in St. John as a way to have a home away from home. There are actually more villa and condo beds available at St. John than there are hotel beds. Private homes and condos offer spaciousness and comfort, as well as privacy and freedom, and come with fully equipped kitchens, dining areas, bedrooms, and such amenities as VCRs and patio grills. Rentals range from large multiroom resort homes to simply decorated one-bedroom condos. Villa rentals year-round average from about $1,200 to $2,000 per week, an affordable option for multiple couples or families looking for a large house. Condos generally range from $105 to $360 per night per unit. For information on privately owned villas and condos on St. John, call **800/USVI-INFO.**

### EXPENSIVE/MODERATE

⑤ **Caribbean Villas & Resorts Management Co., Inc.**

P.O. Box 458, St. John, USVI 00831. ☎ **809/776-6152,** or 800/338-0987 in the U.S. 74 units. A/C Transportation: Taxi. Rates: Most less than $200 per night (a Cruz View

# St. John Accommodations/Sports

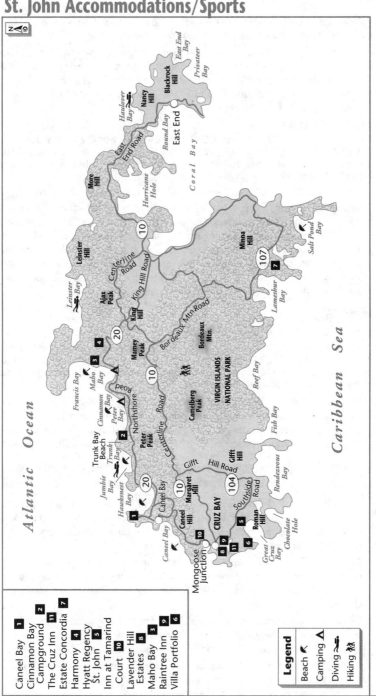

**Legend**

Beach 🏖️
Camping ⛺
Diving 🤿
Hiking 🥾

Caneel Bay **1**
Cinnamon Bay
Campground **2**
The Cruz Inn **11**
Estate Concordia **7**
Harmony **4**
Hyatt Regency
St. John **5**
Inn at Tamarind
Court **10**
Lavender Hill
Estates **8**
Maho Bay **3**
Raintree Inn **9**
Villa Portfolio **6**

two-bedroom unit for four costs $220 in winter, $150 in summer). Private homes are more expensive. Children under 6 stay free. No credit cards. Parking: Free.

Caribbean Villas & Resorts, the island's biggest company, is your best bet if you're seeking a villa or a condo on St. John. This well-run outfit, directed by Richard Clark, offers 74 private villas and condos. Private homes, ranging from two to six bedrooms, renting for around $200 to $1,500 (although prices vary) per night with swimming pools, Jacuzzis, and views.

### ⓢ Lavender Hill Estates

P.O. Box 8306, Cruz Bay, St. John, USVI 00831-8306. ☎ **809/776-6969.** Fax 809/776-6969. 10 units (all with bath). TV TEL Transportation: Taxi. Rates: Winter, $210 one-bedroom unit; $265 two-bedroom unit. Summer, $135 one-bedroom unit; $160 two-bedroom unit. MC, V. Parking: Free.

This outfit offers some of the best condominium values on the island. It's attraction include a swimming pool with a lounging deck in tropical setting. It is a short walk to the shops, markets, restaurants, and safari buses of Cruz Bay. The rates are midway between the campgrounds and inns and the upscale properties of Virgin Grand and Caneel Bay. The units overlook Cruz Bay Harbor, and each one has a spacious central living/dining area opening onto a tiled deck, along with a fully equipped kitchen and one or two bedrooms. Laundry facilities are available. Units are furnished in an attractive, modern Caribbean style.

## MODERATE

### Estate Concordia

P.O. Box 310, Cruz Bay, St. John, USVI 00831. ☎ **212/472-9453,** or 800/392-9004 in the U.S. and Canada. Fax 212/861-6210 in New York City. 9 studios. Rates: Winter, $135–$190 double; summer, $95–$150 double. $25 per day per person extra. Minimum stay seven nights in winter. No credit cards. Parking: Free.

Opened in 1993, this development project was widely praised for its adherence to sustainable development and its integration with the local ecosystem. Elevated modular structures were designed to coexist with the stunning but fragile landscapes of the dry southern edge of St. John. Nestled on a low cliff above a salt

---

### 🟢 Family-Friendly Hotels

**Hyatt Regency St. John**   *(see p. 138)* This hotel has more for kids than any other hotel on the island: there's a supervised activities program for ages 3 to 15 during the summer months, winter weekends, and certain holiday periods. A special children's menu is available in the restaurants.

**Lavender Hill Estates**   *(see p. 140)* Families often save money by staying at one of these condos with a swimming pool. Meals can be prepared in each of the condo's fully equipped kitchen units. Children under 12 stay free; others are charged $25 extra per night.

**Cinnamon Bay Campground**   *(see p. 142)* Tents or cottages come with cooking gear—families have a choice here. Families can even rent a bare site on a beachside campground. The National Park Service is the host.

**Maho Bay**   *(see p. 143)* The tents here are really like small canvas houses with kitchen areas and sundecks. In this laid-back hideaway, children can be taught how to become more sensitive to the environment.

pond, surrounded by hundreds of acres of pristine national park, the secluded location is recommended for those who arrange for their own rental vehicle. Each building was sited to protect mature trees and is interconnected to its neighbors with raised boardwalks, under which the utility and electrical lines are concealed. The developer, Stanley Selengut, is a New York–based entrepreneur whose pioneer work in ecological preservation is well known throughout the region.

The nine units are contained in six postmodern cottages capped with ventilation stacks which cool by means of natural convection. Each unit comes with a kitchen, bathroom, sleeping beds, balcony, ceiling fan, and tile floors. The large airy units usually lack dividing walls and contain either a full kitchen or kitchenette and, in some cases, high-peaked ceilings. Some units have an extra bedroom or a large private bathroom.

Estate Concordia also features a private, deep-water swimming pool and guest laundry facilities. The management will give you ideas about how to tour the natural sights nearby.

### Harmony

P.O. Box 310, Cruz Bay, St. John, USVI 00831. ☎ **212/472-9453,** or 800/392-9004 in the U.S. and Canada. Fax 212/861-6210 in New York City. 12 studios. Rates: Winter, $150–$170 double. Summer, $95–$125 double. $25 per day per person extra. Minimum stay seven nights in winter. No credit cards. Parking: Free.

Built on a hillside above Maho Bay Campground, this small-scale cluster of 12 luxury units in six two-story houses, offers views down to the sea. Designed to combine both ecological technology and comfort, it's one of the few resorts in the Caribbean to operate exclusively on sun and wind power. Its construction guidelines are models of ecologically sensitive development. Most of the building materials are derived from recycled materials, including reconstituted plastic, glass containers, newsprint, old tires, and scrap lumber. The managers and staff are committed to offering an educational experience to to their guests, as well as the services of a small-scale resort. Guests are asked to share their experience of living in an ecologically sensitive resort. They are taught how to operate a user-friendly computer telling them how their unit's energy is being spent and how to give their assessment of the establishment's experimental appliances, furnishings, and supplies.

Units contain queen-size sleep sofas and/or twin beds, tile bathrooms, kitchenettes, dining areas, and outdoor terraces. Guests can walk a short distance downhill to use the restaurant, grocery store, and water-sports facilities at the Maho Bay Campground.

### Villa Portfolio Management

P.O. Box 618, Cruz Bay, St. John, USVI 00831. ☎ **809/693-9100,** or 800/858-7989. A/C Transportation: Taxi. Rates: Winter, $195–$295 single or double ($1,365–$1,675 per week). Summer, $105–$125 single or double ($875–$966 per week). No credit cards. Parking: Free.

This agency offers about a dozen condominium apartments that accept guests for a week or more. The names of the individual building complexes include the Battery Hill Condominiums and the Villa Caribe Condominiums. All units lie a short walk south of Cruz Bay. Each unit has its own self-contained kitchen as well as views of either the town and harbor of Cruz Bay or of the faraway coastline of St. Thomas. Units include one- and two-bedroom town houses, often on more than one level and which usually have verandas, terraces, ceiling fans, and patios. Each is individually furnished in off-whites and pastels.

## BUDGET INNS

Let's face it: Except for the campgrounds recommended below, the tab at most of the establishments on St. John is far beyond the pocketbook of the average traveler. If you're willing to settle for few frills, the following places can provide a low-cost holiday on St. John.

### ⑤ Cruz Inn

P.O. Box 566, Cruz Bay, St. John, USVI 00831. ☎ **809/693-8688,** or 800/666-7688. Fax 809/693-8688. 14 rms (5 with bath and kitchen). Rates (including continental breakfast): Winter, $50 double without bath; $65–$85 efficiency. Summer, $45 double without bath; $60–$75 efficiency. Extra person $15. Housekeeping units require a three-day minimum stay. AE, MC, V. Parking: Free.

This low-priced accommodation overlooking Enighed Pond is a bit of a walk from the Cruz Bay ferry dock. Seven of the guest rooms are in the main building and share two baths; each has an overhead fan and either a double bed or twin beds. Other accommodations are housed in efficiencies and apartments in the complex. Five of the units have cooking facilities, and some are air-conditioned. The inn has a convivial bar and offers weekly entertainment. Tennis courts are available nearby. A food service allows you to order a full breakfast, as well as a take-out lunch or simple dinner.

### ⑤ Inn at Tamarind Court

P.O. Box 350, Cruz Bay, St. John, USVI 00831. ☎ **809/776-6378,** or 800/221-1637. 20 rms (13 with bath), 1 apt, 2 suites. Rates (including continental breakfast): Winter, $48 single without bath; $73 double with bath; $98 apt.; $108 suite. Summer, $38 single without bath; $63 double with bath; $88 apt.; $98 suite. AE, MC, V. Parking: Free.

Right outside Cruz Bay but still within walking distance of the ferryboat dock, this modest establishment consists of a small hotel (where the non-smoking rooms have been renovated) and an even simpler West–Indian inn. Baths at the inn are shared, whereas within the hotel all rooms have private baths. The establishment's social life revolves around its courtyard bar. At Etta's you can enjoy West Indian cuisine and live entertainment on Friday.

### Raintree Inn

P.O. Box 566, Cruz Bay, St. John, USVI 00831. ☎ **809/693-8590,** or 800/666-7449. Fax 809/693-8590. 11 rms (all with bath). A/C TEL Rates: Winter, $70 double; $95 efficiency. Summer, $50 double; $75 efficiency. Efficiencies require a three-day minimum stay. AE, MC, V. Parking: Free.

One block from the ferry stop, next to the Catholic church, the Raintree Inn has simple non-smoking double rooms, some with high ceilings. Linen, towels, and soap are supplied upon request. Three of the rooms have full kitchen, and two twins are in a carpeted loft. A small deck is attached. The inn adjoins a reasonably priced restaurant next door, The Fish Trap (see "Dining," below). Laundry service is available on the premises.

## CAMPGROUNDS

### Cinnamon Bay Campground

P.O. Box 720, Cruz Bay, St. John, USVI 00831. ☎ **809/776-6330,** or 800/223-7637. Fax 809/776-6458. 111 units (none with bath). Transportation: Safari bus from Cruz Bay. Rates: Winter, $86–$95 cottage for two; $67 tent; $15 bare site. Summer, $59–$61 cottage for two; $44 tent; $15 bare site. MAP (five-day minimum) $18.50 per day per person. AE, MC, V. Parking: Free.

Established by the National Park Service in 1964, this is the most complete campground in the Caribbean. Located on the north coast of the island, the site is directly on the beach, amid thousands of acres of tropical vegetation. You have a choice of three accommodations—tent, cottage, or bare site. At the campsites, only bare necessities are provided. The tents are permanently affixed to wooden platforms measuring 10 by 14 feet. Cottages have 15-by-15-feet cement floors and consist of a cross-ventilated shelter with two concrete walls and two screens. They each contain four twin beds; two cots can be added. Each additional occupant is charged $12. Guests who rent both the tents and the showers get free use of a two-burner propane gas stove, cooking utensils, cutlery, plates, and cups. Linen is changed twice weekly. Lavatories, showers, a grocery store, and a cafeteria (serving $12 dinners) are all located nearby. Camping here for more than a two-week period in any given year is illegal.

### ✪ Maho Bay

P.O. Box 310, Cruz Bay, St. John, USVI 00831. ☎ **809/776-6226,** or 800/392-9004; 212/472-9453 in New York. Fax 212/816-6210. 114 tent cottages (none with bath). Transportation: Maho Bay shuttle. Rates: Mid-Dec to Apr, $90 tent cottage for two; minimum stay of seven nights required. May to mid-Dec, $60 tent cottage for two; no minimum stay required. $12 extra for each additional occupant over 16; $10 extra for each additional occupant age 15 and younger. No credit cards. Parking: Free.

Maho Bay is an interesting take on ecotourism that combines propinquity to nature with considerable comfort. *The New York Times* called it "an ecological showplace, one of the best values in the Caribbean." The deluxe campground, an 8-mile drive from Cruz Bay, is set in the Virgin Islands National Park. To preserve the existing ground cover, all 114 tent cottages are on platforms above a thickly wooded slope. Utility lines and pipes are hidden under wooden boardwalks and stairs.

The tent cottages are covered with canvas and screens. Each unit has two movable twin beds, a couch, electric lamps and outlets, a dining table, chairs, a propane stove, and an ice chest (cooler). That's not all—you're furnished linen, towels, and cooking and eating utensils. There's a store where you can buy supplies. You can do your own cooking, although you can eat at the camp's outdoor restaurant. Guests share communal bathhouses.

Maho Bay has an open-air Pavilion Restaurant, which serves breakfast and dinner year-round. Lunches are offered in winter, and the international dinner menu is changed nightly depending on what is fresh. Both meat and vegetarian selections are offered. The Pavilion also functions as an amphitheater and community center where various programs are featured. A new Pavilion, higher up on the hill with panoramic views of the ocean, is also used for a community center, as well as for special occasions such as weddings and group meetings. The camp has an excellent water-sports program.

# 4  Dining

St. John has some posh dining, particularly at Caneel Bay and Hyatt Regency St. John, but it also has some West Indian places with lots of local color and flavor. Many of the restaurants here command high prices, but you can lunch almost anywhere at reasonable rates. Dinner is considered a bit of an event here, since there's not much organized entertainment anywhere.

Prices are considered "expensive" if restaurants charge from $40 to $65 per person for dinner without wine. Those viewed as "moderate" charge from $22 to $35 for dinner. Anything under $20 is "inexpensive." Most of the places in this category can be "inexpensive" if you order the less costly items on the menu, although Caribbean lobsters and steak always cost more.

# LUXURY DINING AROUND THE ISLAND
## EXPENSIVE

### Caneel Bay Beach Terrace Dining Room
Caneel Bay Hotel. ☎ **776-6111.** Reservations required for dinner. Transportation: Taxi. Lunch buffet $22 per person; dinner appetizers $6.50–$12.50, dinner main dishes $28–$38; fixed-price dinner $55. AE, DC, MC, V. Lunch daily 11:30am–2:30pm; dinner daily 7–9pm. INTERNATIONAL/SEAFOOD.

This is the main dining room for the Caneel Bay resort. Located beneath the soaring ceiling of a gazebo-inspired pavilion set midway between the beach and the hotel's reception desk, the Beach Terrace Dining Room serves rich buffets at lunch and more formal à la carte and fixed-price dinners. Men are requested to wear jackets for dinner (especially between November and May).

Although the menu changes nightly according to the available ingredients, your meal might include poached oysters with a sauce of roast fennel and garlic, fresh figs with prosciutto, rack of lamb with green peppercorn sauce, grilled grouper with a roast red pepper sauce, and gingered floating island with an English cream sauces for dessert.

### Le Château de Bordeaux
Junction 10, Centerline Rd., Bordeaux Mountain. ☎ **776-6611.** Reservations recommended. Transportation: Taxi. Appetizers $5.95–$7.95; main dishes $17.95–$26.95. DC, MC, V. Dinner Mon–Sat, two nightly seatings from 5:30–6:30pm and from 7:45–8:45pm. CONTINENTAL/CARIBBEAN.

Set 5 miles east of Cruz Bay near the geographical center of the island close to one of its highest points at an elevation of 1,300 feet, this restaurant is known for its eastward-facing vistas and some of the best high-altitude views in St. John. Although an ice-cream kiosk sells sundaes and milkshakes throughout the day, the true lure is in the evening. Amid a Victorian decor with lace tablecloths, you can enjoy dishes like banana-papaya conch fritters, saffron-flavored pastas, West Indian seafood chowder, smoked salmon, filet mignon, wild game specials, roast rack of lamb, and a changing array of cheesecakes, among other desserts. The specialty drink is passion fruit daiquiri.

### ✪ Ciao Mein
Hyatt Regency St. John, Great Cruz Bay. ☎ **776-7171.** Reservations recommended. Transportation: Taxi. Appetizers $5.75–$10.25; main dishes $20–$26.75. AE, DC, MC, V. Dinner daily 6–9:30pm. ASIAN/ITALIAN.

This restaurant is a direct import of California cuisine and design, with liberal doses of razzmatazz added by Hyatt Hotels. Hypermodern marble tables are placed one floor above the most dramatic lobby in the Caribbean, with views of an architectural style inspired by ancient Egypt or Mesopotamia. Piano music filters from a spotlit dais in the restaurant to the lobby below, as scents from the hotel's gardens filter upward.

You can dine multiculturally here. Start with an order of the Thai spring rolls or perhaps the shredded duck salad. If you feel like Italian, order an antipasto or zuppe minestrone. Chinese specialties include fried whole fish with a julienne of vegetables and crispy duck with Chinese barbecue sauce. Main dishes on the Italian menu feature chicken breast baked with mozzarella and parmesan in a marinara sauce or pan-seared veal Norman with eggplant.

### Ellington's

Gallows Point, Cruz Bay. ☎ **776-7166.** Reservations required for upstairs seating only. Appetizers $6–$10; main dishes $13–$30. AE, MC, V. Breakfast daily 8–11am; dinner daily 6–10pm. CONTINENTAL.

By far one of the most stylish and exciting independent restaurants on St. John, Ellington's is set near the neocolonial villas of Gallows Point. Its putty-colored exterior has the double staircase, fan windows, louvers, and low-slung hip roof of an 18th-century Danish manor house. Drop in for a drink on the panoramic upper deck, which has the finest view anywhere of sunsets over St. Thomas.

The establishment is named after a local radio announcer, raconteur, and mystery writer whose real estate developments helped transform St. John into a stylish enclave for the American literati of the 1950s and '60s. Nicknamed Richard "Duke" Ellington, he entertained his friends, martini in hand, around a frequently photographed table that is currently used in the sunset lounge. Ellington's dining room is very open and is lavishly adorned with tropical hardwoods. The dinner menu changes daily according to what's fresh. Try the fish of the day, perhaps Caribbean lobster, or else one of the steak, pasta, or chicken dishes prepared West Indian style.

### Equators

In the Caneel Bay Hotel, Caneel Bay. ☎ **776-6111.** Reservations necessary. Appetizers $6–$10; main courses $13.50–$30. AE, MC, V. Dinner only, Tues–Sun 6:30–10pm. CARIBBEAN/LATIN/THAI.

This restaurant lies within the bougainvillea-cloaked tower of a former 18th-century sugar mill. At the tower's base, pools of water accented with water lilies fill what used to serve as crystallization pits for hot molasses. A flight of stairs leads to a monumental circular dining room with a wraparound veranda and sweeping views westward over a park and the sea. In the restaurant's center rises the stone column that horses and mules once circumambulated to crush sugarcase stalks.

The cuisine is considered the most experimental and the most successful on St. John; it is the result of thousands of dollars invested by the upscale Rosewood Hotels & Resorts chain which owns the restaurant. Dinner include teriyaki tuna with a picked lobster hand roll and tempura vegetables; pepper-cured tandoori lamb on Egyptian cous-cous with mango-pickles; wok-fried whole catfish with Polynesian ponzu and fried rice; and sugarcane-glazed salmon steak on habañero peppers and mashed potatoes served with a guava-flavored rum sauce. Dessert might be a lime-lychee-nut layer cake with guava sorbet.

### ✪ Paradiso

Mongoose Junction. ☎ **776-8806.** Reservations recommended. Appetizers $3.50–$7.95; main dishes $15–$26.50. AE, MC, V. Dinner only, daily 6–10pm. Bar daily 4:30pm–12:30am. ITALIAN/AMERICAN.

The most talked-about restaurant on St. John, Paradiso is located among the catwalks and lattices of the island's major shopping center, Mongoose Junction. The

## 😊 Family-Friendly Restaurants

**Café Roma** *(see p. 146)* is a family favorite. Treat your child to a "white pizza" made without tomato sauce.

**Mongoose Restaurant** *(see p. 146)* The best choice for children if you're visiting Cruz Bay. At this tropical stage setting, kids munch on the well-stuffed sandwiches and island fish cakes.

**Pusser's** *(see p. 148)* Families like this place for its succulent barbecued chicken, and no kid can resist its frozen mud pie.

decor includes lots of brass, glowing hardwoods, and nautical antiques. Paradiso has what might be the most beautiful bar on the island. It's crafted from mahogany, purpleheart, and angelique.

Menu items include an array of pastas, Caesar salads, a platter of smoked seafood, baked stuffed sole with a lobster cream sauce, lobster fra diavolo (with seafood and red chilies), and a selection of daily specials whose availability depends on their arrival that day from the U.S. mainland. The house drink is Paradiso Punch, the bartender's version of plantation punch.

## MODERATE

### Café Roma

Cruz Bay. ☎ **776-6524.** Reservations not required. Appetizers $2.75–$8; main dishes $12–$15.50. AE, MC, V. Dinner daily 5–10pm. ITALIAN.

Diners climb a flight of concrete steps to reach this rustic, air-conditioned Italian restaurant and pizza parlor. You may want to arrive early and have a strawberry colada then enjoy a selection of pastas or veal and chicken dishes. Ask about their "white pizza," made without tomato sauce. Italian wines are sold by the glass or bottle, and you can end the evening with an espresso.

### Don Carlos Mexican Seafood Cantina

10–19 Estate Carolina, Coral Bay. ☎ **776-6866.** Reservations required during winter. Appetizers $5.95–$8.95; main dishes $9.95–$17.95. AE, MC, V. Daily 11am–9 or 10pm. Bar daily 11am–10:30pm. MEXICAN.

An open-sided pavilion at the edge of the sea overlooking Coral Bay, this establishment is one of the best Mexican restaurants in the Virgin Islands. It's a branch of an award-winning chain of Stateside restaurants known for their fajitas and foaming margaritas. Amid a decor of Mexican weavings and a prominent bar, you can order Mexican-style conch fritters served with avocado slices and salsa ranchero; at least four kinds of what the owners claim are the most famous fajitas north of the Mexican border; and swordfish Vera Cruz, chargrilled with beans, rice, and tomato-onion salsa. The most popular drink? A jumbo, 36-ounce margarita concocted for two, priced at $14 each.

### Mongoose Restaurant, Café, and Bar

Mongoose Junction. ☎ **776-7586.** Reservations required during winter. Lunch appetizers $3–$8; salads, burgers, and sandwiches $5–$9; dinner appetizers $3–$10; main dishes $8–$20. AE, DC, MC, V. Breakfast daily 8:30–11:30am; lunch daily 11:30am–5pm; dinner daily 5–10pm. Bar daily 11am–10pm. CARIBBEAN.

Some visitors compare the soaring interior design here to a large Japanese birdcage because of the strong vertical lines and the 25-foot ceiling. Set among trees and

# St. John Dining

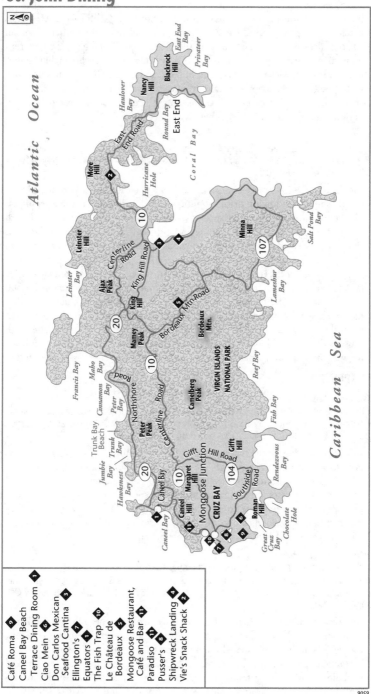

Café Roma ◆9
Caneel Bay Beach
Terrace Dining Room ◆1
Ciao Mein ◆6
Don Carlos Mexican
Seafood Cantina ◆3
Ellington's ◆7
Equators ◆4
The Fish Trap ◆10
Le Château de
Bordeaux ◆5
Mongoose Restaurant,
Café and Bar ◆11
Paradiso ◆11
Pusser's ◆8
Shipwreck Landing ◆4
Vie's Snack Shack ◆2

9059

built above a stream, it's very reminiscent of northern California. Some guests perch at the open-centered bar for a drink and sandwich, while others sit on an adjacent deck where a canopy of trees filters the tropical sunlight. The bar offers more than 20 varieties of frothy island-inspired libations. Lunches include soups, well-stuffed sandwiches, salad platters, burgers, and pastas. Dinner is more formal, with specialties such as grilled steaks, fresh catch of the day, surf and turf, seafood creole, and island fish cakes. This establishment's Sunday brunch is mobbed with St. Johnians who clamor for eggs Benedict.

### Pusser's

Wharfside Village, Cruz Bay. ☎ **693-8489.** Reservations recommended. Appetizers $4.95–$8.95; main dishes $12.95–$24.95. AE, MC, V. Lunch daily 11am–3pm; dinner daily 6–10pm. INTERNATIONAL/CARIBBEAN.

More than any other place in St. John, Pusser's re-creates the days of the English clipper ships, with English maritime antiques, dark hardwood, and masses of polished brass jutting out from unexpected corners. Its two levels combine a pub with a store selling its own line of clothing and gift items. Its veranda high above the shoreline of Cruz Bay is immediately obvious to passengers on the ferryboat from St. Thomas.

The establishment (now a chain throughout the Caribbean) is named after the famous blend of five different rums that the Royal Navy served its sailors for 300 years. At tables near the bar, you can order Cajun barbecued chicken, shrimp diablo, lobster medaillons, or New York strip steak. Pusser's famous frozen mud pie is the most popular dessert, followed by Pusser's Coffee—roasted coffee with Pusser's Rum and a bit of brown sugar and whipped cream. If you're in your bathing suit and want only a hamburger or fast food for lunch, try Pusser's Beach Bar.

## INEXPENSIVE

### The Fish Trap

In the Raintree Inn, Cruz Bay. ☎ **693-9994.** Reservations not required, except for parties of six or more. Appetizers $2.95–$8.95; main dishes $15.95–$22.95; pastas and burgers $8.95–$17.95. AE, MC, V. Dinner Tues–Sun 4:30–9:30pm. SEAFOOD.

In an inn standing in the center of the island's main town. The Fish Trap enjoys both local and foreign patronage (see "Accommodations," above for a hotel review). It's known for its wide selection of seafood but also serves vegetarian food and burgers. In a tropical setting in the midst of coconut, palm and banana trees, most diners begin with the conch fritters or the Fish Trap chowder. Then they might try a tasty seafood combo, blackened sea scallops, or shrimp Palermo (with olive oil, garlic, and parsley). All desserts are prepared fresh.

### Shipwreck Landing

34 Freeman's Ground, Rte. 107, Coral Bay. ☎ **693-5640.** Reservations not required. 8 miles east of Cruz Bay on the road to Salt Pond Beach. Appetizers $3.50–$8.50; main dishes $11.25–$17.50. MC, V. Restaurant daily 11am–10pm. Bar daily 11am–11pm. SEAFOOD/ CONTINENTAL.

Run by Pat and Dennis Rizzo, this is an attractive place to head for after an island sightseeing tour. You dine amid palms and tropical plants on a veranda overlooking the sea. The intimate bar specializes in tropical frozen drinks, and the kitchen prepares such items as chicken Caribbean Bleu, blackened red snapper, and surf and turf, along with daily seafood specials. Some Mexican and Asian dishes are also served. Music is often featured on Tuesday, Thursday, and Sunday in winter.

# EAST END

## BUDGET

### ⑤ Vie's Snack Shack

East End Rd. ☎ **693-5033.** Reservations not required. Appetizers $3.25; main dishes $5–$6.50. No credit cards. Daily 10am–5pm, but call first! WEST INDIAN.

The owner of this plywood-sided hut on the island's East End is one of the best local chefs in St. John. Her famous garlic chicken is considered the best on the island. She also serves conch fritters, johnnycakes, and coconut and pineapple tarts. While the place is open most days, it's wise to call first, since, Vie warns, "Some days, we might not be here at all." Vie's is about 12½ miles east of Cruz Bay.

## PICNIC FARE & WHERE TO EAT IT

Most picnickers trek up to mountain panoramas or down to low-lying, semiconcealed beaches along the island's eastern end. If you don't care about privacy, a good spot is Trunk Bay, where the National Park Service maintains picnic tables.

The best place to buy your picnic fixings is **The Dell,** at the Hyatt Regency St. John in Great Cruz Bay (☎ 776-7171). Decorated like a brightly painted West Indian cottage, it carries everything you'll need, including an array of international cheeses, sausages, and salamis; fresh pastries; French bread; English crackers; pizza; and sandwiches. Virtually anything you buy here can be wrapped for a picnic lunch, including wines from around the world.

# 5 Attractions

## ON YOUR OWN

The ferry from St. Thomas docks at the main town, **Cruz Bay.** In this West–Indian village there are interesting bars, restaurants, boutiques, and pastel-painted houses. It's pretty sleepy, but it's a pleasant place to visit after the fast pace of St. Thomas. The **Elaine I. Sprauve Museum** (☎ 776-6359) at Cruz Bay is small but contains some local artifacts that will teach you about the islands history. It's located in the public library; it's open from 9am to 5pm Monday through Friday.

Most cruise-ship passengers dart through Cruz Bay and head for the island's biggest attraction, **Virgin Islands National Park.** But before going to the park, you

### ❓ Did You Know?

- Caneel Bay, the chic resort, is the site of the former Pieter Duerloo plantation, where slaves revolted against white settlers.
- The mongoose was brought to St. John to kill rats. It has practically been adopted as the island mascot—watch for them darting across roads.
- St. John was once a volcano.
- The only Danes left on the former Danish colony of St. John are dogs.

may want to stop at the Visitor's Center at Cruz Bay (see "Organized Tours," below), which is open daily from 8am to 4:30pm. There you'll see some exhibits and learn more about what you can see in the park.

The Virgin Islands National Park is the only national park in the Caribbean. It totals 12,624 acres, including submerged lands and waters adjacent to St. John, and has a 20-mile trail system.

If your time on St. John is limited, try at least to visit the **Annaberg Ruins,** Leinster Bay Road, where the Danes maintained a thriving plantation and sugar mill after 1718. It's located off North Shore Road east of Trunk Bay on the north shore. On varying days of the week, park rangers give guided walks of the area.

✪ **Trunk Bay** is considered one of the world's most beautiful beaches. It's also the site of one of the world's first marked underwater trails (bring your mask, snorkel, and fins). It lies to the east of Cruz Bay along North Shore Road. Beware of pickpockets.

**Fort Berg** (also called Fortsberg), at Coral Bay, dating from 1717, played a disastrous role during the 1733 slave revolt. The fort may be restored as a historic monument.

### THE TOP 10 THINGS TO DO ON YOUR OWN

1. Snorkel along the underwater trail at Trunk Bay.
2. Camp at Cinnamon Bay or Maho Bay campgrounds.
3. Hike the Reef Bay Trail through the Virgin Islands National Park.
4. Rent a four-wheel-drive vehicle and tour the rugged terrain of the island.
5. Shop duty-free at Mongoose Junction in Cruz Bay.
6. Visit Annaberg ruins and watch sugar being made.
7. Dine at Le Château de Bordeaux for its view; arrive long before sunset.
8. Sail to the British Virgin Islands from Coral Bay.
9. Walk along some of the Caribbean's most beautiful beaches.
10. Hike to Ram's Head, a scenic overlook on the island's southern shore.

## ORGANIZED TOURS

Park rangers conduct several different tours of the Virgin Islands National Park on Monday and Wednesday. You must make a reservation to participate in the $2^1/_2$-mile Reef Bay Trail hike through old sugar mill ruins and mysterious petroglyphs. Call **776-6330** for reservations. Other conducted programs include shore walks, a three-hour historic bus tour, snorkel tours, and informal evening lectures.

The **St. John Taxi Association** (☎ 776-6060) conducts a historical tour of St. John, and includes a swim at Trunk Bay and a visit to the Caneel Bay resort. The cost is $40 to $45 for two people. Depending on demand, tours depart Cruz Bay daily.

Tourists are encouraged to drop by the **Cruz Bay Visitor Center** upon their arrival on the island. At the center, you can pick up a park brochure, which includes a map, and the *Virgin Islands National Park News*, which has the latest information on activities in the park. For more information, call **776-6201.**

Maps of the island's hiking trails are readily available from the National Park Headquarters at Cruz Bay (see "On Your Own," above). One of our favorite tours requires only about a half-mile stroll (about 30 minutes round-trip, not including stops) and departs from clearly marked points along the island's north coast, near the junction of routes 10 and 20. Identified by the National Park Service as trail no. 10 (The Annaberg Historic Trail), it crosses the partially restored ruins of an 18th-century manor house overlooking the island's north coast. Signs along the way give historical and botanical data.

If you want to prolong your experience, trail no. 11 (The Leinster Bay Trail), begins near the point where trail no. 10 ends. Following the edge of Watermelon Bay, it leads past mangrove swamps and coral inlets rich with plant and marine life; markers identify some of the plants and animals.

## DRIVING TOUR
### St. John

**Start:**  Ferry docks in Cruz Bay.
**Finish:**  Ferry docks in Cruz Bay.
**Time:**  3 to 7 hours, depending on beach time, bar stops, and pedestrian detours.
**Best Times:**  Any warm sunny day.
**Worst Times:**  Any rainy day when you are likely to get stuck in the mud on bad roads.

*Important Note:* Before you begin this tour, make sure you have at least three-quarters of a tank of gas, since there are only two gas stations on St. John, one of which is often closed. The more reliable of the two stations is in the upper regions of Cruz Bay, beside Route 104. Ask for directions when you pick up your rented vehicle. *Remember to drive on the left!*

Head out of Cruz Bay, going east on Route 20. Within about a minute, you'll pass the catwalks and verandas of:

**1. Mongoose Junction.** Considered a sightseeing attraction as well as a shopping emporium, it contains some unusual art galleries and jewelry shops. (See "Shopping," below.)

Two miles northeast of Cruz Bay, you'll see a pair of unmarked stone columns on your left and an area of immaculate landscaping. This is the entrance to the island's most legendary resort:

**2. Caneel Bay.** Past the security guard, near the resort's parking lots, is a gift shop and a handful of bars and restaurants. In a mile, you'll see the first of many stunning vistas. Along the entire trajectory note the complete absence of billboards and electrical cables (a rule rigidly enforced by the National Park Service). In less than three miles, you'll come to:

**3. Hawksnest Beach,** whose palms and salt-tolerant wild figs are maintained by the National Park Service (NPS). Stop to read the ecological signs and perhaps wet your feet in the water. There are some squat toilets (with lots of flies) at this point if you need them. Continuing your drive, you'll pass, in this order, Trunk Bay, Peter Bay (private), and Cinnamon Bay, all of which have sand, palm trees, and clear water. A few steps from the entrance to the Cinnamon Bay Campground is a redwood sign marking the beginning of:

**4. The Cinnamon Bay Trail.** Laid out for hikers by the National Park Service, this 1.2-mile walk takes about an hour. Its clearly marked paths lead through shaded forest trails along the rutted cobblestones of a former Danish road, past ruins of abandoned plantations.

A short drive beyond Cinnamon Bay is the sandy sweep of Maho Bay, site of one of the most upscale campgrounds in the Caribbean.

Shortly after Maho Bay, the road splits. Take the left fork, which merges in a few moments with an extension of Centerline Road. Off this road, on your left will appear another NPS signpost marked DANISH ROAD, indicating a five-minute trek along a potholed road to the ruins of an 18th-century school.

At the next fork, bear right toward Annaberg. (Make sure you don't go toward Francis Bay.) You'll pass the beginning of a 0.8-mile walking trail to the Leinster Bay Estate, which leads to a beach said to be good for snorkeling. Within less than a minute, you'll reach the parking lot of the:

5. **Annaberg Historic Trail.** The highlight of this driving tour, the Annaberg Trail leads pedestrians within and around the ruined buildings of the best-preserved plantation on St. John. During the 18th and 19th centuries, the smell of boiling molasses permeated the air here during the era of slavery. About a dozen National Park Service plaques identify and describe each building within the compound. The walk around the grounds takes about 30 minutes. From a terrace near the ruined windmill, a map identifies the British Virgin Islands to the north, including Little Thatch, Tortola, Watermelon Cay, and Jost Van Dyke.

After your visit to Annaberg, retrace your route to its first major division, and take the left fork. Soon a road sign will identify your road as Route 20 East. Stay on this road, forking left wherever possible, until you come after many bends in the road to sandy bottomlands that contain an elementary school, a baseball field, and, on a hilltop, a simple barnlike building known as the:

6. **Emmaus Moravian Church,** with its yellow clapboards and red roof. (It's often closed to visitors.) Near its base yet another NPS walking trail begins (the $1^1/_2$-mile Johnny Horn Trail), known for its scenic views and steep hills. You will by now be about $12^1/_2$ miles east of Cruz Bay.

The roads at this point are not very clearly marked. Do not drive beyond the elementary school below the church. That road, although beautiful, is long and leads only to the barren and rather dull expanses of the island's East End. Instead, backtrack a very short distance to a cluster of signs that point to the restaurant the Still and Shipwreck Landing. Follow these signs heading south about a mile to:

7. **Coral Bay.** Claimed by the Danes in the 1600s, the bay still contains a crumbling stone pier used to unload Danish ships. It was also the site of the first plantation on St. John. Established in 1717 (and long ago abandoned), it predated the far better-developed facilities of Cruz Bay. Coral Bay was visited by a Danish princess in the early 1700s.

Prized by yachting enthusiasts, the bay shelters a closely knit community of boaters who moor and live on their yachts here between excursions to other parts of the Caribbean. Ringing the bay's perimeter is a widely spaced handful of restaurants and bars.

☕ **TAKE A BREAK**   **8. Don Carlos Mexican Seafood Cantina,** 10–19 Estate Carolina (☎ 776-6866), is an open-sided timbered pavilion close to the emerald waters of Coral Bay. The bar serves up jumbo 36-ounce margaritas, not recommended for the driver.

After your break, continue driving south along Coral Bay, perhaps stopping in at another of the two or three shops and bars beside the road. (Shipwreck Landing, described in "Dining," above, is a good choice for lunch or dinner.)

# Driving Tour—St. John

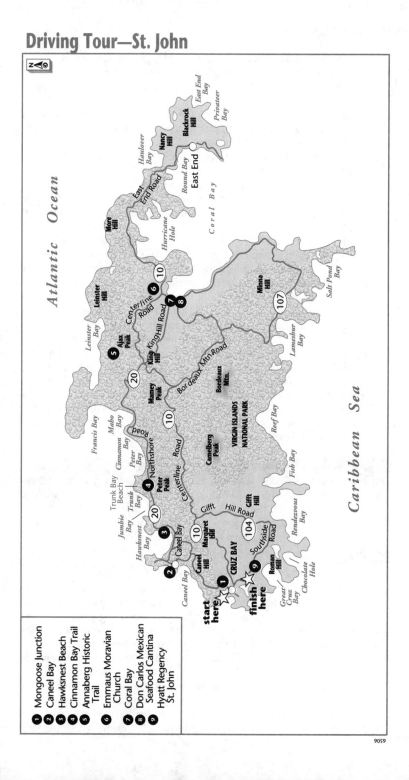

1. Mongoose Junction
2. Caneel Bay
3. Hawksnest Beach
4. Cinnamon Bay Trail
5. Annaberg Historic Trail
6. Emmaus Moravian Church
7. Coral Bay
8. Don Carlos Mexican Seafood Cantina
9. Hyatt Regency St. John

9059

After you pass Shipwreck Landing, the road is passable for only another five or six miles. If you want, you can sightsee for a few miles along the eastern coastline (there are some churches and houses along the way), but eventually you'll have to retrace your route.

Road signs on this end of the island are notoriously bad, so it's wise to ask directions at one of the Coral Bay bars, restaurants, or shops before making any firm conclusions about road conditions.

Backtrack north along Coral Bay to a point near the Emmaus Moravian Church (see 6), which you'll see in the distance. At the cluster of restaurant signs, turn left onto Route 10 West (Centerline Road), which has high-altitude views in all directions as you follow it back toward Cruz Bay. (An alternate, although much steeper, way is Route 108, which merges later with Route 10 West.)

Within seven or eight miles, Route 10 merges with Route 104 (Gifft Hill Road) just after the island's only hospital, the St. John Myrah Keating Smith Community Health Clinic. Take Route 104, and begin one of the steepest descents with the greatest number of blind curves of your driving tour. (Use low gear whenever possible, and honk around blind curves.) When the land levels off, you'll see, on your left, the entrance to one of the most imaginative pieces of modern architecture on the island, the deluxe postmodern:

**9. Hyatt Regency St. John.** If you're a gardening or architecture enthusiast, stop in for a look at a hotel whose inspirations included ancient Mesopotamia, colonial Denmark, and the coast of California. What makes all of this even more impressive is the fact that it was built upon land that was considered unusable swampland only a few years ago. A staff member will direct you to the hotel's scattering of bars (perhaps the Poolside Splash Bar) for a midafternoon quaff.

From here, your return to Cruz Bay involves only a short drive along Route 104, through a slightly urbanized periphery of private homes.

## 6 Sports A to Z

Don't visit St. John to play golf. Rather, anticipate some of the best snorkeling, scuba diving, swimming, fishing, hiking, sailing, and underwater photography in the Caribbean. The island is known for its coral-sand beaches; winding mountain roads; trails past old, bush-covered sugarcane plantations; and hidden coves.

### BEACHES

✪ **Trunk Bay** on the northwest coast of the island, is the biggest attraction on St. John and a beach lover's find. Trouble is the word is out. It's likely to be overcrowded, and there are pickpockets. Against a backdrop of sea grape and palm, the beach has lifeguards and offers rentals, such as snorkeling gear. Beginning snorkelers in particular are attracted to its underwater trail near the shore. Both taxis and safari buses meet the ferry as it docks at Cruz Bay from Red Hook on St. Thomas. Round-trip passage is provided to Trunk Bay, where most people are headed.

**Caneel Bay,** stamping ground of the rich and famous, has seven beautiful beaches on its 170 acres—but only one open to the public. That's **Hawksnest Beach,** a little gem of white sand beloved by St. Johnians. The beach is a bit narrow and windy but beautiful, as filmmakers long ago discovered. Close to the

## Nature Walks

Home of the largest U.S. National Park in the Caribbean, St. John is blessed with over 120 of clearly marked walking paths. At least 20 of these trails originate from designated points along either the North Shore Road (Route 20) or from points along the island's main east-to-west artery, Centerline Road (Route 10). Each trail's origin is marked, and each presents a pre-planned itinerary which usually lasts from 10 minutes to two hours. This part of St. John is moist and semitropical.

Another series of hikes traversing the more arid eastern section of St. John originate at clearly marked points along the island's southeastern tip off of Route 107. Many of the trails cross the grounds of 18th-century plantations, often circum-navigating ruined schoolhouses, rum distilleries, molasses factories, and great houses, many of them verdantly overgrown with encroaching vines and trees.

Maps of the island's hiking trails are readily available from the National Park Headquarters at Cruz Bay (see "On Your Own," above). One of our favorite tours requires only about a half-mile stroll (about 30 minutes round trip, not including stop) and departs from clearly marked points along the island's north coast, near the junction of Routes 10 and 20. Identified by the National Park Service as trail no. 10 (The Annaberg Historic Trail), it crosses partially restored ruins of an 18th-century house overlooking the island's north coast. Signs along the way give historical and botanical data.

If you want to prolong your experience, trail no. 11 (The Leinster Bay Trail), begins near the point where trail no. 10 ends. Following the edge of Watermelon Bay, it leads past Mangrove swamps and coral inlets rich with plant and marine life, markers identify some of the plants and animals.

---

road are barbecue grills, and there are portable toilets. Safari buses and taxis from Cruz Bay will take you along the North Shore Road.

The campgrounds of **Cinnamon Bay** and **Maho Bay** (see "Accommodations," above) both have their own beaches where forest rangers sometimes have to remind visitors to put their bathing suits back on. Snorkelers find good reefs here. Changing rooms and showers are available.

**Salt Pond Bay** is known to locals but often missed by visitors. The bay here is tranquil, but there are no facilities. The Ram Head Trail, which begins here and wind for a mile, leads to a panoramic belvedere overlooking the bay.

# SPORTS

## HIKING

Hiking is popular here, and a network of trails covers the National Park. We, however, suggest a tour by Jeep first, just to get your bearings. At the Visitor's Center at Cruz Bay (see "Organized Tours" under "Attractions," above), ask for a free trail map of the park. It's best to set out with someone experienced in the mysteries of the island. Both **Maho Bay** and **Cinnamon Bay** conduct nature walks (see "Frommer's Nature Notes," above). For more information on specific trains, see "Nature Walks," above.

## TENNIS

**Caneel Bay** (☎ 776-6111) has seven courts and a pro shop. The courts aren't lit at night, and nonguests are not welcome. There are two public courts at Cruz Bay. **Hyatt Regency St. John,** Great Cruz Bay (☎ 693-8000), has six tennis courts, all lit at night.

## WATERSPORTS

St. John's warm, sparkling, and clear water is ideal for all water sports. **Cinnamon Bay Watersports Center,** on Cinnamon Bay Beach (☎ 776-6330), offers windsurfing, kayaking, and sailing.

The windsurfing here is superlative, both for the beginner and the expert. High-quality equipment is available for all levels, even for kids. You can rent a board at $12 an hour; a two-hour introductory lesson costs $40.

Want to paddle to a secluded beach, explore a nearby island with an old Danish ruin, and jump overboard anytime you like for snorkeling or swimming? Then try a kayak; one- and two-person kayaks are available for rent at $10 to $17 per hour.

You can also sail away in a 12- or 14-foot Hobie mono-hull sailboat, which rents for $20 to $30 per hour.

Bicycles, though landbound are also available at $10 per hour. While St. John's steep hills and off-road trails can challenge the best of riders, there are more moderate rides to the ruins at Annaberg or the beaches at Maho, Francis, Leinster, or Watermelon Bay.

You can also take half- and full-day boat charters, including trips to The Baths at Virgin Gorda on Tuesday. The cost of this full-day adventure is $65 per person. An Around St. John Snorkel Excursion costs $40 per person, and a Sunset Cocktail Cruise also goes for $40 per person. Call Captain Robert Conn at 776-6462 or 771-3996 for more details.

You can obtain snorkeling equipment from the **Watersports Beach Shop,** part of the Cinnamon Bay Watersports, for $4 per day.

Divers can ask about scuba packages at **Low Key Watersports,** Wharfside Village (☎ 693-8999, or 800/835-7718). All wreck dives are two-tank, two-location dives. A one-tank dive costs $55 per person, with night dives going for $65. Snorkel tours are also available at $25 per person. The center uses its own custom-built dive boats and offers water-sports gear, including masks, fins, snorkels, and dive skins. It also arranges day-sailing charters and deep-sea sportfishing.

**Cruz Bay Watersports,** Cruz Bay (☎ 776-6234), is a PADI and NAUI five-star diving center on St. John. Certifications, arranged through a divemaster, cost $350 to $495. The center operates four custom dive boats every day of the year run by a staff of 10 instructors. Certification classes are offered daily; there are also daily two-tank reef dives with all the necessary dive gear for $70 to $78. Beginner scuba lessons start at $65, wreck dives (Wednesday and Friday), night dives, and dive packages are also available.

# 7 Shopping

Compared to St. Thomas, the shopping on St. John isn't stellar, but it's interesting. The boutiques and shops of **Cruz Bay** are quite special. Most of the shops are clustered at **Mongoose Junction,** a woodsy area beside the roadway, about a five-minute walk left (or northeast) from the ferry dock. In addition to shops, this complex also has some good restaurants (see "Dining," above).

## Bamboula
Mongoose Junction. ☎ **693-8699.**

Bamboula has an exotic and very appealing collection of gifts from Guatemala, Haiti, India, Indonesia, and Central Africa.

## The Canvas Factory
Cruz Bay. ☎ **776-6196.**

This shop produces its own handmade, rugged, and colorful canvas bags in the factory at Mongoose Junction. Their products range from canvas sailing hats to handsome luggage. Among the many items for sale is an extensive line of island-made 100% cotton clothing.

## The Clothing Studio
Mongoose Junction. ☎ **776-6585.**

At the Caribbean's oldest hand-painted-clothing studio (in operation since 1978), you can watch talented artists create original designs on fine tropical clothing, including swimwear; daytime and evening clothing; and articles for babies, children, men, and women. They will ship items around the world.

## Donald Schnell Studio
Mongoose Junction. ☎ **776-6420,** or 800/253-7107.

This working studio and gallery features one of the finest collections of handmade pottery, sculpture, and blown glass in the Caribbean. Especially noted for their rough-textured coral work, the artists here can be seen producing their crafts daily. Water fountains are a specialty item, as are lighting fixtures and signs. The coral pottery dinnerware is also unique and popular. Go in and discuss any particular design you may have in mind; they enjoy designing to please customers. The studio will mail works all over the world.

## Fabric Mill
Mongoose Junction. ☎ **776-6194.**

This shop features silk-screened and batik fabrics from around the world. Vibrant rugs and linens for the bed, bath, and table are the perfect items to bring home. Whimsical soft sculpture, sarongs, scarves, and handbags are also made in the studio of the shop.

## Pusser's of the West Indies
Wharfside Village, Cruz Bay. ☎ **693-8489.**

Before you set sail for St. Thomas, pay a visit to Wharfside Village, just a few steps from the ferry dock, and explore this pastel complex of courtyards, alleys, and shady patios with boutiques, restaurants, fast-food joints, and bars.

Pusser's offers a large collection of classically designed travel and adventure clothing, along with unusual accessories. Clothing for women, men, and children is displayed, including T-shirts carrying Pusser's colorful emblem.

## R and I Patton Goldsmithing
Cruz Bay. ☎ **776-6548.**

R and I Patton Goldsmithing has been on the island since 1973. Located at the entrance to Mongoose Junction, it has a large selection of island-designed jewelry in sterling, gold, and precious stones.

### The Shop at Caneel Bay

Caneel Bay Resort, Caneel Bay. ☎ **776-6111.**

The shop's location within a palatial outbuilding on the manicured grounds of the most legendary resort on St. John guarantees both an upscale clientele and an upscale assortment of merchandise. Scattered over two simple, elegant floors are the usual drugstore items, books, sundries, and handcrafts you'd expect at a Caribbean resort hotel, as well as some unusual artworks and pieces of expensive jewelry. There are also racks of resortwear and sportswear for men, women, and children.

## 8  St. John After Dark

Bring a good book. St. John is not St. Thomas after dark, and everybody here seems to want to keep it that way. Most people are content to have a long leisurely dinner and then head for bed.

Among the hotels, the **Hyatt Regency St. John** in season has the most activity, including live music for dancing. The crowd at **Caneel Bay** (especially the older guests, attracted to the place in winter) tends to be conservative, and likes to retire early. There are sometimes island events, such as a fish fry—ask at the tourist office (see "Orientation," earlier in this chapter).

Among the popular bars of Cruz Bay, **Pusser's** at Wharfside Village has the most convivial atmosphere. The **Caneel Bay Bar,** at the Caneel Bay resort (☎ **776-6111**), open daily from 11am to 11:30pm, presents live music nightly from 8:30 to 11pm. The most popular drinks (from $4) include a Cool Caneel (local rum with sugar, lime, and anisette) and the trademark of the house, a Plantation Freeze (lime and orange juice with three different kinds of rum, bitters, and nutmeg).

# 6

# The U.S. Virgin Islands: St. Croix

**M**easuring 84 square miles, St. Croix is the largest of the U.S. Virgin Islands. Columbus named it Santa Cruz (Holy Cross) when he stopped here on November 14, 1493. Columbus anchored his ship off the north shore but was driven away by the spears, arrows, and axes of the Caribs.

Despite the efforts of the Caribs to keep them out, settlers began arriving—first the Dutch, who were driven out by the English, then the Spanish, who were kicked out by the French. The latter laid claim to the island in 1650.

The Danes purchased St. Croix in 1773, slave labor and sugarcane fields by the island's during the golden era of both planters and pirates. The sugar boom went bust due to eventual slave uprisings, the introduction of the sugar beet in Europe, and the slave emancipation of 1848. Even though seven different flags have flown over St. Croix, the nearly two-and-a-half centuries of Danish influence marked the island.

Today, tourists flock to St. Croix for some of the best beaches in the Virgin Islands and for its ideal weather. At the east end, which, incidentally, is the easternmost point of the United States, the terrain is rocky and arid. The west end is lusher, with a rain forest of mango, mahogany, tree ferns, and dangling lianas. Between the two extremes are rolling hills, pastures, and, increasingly, miles of condos.

## 1 Orientation

### ARRIVING
### BY PLANE

**American Airlines** (☎ **800/433-7300**) currently offers the most frequent and most reliable flights to St. Croix. Passengers who want night flights go through one of the airline's many connections from either JFK or from Newark, New Jersey through San Juan, Puerto Rico. From San Juan, there are about eight nonstop American Eagle flights daily to St. Croix.

There is one flight daily to St. Croix from Miami, with one stop (but no change of plane) in St. Thomas. A daily nonstop flight to St. Thomas departs from New York's JFK daily at 9:15am, with continuing service to St. Croix.

## What's Special About St. Croix

Beaches
- Cormorant Beach, 5 miles northwest of Christiansted, with some 1,200 feet of white sands and palm trees.
- Sandy Point, the biggest beach in the U.S. Virgin Islands, with shallow, calm waters.
- Cane Bay, adjoining Route 80 on the north shore—a favorite of snorkelers and divers attracted to its rolling waves and coral gardens, with a "dropoff wall."

Great Towns/Villages
- Christiansted, capital of St. Croix, a seaport filled with handsome 18th-century Danish Colonial buildings.
- Frederiksted, a gingerbread-studded monument to the former Danish mercantile prosperity.

Historic Buildings
- Government House, in Christiansted, former seat of the Danish governor-general and a courtyard evocative of old- fashioned Europe.
- Fort Christiansvaern, built on the foundations of a 1645 French fortress, offering fine harbor views from the battlements.
- Estate Whim Plantation Museum, a unique sugar plantation great house, a vestige of the slavery era.

Unless they go through Miami or San Juan, passengers from the Midwest and Middle South often transfer through American's hub in Raleigh-Durham, North Carolina. From Raleigh-Durham, a daily nonstop flight, as well as a daily one-stop flight (with a touchdown in St. Thomas but no change of plane) both continue to St. Croix.

American's least expensive round-trip fare to St. Croix from any of its departure points is a SuperSaver fare, requiring a 14-day advance payment, a delay of between 3 to 30 days before activating the return portion, and a payment of a $35 penalty for any alterations in the itinerary. From New York, this fare is between $353 and $446 round-trip, depending on the season and the flight dates.

**Delta** (☎ 800/221-1212) offers daily flights to St. Croix from Atlanta. Flights usually touch down in St. Thomas before continuing on to St. Croix. From St. Croix, flights turn around and head back to their point of origin, stopping first in St. Thomas. Convenient connections are available through San Juan from virtually anywhere on Delta's vast network. Fares are competitive with those of American and sometimes match them dollar for dollar.

Travelers from the South and Midwest have better access to St. Thomas and St. Croix since **United Airlines** (☎ 800/241-6522) formed an alliance with **Sunaire Express Airlines** (☎ 800/495-2840). Sunaire Express is a St. Croix–based commuter airline. The two companies agreed to a code-share that lists Sunaire flights from Puerto Rico to the U.S. Virgin Islands as connecting United Airlines flights. Passengers flying from Chicago, Miami, and other United Airlines points of origin to Puerto Rico are able to board any of the 18 daily flights to St. Croix and St. Thomas on Sunaire. Under the agreement, the carriers coordinate their schedules and provide quick transfers of passengers and luggage.

> ## ❓ Did You Know?
>
> • Columbus was driven away by a rain of arrows by the Carib Indians.
> • Under FDR's New Deal, the federal government produced a rum here called "Government House." FDR designed the label himself.
> • Alexander Hamilton once worked in a hardware store on St. Croix.

**Virgin Islands Paradise Airways** (☎ 800/299-USVI) flies daily to St. Thomas and St. Croix; nonstop flights originate in Miami and Newark, New Jersey. A professional crew, clad in island-style clothing, serves Virgin Island cuisine, including pâtés and Cruzan rum, to guests aboard the 727-200s. Caribbean music serenades passengers, while a TV screen provides previews of places to see and things to do in St. Thomas, St. John, and St. Croix. *Black Enterprise* magazine listed the airline's parent company, NavCom Systems, Inc., 59th on their list of 100 top black-owned companies.

Transit time, including ground time, to St. Croix from New York is 4 hours, from Chicago $5^1/_2$ hours, from Miami $3^1/_2$ hours, and from the nearby island of Puerto Rico, 20 minutes.

*A final reminder:* Often, an airline can arrange discounted hotel accommodations in conjunction with air passage if both are booked simultaneously. Ask an airline reservations agent to explain the various options.

## BY BOAT

There is no ferry from St. Thomas to St. Croix. However, many cruise ships stop over in St. Croix (see "Getting There," Chapter 3).

## ISLAND LAYOUT

St. Croix has only two sizeable towns: Christiansted on the north-central shoreline and Frederiksted in the southwest. The airport on St. Croix, Alexander Hamilton Airport, opens onto the south coast, lying directly west of the Hess Oil Refinery, the major industry on the island. There is no road that encircles the coast.

To continue east from Christiansted, take Route 82 or the East End Road. Route 75 will take you west from Christiansted through the central heartland all the way to the Hess Oil Refinery. Melvin H. Evans Highway, Route 66, runs along the southern part of the island. You can connect with this route in Christiansted and head west all the way to Frederiksted.

### FREDERIKSTED

Frederiksted is so tiny that it's almost impossible to get lost. Most visitors head for the central historic district, where the Frederiksted Pier juts out into the sea. The two major streets, both of which run parallel to the water, are Strand Street and King Street. Farther back are Queen Street, Prince Street, Hospital Street, and New Street, the last of which runs beside the cemetery. These streets are crisscrossed by such side streets as Queen Cross Street, King Cross Street, Hill Street, and Market Street.

### CHRISTIANSTED

The historic district—the only part of the capital of interest to most visitors—is in the center bordering Veterans Drive, which runs along the waterfront. The district is split by Kronprindsens Gade (Route 308), which runs completely through the district. Kronprindsens Gade (also called Main Street) is connected to Veterans Drive by a number of shop-filled little streets, including Gutters Gade, Trompeter Gade, and Raadets Gade. The Visitor's Information Center lies at the end of King Street (Kongens Gade) near the water.

Nearby Fort Christiansvaern also opens onto the water. The center of Christiansted can get very congested at times, and driving around is difficult because of the one-way streets. It is usually more practical to park your car and cover the relatively small district on foot. You will find open-air parking on both sides of Fort Christiansvaern.

### FINDING AN ADDRESS

In both Christiansted and Frederiksted, buildings are numbered consecutively on one side, stretching all the way to the limits of these towns. Then the numbers "cross the street" and begin numbering on the opposite side. That means that even and odd numbers appear on the same side of the street. The numbering system begins in Christiansted at the waterfront. In Frederiksted, the first number appears at the north end of town for streets running frederh-south. Numbering begins at the waterfront for streets running east-west.

## 2 Getting Around

### BY TAXI OR BUS

At the airport, you'll find official **taxi** rates posted. Per-person rates require a minimum of two passengers; one passenger pays double the fares listed. Expect to pay about $5 per person from the airport to Christiansted and about $8 for one or two from the airport to Frederiksted. Because the cabs are unmetered, be sure to agree on rate before you get in.

The **St. Croix Taxicab Association,** which offers door-to-door service, can be reached by calling **778-1088.**

Air-conditioned **buses** run between Christiansted and Frederiksted about every 40 minutes daily between the hours of 6am and 9pm. Originating at Tide Village to the east of Christiansted, buses go along Route 75 to the Golden Rock Shopping Center. Then they make their way to Route 70, with stopovers at the Sunny Isle Shopping Center, La Reine Shopping Center, St. George Village Botanical Garden, and Whim Plantation Museum before reaching Frederiksted. Bus service is also available from the airport to both Christiansted and Frederiksted. The fare is $1. For more information, call **773-7746.**

---

### 🕐 In Their Footsteps

**Alexander Hamilton** (1755–1804) American statesman from the West Indies who served brilliantly in the American Revolution. He wrote many of the articles contained in the Federalist Papers and became Secretary of the Treasury to George Washington. He was noted for both his literary and oratorical skills. **Birthplace:** The British-held island of Nevis on January 11, 1755. **Residence:** St. Croix. **Final Days:** In a duel fought with Aaron Burr, Hamilton was mortally wounded and died on July 12, 1804.

## BY CAR, MOTORCYCLE, OR SCOOTER

This is a suitable means of exploring for some, but know that if you're going into the "bush country," you'll find the roads very difficult. Sometimes the government smoothes the roads out before the rain season begins, but they deteriorate rapidly.

St. Croix offers moderately priced **car rentals.** Cars with automatic transmissions and air conditioning are available, even among some of the lowest-priced rentals.

However, because of the island's higher than normal accident rates (which is partly the result of tourists forgetting that they have to drive on the left-hand side of the road), insurance costs are a bit higher than usual. **Budget** (☎ **809/778-9636,** or **800/472-3325), Hertz** (☎ **809/778-1402,** or **800/654-3001),** and **Avis** (☎ **809/778-9365,** or **800/331-2112)** all maintain their headquarters at the island's airport; look for their kiosks near the baggage claim areas.

Each of the three companies offers Suzuki Swifts, Suzuki Esteems, and Ford Escorts, usually with automatic transmission and air conditioning. Rates vary from company to company. During a recent spot check, Budget was offering cars for $198 to $270 for five to six days; Hertz, $240 to $370 weekly; and Avis $189 to $269 weekly.

To rent a car at any of these companies, you must be between the ages of 25 and 70 or 75 years old and present a valid driver's license and a credit card at the time of rental.

Collision-damage insurance can be arranged for an additional fee of between $9.95 and $11.95 a day, depending on the company. Considering the dangers, the bad lighting, and most tourists' unfamiliarity with left-hand driving, it's a wise investment. In certain instances, your credit-card issuer might automatically have grant you collision-damage protection if you pay for the rental with the appropriate credit card. Verify coverage in advance directly with your credit-card issuer. Additional forms of supplementary insurance offered by each of the companies include personal accident insurance.

Remember to *drive on the left* and to take more precautions than usual because of the unfamiliarity of the roads. A 35 m.p.h. speed limit is called for in most rural areas, certain parts of the major artery, Route 66, the Melvin H. Evans Highway, are 55 m.p.h. In towns and urban areas, the limit is 20 m.p.h.

You can rent motorcycles and scooters at **A & B Honda Motorcycles & Scooter Rentals,** 26 Bassin Triangle (☎ **809/778-8567),** in Christiansted.

## ON FOOT

St. Croix is too big to tour on foot, and you'll need a rented car or taxi to get about in lieu of the totally inadequate public transportation. The historic districts of Christiansted and Frederiksted, however, are relatively small and can only be explored on foot.

## FAST FACTS: St. Croix

**American Express**   The American Express travel representative is Southerland, Chandler's Wharf, Gallows Bay (☎ **773-9500).**

**Area Code**   The area code is **809.** You can call direct from the U.S. mainland.

**Banks**    Several major banks are represented in St. Croix. Most banks are open Monday through Thursday from 9am to 3pm and Friday from 9am to 4:30pm. First Pennsylvania Bank has a branch at 12 King's St. (☎ 773-0440), in Christiansted.

**Bookstores**    The Writer's Block, 36C Strand St. (☎ 773-5101), in Christiansted, will supply you with a selection of titles to read on the beach or around the pool.

**Business Hours**    Typical business hours are Monday through Friday from 9am to 5pm, Saturday from 9am to 1pm.

**Car Rentals**    See "Getting Around," earlier in this chapter.

**Climate**    See "Where to Go," in Chapter 3.

**Crime**    At night, parts of Christiansted and Frederiksted are considered unsafe. Stick to the heart of Christiansted, exercise caution, and avoid wandering anywhere around Frederiksted at night.

**Currency**    See "Visitor Information, Entry Requirements & Money," in Chapter 3.

**Customs**    See "Visitor Information, Entry Requirements & Money," in Chapter 3.

**Documents Required**    See "Visitor Information, Entry Requirements & Money," in Chapter 3.

**Dentist**    Go to the Sunny Isle Medical Center, Sunny Isle (☎ 778-6356). Call first for an appointment.

**Doctors**    A good local doctor is Dr. Frank Bishod, Sunny Isle Medical Center (☎ 778-0069). Call for an appointment.

**Drugstores**    Try the Golden Rock Pharmacy, Golden Rock Shopping Center (☎ 773-7666), or People's Drugstore, Sunny Isle Shopping Center (☎ 778-5537), which also has a more convenient branch at 1A King St. (☎ 778-7355), in Christiansted.

**Embassies and Consulates**    St. Croix has no embassies or consulates. Go to one of the local U.S. government agencies if you have a problem.

**Emergencies**    Police, **915;** fire, **921;** ambulance, **922.**

**Etiquette**    Cruzans tend to be fairly conservative about dress. When walking the streets or visiting public places such as restaurants, don't appear in skimpy swimwear.

**Eyeglasses**    The best place to go is Southern Optical, Sunny Isle Professional Building, Sunny Isle (☎ 778-6565).

**Hairdressers**    The best place is Spencer's Beauty, Hair & Health Spa, 14A La Grande Princesse (☎ 773-1000), in The Pink Building on Northside Road, Route 75, in Christiansted. It's open daily from 9am to 8pm. Call for an appointment. It has a hair salon, a nail salon, and a center offering skin and body care. All kinds of hair care, including textured perms, are also offered at Head Quarters, Caravelle Hotel, Queen Cross Street (☎ 773-2465), in Christiansted.

**Hitchhiking**    It isn't illegal, but it isn't commonly practiced. You'll probably wait a long time for a ride. We don't recommend it.

**Holidays** See "When to Go," in Chapter 3.

**Hospitals** The principal facility is St. Croix Hospital, Estate Ruby (☎ **778-6311**).

**Information** The U.S. Virgin Islands Division of Tourism has offices in Christiansted at The Old Scalehouse, King Street (☎ **773-0495**), and at the Customs House Building, Strand Street (☎ **772-0357**), in Frederiksted.

**Laundry** Try Tropical Cleaners & Launderers, 16–17 King Cross (☎ **773-3637**), in Christiansted.

**Liquor Laws** You must be at least 21 years of age to purchase liquor.

**Lost Property** Go to the police station (see below).

**Mail** Postal rates are the same as on the U.S. mainland.

**Maps** Tourist offices provide free maps to the island. *St. Croix This Week,* which is distributed free to cruise-ship passengers and air passengers, has detailed maps of Christiansted, Frederiksted, and the entire island, pinpointing individual attractions, hotels, shops, and restaurants. If you plan to do extensive touring of the island, purchase *The Official Road Map of the U.S. Virgin Islands,* available at island bookstores.

**Newspapers and Magazines** Newspapers, such as *The Miami Herald,* are flown into St. Croix daily. St. Croix also has its own newspaper, *St. Croix Avis. Time* and *Newsweek* are widely sold as well. Your best source of local information is *St. Croix This Week,* which is distributed free by the tourist offices.

**Photographic Needs** V.I. Express Photo, 2A Strand St. (☎ **773-2009**), in Christiansted, offers one-hour photo finishing. You might also try Fast Foto, 1116 King St. (☎ **773-6727**), in Christiansted.

**Police** The Police Headquarters (☎ **915**) is on Market Street in Christiansted.

**Post Office** The U.S. Post Office is on Company Street (☎ **773-3586**), in Christiansted.

**Radio and TV** Local radio stations include WVGN-105FM and WJKC Isle 95 FM. The local television station is WSVI-TV Channel 8.

**Religious Services** Places of worship in Christiansted include Lutheran Church Lord God of Saboath, 52 King St. (☎ **773-1320**). In Frederiksted, St. Patrick's Catholic Church is at 5 Prince St. (☎ **772-0138**), and St. Paul's Anglican Church is at 28 Prince St. (☎ **772-5818**).

**Restrooms** There are few public restrooms, except at the major beaches and airport. Most people use the restrooms in commercial establishments, which, technically, businesses have a right to reserve for customers. In Christiansted, the National Park Service maintains some restrooms within the public park beside Fort Christiansvaern.

**Safety** St. Croix is safer than St. Thomas. Possessions should never be left unattended, especially on the beach. Exercise extreme caution at night around Christiansted and Frederiksted. Avoid night strolls along beaches or drives along little-used roads.

**Shoe Repair** Go to Rodriguez Shoe Repair, Bassin Triangle (no phone).

**Taxis** Summon a taxi by calling **778-0599** or **778-1088**.

**Telephone, Telex, and Fax**    A local call at a phone booth costs 25¢. You can dial direct to St. Croix from the mainland by using the 809 area code. Omit the 809 for local calls. The bigger hotels will send telex and fax, or you can go to the post office (see above).

**Tipping**    As a general rule, it is customary to tip 15%. Most hotels add a 10% to 15% surcharge to cover service. When in doubt, ask.

**Water**    Water is generally considered safe, but you are asked to conserve. If you have a delicate stomach, stick to bottled water.

**Yellow Pages**    See "Fast Facts: The U.S. Virgin Islands," in Chapter 3.

## 3  Accommodations

The charming old waterfront inns are at Christiansted, while the deluxe resorts lie mainly along the North Shore. You can also stay at a former plantation turned to better use, or in a unit in a condo complex. Rates for the most part are steep, and all rooms are subject to a 7.5% tax.

Hotels considered "very expensive" charge from $195 to $345 for a double room in winter. Those rated "expensive" ask upward of $180. Rooms in the "moderate" classification generally go for for $120 to $165 for doubles, although some units here can also climb much higher. "Inexpensive" hotels charge from $69 to $120 for a double.

In summer, St. Croix accommodations are better bargains, as hotels slash prices by about 20% to 50%.

For an explanation of the abbreviations AP, CP, EP, and MAP, see "Tips on Accommodations," in Chapter 3.

## NORTH SHORE
### VERY EXPENSIVE

**Buccaneer**
P.O. Box 25200, Rte. 82 (East End Rd.), Estate Shoys, Gallows Bay, St. Croix, USVI 00824. ☎ **809/773-2100**, or 800/255-3881. Fax 809/773-0010. 150 rms (all with bath). A/C TEL Rates (including breakfast): Winter, $175–$320 single; $195–$340 double; summer, $145–$215 single; $165–$235 double. AE, DC, MC, V. Parking: Free.

Located two miles east of Christiansted, this large, family-owned resort has been in operation since 1948. Its 340 acres contain three of the island's best beaches: Bogart, Cutlass, and Whistles.

The property was once a cattle ranch and a sugar plantation. Its first estate house, dating from the mid-17th century, stands near a freshwater swimming pool. Pink and patrician, the hotel offers a choice of accommodations in its main building or in one of the beachside properties. The baronially arched main building has a lobby opening onto a few terraces with a sea vista on two sides and Christiansted to the west. The interiors of the accommodations effectively use tropical furnishings to provide fresh, modern, comfortable bedrooms which range from deluxe to standard.

**Dining/Entertainment:** Breakfast and dinner are served at the Terrace Dining Room and at the Little Mermaid Restaurant. Lunch is also served at the Mermaid and the Grotto, where hamburgers and hot dogs are available. The hotel's gourmet restaurant, Brass Parrot, is recommended (see "Dining," below). There is entertainment nightly at the Terrace Lounge, with a variety of music ranging from Jimmy Hamilton's jazz to steel drums.

**Services:** The hotel offers the best sports program on St. Croix and arranges trips to Buck Island.

**Facilities:** Swimming pool, eight championship tennis courts, fitness center and health spa, 18-hole golf course, 2-mile jogging trail.

### Carambola Beach Resort

P.O. Box 3031, Kingshill, St. Croix, USVI 00851. ☎ **809/778-3800,** or 800/333-3333 in the U.S. and Canada. Fax 809/778-1682. 153 rms. A/C TV TEL Rates: Winter, $205–$345 single or double; off-season, $178–$280 single or double. Breakfast $12 extra. AE, MC, V. Parking: Free.

Set on 28 acres above Davis Bay on the island's sparsely populated north shore, the resort is a 30-minute drive from Christiansted. The hotel reopened in 1993 after renovations and three-year closing after it was done in by Hurricane Hugo. Today, it's owned by the Kentucky-based Sargasso Corporation and is operated as a Radisson. It is the island's only chain hotel and one of the largest properties in St. Croix. The resort sometimes offers package tours. It is adjacent to the well-known golf course designed by Robert Trent Jones, Sr.

Guests are housed in red-roofed, two-story outbuildings, each of which contains six units. Accommodations are furnished in rattan and wicker, with pastel colors and a partially concealed balcony overlooking either the garden or sea.

**Dining/Entertainment:** Diners can choose from a trio of restaurants which are are open to the public. The Saman Room offers breakfast and lunch daily; dinner is served only on Sunday, Monday, and Wednesday nights. In the air-conditioned Mahogany Room, dinner is served on Tuesday, Thursday, and Saturday nights. Sandwiches and salads are offered daily in the New York Deli, and the hotel's Sunday brunch from 11am to 2pm has already become an island tradition. On Friday night there is a pirate's buffet from 7 to 9pm.

**Services:** Room service, babysitting, concierge for the arrangement of tours, car rentals.

**Facilities:** A large swimming pool, four turf tennis courts, 18-hole golf course.

### ✪ Cormorant Beach Club

4126 La Grande Princesse, St. Croix, USVI 00820. ☎ **809/778-8920,** or 800/548-4460. Fax 809/778-9218. 34 rms, 4 suites (all with bath). A/C TEL Rates: Winter, $185–$200 single; $210–$230 double; $245–$265 triple; $295 suite. Off-season, $120–$160 single; $140–$190 double; $165–$230 triple; $300 suite. AE, DC, MC, V. Parking: Free.

Surrounded by king palms on a 12-acre site about three miles northwest of Christiansted on Route 75, this resort strikes a perfect balance between seclusion and accessibility. Long Reef, one of the better-known zoological phenomena of the Caribbean, lies a few hundred feet from the hotel's sandy beachfront. The hotel's social life revolves around a wood-sheathed, high-ceilinged clubhouse, whose walls were removed to give guests a firsthand taste of the salty air. Off the central core are a library, the largest freshwater pool on St. Croix, and a tasteful, airy dining room where half a dozen large fan-shaped windows offer a view of the beach.

The rooms are located in well-maintained outbuildings. Each contains a spacious bath, a tasteful decor of cane and wicker furniture, and bouquets of seasonal flowers. In winter, children under five are politely discouraged.

**Dining/Entertainment:** Dinners, served à la carte, are elegantly lighthearted affairs. The food is among the best on the island (see "Dining," below). Weekly steel bands and dance combos are regularly featured. You can stay here on the CBC (Cormorant Beach Club) meal plan including a gourmet breakfast, complete lunch, and all drinks until 5pm for only $37.50 per person per day. The AIP (All-Inclusive Plan) adds to the CBC plan an open dinner menu and all beverages until closing for $77.50 per person per day. Thursday night is Caribbean Grill Night with a buffet and entertainment, and the Sunday brunch is rated the best on the island.

**Services:** Laundry; arrangements for golf, horseback riding, sailing, and scuba diving.

**Facilities:** Freshwater swimming pool, two tennis courts, snorkeling, croquet, library just off the lobby.

# EAST END
## VERY EXPENSIVE

### Villa Madeleine

P.O. Box 3109, Gallows Bay, St. Croix, USVI 00822. ☎ **809/778-7377,** or 800/548-4461. Fax 809/773-7515. 43 villas (all with bath). A/C TV TEL Rates: Winter, $425 two-bedroom villa for four; summer, $300 two-bedroom villa for four. AE, DC, MC, V. Parking: Free.

Villa Madeleine was built in 1990 on a $6^1/_2$-acre plot of some of the most desirable land on the island. The hotel is about 8 miles east of Christiansted at the pinnacle of the rocky spine that divides the east end of the island into north- and south-facing watersheds. Its focal point is a great house whose Chippendale balconies and foursquare proportions recall the Danish Colonial era. The landscaped property is dotted with serpentine paths and flowering shrubbery.

Villas are completely detached structures with their own pools. Thanks to the sloping terrain, each villa is hidden from the others and contains a well-equipped kitchen, queen-size or twin beds, marble bathrooms, and an elegant decor. Beach lovers will willingly travel one-third of a mile to the nearest beach.

Children under 12 years of age are discouraged.

**Dining/Entertainment:** Café Madeleine (see "Dining," below) serves Italian cuisine. The resort also has a piano bar with nautical decorations and a billiard table.

**Services:** Concierge, room service, daily chamber and pool service, laundry, babysitting.

**Facilities:** Small library with writing tables, game room for cards and billiards, access to nearby tennis courts.

# CHRISTIANSTED
## MODERATE

### ⑤ Anchor Inn

58 King St., Christiansted, St. Croix, USVI 00820. ☎ **809/773-4000,** or 800/524-2030. Fax 809/773-4408. 31 units (all with bath). A/C MINIBAR TV TEL Rates: Winter, $95–$125 single; $115–$145 double; $135–$165 triple; summer, $80–$95 single; $90–$105 double; $110–$125 triple. Extra person $20. Breakfast $6 extra. AE, DC, MC, V. Parking: Free.

One of the few hotels on the waterfront, the Anchor Inn is set in a quiet courtyard close to the Government House and the Old Danish Customs House. It's also right in the heart of the shopping district. The space is so compact and intimate that you might not expect it holds 31 units, each with a refrigerator, radio, and small porch. A few larger units (without porches) have king- and queen-size beds;

some are small and have no view. Furnishings are conventional but warm. Directly on the waterfront there are a sundeck and small swimming pool, as well as the Anchor Inn's own boardwalk, from which catamarans and glass-bottom boats run daily to Buck Island.

**Dining/Entertainment:** Antoine's Restaurant & Bar, on the hotel's second level, overlooks the historic harbor.

**Services:** Honeymoon and family package tours.

**Facilities:** Deep-sea fishing boats, scuba-dive shop.

### Caravelle

44A Queen Cross St., Christiansted, St. Croix, USVI 00820. ☎ **809/773-0687,** or 800/524-0410. Fax 809/778-7004. 43 rms (all with bath). A/C TV TEL Rates: Winter, $115–$125 single; $125–$135 double. Summer, $85–$95 single; $95–$105 double. Breakfast $6 extra. AE, DC, MC, V. Parking: Free.

The biggest hotel in the historic core of Christiansted, Caravelle usually caters to a clientele of international businesspeople who prefer to be near the center of town. There's an Andalusian-style fountain in the lobby, and the restaurant, Banana Bay Club, is a few steps away. Many sports activities, such as sailing, deep-sea fishing, snorkeling, scuba, golf, and tennis, can be arranged at the reception desk. A swimming pool and sundeck face the water, and all the shopping and activities of the town are close at hand. Accommodations, which are generally spacious and comfortably furnished, are priced according to their views.

### King Christian Hotel

59 King's Wharf, P.O. Box 3619, Christiansted, St. Croix, USVI 00822. ☎ **809/773-2285,** or 800/524-2012. Fax 809/773-9411. 39 rms (all with bath). A/C TV TEL Rates: Winter, $90–$120 single; $95–$130 double. Summer, $85–$95 single; $85–$102 double. AE, DC, MC, V. Parking: Public lot off King Street.

Dating from the days of Danish rule, this pink hotel stands on the harborfront in the center of Christiansted. Each of the 24 front rooms has two double beds or one king-size bed, a refrigerator, a room safe, and a private balcony overlooking the harbor. Fourteen no-frills economy-wing rooms have either two single beds or one king-size bed but no view or balcony.

You can relax on the sundeck, shaded patio, or in the freshwater pool. The staff will make arrangements for golf, tennis, horseback riding, and sightseeing tours, and there's a beach just a few hundred yards across the harbor, reached by ferry.

---

### 👪 Family-Friendly Hotels

**Anchor Inn** *(see p. 168)* This inn is a good choice for families who don't want to spend money on a rental car located in the heart of Christiansted, the hotel lets children under 12 stay free in a room with their parents. The inn is directly on the waterfront from which boats run to Buck Island.

**Colony Cove** *(see p. 174)* Families staying at Colony Cove have their own kitchens, clothes washers, and dryers. The hotel is near a beach and has a swimming pool.

**Chenay Bay Beach Resort** *(see p. 173)* Guests have their own cottages, with kitchenettes overlooking the Caribbean. The resort has a swimming pool and a fine beach nearby.

| Hotels of St. Croix at a Glance | Access for Disabled | Air Conditioning in Bedrooms | Childcare Facilities | Children Are Welcome | Convention Facilities | Credit Cards Accepted | Directly Beside Beach | Fitness Facilities | Golf Course Nearby | Live Entertainment | Marina Facilities | Restaurant & Bar | Spa Facilities | Swimming Pool | Tennis Courts | TV in Bedrooms | Watersports |
|---|---|---|---|---|---|---|---|---|---|---|---|---|---|---|---|---|---|
| Anchor Inn | | ✓ | | ✓ | | ✓ | | | | ✓ | | ✓ | | ✓ | | ✓ | |
| Buccaneer | ✓ | ✓ | | | ✓ | ✓ | ✓ | ✓ | ✓ | ✓ | | ✓ | ✓ | ✓ | ✓ | ✓ | ✓ |
| Cane Bay Reef | | | | ✓ | | ✓ | ✓ | | ✓ | | | ✓ | | ✓ | | | ✓ |
| Carambola | ✓ | ✓ | | ✓ | | ✓ | ✓ | | ✓ | ✓ | | ✓ | | ✓ | ✓ | ✓ | ✓ |
| Caravelle | | ✓ | | ✓ | | ✓ | | | | | | ✓ | | ✓ | | ✓ | |
| Chenay Bay | | ✓ | | ✓ | | ✓ | | | ✓ | | | ✓ | | ✓ | ✓ | | ✓ |
| Colony Cove | | ✓ | | ✓ | | ✓ | ✓ | | | | | ✓ | | ✓ | ✓ | ✓ | ✓ |
| Cormorant | ✓ | ✓ | | ✓ | | ✓ | ✓ | ✓ | ✓ | | | ✓ | | ✓ | ✓ | | ✓ |
| Danish Manor | | ✓ | | ✓ | | ✓ | | | | | | ✓ | | | | ✓ | |
| Hilty House | | | | | | | | | | | | | | ✓ | | | |
| King Christian Hotel | | ✓ | | ✓ | | ✓ | | | | | ✓ | ✓ | | ✓ | | ✓ | ✓ |
| Pink Fancy | | ✓ | | ✓ | | ✓ | | | | | | | | ✓ | | ✓ | |
| Sprat Hall Plantation | ✓ | ✓ | | ✓ | | ✓ | | | | | | ✓ | | | | ✓ | ✓ |
| Sugar Beach Condos | | ✓ | | ✓ | ✓ | ✓ | ✓ | | | | | | | ✓ | ✓ | | |
| The Frederiksted | | ✓ | | ✓ | | ✓ | | | | | | | | ✓ | | ✓ | |
| Villa Madeleine | | ✓ | | ✓ | | ✓ | | | ✓ | | | ✓ | | ✓ | | ✓ | |
| Waves at Cane Bay | ✓ | ✓ | | ✓ | | ✓ | ✓ | | ✓ | | | ✓ | | | | ✓ | ✓ |

Mile Mark Charters, a water-sports center, offers daily trips to Buck Island's famous snorkeling trail, as well as a complete line of water sports. Special events are organized on request. The hotel is also the headquarters of Dive St. Croix, which operates a 46-foot dive boat (see "Sports A to Z," below).

Also on the premises is the Chart House, one of the best restaurants on St. Croix, noted for its salad bar and steaks. It's an easy walk to several nearby cafés that serve breakfast.

## INEXPENSIVE

### ⓢ Danish Manor Hotel

2 Company St., Christiansted, St. Croix, USVI 00820. ☎ **809/773-1377,** or 800/524-2069. Fax 809/773-1913. 34 rms, 2 suites. A/C TV TEL Rates (including continental breakfast): Winter, $59–$85 single; $69–$95 double; $95–$130 suite; summer, $49–$85 single; $59–$85 double; $85–$100 suite. AE, DC, MC, V. Parking: Public lot off King Street.

Built around a Danish courtyard and a freshwater pool in the heart of town between King and Queen Streets, this compound combines the very old with the very new. The hotel was erected on the site of a counting house once used by the Danish West Indies Company. An L-shaped, three-story addition stands in the rear;

# St. Croix Accommodations/Sports

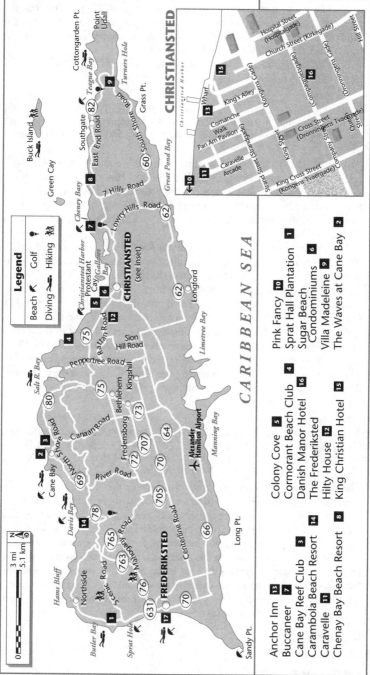

**Legend**

Beach | Golf | Diving | Hiking

**CHRISTIANSTED**

Anchor Inn **13**
Buccaneer **7**
Cane Bay Reef Club **3**
Carambola Beach Resort **14**
Caravelle **11**
Chenay Bay Beach Resort **8**

Colony Cove **5**
Cormorant Beach Club **4**
Danish Manor Hotel **16**
The Frederiksted **12**
Hilty House **12**
King Christian Hotel **15**

Pink Fancy **10**
Sprat Hall Plantation **1**
Sugar Beach Condominiums **6**
Villa Madeleine **9**
The Waves at Cane Bay **2**

8896

its spacious rooms have air conditioning and ceiling fans. All units overlook the courtyard, which is dominated by an ancient mahogany tree. The entrance to the courtyard is through old arches. Guests can swim at the beach in Christiansted harbor, about a five-minute ferry ride from the hotel.

**Dining/Entertainment:** The hotel has a courtyard bar for guests and the popular Italian/seafood restaurant Tutto Bene (see "Dining," below).

### ✪ Hilty House

P.O. Box 26077, Questa Verde Rd., Gallows Bay, St. Croix, USVI 00824. ☎ and fax **809/773-2594.** 4 rms (all with bath), 2 cottages. Rates (including continental breakfast): Winter, $75 single; $99 double; $105–$125 cottage; summer, $60 single; $80 double; $85–$95 cottage. No credit cards. Parking: Free.

Jacquie and Hugh Hoare-Ward own this bed and breakfast in a two-hundred-year-old building that was once a rum distillery. Hilty House is located on the east side of St. Croix atop a hill surrounded by mountains and hills. The airport, 7 miles away, a 15-minute ride; the nearest beach a 10-minute drive. Upon, their arrival, guests pass through a shaded courtyard to a set of iron gates that lead to the inn's gardens.

The plantation-style house is beautifully appointed with hand-painted Italian tiles. The interior has a high-ceilinged living room and an enormous fireplace that houses a spit. The master bedroom, the most lavish room, holds a four-poster bed and sunken shower over which hangs a chandelier. There are also two self-catering cottages that can be rented with a required minimum stay of three nights. The Danish Kitchen, one of the cottages, has a covered porch, TV, and telephone.

A continental breakfast is included in the room rates only, not in the cottage rates. Dinner, a three-course meal with a set price of $25, is only served on Monday nights. Guests can swim in the large pool decorated with hand-painted tiles. The atmosphere is very homey, and the place gives off a warm feeling. No children under 12 are allowed, and no more than three people are allowed in one room.

### ⓢ Pink Fancy

27 Prince St., Christiansted, St. Croix, USVI 00820. ☎ **809/773-8460,** or 800/524-2045. Fax 809/773-6448. 12 units (all with bath). A/C TV TEL Rates (including continental breakfast): Winter, $75–$90 single; $90–$120 double. Summer, $65–$75 single; $75–$90 double. Children under 12 stay free in parents' room. AE, MC, V.

The Pink Fancy underwent restoration to become this small, unique private hotel. Although the hotel is located in a somewhat seedy part of Christiansted, it lies within walking distance of restaurants, duty-free shops, and historical sites. The oldest part of the four-building complex is a 1780 Danish town house. Years ago, the building served as a private club for wealthy planters. Fame came to the structure when Jane Gottlieb, the Ziegfeld Follies star, opened it as a hotel in 1948. In the 1950s, the hotel became a mecca for writers and artists, including playwright Noël Coward. All the rooms are equipped with kitchenettes. A freshwater swimming pool forms the center of the courtyard. Other than breakfast and a 24-hour honor bar, you're on your own for meals.

## FREDERIKSTED
### MODERATE

#### Sprat Hall Plantation

Rte. 63, P.O. Box 695, Frederiksted, St. Croix, USVI 00841. ☎ **809/772-0305,** or 800/843-3584. 17 units (all with bath). A/C TV Rates (including continental breakfast):

Winter, $110–$120 single; $120–$130 double; $150 suite (without breakfast); $170 cottage (without breakfast); $160 great house room. Summer, $90–$100 single; $100–$110 double; $130 suite (without breakfast); $170 cottage (without breakfast); $140 great house room. AE. Parking: Free.

This resort, located 1 mile north of Frederikstad, is the oldest plantation great house (and the only French-built plantation house left intact) in the Virgin Islands. Dating from the island's French occupation of 1650 to 1690, the plantation set on 20 acres fringed by private white sandy beaches. The plantation has room for about 40 people, depending on how many guests use the cottage units.

The units in the great house have been designated for nonsmokers because of the value of their antiques. An annex originally built in the 1940s contains simply furnished units with ocean views. If you want a sense of the region's history, you should insist on a room in the great house. Our readers who wound up in one of the rather plain and dingy cottages have repeatedly complained about their rooms. Check out the cottages before you decide to stay in them.

**Dining/Entertainment:** Both the Beach Restaurant (which serves lunch) and the Sprat Hall Restaurant serve good food often made from the plantation's own gardens and fresh local fish. Dress is semi-formal, and only people staying at the hotel and their guests can eat here. Lunches at the beach club (see below) are open to everyone.

**Facilities:** Equestrian stable (see "Sports A to Z," below), hiking, birdwatching, snorkeling, swimming, shore fishing, jetskiing, and waterskiing.

## INEXPENSIVE

### The Frederiksted

20 Strand St., Frederiksted, St. Croix, USVI 00840. ☎ **809/772-0500,** or 800/524-2025 in the U.S. Fax 809/778-4009. 40 rms. A/C TV TEL Rates: Winter, $85–$95 single; $95–$105 double. Summer, $75–$85 single; $85–$95 double. Breakfast $4–$7 extra. AE, DC, MC, V. Parking: Free.

For those who'd like to stay in Frederiksted, the second city of St. Croix, this contemporary four-story inn might be just the place. The closest beach, however, is a long walk away on the other side of town. The hotel lies about a 10-minute ride from the airport. The outdoor tiled courtyard has a tiny swimming pool and a bar where breakfast is served. Bedrooms are decorated in a tropical motif of pastels and are equipped with small refrigerators for drinks as well as a wet bar. The best bedrooms—and the most expensive—are those with ocean views.

# SELF-SUFFICIENT UNITS AROUND THE ISLAND
## EXPENSIVE

### Chenay Bay Beach Resort

P.O. Box 24600, Rte. 82, East End Rd., Chenay Bay, St. Croix, USVI 00824. ☎ **809/ 773-2918,** or 800/548-4457. Fax 809/773-2918. 50 cottages (all with bath). A/C TEL Rates (with EP): Winter, $180–$225 single or double; summer, $130–$165 single or double. Extra person $25. AE, MC, V. Parking: Free.

This rustic, casual resort is nestled on a beachside of 30 acres; Chenay Bay, 4 miles east of Christiansted, is one of the island's finest beaches for swimming, snorkeling, and windsurfing. Each of the West–Indian style cottages, new or newly renovated, contains a fully equipped kitchenette and ceiling fan, and most have air conditioning. The establishment is owned and managed by Richard and Vicki Locke, veterans of the Caribbean hotel business.

**Dining/Entertainment:** The Beach Bar and Grill is open for casual dining daily from 9am to 9pm. The hotel has a popular Tuesday West Indian buffet and a pig roast. On Saturday night, "Caribbean Kaleidoscope" features a mélange of West Indian cuisine and entertainment.

**Facilities:** Freshwater pool overlooking the Caribbean; two tennis courts; free tennis, snorkeling, kayaks, floating mats, daily shuttles to the grocery store. The resort has one of the best children's programs on the islands, in effect in summer and over holiday periods.

### Colony Cove

3221 Estate Golden Rock, St. Croix, USVI 00820. ☎ **809/773-1965,** or 800/828-0746. Fax 809/773-5397. 60 rms (all with bath). A/C TV TEL Rates: Winter, $185–$245 single or double; summer, $125–$155 single or double. Extra person $20. AE, MC, V. Parking: Free.

Of all the condo complexes of St. Croix, this one, located about 1 mile west of Christiansted, is perhaps the most like a full-fledged hotel. It's next to a palm-dotted beach and is composed of a quartet of buff-colored three-story buildings with angular façades surrounding an oval-shaped swimming pool. Each unit contains a clothes washer and dryer, a kitchen, an enclosed veranda or gallery, ceramic-tile floors, two air-conditioned bedrooms, and a pair of bathrooms. The complex also has a good restaurant and two tennis courts.

## MODERATE

### ⑤ Cane Bay Beef Club

P.O. Box 1407, Kingshill, St. Croix, USVI 00851. ☎ **809/778-2966,** or 800/253-8534. 9 suites. Rates: Winter, $125–$165 single or double; summer, $85–$110 single or double. Extra person $15 a night. MC, V. Parking: Free.

Since 1975, Carl Seiffer has run one of the little gems of the island, offering nine large-size suites, each with a living room, a full kitchen, a bedroom, a bath, and a balcony overlooking the water. Trade winds make air conditioning unnecessary, although two units contain air conditioning. The decor is breezy and tropical, with cathedral ceilings, overhead fans, and Chilean tiles. The hotel is located on the north shore of St. Croix, about a 20-minute taxi ride from Christiansted. The hotel fronts a rocky beach near The Waves at Cane Bay (see hotel recommendation below). Guests introduce themselves around the pool, and local rum drinks are served at the patio bar.

**Dining/Entertainment:** The hotel's dining choice is the No Name Bar & Grille, where a sample dinner menu always includes grilled fresh fish (perhaps dolphin, wahoo, swordfish, or halibut). Other dishes might include an old-fashioned pot roast or various stir fries. When available, fresh stuffed lobster is prepared.

### Sugar Beach Condominiums

3245 Estate Golden Rock, St. Croix, USVI 00820. ☎ **809/773-5345,** or 800/524-2049. Fax 809/773-1359. 46 units (all with bath). A/C TEL Rates: Winter, $150–$200 studio or one-bedroom unit for two; $250 two-bedroom unit for four; $300 three-bedroom unit for six. Summer, $110–$145 studio or one-bedroom unit for two; $180 two-bedroom unit for four; $250 three-bedroom unit for six. AE, MC, V. Parking: Free.

These modernized, one-, two-, and three-bedroom apartments are strung along 500 feet of sandy beach on the north coast off North Shore Road. Their proximity to a housing development is a turn-off for some visitors. When you tire of the sand, you can swim in the freshwater pool nestled beside a sugar mill, where rum was made three centuries ago. The apartments, roofed in red tiles, have enclosed balconies to provide privacy. All units open toward the sea, are tastefully decorated, and have completely equipped kitchens. Chamber service is extra. The property has two Laykold tennis courts, and the Carambola golf course is a few minutes away.

### ⑨ The Waves at Cane Bay

P.O. Box 1749, Kingshill, St. Croix, USVI 00851. ☎ **809/778-1805**, or 800/545-0603. Fax 809/778-1805. 12 units (all with bath). A/C TV Rates: Winter, $130–$195 single or double; summer, $85–$120 single or double. Extra person $20: AE, DC, MC, V. Parking: Free.

This intimate and tasteful property, run by Suzanne and Kevin Ryan, is 8 miles east of the airport, midway between the island's two biggest towns. It sits on a narrow but well-landscaped plot of oceanfront property on Cane Bay, the heart of some of the best scuba and snorkeling on the island. The rooms are in angular two-story units that have screened-in verandas almost directly above the ocean. The Ryans welcome their guests as part of their extended family by hosting cocktail parties on their waterside terrace, and by adding many homelike touches to their guests accommodations.

Each accommodation is high-ceilinged, with fresh flowers, a well-stocked kitchen, a private library, and thick towels; some are air conditioned. A two-room villa next to the main building has a large oceanside deck. The social center is a beachside bar ringed with stone and coral. An all-you-can-eat barbecue dinner is featured one night a week for $12 per person. Don't overlook the possibility of a game of golf or tennis at nearby Carambola. A full PADI dive center operates on the property, providing everything from rented tanks to individual scuba lessons.

## 4 Dining

Don't limit yourself to your hotel for dining. Head for one of the island's many independently owned restaurants—they are among the best in the Caribbean.

Restaurants considered "expensive" charge from $40 for a meal; those ranked "moderate" ask from $20 to $25, and anything under that is considered "inexpensive." In all cases, drinks are extra.

## NORTH SHORE
### EXPENSIVE

#### Brass Parrot

In the Buccaneer, Rte. 82 (East End Rd.), Estate Shoys. ☎ **773-2100.** Reservations recommended. Leave Christiansted heading east (there's only one road that goes this way); turn left at the pink-and-white entrance about 2 miles out of town. Appetizers $5.50–$8; main dishes $19–$24. AE, DC, MC, V. Dinner Thurs–Mon 6:30–9:30pm. INTERNATIONAL.

Set in the pink great house of this superlative resort, the Brass Parrot is one of the most elegant restaurants on the island. Views open onto the sea, as well as onto the lights of Christiansted. The restaurant remains popular with locals and visitors alike. The chef specializes in seafood, but there are plenty of other choices on the menu, accompanied by an extensive and reasonably priced wine list. The menu changes with the season, but dishes tend to be innovative, offering products native to the Caribbean Basin such as sweet-potato soup topped with fresh ginger whipped cream. For appetizers, try the Caribbean-style saltfish wontons with pineapple dipping sauce or the smoked black-bean soup topped with grilled tender strips of marinated chicken. Main dishes have included grilled Jamaican jerk

Cornish hen or cinnamon-crusted seared tuna over crisp rice noodles with red pepper sauce. The best steaks and chops are flown down from Chicago. No smoking is allowed inside the restaurant, and slacks and collared shirts are required for men.

### Cormorant Beach Club Restaurant

4126 La Grande Princesse. ☎ **778-8920.** Reservations required. Take Rte. 75, 3 miles northwest of Christiansted. Appetizers $6–$12; main dishes $18–$30; Caribbean grill night $26. Sun brunch $22. AE, DC, MC, V. Lunch daily 11am–2pm; dinner daily 6:30–9:30pm; brunch Sun 11:30am–2:30pm. CONTINENTAL/CARIBBEAN.

This restaurant just might be the most elegant hotel dining experience on St. Croix. Enjoy the sea breeze and listen to the swaying palm trees as you dine on the beach. Entertainment is featured on Thursday evening–a taste of the Caribbean with steel drum, calypso, and limbo dancers. On Friday a jazz band performs, and light jazz is also played during Sunday brunch. The restaurant, like many hotels, has a history of changing chefs who are usually good. Menu items are always changing but appetizers usually include shrimp and prawns, a selection of soups (perhaps island seafood chowder), and Cormorant's classic Caesar salad. Main dishes are likely to include a pasta special of the night and the usual run of chicken breasts, filet mignons, lobster, and, perhaps as a taste of the West Indies, conch in butter sauce.

## INEXPENSIVE

### ⑤ Oskar's Bar and Restaurant

4A La Grande Princesse, Rte. 75. ☎ **773-4060.** Reservations not required. Transportation: Taxi. Soups $2.50; main dishes $8–$13. No credit cards. Lunch Mon–Sat 11am–2:30pm; dinner Mon–Sat 5:30–9pm. CONTINENTAL.

Set in a simple concrete building just west of Christiansted, this inexpensive restaurant is often filled when better-known (and more expensive) establishments are empty. The restaurant was established in 1974 by Oskar Bütler, an expatriate Swiss who freely admits he's never changed his highly successful menu since he opened the restaurant. After beginning with soup, try the special of the day such as roast pork with gravy accompanied by mashed potatoes and corn. To go continental, order bratwurst with sauerkraut, filet mignon, or wienerschnitzel. Finish your repast with Swiss chocolate cake.

## EAST END
## EXPENSIVE

### Café Madeleine

Gallows Bay. ☎ **778-7377.** Reservations recommended. Appetizers $7.50–$12; main dishes $22–$33. AE, DC, MC, V. Dinner Wed–Sun 6–9:30pm. ITALIAN.

Located in the great house built by the Roncari family in 1990 in colonial style, Café Madeleine, 8 miles east of Christiansted, offers a mountaintop panorama of both the north and south sides of the island. The lavish decor was created by a battalion of hardworking decorators. Diners have a choice of either indoor or terrace dining. Don't overlook a before-dinner drink at the mahogany-trimmed bar, where a scale model of a Maine schooner, bolted against mahogany paneling, creates a private club aura.

The cuisine is inspired by the recipes of northern Italy accented by a generous dose of experimental nouvelle cuisine. Menu choices might include baked artichoke hearts; oysters Mario; filet of red snapper milanese; veal scallopini alla Madeleine; and some of the most unusual pastas in the world, including a version of key lime fettuccine with raspberry sauce and wild mushroom ravioli.

## MODERATE

### Duggan's Reef

East End Rd., Teague Bay. ☎ **773-9800.** Reservations required for dinner. Take Rte. 82 7 miles east of Christiansted; park in the public lot near the public beach at Teague Bay. Appetizers $3.50–$9.50; main dishes $14.50–$29; pastas $16.50–$24. AE, MC, V. Lunch daily noon–3pm; dinner daily 6–9:30pm. Bar daily 11am–11:30pm. CONTINENTAL/ CARIBBEAN.

Set only 10 feet from the still waters of Reef Beach and open to the sea breezes, Duggan's Reef is an ideal perch for watching the windsurfers and Hobie Cats careering through the nearby waters. The restaurant, owned for more than a decade by Boston-born Frank Duggan, is considered the most popular in St. Croix— all visitors seemingly dine here at least once during their stay on the island. At lunch, a simple array of salads, crêpes, and sandwiches is offered. At night, a more elaborate menu contains the popular house specialty—Duggan's Caribbean lobster pasta and Irish whiskey lobster. The local seafood is fresh and depends on the day's catch—in other words, fresh fish or no fish. That catch of the day can be baked, grilled, or blackened in the Cajun style. It also can be served island style (with tomato, pepper, and onion sauce). Begin with fried calamari or else a conch chowder before sampling a pasta dish such as seafood diavolo. Main dishes include New York strip or veal piccata.

### The Galleon

East End Rd., Green Cay Marina, 50 Estate Southgate. ☎ **773-9949.** Reservations recommended. Appetizers $5–$8.50; main dishes $13.50–$29. AE, MC, V. Dinner daily 6–10pm. Closed Sun–Mon in summer. FRENCH/ITALIAN.

Overlooking the ocean on Route 82, a five-minute drive east of Christiansted, the Galleon enjoys a fine reputation—and deservedly so. The best cooking of northern Italy and of France is offered at this casual but elegant spot. The osso buco is just as good as that served in Milan. Freshly baked bread, two fresh vegetables, and rice or potatoes accompany main dishes. The menu always includes at least one local fish, such as wahoo, tuna, grouper, swordfish, snapper, or dolphin. If you prefer the classics, you might order a perfectly done rack of lamb carved at your table. Chilled soup, fruit salads, and croissants complement any meal. Music from a baby grand accompanies your dinner.

## CHRISTIANSTED

## EXPENSIVE

### Antoine's

58A King St. ☎ **773-0263.** Reservations required in winter. Appetizers $3.75–$5.75; main dishes $13–$20. AE, MC, V. Lunch daily 11am–2:30pm; dinner daily 6:30–9:30pm. GERMAN/ ITALIAN/CARIBBEAN.

Set directly on King's Wharf, Antoine's overlooks Christiansted's harbor and marina. Many visitors come just to patronize the bar, which dispenses more than 35 different kinds of frozen blender drinks and the island's largest selection of beer. In addition to a covered terrace, there's a satellite bar in the rear, decorated with a windsurfer suspended from the ceiling, and a cubbyhole Italian restaurant, Pico Bellmo, serving dinner only Thursday through Sunday. Regardless of where you decide to eat, you can order from a range of pasta and fish dishes, even in the bar. Try the fish chowder and, if available, lobster or the catch of the day. German fare such as golden schnitzels and goulash is served daily.

## ✪ Indies

55-56 Company St., ☎ **692-9440.** Reservations recommended. Appetizers $6.50–$8.50; main dishes $16–$21; lunch platters $6–$9.50. AE, MC, V. Lunch Mon–Fri 11:30am–2:30pm; dinner daily 6–9:30pm. CARIBBEAN/INTERNATIONAL.

Set in a 19th-century courtyard ringed with multicolored gingerbread houses and antique cobblestones, Indies is one of the most noteworthy restaurants on St. Croix. The restaurant's creative vision comes from San Francisco–born Catherine Plav-Driggers, who is assisted by her husband, Curtis. She prepares an island-inspired menu of fresh ingredients and keeps her prices reasonable. The dinner menu changes nightly. The dining room lies adjacent to a carriage and cookhouse from the 1850s in a sheltered courtyard protected from the noise of the street outside. Menu items include spring rolls, spicy Caribbean chicken, grouper (cooked in coconut milk, shrimp, scallions, tomato, and ginger), and grilled tenderloin of beef with corn-based custard and fried-onion chutney. Dessert might be a key lime pie or coconut mousse. The wine list, mostly California vintages, is especially attractive.

## ✪ Kendricks

52 King St. ☎ **773-9199.** Reservation recommended. Appetizers $4–$9; main dishes $14–$25. AE, MC, V. Dinner Mon–Sat 6–10pm. Closed June. CONTINENTAL.

This fine restaurant is housed in a 19th-century brick building in the heart of town. Climb a flight of brick stairs to the second-floor dining room, which has a view of old Christiansted with the distant sea beyond the rooftops. David and Jane Kendrick's appetizers might include Mediterranean-American shrimp with an orange pistachio couscous, Caribbean lobster cakes, or a warm chipotle pepper soup with onions and garlic. Pasta dishes are always featured, and Kendrick's Cordon Bleu (boneless breast of chicken stuffed with lobster, mango, and Monterey Jack cheese) often appears as a main course. Other main dish selections are herb-crusted rack of lamb with roasted garlic and a fresh thyme sauce and sautéed medallions of veal with grilled baby artichokes.

## Top Hat

52 Company St. ☎ **773-2346.** Reservations recommended. Appetizers $5.50–$10; main dishes $14.50–$30; three-course fixed-price menu $20. AE, DC, MC, V. Lunch Tues–Fri 11:30am–2pm; dinner Mon–Sat 6–10pm. Closed May–June. CONTINENTAL/SCANDINAVIAN.

On the second floor of a restored old merchant's house opposite Market Square, the Top Hat has been operated by Scandinavians Bent and Hanne Rasmussen since 1970. Look for daily specials, such as fresh seafood. A good selection of homemade desserts is offered, and the changing menu is backed up by a selection of wines. Try such well-prepared dishes as crisp roast duck in the Danish style with apples, prunes, red cabbage, sugar-brown Irish potatoes, and a demiglacé sauce; gravlax; herring; chilled cucumber soup; local dolphin sautéed with butter and lime; and an excellent version of wienerschnitzel. A longtime favorite is frikadeller with Danish meatballs, red cabbage, and mashed potatoes.

## MODERATE

### Bombay Club

5A King St. ☎ **773-1838.** Reservations not required. Appetizers $3–$6.50; main dishes $8.75–$16. AE, MC, V. Restaurant daily 11am–10pm. Bar daily 11–1am. INTERNATIONAL.

The owners have managed to squeeze a lot of miscellany into what has become one of the most enduring restaurants in Christiansted. Concealed from the street by the brick foundations of an 18th-century planter's town house, the restaurant welcome diners with a large photograph of John Lennon near the entrance, original paintings, and tropical plants. You enter through a low stone tunnel that leads to the bar and a courtyard with tables. The food, while simple, is plentiful, flavorful, and reasonably priced. Menu items include the catch of the day and regional dishes such as conch, veal, beef filet, and pasta.

### The Chart House

59 King's Wharf. ☎ **773-7718.** Reservations recommended on weekends. Appetizers $4.95–$8.95; main dishes $12.95–$37.95. AE, DC, MC, V. Dinner daily 6–10pm; bar daily 5–10pm. STEAKS.

This nautically decorated restaurant on the wharf under the King Christian Hotel has a classy decor of varnished hardwoods, polished brass, and wicker chairs. The Chart House is an exception to the blandness of most chain restaurants.

To begin with, the Chart House has the best salad bar on the island, and many people come here just for that. Try the celebrated prime rib, a huge slab of seasoned meat, the lobster, or the barbecued beef ribs. The mud pie is also justly renowned.

### Comanche Club

1 Strand St. ☎ **773-2665.** Reservations recommended. Appetizers $3.50–$10.50; main dishes $7.75–$14.75. AE, V. Breakfast daily (Nov–May only) 7–10:30am; lunch daily 11:30am–2:30pm; dinner daily 6–11pm. WEST INDIAN/CONTINENTAL.

One of the most popular restaurants on the island, Comanche is relaxed yet elegant. The specialties are eclectic—there's everything from fish and conch chowder to shark cakes. Each night, a different special is featured. There's also a good selection of Cruzan dishes—one for every night of the week. Salads and a cold buffet are traditionally featured; the Comanche curries have won over devotees. Island fish are generally sautéed with lemon butter and capers; typical West Indian dishes include conch creole with fungi. Fish cakes with seasoned rice is the Friday night specialty, and the most popular desserts are Comanche cheesecake or key lime pie.

### ❸ Dino's

4C Hospital St. ☎ **778-8005.** Reservations required. Appetizers $4.50–$10; main dishes $13–$19. AE. Dinner Mon–Sat 6–10pm. ITALIAN.

This Mediterranean-style bistro is housed in a 200-year-old brick building with two different sections: an air-conditioned interior and an open-air terrace. Veal prepared in at least three different ways, including saltimbocca. The local fish du jour is prepared Caribbean style—sautéed with tropical fruits, tomato, ginger, and cilantro. But Dino's is mainly known for its homemade pastas, including traditional dishes like fettuccini Alfredo. More creative pastas include fettuccini Caribbean with chicken, rum, black beans, ginger, cilantro, and sweet and hot pepper. The list of homemade desserts changes daily.

## Ⓢ Luncheria

Apothecary Hall Courtyard, 2111 Company St. ☎ **773-4247.** Reservations not required. Appetizers $2.50–$6.75; main dishes $4.25–$7.75. No credit cards. Mon–Fri 11am–9pm, Sat noon–9pm. MEXICAN.

In a historic courtyard in the center of town, this Mexican restaurant offers some of the best priced food on the island. You get the usual array of tacos, tostadas, burritos, nachos, and enchiladas. Specialties include chicken fajitas, enchiladas verde, and *arroz con pollo* (spiced chicken with brown rice). Daily specials feature both low-calorie and vegetarian choices, and the chef's refried beans are lard free. Whole-wheat tortillas are offered. Check the board for daily specials, and indulge in the complimentary salsa bar.

### Serendipity Inn

Mill Harbour Condominiums, Mill Harbour. ☎ **773-5762.** Reservations required for dinner and Sun brunch. Appetizers $4.50–$5.75; main dishes $14.50–$19.50; Sunday brunch main dishes $4.50–$7.50. AE, DC, MC, V. Lunch daily 11am–3pm; dinner daily 6:30–9:30pm; brunch Sun 10:30am–2:30pm. Bar daily 11am–midnight. INTERNATIONAL.

This beach and poolside restaurant lies just west of Christiansted in the Mill Harbour Condominiums. Surrounded by iron gates and brick walls, the restaurant offers a spacious courtyard fronting the lagoon. At lunch you can enjoy light fare such as homemade soups, freshly made salads, and sandwiches. Daily specials are regularly featured. On Friday night a barbecue, including chicken and ribs, along with salad, costs only $10. For dinner, begin with calamari or nachos grande, then try the chef's fresh catch of the day, seafood pasta, or perhaps steak au poivre.

## Ⓢ Tivoli Gardens

39 Strand St., upstairs in the Pan Am Pavilion. ☎ **773-6782.** Reservations recommended after 7pm. Appetizers $3.50–$7; main dishes $13–$19. AE, MC, V. Lunch Mon–Fri 11:15am–2:30pm; dinner daily 6–9:30pm. INTERNATIONAL.

This large second-floor porch festooned with lights affords the same view of Christiansted Harbor that a sea captain might have. The well-known local gathering place, run by Gary Thomson, has white beams, trellises, and hanging plants that evoke its namesake, the pleasure gardens of Copenhagen. The menu lists everything from escargots provencale to goulash inspired by a recipe concocted in the days of the Austro-Hungarian Empire. The Thai curry is excellent. For dessert, those in the know order a wicked, calorie-laden chocolate velvet cake. Often there is live music and dancing after 7pm.

### Tutto Bene

2 Company St. ☎ **773-5229.** Reservations recommended for parties of 5 or more. Appetizers $4.95–$7.95; main dishes $10.95–$18.95. AE. Dinner daily 6–10pm. ITALIAN.

Located on the street level of a building in the heart of town, this restaurant evokes the atmosphere of a cozy village inn on the Mediterranean. If you don't feel like eating, there's a full-service mahogany bar in back doing a brisk business of its own. You'll find wooden tables covered with painted tablecloths, warm colors, and, often, lots of hubbub. Menu items are written on a pair of oversize mirrors against one wall, and include pastas; fish prepared with parmigiana; seafood Genovese (mussels, clams, shrimp, and white wine and pesto sauce over linguini); and chicken alla Napoli (with sausages and peppers).

# St. Croix Dining

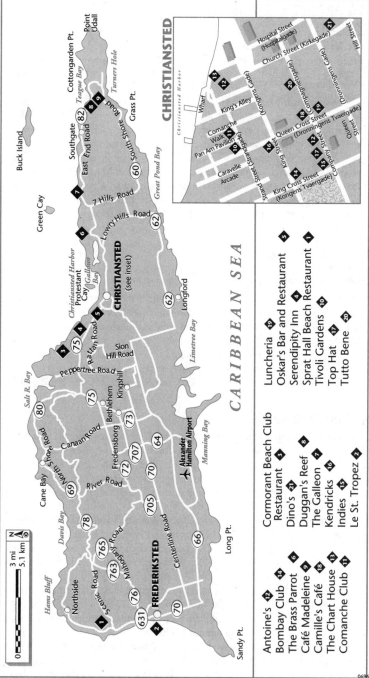

**CHRISTIANSTED**

Antoine's 🔷12
Bombay Club 🔷14
The Brass Parrot 🔷6
Café Madeleine 🔷9
Camille's Café 🔷18
The Chart House 🔷13
Comanche Club 🔷11

Cormorant Beach Club Restaurant 🔷3
Dino's 🔷22
Duggan's Reef 🔷8
The Galleon 🔷7
Kendricks 🔷16
Indies 🔷15
Le St. Tropez 🔷2

Luncheria 🔷19
Oskar's Bar and Restaurant 🔷5
Serendipity Inn 🔷4
Sprat Hall Beach Restaurant 🔷1
Tivoli Gardens 🔷10
Top Hat 🔷17
Tutto Bene 🔷20

0696

# IN & AROUND FREDERIKSTED
## MODERATE

### Le St. Tropez
Limetree Court, 67 King St., Frederiksted. ☎ **772-3000.** Reservations recommended. Appetizers $4.50–$11.50; main dishes $13.50–$19. AE, MC, V. Lunch Mon–Fri 11:30am– 2:30pm; dinner Mon–Sat 6–9pm. FRENCH/MEDITERRANEAN.

The most popular bistro in Frederiksted, Le St. Tropez is presided over by Danielle and André Ducrot. Since it's small, it's always better to call ahead for a table. If you're visiting for the day, make this bright little café your luncheon stopover; enjoy crêpes, quiches, soups, and salads in a sunlit courtyard or on the covered terrace. At night, the atmosphere glows with candlelight. Begin with mushrooms aïoli, escargots provencale, or one of the freshly made soups. Main dishes are likely to include medallions of beef with two mushrooms, the fish of the day, and a magret of duck. Ingredients are always fresh; look for the daily specials, perhaps coq au vin. After dinner you can take a stroll through their gift shop.

## INEXPENSIVE

### Sprat Hall Beach Restaurant
Rte. 63. ☎ **772-5855.** Reservations not required. Lunch $3.50–$15. No credit cards. Wed– Sun 9am–4pm; hot food Wed–Sun 11:30am–2:30pm. CARIBBEAN.

One mile north of Frederiksted, this restaurant is an informal spot on the western coast of St. Croix near Sprat Hall Plantation (see "Accommodations," above). It's about the best place on the island to combine lunch and a swim. Sprat Hall has been feeding both locals and visitors since 1948. Try local dishes such as conch chowder, pumpkin fritters, tannia soup, and the fried fish of the day. If you'd like more standard fare, there are also salads and burgers. The bread is baked here fresh daily. The restaurant is directed by Cruzan-born Joyce Merwin Hurd and her husband Jim.

# SPECIALTY DINING

For Sunday brunch, try the **Cormorant Beach Club Restaurant,** 4126 La Grand Princesse (☎ 778-8920), open from 11:30am to 2pm. The cost is $22 for adults, $16 for children. Sample Cruzan-style fish, West Indian curried lamb, shrimp salad, salade niçoise, barbecued ribs, eggs Benedict, salmon mousse, and johnnycakes. Wash it all down with a mimosa or a glass of champagne while you're entertained by jazz band.

A local favorite is the New York deli-style **Camille's Café** (☎ 773-2985), at the corner of Queen Cross and Company St. Formerly called the Ritz Café, Camille's is a favorite gathering place for locals. Its brick walls and beamed ceilings were part of the original 18th-century house. Fresh daily salad specials are featured, as are soups and sandwiches. Appetizers go for $3.50 to $4, and main courses are $9.95 to $13.95. The international menu includes fresh fish, filet mignon, lobster, and chicken. Its fixed-price dinner, at $13.95, is one of the best dining values in Christiansted. Camille's is open Monday through Saturday from 7:30am to 10pm. Reservations are not needed.

Camille's is also a good place to buy picnic fare. Sandwiches (from $3.95 to $8.95) include crunchy vegetarian delight, salami, and other deli favorites, and all come with garnishes. The special "Buck Island Lunch," named after an ideal spot for a picnic (see "An Easy Excursion," below), can be picked up at 7:30am.

# 5 Attractions

## THE TOP 10 THINGS TO DO ON ST. CROIX

1. Take a walking tour of historic Christiansted along the waterfront.
2. Spend a day and a half at Buck Island—snorkeling the water trail, hiking, and sitting on the beach.
3. Explore natural sights: Sandy Point, Buck Island Reef National Monument, Salt River.
4. Go on a rain forest drive in St. Croix's northwest corner.
5. Visit the Estate Whim Plantation Museum—a restored sugar plantation and great house.
6. See the Salt River Bay National Historical Park and Ecological Preserve, where Columbus landed in 1493.
7. Tour the historic sites in Frederiksted, on the western edge of St. Croix.
8. Go horseback riding through the rain forest or along the coast, perhaps by moonlight.
9. Hike along nature trails.
10. Shop duty free in the center of Christiansted.

Many visitors like to explore St. Croix on a **taxi tour** (☎ 778-1088), which for a party of two costs from $20 per hour. The fare should be negotiated in advance. Extra fees are charged for the following sights: $5 for the botanical gardens, $5 for the Whim Estate House, and $3 for the rum distillery.

Check with your hotel desk to see if you can go on an organized tour. The tours operate according to demand, with fewer departures in summer than in winter. A typical four-hour tour costs $25 per person, and many are conducted at least three times a week during the winter. Tours usually go through old Christiansted and visit the botanical gardens, Whim Estate House, the rum distillery, the rain forest, the St. Croix Leap mahogany workshop, and the site of the ill-fated Columbus landing at Salt River. Call **Travellers' Tours,** Alexander Hamilton Airport (☎ 778-1636), for more information.

## CHRISTIANSTED

This picture-book harbor town of the Caribbean is an old Danish port in the process of being handsomely restored. Located on the northeastern shore of the island on a coral-bound bay, the town is filled with Danish buildings, most erected by prosperous merchants in the booming mercantile days of the 18th century. Built of solid stone, these red-roofed structures are often washed in pink, ocher, or yellow; their walls are so thick that the buildings keep cool. The whole area around the harborfront has been designated as a historical site supervised by the National Park Service.

If you're an independent traveler, consider the walking and driving tours below. However, if you'd like guidance, you can take a walking tour of both Christiansted and Frederiksted from **Take-a-Hike,** (☎ 778-6997), which gives guided one-hour walks of both towns. Tours leave Monday and Thursday at 10am from the Visitors' Bureau in Christiansted. The Christiansted tour costs $5.50, the

Frederiksted tour is $6.50. Children are charged $3.50 for either tour. Take-a-Hike also conducts nature hikes; inquire about them if you're interested.

## WALKING TOUR
### Christiansted

**Start:**  Visitors' Bureau.
**Finish:**  Christiansted harborfront.
**Time:**  1¹/₂ hours.
**Best Times:**  Any day 10am to 4pm.
**Worst Times:**  Monday to Friday 4 to 6pm.

Begin your tour at:

1. **The Visitors' Bureau,** a yellow-sided building with a cedar-capped roof near the harborfront. It was originally built as the Old Scalehouse in 1856 to replace a similar, older structure which burned down. In its heyday, all taxable goods leaving and entering Christiansted's harbor were weighed here. The scales which once stood could accurately weigh barrels of sugar and molasses up to 1,600 pounds each.

   In front of the Scalehouse lies one of the most charming squares in the Caribbean. Its old-fashioned asymmetrical allure is still evident despite the masses of cars.

   With your back to the Scalehouse, turn left and walk through the parking lot to the foot of the white-sided gazebo-inspired band shell that sits in the center of a park named after Alexander Hamilton. The yellow-brick building with the ornately curved brick staircase is the:

2. **Old Customs House** (currently the headquarters of the National Park Service). The gracefully proportioned 16-step staircase was added in 1829 as an embellishment to an older building. (There are public toilets on the ground floor.)

   Continue climbing the hill to the base of the yellow-painted structure which is:

3. **Fort Christiansvaern.** Considered the best-preserved colonial fortification in the Virgin Islands, the fort is maintained as a historic monument by the National Park Service. Its original four-sided, star-shaped design was in accordance with the most advanced military planning of its era. The fort is the site of the St. Croix Police Museum, which traces police work on the island from the late 1800s to the present. Photos, weapons, and artifacts create the police force's past.

   Exit from the fort, and head straight down the tree-lined path toward the most visible steeple in Christiansted. It caps the appropriately named:

4. **Steeple Building** (Church of Lord God of Sabaoth), completed in 1753 as St. Croix's first Lutheran church, and embellished with a steeple in 1794–96. The building was deconsecrated in 1831, and served at various times as a bakery, a hospital, and a school. The building contains a museum devoted to local history.

   Across Company Street from the Steeple Building is a U.S. post office. The building that contains it was built in 1749 as:

5. **The West Indies and Guinea Warehouse.** The structure was once three times larger than it is today and included storerooms and lodgings for staff. Go to the building's side entrance, on Church Street, and enter the rear courtyard if the

# Walking Tour—Christiansted

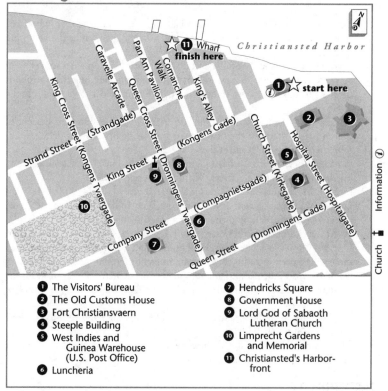

**1** The Visitors' Bureau
**2** The Old Customs House
**3** Fort Christiansvaern
**4** Steeple Building
**5** West Indies and Guinea Warehouse (U.S. Post Office)
**6** Luncheria
**7** Hendricks Square
**8** Government House
**9** Lord God of Sabaoth Lutheran Church
**10** Limprecht Gardens and Memorial
**11** Christiansted's Harborfront

iron gate is open. For many years, this was the site of some of the largest slave auctions in the Caribbean.

From the post office, retrace your steps to Company Street and head west for one block. On your left, you'll pass the entrance to Apothecary Hall, 2111 Company St., which contains a charming collection of shops and restaurants.

☕ **TAKE A BREAK** If you need refreshment, try **6. Luncheria,** Apothecary Hall Courtyard, 2111 Company St. (☎ **773-4247**). Housed in an extension of an 18th-century building, the bar's tables are grouped in a courtyard shaded by trees. The owners are considered the margarita specialists of the island, stocking more types of tequila (15 plus) than any other bar in the neighborhood. Most margaritas cost from $3 each. Specializing in Mexican fare, Luncheria serves burritos, tostadas, enchiladas, and tacos, as well as daily specials and vegetarian meals. See separate recommendation under "Dining."

Exit Apothecary Hall and turn left onto Company Street. Cross Queen Cross Street (Dronningens Tvergade). Half a block later, you'll arrive at the island's largest outdoor market:

**7. Hendricks Square** (Christian "Shan" Square), which was rebuilt in a timbered, 9th-century style after the 1989 hurricane. Fruits and vegetables are sold here Monday to Saturday from 7am to 6pm.

Retrace your steps half a block along Company Street, and turn left onto Queen Cross Street. Head downhill toward the harbor, walking on the right-hand side of the street. Within half a block, you'll reach an unmarked arched iron gateway, set beneath an arcade. If it's open, enter the charming gardens of:

8. **Government House.** Evocative of Europe, the garden: contain a scattering of very old trees, flowerbeds, and walkways. The antique building that surrounds the gardens was formed from the union of two much older town houses in the 1830s.

Exit the same way you entered, turn right, and continue your descent of Queen Cross Street. At the first street corner (King Street), turn left, and admire the neoclassical façade of the:

9. **Lord God of Sabaoth Luthern Church,** established in 1734. Continue walking southwest along King Street. Within two blocks is the:

10. **Limprecht Gardens and Memorial.** For 20 years (1888–1908) Peter Carl Limprecht served as governor of the Danish West Indies. Today, an occasional chicken pecks at seedlings planted near a Danish-language memorial to him.

At the end of the park, retrace your steps to King Cross Street, and go left. One very short block later, turn right onto Strand Street, which contains some interesting stores, including at least two different shopping arcades. The streets will narrow, and the pedestrian traffic will be more congested. Pass beneath the overpass belonging to a popular bar and restaurant, the Comanche Club (see "Dining," above).

Continue down the meandering curves of King's Alley and within one block you'll be standing beside:

11. **Christiansted's harborfront,** where you can end your tour by strolling on the boardwalk of the waterside piers.

## FREDERIKSTED

This old Danish town at the western end of the island, about 17 miles from Christiansted, is a sleepy port that only comes to life when a cruise ship docks at its shoreline. In 1994, a 1,500-foot pier opened to accommodate the largest grade of cruise ship; the old pier had suffered damage from Hurricane Hugo in 1989. The pier facility is designed for two large cruise vessels and two mini cruise vessels which run simultaneously.

The town is not new to natural disasters. Frederiksted was destroyed by a fire in 1879, and the citizens rebuilt it, using wood frame and clapboards on top of the old Danish stone and yellow-brick foundations.

Most visitors begin their tour at russet-colored **Fort Frederick,** next to the pier. Some historians claim that this was the first fort to sound a foreign salute to the U.S. flag, in 1776. It was here on July 3, 1848, that Governor-General Peter von Scholten emancipated the slaves in the Danish West Indies. The fort, at the northern end of Frederiksted, has been restored to the way it looked in 1840. You can explore the courtyard and stables, and an exhibit area has been installed in what was once the Garrison Room.

Just south of the fort, the **Customs House** is an 18th-century building with a 19th-century two-story gallery. Here you can go into the **Visitor's Bureau** and pick up a free map of the town.

Nearby, privately owned **Victoria House,** Market Street, is a gingerbread-trimmed structure built after the fire of 1879. Some of the original 1803 structure was preserved when it was rebuilt.

# Frederiksted

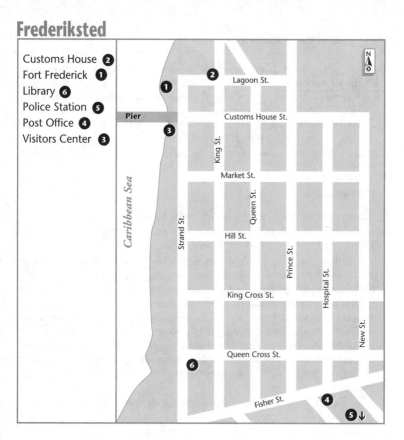

Customs House ❷
Fort Frederick ❶
Library ❻
Police Station ❺
Post Office ❹
Visitors Center ❸

Lagoon St.

Customs House St.

Pier

King St.

Market St.

Queen St.

Strand St.

Hill St.

Prince St.

Hospital St.

King Cross St.

New St.

Queen Cross St.

Fisher St.

Caribbean Sea

Along the waterfront Strand Street is the **Bellhouse,** once the Frederiksted Public Library. One of its owners, G. A. Bell, ornamented the steps with bells. The house today is an arts and crafts center and a nursery. Sometimes a local theater group presents dramas here.

Other buildings of interest include the **Danish School,** Prince Street, which was adapted in the 1830s into a building designed by Hingelberg, a well-known Danish architect. Today it's the police station and welfare department.

Two churches are of interest. **St. Paul's Anglican Church,** 28 Prince St., was founded outside the port in the late 18th century; the present building dates from 1812. **St. Patrick's Catholic Church,** 5 Prince St., was built in the 1840s.

On the waterfront in Frederiksted, you can visit the pint-sized but interesting **St. Croix Aquarium,** housing some 40 species of marine animals and more than 100 species of invertebrates. With constant rotation, each creature can adjust easily back to its natural habitat, as hundreds of species pass through the tanks each year. A touch pond teems with starfish, sea cucumbers, brittle stars, and pencil urchins. The aquarium allows you to become familiar, with marine life before you see it while scuba diving or snorkeling. The aquarium is open Wednesday through Sunday from 11am to 4pm; admission is $3 for adults and $1.50 for children.

## AROUND THE ISLAND

North of Frederiksted, you can drop in at **Sprat Hall,** the island's oldest plantation, or else continue to the rain forest, which covers about 15 acres, including the 150-foot-high **Creque Dam.** Mahogany trees and yellow cedar grow in profusion, as do wild lilies. The terrain is privately owned, but the owner lets visitors go inside to explore.

Most people want to see the jagged estuary of the northern coastline's **Salt River,** but other than bird life, there isn't much to see. This is where Columbus landed for a brief moment before being driven off by Caribs. A modest marker indicates the area, which is now a national park. In the area are burial grounds, extensive mangroves, an old earthworks fort, and Native American ceremonial ball court.

The St. Croix Environmental Association conducts tours of the area; call **773-1989** for details.

## St. George Village Botanical Garden of St. Croix

Estate St. George. ☎ **772-3874.** $5 adults; $1 children 12 or under. Dec 1–Apr 30, daily 9am–5pm; May 1–Nov 30, Tues–Sat 9am–4pm.

Just north of Centerline Road, 4 miles east of Frederiksted at Estate St. George, is a botanical garden bursting with tropical trees, shrubs, vines, and flowers. The garden is a delight for the eye and camera—from the entrance drive bordered by royal palms to the tropical rain forest and the cactus garden. Botanical collections include orchids, ferns, bromeliads, dry-growing palms, aroids, and ginger plants. Ruins of a 19th-century sugar plantation form the background of the gardens. Several buildings have been restored to illustrate plantation life, including the blacksmith shop and the superintendent's house. Other restored buildings are used as a gift shop, nursery, library, herbarium, and visitors' orientation center.

Self-guided walking tour maps are available at the entrance to the administration building.

## Cruzan Rum Factory

West Airport Rd., Route 64. ☎ **772-0280.** $2. Mon–Fri 9am–11:30am and 1–4:15pm.

This factory distills the famous Virgin Islands rum, which is considered by residents to be the finest rum in the world. Guided tours depart from the visitors' pavilion; call for reservations and information.

## Estate Whim Plantation Museum

Centerline Rd. ☎ **772-0598.** $5 adults, $1 children. Mon–Sat 10am–4pm.

Located about 2 miles east of Frederiksted, this museum was restored by the St. Croix Landmarks Society and is unique among the many sugar plantations dotting the island of St. Croix. The great house is composed of only three rooms. Surrounded by three-foot-thick walls made of stone, coral, and molasses, the house resembles a European château in miniature.

In 1992, a division of Baker Furniture Company, Milling Road, used the Whim Plantation's collection of models for one of its most successful lines of reproductions, the "Whim Museum–West Indies Collection." A showroom in the museum sells reproductions, including pineapple-capped four-poster beds, cane-bottomed planters' chairs with built-in leg rests, and Caribbean adaptations of Empire-era chairs with cane-bottomed seats.

A woodworking shop on the plantation displays tools and techniques from the 18th century. Other sights include the estate's original kitchen, a gift shop, and a reproduction of a typical town apothecary. You can also visit the ruins of the plantation's sugar-processing plant, complete with a restored windmill.

# Driving Tour—East St. Croix

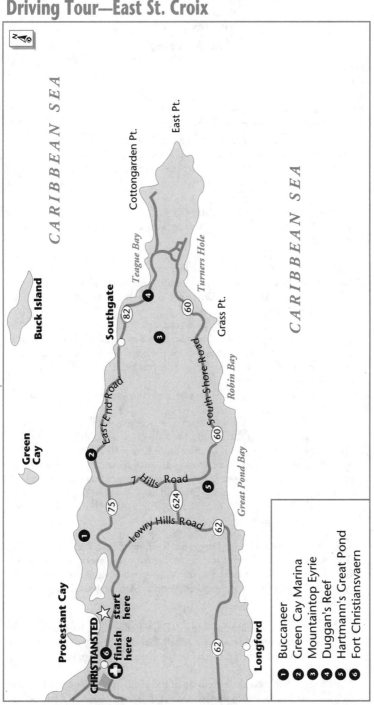

## DRIVING TOUR
### East St. Croix

**Start:** Buccaneer.
**Finish:** Fort Christiansvaern.
**Time:** 1¹⁄₂ hours.
**Best Times:** Early morning or late afternoon.
**Worst Times:** Any evening after 5pm.

Head east from Christiansted on Route 75. (Sometimes referred to as East End Road.) Within a few miles, it will become Route 82. If you get confused at any time during this tour, remember the ocean should always be on your left.

Landmarks you'll pass on your way out of town will include Gallows Point and:

**1. Buccaneer.** A hotel where you might want to return for one of the nightly musical performances that are among the best on the island (see "Accommodations," above).

Suddenly, the landscape will open onto verdant countryside. Cows graze peacefully on a rolling landscape that may remind you of the Scottish lowlands. Accompanying the cows are tickbirds, which feed on ticks buried in the cows' skin. An occasional traffic mini-jam might form as herds of goats cross the road.

Continue driving and you'll pass:

**2. Green Cay Marina,** identified by a road sign; you might want to visit the marina to admire the yachts bobbing at anchor or perhaps to have a swim at Chenay Bay. Nearby monuments include the Southgate Baptist Church and a handful of stone towers that once housed the gear mechanisms of windmills that crushed the juice from sugarcane.

As the vistas unfold, you'll pass by scatterings of bougainvillea-covered private villas.

About 7 miles along the route from Christiansted, you'll see the:

**3. Mountaintop Eyrie** of the island's most prominent socialite, the Contessa Nadia Farbo Navarro, the Romanian-born heiress to a great fortune. This opulent castle is the most outrageously unusual, most prominent, and most talked-about villa on St. Croix. Understandably, its privacy is rigidly maintained.

A couple of miles farther along East End Road, you'll reach one of the most popular windsurfing beaches in St. Croix, Teague Bay. This is a good spot to take a break.

☕ **TAKE A BREAK    4. Duggan's Reef,** East End Road, Teague Bay (**773-9800**), offers flavorful lunches, more formal dinners, fruit daiquiris, and a bar only 10 feet from the waves. Many guests claim this is the best way to experience windsurfing without getting on a sailboard. See "Dining," above, for details.

After your stop, continue driving east along Route 82 to the area that most residents consider the most peaceful and dramatic on the island. It is especially memorable at sunset, when the vistas are highlighted and the sun is against your back.

At Knight Bay, near the eastern tip of the island, turn right onto Route 60 (South Shore Road), and head west. One of the several lakes you'll pass is:

5. **Hartmann's Great Pond** (also known as Great Pond), a favorite of nesting sea-birds. The sea vistas and the rolling grasslands are spectacular.

Route 60 merges with Route 624 a short distance north of Great Pond. Fork left onto Route 624, and, a short distance later, right onto Route 62 (Lowry Hill Road). You will travel the mountainous spine of the island through districts named after former farms, such as Sally's Fancy, Marienhøj, and Boetzberg.

Within 2 miles, Lowry Hill Road merges with Route 82 again. Fork left, and follow it as it turns into Hospital Gade and leads to the center of Christiansted. To your right will appear:

6. **Fort Christiansvaern,** as you pull into the parking lot in front of Christiansted's tourist office (Old Scalehouse).

## EXPLORING THE RAIN FOREST

Unlike the rest of St. Croix, a verdant portion of the island's western district is covered with dense forest–very different landscape than the scrub-covered hills covering other parts of the island. Located in the island's sparsely populated northwestern corner north of Fredericksted, the area grows thick with mahogany trees, kapok (silk-cotton) trees, turpentine (red-birch) trees, samaan (rain) trees, and all kinds of ferns and vines. Sweet limes, mangoes, hog plums, and breadfruit trees, all of which have grown in the wild since the days of the plantations, are interperse among the forest's larger trees. Crested hummingbirds, pearly-eyed thrashers, green-throated caribs, yellow warblers, and perky but drably camouflaged banana quits nest in the trees.

Although the district is not actually a tropical rain forest, it's known as the "Rain Forest." To experience the charm of the areas some visitors opt to drive along Route 76 (which is also known as Mahogany Road), stopping their car beside the footpaths which meander off on either side of the highway into dry river beds and

---

## A Wildlife Refuge

One of the most rarely visited parts of St. Croix, the island's southwestern tip is composed of salt marshes, tidal pools, and low vegetation inhabited by birds, turtles, and other forms of wildlife. More than 3 miles of ecologically protected coastline lie between Sandy Point (the island's most westerly tip) and the shallow waters of the Westend Saltpond.

Home to colonies of green and hawksbill turtles, the site is also a resting ground for leatherback turtles. It is one of only two such places in U.S. waters. The site is also home to thousands of birds, including herons, brown pelicans, Caribbean martins, black-necked stilts, and white-crowned pigeons. Sandy Point gave its name to a rare form of orchid, a brown and/or purple variety.

Part of the continued viability of the site as a wildlife refuge depends on its inaccessibility, except on Saturday and Sunday from 6am to 6pm. The site is most easily reached by driving to the end of Route 66 (Melvin Evans highway) and continuing down a gravel road. Earthwatch, a nonprofit organization staffed mostly by volunteers working cooperatively with advisors from universities around the world, maintains a monitoring program here. For inquiries about guided weekend visits to the site, call the St. Croix Environmental Association at **773-1989.**

glens. (It's advisable to stick to the best-worn of the footpaths and to retrace your steps.)

You can also hike along the highways on the island's western sector, where few cars ever venture. Three of the most viable for hiking are the Creque Dam Road (Routes 58/78), the Scenic Road (Route 78), and the Western Scenic Road (Routes 63/78).

Consider beginning your trek near the junction of Creque Dam Road and Scenic Road. (Although cars can enter here, they rarely do.) Beginning at this junction, your trek will cover a broad triangular swath, heading north and then west along Scenic Road. First, the road will rise, and then it will descend toward the coastal lighthouse of the island's extreme northwestern tip, Hamm's Bluff. Most trekkers decide to retrace their steps after about 45 minutes of northwesterly hiking. Real diehards, however, will continue trekking all the way to the coastline, then head south along the coastal road (Butler Bay Road), and finally head east along Creque Dam Road to their starting point at the junction of Creque Dam Road and Scenic Road. Embark on this longer expedition only if you're really prepared for a prolonged hike lasting about five hours.

## ESPECIALLY FOR KIDS

**Fort Christiansvaern**    *(see p. 184)* Children are taken through dungeons and around battlements, and even shown how soldiers of yesteryear fired a cannon.

**St. George Village Botanical Garden of St. Croix**    *(see p. 188)* Kids wander this sunny spot built around the ruins of a sugarcane workers' village from the 1800s.

**Buck Island**    *(see p. 200)* The boat ride to Buck Island's 850 mostly underwater acres is a great amusement for kids. Equally appealing are the island's white sandy beaches, its profuse wildlife, and the picnic you've brought along.

# 6  Sports A to Z

## BEACHES

While beaches are the big attraction in St. Croix, getting to them from Christiansted, the center of most of the hotels, isn't always easy. It can also be expensive, especially if you want to go back and forth every day.

In Christiansted, take the ferry to the **Hotel on the Cay,** which occupies its own tiny island in the middle of the harbor. There you'll find a sandy bottom, a bar, restaurant facilities, and windsurfers.

**Cramer Park,** at the northeast end of the island, is a special public park operated by the Department of Agriculture. Lined with sea grape trees, the beach also has a picnic area, a restaurant, and a bar.

We highly recommend **Cane Bay** and **Davis Bay**—they're the kind of beaches you'd expect to find on a Caribbean Island (with palms, white sand, good swimming, and snorkeling). Cane Bay, which adjoins Route 80 on the north shore, attracts snorkelers and divers with its rolling waves, coral gardens, and dropoff wall. Davis Bay, which doesn't have any reefs to block the ocean swells, draws bodysurfers and has an alluring white sand beach. Changing facilities aren't available. It's off the South Shore Road (Route 60), in the vicinity of the Carambola Beach Resort.

Windsurfers like **Reef Beach,** opening onto Teague Bay along Route 82, a half-hour ride from Christiansted. Food can be ordered at Duggan's Reef. On

Route 63, a short ride north of Frederiksted, **Rainbow Beach** lures people with its white sand and ideal snorkeling conditions. In the same vicinity, also on Route 63, about five minutes north of Frederiksted, **La Grange** is another good beach. Lounge chairs can be rented, and there's a bar nearby.

At the **Cormorant Beach Club** (see "Accommodations," above), about 5 miles west of Christiansted, some 1,200 feet of white sands are shaded by palm trees. Since a living reef lies just off the shore, snorkeling conditions are ideal. **Grapetree Beach** offers about the same footage of clean white sand on the eastern tip of the island (Route 60). Follow the South Shore Road to reach it. Water sports are popular here.

**Buccaneer Beach,** 2 miles east of Christiansted, is another beach awaiting the explorer.

**Sandy Point,** lying directly south of Frederiksted, has the largest beach in all of the U.S. Virgin Islands. Its waters are shallow and calm, perfect for swimming. Sandy Point juts out from southwestern St. Croix like a small peninsula. It is reached by taking the Melvin Evans Highway (Route 66) west from the Alexander Hamilton Airport.

# SPORTS

## FISHING

The fishing grounds at Lang Bank are about 10 miles from St. Croix. Here you'll find kingfish, dolphin fish, and wahoo. Using light-tackle boats gliding along the reef, you'll probably turn up jack or bonefish. At Clover Crest, in Frederiksted, Cruzan anglers fish right from the rocks.

Serious sportfishermen can board the *Shenanigan's*, a 42-foot Hatteras convertible, available for half- or full-day charters with bait and tackle included. It's anchored at St. Croix Marina, Gallows Bay. Reservations can be made during the day by calling **773-7165,** or **773-4141** at night.

## GOLF

St. Croix has the best golf in the U.S. Virgins. In fact, guests staying on St. John and St. Thomas often fly over for a day's round. On the island are two 18-hole golf courses. ♻ **Carambola Golf Course** (☎ **778-5638**), on the northeast side of St. Croix, was designed by Robert Trent Jones, Sr., who called it "the loveliest course I ever designed." The course, formerly Fountain Valley, looks like a botanical garden with its bamboo, saman trees, and palms. Its collection of par-3 holes is known to golfing authorities as the best in the tropics. The course record at Carambola, site of "Shell's Wonderful World of Golf," is 66, set by Tom Kite in 1987. Greens fees are $55 for 18 holes. The rental of a golf cart is mandatory at $18 per 18 holes.

The other major course is at the **Buccaneer** (☎ **773-2100, ext. 738**), 2 miles east of Christiansted (see "Accommodations," above). The Buccaneer is a challenging 6,200-yard, 18-hole course that allows the player to knock the ball over rolling hills right to the edge of the Caribbean. The vistas are truly spectacular. Nonguests who reserve pay $30 for greens fees and $13 for a cart. A golf pro is available for lessons, and there is a pro shop.

**The Reef at Teague Bay,** in the east end (☎ **773-8844**), is a popular 3,100-yard, 9-hole course; greens fees are $14, and carts cost $8. The course's longest hole is a 579-yard par 5.

## HORSEBACK RIDING

Specializing in nature tours, **✪ Paul and Jill's Equestrian Stables,** Sprat Hall Plantation, Rte. 63 (☎ 772-2880), is the largest equestrian stable in the Virgin Islands. It's about a 35- to 40-minute ride from Christiansted by car. Set on the sprawling grounds of the island's oldest plantation great house, it's operated by Paul Wojcie and his wife, Jill Hurd, one of the daughters of the establishment's original founders. The stables are known throughout the Caribbean for the quality of the horses and the beautiful trail rides through the forests, past ruins of abandoned 18th-century plantations and sugar mills, to the tops of the scenic hills of St. Croix's western end. All tours are accompanied by operators who give a running commentary on island fauna, history, and riding techniques. Beginners and experienced riders alike are welcome.

A two-hour trail ride costs $50 per person; discounts are granted to residents staying at Sprat Hall Plantation. Tours usually depart at 10am and 4pm, with slight seasonal variations. Reservations at least three days in advance are important from December through April.

## SNORKELING & SCUBA

Sponge life, black-coral trees (considered the finest in the West Indies), and steep dropoffs into water near the shoreline have made St. Croix a diver's mecca.

**Buck Island,** with an underwater visibility of more than 100 feet, is the site of the nature trail along the underwater national monument; it's the major diving attraction on St. Croix (see "An Easy Excursion," below). All the minor and major travel agencies offer scuba and snorkeling tours to Buck Island.

Divers also like to go to **Pillar Coral,** with its columns of coral spiraling up to 25 feet and **North Cut,** one of the tallest, largest coral pinnacles in the West Indies. **Salt River Dropoff** plunges to depths of well over 1,000 feet, as does **Davis Bay Dropoff,** with its unique coral and rock-mound structures twisted into grotesque shapes.

**Dive St. Croix,** 59 King's Wharf (☎ 773-3434, or 800/523-DIVE), operates the 46-foot dive boat *Betty Ann.* The staff offers complete instruction from resort courses through full certification, as well as night dives, underwater photography, and rentals of underwater cameras. A resort course, including all equipment, and a one-tank boat dive, is $50. A two-tank boat dive for the certified diver goes for $75.

**V. I. Divers, Ltd.,** Pan Am Pavilion, 1102 Strand St., Christiansted (☎ 773-6045, or 800/544-5911), is a PADI five-star dive center established in 1971. *Skin Diver* magazine called its tours one of the "10 top dives in the Caribbean." An introductory resort course costs $85; a two-dive boat tour goes for $70.

## TENNIS

Some authorities rate the tennis at the **Buccaneer** (☎ 773-2100, ext. 736) as the best in the West Indies. The eight courts, two of which are lit for night games, are open to the public. Nonguests pay $10 per person per hour. You must call to reserve a court. A tennis pro is available for lessons, and there is a pro shop.

The **Carambola Golf Club** (☎ 778-0797), has five clay courts, two of which are lit for night games. The courts are reserved for hotel guests or residents of the nearby condos. There are a pro shop and a tennis pro for lessons.

## WINDSURFING

The best place for this increasingly popular sport is the **Tradewindsurfing Water Sports Center** (☎ 773-2035), located on a small offshore island in Christiansted harbor and part of the Hotel on the Cay. They give lessons and are open daily from 10am to 5pm. Renting a sailboat costs $60 for two hours.

# 7  Shopping

## CHRISTIANSTED

In Christiansted, the core of shopping on the island, the emphasis is on hole-in-the-wall boutiques, selling one-of-a-kind merchandise. Handmade items are popular. Of course, the same duty-free stipulations (see "Visitor Information, Entry Requirements & Money," in Chapter 3) apply to shopping in St. Croix.

Knowing it can't compete with Charlotte Amalie, Christiansted has forged its own kind of creativity, and by word of mouth, has now become the chic spot for merchandise in the Caribbean. All the shops are easily compressed into half a mile or so. On a day's tour (or half-day tours), you'll be able to inspect most of the stores.

### SHOPPING A TO Z

#### Art and Miscellanies

**American West India Company**
1 Strand St. ☎ **773-7325.**

Occupying the two floors of a town house from around 1733 located in downtown Christiansted, the American West India Company offers a broad collection of luxury products made in the Caribbean. Merchandise includes artwork from Haiti, gourmet foods, limited-production rums and liqueurs, sea island cotton clothing, T-shirts with unique Caribbean designs, ceramic figurines, and island-made jewelry.

**Folk Art Traders**
1B Queen Cross St. ☎ **773-1900.**

Since 1985, the operators of this store have traveled throughout the Caribbean to acquire a unique collection of local art and folk-art treasures. Their finds include carnival masks, pottery, ceramics, and original paintings, and hand-wrought jewelry. The merchandise is from all parts of the Caribbean, from batiks from Barbados to high-quality iron sculpture from Haiti. There is no other store in the Virgin Islands that caters so well to the Caribbean aficionado.

#### Crafts

See Folk Art Traders under "Art and Miscellanies," above.

**Java Wraps Home Store**
51 ABC Company St. ☎ **773-2920.**

At Java Wraps, textiles from the home cascade from antique Dutch Colonial chests, and old teak tables are laden with hand-drawn batik tablecloths, napkins, and card placements. There's also a collection of intricately patterned, hand-batik quilted bedcovers. Their wood carvings make unusual gifts. Grace your table with island-inspired hand-painted fish plates, large banana leaf trays, and coral reef salad bowls.

## Crystal

One of the best selections is at Little Switzerland (see "Jewelry," below).

## Fashions

### Java Wraps

Stand Street, Pan Am Pavilion. ☎ **773-3770.**

Known for their resortwear for women, men, and children, this shop is a kaleidoscope of colors and prints. You half expect Dorothy Lamour to appear at any minute. In fact, a modern-day Dorothy (actually a local salesperson) demonstrates how to wrap and tie beach pareos and sarongs. Men's shirts are a collection of tropic and ethnic prints, and there's also a children's selection.

## Gifts

### Many Hands

In the Pan Am Pavilion. ☎ **773-1990.**

Many Hands is devoted exclusively to Virgin Islands handicrafts. The merchandise includes West Indian spices and teas, shellwork, stained glass, hand-painted china, pottery, and handmade jewelry. Be sure to see their collection of local paintings and their year-round Christmas tree.

### Only in Paradise

5 Company St. ☎ **773-0331.**

This spacious, air-conditioned store offers a choice assortment of gifts, such as art glass, linens, fine and costume jewelry, and decorative items, as well as pearls—cultured, freshwater, or baroque. Its boutique, out back in a secluded courtyard, offers leather goods and cotton lingerie.

### The Royal Poinciana

Strand St. ☎ **773-9892.**

Probably the most interesting gift shop on St. Croix, The Royal Poinciana is the creative statement of Carl Brown and Jack Rahn. Within a decor like that of an antique apothecary shop, you'll find Caribbean-inspired items such as hot sauces, seasoning blends for gumbos, island herbal teas, Antillean coffees, a scented array of soaps, toiletries, lotions, and shampoos, and museum-reproduction greeting cards and calendars.

## Jewelry

### Colombian Emeralds

43 Queen Cross St. ☎ **773-1928.**

Colombian Emeralds specializes in stunning emeralds. In addition, there are rubies and diamonds and a large selection of other gemstones, including ametrine, blue topaz, opals, and amethyst. The staff will show you the large range of 14-karat gold jewelry. Check out the good deals in watches, including Seiko quartz.

### Little Switzerland

1108 King St. ☎ **773-1976.**

This store is one of the best sources on the island for crystal, figurines, watches, china, perfume, flatware, and fine jewelry. Little Switzerland specializes in all the big names, such as Paloma Picasso leather goods. If you want to buy a luxury item such as a Rolex watch or heirloom crystal, made by Lalique, Swarovski, and Baccarat, this is the place. Some items—at least a few—are said to sell for prices often 30% less than or the U.S. mainland.

## Pegasus Jewelers

58 Company St. ☎ **773-6926.**

Both a trusted retail outlet and a workshop, Pegasus specializes in diamonds, gold, and gemstones. They offer earrings, pendants, bracelets, and many one-of-a-kind pieces; tariffs are based on the fluctuating price of gold. They also have a varied selection of handcrafted gold, diamond, pearl, and coral jewelry. The shop also offers the finest collection of antique coins on the island.

## Liquor

Duty-free liquor purchases can be made at American West India Company (see "Art and Miscellanies," above).

The largest supply of discounted liquor is found not in Christiansted, but at **Woolworth's,** Sunny Island Shopping Center, Centerline Rd. ( ☎ **778-5466**), which is a department store. The liquor is duty free.

## Perfume

### St. Croix Perfume Center

1114 King St. ☎ **773-7604,** or 800/225-7031.

Here you'll find the largest duty-free assortment of men's and women's fragrances in St. Croix, usually at 30% below U.S. mainland prices. For a minimum charge of $5, this store will ship perfumes anywhere in the world. Each duty-free shipment should be for your personal use and should be valued at less than $100.

### Violette Boutique

In the Caravelle Arcade, 38 Strand St. ☎ **773-2148.**

This small department store, carrying a cosmopolitan line of perfume and luxury goods, stocks exclusive fragrances and hard-to-find bath lines. They also have the latest in Cartier, Fendi, Pequignet, and Gucci. A wide selection of famous cosmetic names are featured, and Fendi has its own bags and accessories section.

## Sportswear

### Down Island Clothing

West Indian Townhouse, King St. ☎ **773-9235.**

For a fashionable island look, head here for one-of-a-kind dresses, sandals, accessories, casuals, and swimwear. Located atop the Bombay Club, the store captures the light, laid-back spirit of St. Croix resort fashion better than any other clothing shop on the island.

### Simply Cotton

36C Strand St. ☎ **773-6860.**

Selling items made of 100% cotton, this store is ideal place to purchase casual fashions for both women and children. The makings of a tropical wardrobe, including skirts, washable tops, shorts, jackets, and pants are all here. The store even sells reasonably priced, casual nighttime wear.

## Toys

### Land of Oz

2126 Company St. ☎ **773-4610.**

Located opposite Market Square Mall, Land of Oz is one of the most enchanting stores for "children of all ages" in the Caribbean. Variety is the keynote of this establishment, which sells some 3,000 unusual items from around the world. They'll ship purchases for you.

## AROUND THE ISLAND

If you're touring western St. Croix in the vicinity of Frederiksted, you might want to stop off at the following offbeat shops.

### St. Croix Leap
Mahogany Rd., Rte. 76. ☎ **772-0421.**

In this open-air shop, you can see stacks of rare wood being tastefully fashioned into various objects. The shop is a St. Croix Life and Environmental Arts Project, dedicated to the natural environment through manual work, conservation, and self-development. The end result is a fine collection of Cruzan mahogany serving boards, tables, wall hangings, and clocks. St. Croix Leap is 15 miles from Christiansted; to reach it, drive drive 2 miles up Mahogany Road from the beach north of Frederiksted. Large mahogany signs and sculptures flank the driveway. Bear to the right to reach the woodworking area and gift shop. For inquiries, write to Leap, P.O. Box 245, Frederiksted, St. Croix, USVI 00841-0245. The site is open daily but does not keep set hours—"not too early, not too late."

### Whim Gift Shop
In the Estate Whim Plantation Museum, Centerline Rd. ☎ **772-0598.**

Be sure to browse through this museum gift shop located east of Frederiksted. The selection appeals to a wide age spectrum. Many of the goods are imported, but several are Cruzan made; some are specially crafted for the Whim Gift Shop. When you buy something, you contribute to the upkeep of the museum and the grounds.

## 8 St. Croix After Dark

St. Croix doesn't have as much nightlife as St. Thomas, which is just the way permanent residents want it. To find the action, you might have to hotel- or bar-hop. If he's playing, the man to seek out is Jimmy Hamilton, Duke Ellington's "Mr. Sax." He and his quartet are a regular feature of St. Croix nightlife. Ask at your hotel if he is appearing on the island.

Also try to catch a performance of the **Quadrille Dancers,** the cultural attraction of St. Croix. Their dances have changed little since plantation days. The women wear long dresses, white gloves, and turbans, and the men are attired in flamboyant shirts, sashes, and tight black trousers. When you've learned their steps, you're invited to join the dancers on the floor. Ask at your hotel if and where they are performing.

## THE PERFORMING ARTS

### Island Center
Sunny Isle. ☎ **778-5272.** Tickets $5–$25. Call the theater for performance times. Transportation: Taxi.

This 1,100-set amphitheater one-half mile north of Sunny Isle continues to attract big-name entertainers to St. Croix. Its program is widely varied, ranging from jazz, nostalgia and musical revues, to Broadway plays, such as *The Wiz.* Consult

*St. Croix This Week* or call the center to see what's being presented. The Caribbean Community Theatre and Courtyard Players perform regularly.

## THE CLUB & MUSIC SCENE

### The Terrace Lounge

Buccaneer, Estate Shoys. ☎ **773-2100**. $4 nonguests. Drinks $4. Daily 8–11pm. Transportation: Taxi.

Contained within a satellite lounge of the main dining room of one of St. Croix's most upscale hotels (see "Accommodations," above), the Terrace Lounge welcomes some of the Caribbean's finest entertainers. Jimmy Hamilton, who used to play with Duke Ellington, is the highlight. Guests staying at the Buccaneer pay only for their drinks. The house specialty is a Caribbean Sunset. The music includes jazz, calypso, reggae, and contemporary.

### Cormorant Beach Club Bar

4126 La Grande Princesse. ☎ **778-8920**. Drinks from $3.50. Daily 5pm–"whenever."

One of the most romantic bars on the island sits near the sands of the beach of La Grande Princesse this hotel bar northwest of Christiansted. (For a hotel review, see "Accommodations," above). Guests sit at tables overlooking the ocean or around an open-centered mahogany bar whose perimeter is defined by the open-air supports of an enlarged gazebo enhanced by wicker love seats, comfortable chairs, and soft lighting. After drinks, you can move into the adjacent restaurant (see "Dining," above) for dinner. Excellent tropical drinks are mixed here, such as the house specialty, a Cormorant cooler made with champagne, pineapple juice, and Triple Sec.

### The Wreck Bar

5 A-B Hospital Street, Christiansted. ☎ **773-6092**. Mon–Sat 4pm–at least 1:30am.

The bar has had only three owners in its 16-year history; the chain of command has maintained the same name and reputation for margaritas which are "absolutely habit forming." The decor, inspired by the TV series "Gilligan's Island," boasts a retractable awning extends over the open-air dance floor whenever it rains and an indoor-outdoor area decorated in ample amounts of bamboo and thatch. Bill and Penny are the married couple which maintains the place's sense of irreverent fun. Margaritas cost from $3 each.

### Hondo's Nightclub

53 King St. ☎ **778-8103**. $3 women, $5 men. Wed–Thurs 9pm–2am; Fri–Sat 9pm–4am.

Simply called "Hondo's" by its habitués, this is a late-night hot spot featuring either live or recorded music. No one's exactly sure what is happening around here on any given night. Be careful going through the streets late at night. Drinks cost from $3, but are reduced to $1.75 at happy hour from 9 to 10pm.

## 9  Networks & Resources

## FOR STUDENTS & ENVIRONMENTALISTS

### St. Croix Environmental Association

6 Company St. ☎ **773-1989**.

Although the schedules of its events and tours vary according to staff availability and public demand, the association offers regularly scheduled hikes from December through March. This is the most visible environmental group on St. Croix. They coordinate movements to restrict development in environmentally or culturally sensitive areas, test waters for sources of pollution, help reforest the land, and have ongoing in-school and public education programs.

In addition to in-season hikes, their programs include lectures, slide shows, and films on environmental issues. Prices for events vary, and contributions are accepted. The association disseminates information only about St. Croix, not about St. John or St. Thomas.

## FOR GAY MEN & LESBIANS

The only gay scene of any significance is in Frederiksted, on the western shore of the island. Life is relatively quiet here, and the gay scene is subdued. Gay men or lesbians mainly come here to relax and rest and enjoy the beaches—not to indulge in any frenzied nightlife.

Two or three inns in Frederiksted are popular with gays, although the clientele in all of these is mixed, attracting both gays and nongays. The best of these is **King Frederik on the Beach Resort,** Frederiksted Beach, P.O. Box 1908, Frederiksted, St. Croix, USVI (☎ **772-1205,** or **800/524-2018**), a small hotel lying one-half mile from the town's shopping and dining areas. It has 17 bedrooms, all with kitchenettes, private baths, and chamber service. In winter, a single or double ranges from $75 to $180 daily; the price is lowered in summer to $50 to $110 (either single or double). Coffee and continental breakfast are provided free, and the very popular gourmet patio restaurant provides lunch, dinner, and a well-attended Sunday brunch. The hotel accepts major credit cards.

## 10  An Excursion to Buck Island

The crystal-clear water and the white coral sand of ✪ **Buck Island,** 1¹/₂ miles off the northeast coast of St. Croix, are legendary. Only one-third mile wide and 1 mile long, the island and much of its offshore reef have been administered by the National Park Service since 1948, much to the delight of environmental groups. The endangered brown pelican produces young here, and marine life in the outlying waters is thriving.

Today, the park covers about 850 acres of land and water surface. The island contains picnic tables, barbecue pits, and a hiking trail through tropical vegetation. Facilities include restrooms and a small changing room. Offshore, there are two underwater trails for snorkeling above the coral, amazing schools of fish, and many other deeper labyrinths and underwater grottoes for more serious divers. Among the attractions are "forests" of elkhorn coral and thousands of colorful reef fish.

**Mile Mark Watersports,** in the King Christian Hotel, 59 King's Wharf (P.O. Box 3045), Christiansted, St. Croix, USVI 00820 (☎ **773-2628,** or **800/524-2012**), offers twice-daily tours to the aquatic wonders of Buck Island. They offer two ways to reach the reefs. One is to board a glass-bottom boat which departs twice daily from a point in front of the King Christian Hotel. The boat runs from 9:30am to 1pm and 1:30 to 5pm; the cost is $35 per person, all snorkeling equipment included. For a more romantic journey, board one of the company's wind-powered sailboats, which offers sea breezes and the thrill of using wind power to reach the reef. A full-day tour in the company's 40-foot catamaran can take up to 20 participants to Buck Island's reefs. Included in the tour are a West Indian barbecue picnic on the isolated sands of Buck Island's beaches, complimentary rum punches, and plenty of opportunities for snorkeling. Operating daily from 10am to 4pm, the trip costs is $40 for adults and $25 for children under 14.

**Captain Heinz,** P.O. Box 25273, Christiansted, St. Croix, 00824 (☎ **773-3161,** or **773-4041**), is an Austrian-born skipper with some 20 years of sailing experience. His trimaran, *Teroro II*, Leaves Green Cay Marina "H" Dock at 9am and 2pm and is never filled with more than 24 passengers, who pay $40 per person. All gear and safety equipment are provided. The captain sailed the first *Teroro* across the Atlantic, and he's not only a skilled sailor, but also is a considerable host. He will even take you around the *outer* reef, which the other guides do not, for an unforgettable underwater experience.

---

## A Walking Tour of Buck Island

A radically different kind of walking tour than trekking through the rain forest (see "Exploring the Rain Forest" in "Attractions," above) traverses Buck Island, a sunbaked, low-lying stretch of sand and coral rock off the island's northeastern coast. Here the climate is considerably drier than the rain forest, although the interest on this walk revolves around the marine life in the sunflooded, shallow waters off the rocky coastline of this long and narrow offshore island.

During the 19th century, goats overgrazed the island's surface, reducing the land to the barren condition you'll find it in today. Despite its arid land, the island is eminently suitable for pedestrian hikes. Just don't rush to touch every plant you see. The island's western edge has groves of poisonous machineel trees, whose leaves, bark, and fruit contain toxins that cause extreme irritation if they come into contact with human skin.

Most visitors to Buck Island come for its ring of beaches and its offshore snorkeling; a circumnavigation of the island on foot will take about two hours. Although Buck Island is only accessible via chartered tours and boat trips (see above), it is one of the most-visited rock spits in the Caribbean.

Managed and protected by the National Park Service, Buck Island has a trail which meanders from several points along its coastline to its sunflooded summit, which affords views over nearby St. Croix.

Of arguably greater interest on Buck Island is the underwater snorkeling trail which rings part of the island. With a face mask, swim fins, and a snorkel, you'll be treated to some of the most spectacular underwater views in the Caribbean. Plan on spending at least two-thirds of a day at this extremely famous ecological site.

# 7

# The British Virgin Islands

In the northeast corner of the Caribbean, about 60 miles east of Puerto Rico, the British Virgin Islands consist of 40 odd islands, some no more than rocks or spits of land. Only a trio of the British Virgins is of any significant size—Virgin Gorda ("Fat Virgin"), Tortola ("Dove of Peace"), and Jost Van Dyke. These islands, craggy and volcanic in origin, are just 15 air minutes from St. Thomas. There is also regularly scheduled ferry service between St. Thomas and Tortola.

With its small bays and hidden coves, once havens for pirates, the British Virgin Islands are considered by the yachting set to be among the world's loveliest cruising grounds. Despite predictions that mass tourism is on the way, these islands are still an escapist's paradise.

The smaller islands have colorful names such as Fallen Jerusalem and Ginger. Norman Island is said to have been the prototype for Robert Louis Stevenson's *Treasure Island.* On Deadman Bay, a barren islet, Blackbeard marooned 15 pirates and a bottle of rum, which gave rise to the well-known ditty.

*Note:* The British Virgin Islands use the U.S. dollar as their form of currency. British pounds are not accepted.

## GETTING THERE

Your gateway to the BVI will most likely be either Tortola or Virgin Gorda, which have the most hotels and services. If you're going to any of the other islands, make sure you carry adequate stocks of prescribed medicines or other items you need, because supplies and services in these islands tend to be severely limited or non-existent.

Before you go, you can obtain **information** about the British Virgin Islands from the **BVI Tourist Board,** 370 Lexington Ave., Suite 313, New York, NY 10017 (☎ **212/696-0400,** or **800/835-8530**); or from the **BVI Tourist Board,** 1686 Union St., San Francisco, CA 94123 (☎ **415/775-0344,** or **800/835-8530**). In the United Kingdom, contact **FCB Travel Marketing,** 110 St. Martin's Lane, London WC2N 4DY (☎ **0171/240-4259**).

### BY PLANE

There are no direct flights from North America to Tortola, but you can make easy connections through San Juan, St. Thomas, or St. Croix.

## What's Special About the British Virgin Islands

Discoveries

- Guana Island, boasting the richest fauna in the West Indies for an island of its size.
- Sage Mountain National Park, on Tortola, which contains the highest mountain in the Virgin Islands (1,780 feet)
- The Baths, Virgin Gorda—clusters of massive prehistoric rocks forming cool, inviting grottoes ideal for swimming and snorkeling.
- The wreck of the RMS *Rhone,* off Salt Island, a royal mail steamer from 1867—the most celebrated dive site in the West Indies.

Beaches

- Cane Garden Bay, on Tortola, which some beach aficionados rank as fine as St. Thomas's celebrated Magens Bay Beach.
- Apple Bay (also called Cappoon's Bay), a surfer's favorite west of Road Town on Tortola.

Great Towns/Villages

- Road Town, capital of Tortola and of the BVI, center for stocking up on supplies for those visitors heading for the remote islands.

Your best bet to reach Beef Island/Tortola is to take one of **American Eagle's** (☎ 800/433-7300) six daily flights from San Juan, Puerto Rico. San Juan is serviced by dozens of daily nonstop flights from North America, including Boston; Toronto; New York; Chicago; Miami; and Raleigh-Durham, North Carolina. You can also fly American to St. Thomas and take an American Eagle flight to Tortola.

Another choice, if you're on one of Tortola's neighboring islands, is **LIAT** (Leeward Islands Air Transport). This Caribbean carrier flies to Tortola from St. Kitts, Antigua, St. Maarten, St. Thomas, and San Juan, in small planes not known for their frequency or careful scheduling. LIAT does not maintain its own toll-free number, so all reservations are made through travel agents or through the larger U.S.-based airlines which connect with LIAT hubs. Call **809/462-0701** for more information.

Flying time to Tortola from San Juan is 30 minutes; from St. Thomas, 15 minutes; and from the most distant of the LIAT hubs (Antigua), 60 minutes.

### BY BOAT

You can go from Charlotte Amalie on St. Thomas by **public ferry** to West End and Road Town on Tortola. The 45-minute voyage goes along Sir Francis Drake Channel through the islands. Services making this run include: **Native Son** (☎ 495-4617), **Smith's Ferry Service** (☎ 495-4495), and **Inter-Island Boat Services** (☎ 776-6597). The latter travels a somewhat obscure route from St. John to the West End in Tortola. This service depart three times a day and four times a day on Friday.

## GETTING AROUND
### BY BOAT OR BUS

In Tortola, **Smith's Ferry** (☎ 54495) and **Speedy's Fantasy** (☎ 55240) operate ferry links to the Virgin Gorda Yacht Club (the trip lasts one-half hour). The

**North Sound Express** (☎ **52271**), near the airport on Beef Island, has daily connections to the Bitter End Yacht Club on Virgin Gorda. **Peter Island Boat** (☎ **42561**) also shuttles between Road Town on Tortola and Peter Island at least seven times a day.

Bus service exists only on Tortola and Virgin Gorda. See the specific section on each island, below, for further details.

# 1 Anegada

The most northerly and isolated of the British Virgins, 30 miles east of Tortola, Anegada (pop. 250) has more than 500 wrecks lying off its notorious Horseshoe Reef. It's different from the other British Virgins in that it's a flat coral-and-limestone atoll with a 2,500-foot airstrip. At its highest point, it reaches only 28 feet; Anegada hardly appears on the horizon, which explains why it has always been so notoriously dangerous to sailing craft. It is 11 miles long and 3 miles wide.

Many of the inhabitants of Anegada have looked unsuccessfully for the legendary hidden treasure on sunken ships including the *Paramatta,* which has rested on the sea bottom for more than a century.

At the northern and western ends of the island, there are some good beaches, which might be your only reason for coming here. This is a remote little corner of the Caribbean. Don't expect any frills, and be prepared to put up with some hardships, such as mosquitoes.

Most of the island, declared off-limits to development, has been reserved for birds and other wildlife. The BVI National Parks Trust has established a bird sanctuary which is the protected home of a flamingo colony, several different varieties of heron, as well as ospreys and terns. The trust has also designated much of the interior of the island as a preserved habitat for some 2,000 wild goats, donkeys, and cattle. The refuge is giving a new lease on life to the rock iguana, an endangered, fierce-looking, but actually harmless reptile that can grow to a length of five feet and weigh up to 20 pounds. Though rarely seen, these creatures have called Anegada home for thousands of years. The environment they share with the other wildlife has hardly changed in all those years.

## GETTING THERE & GETTING AROUND

**Gorda Aero Service** (☎ **809/495-2271**) is the only carrier which flies from Tortola to Anegada. Using six- to eight-passenger prop planes, it operates four times a week. The fare is $54 per person round trip. Flights run on Monday, Wednesday, Friday, and Sunday. In addition, **Fly BVI** (☎ **809/495-1747**), operates a charter/sightseeing service to and from Anegada from Beef Island off Tortola. The one-way cost is $125 for two to three passengers.

Tony's Taxis, which you'll easily spot when you arrive, will take you around the island. It's also possible to rent bicycles. Ask around.

### Impressions

*Question: Where are the British Virgin Islands?*

*Answer: I have no idea, but I should think that they are as far as possible from the Isle of Man.*

—Sir Winston Churchill

---

### ❓ Did You Know?

- Richard Humphreys, a Tortola-born man, founded the first black university in the United States.
- William Thornton, a BVI citizen, designed the U.S. Capitol Building.
- As late as 1869, the steamship *Telegrafo* was held in Tortola and officially charged with piracy.
- Tortola in 1756 had 181 free men and 3,864 slaves—about 21 slaves to each planter.
- In 1752, the BVI was the major Caribbean supplier of cotton to Britain.
- In 1831, free blacks living in the BVI were accorded the full legal rights of British subjects.
- The wreckage of the HMS *Nymph*, which sank off Road Town in 1783, was discovered in 1969.
- In the late 1960s, the British foreign secretary offered to sell the BVI to the United States.

---

## WHERE TO STAY & DINE

The Anegada Reef Hotel is the only major accommodation on the island. Neptune's Treasure, below, rents tents to stay in overnight.

### Anegada Reef Hotel

Setting Point, Anegada, BVI. ☎ **809/495-8002.** Fax 809/495-9362. 12 rms (all with bath). A/C Rates (with AP): Winter, $180 single; $230 double. Summer, $160 single; $215 double. No credit cards.

Anegada Reef Hotel is one of the most remote places, listed in this guide, and guests who stay here are in effect "hiding out." It is a favorite of the yachting set, who enjoy the hospitality provided by Lowell Wheatley. He offers large rooms with private porches opening onto the beach. Guests can easily go inshore and deep-sea fishing (also bonefishing), as well as diving and snorkeling.

On party nights, Mr. Wheatley hosts a fungi band, or he makes a barbecue on the beach. If you're going over for the day, you can order lunch at the beach bar. At night, the barbecued lobster is a favorite. If you plan to dine at the Reef, make a reservation by 4:30pm; dinner costs from $16 to $30 and is served at 7:30pm nightly. Many patrons arrive by boat for the lobster dinners.

### Neptune's Treasure

Between Pomato and Saltheap Points. VHF Ch. 16 or 68, or radio 4-3111. Seafood cuisine. Reservations recommended. Transportation: Taxi. Breakfast from $5; fixed-price lunch $6; fixed-price dinner $10–$20. No credit cards. Open daily 8am–9pm.

While on Anegada, you may want to visit this seaside restaurant which serves fresh fish and lobster that the owners catch themselves. The family that runs the restaurant helpfully explains how to explore the island. Live combos entertain Thursday. The family also rents tents with single or double air mattresses. You can take a taxi to one of their sandy beaches and go snorkeling along their reefs.

*Note:* The restaurant doesn't have a telephone. In its place is a radio contact number used by boaters.

# 2 Jost Van Dyke

This rugged island (pop. 130) on the seaward (west) side of Tortolac was probably named after a Dutch settler. On the south shore of this 4-square-mile mountainous island are some good beaches, at White Bay and Great Harbour. The island has only a handful of places to stay but has several dining choices, as it's a popular stopover point, not only for the yachting set but also for many cruise ships. The island is only tranquil when cruise ships aren't here.

In the 1700s, a Quaker colony settled here to develop sugarcane plantations. One of the colonists, William Thornton, won a worldwide competition to design the Capitol in Washington, D.C. Smaller islands surround the place, including little Jost Van Dyke, the birthplace of Dr. John Lettsom, founder of the London Medical Society.

## GETTING THERE

Guests heading for any point on Jost Van Dyke usually arrive via ferryboat from either St. Thomas or Tortola. (Be warned that departure times can vary widely throughout the year and at times do not adhere very closely to what is printed in the timetables.) Ferryboats from St. Thomas depart from Red Hook three days a week (Friday, Saturday, and Sunday) about twice a day. More convenient (and more frequent) are the daily ferryboat shuttles which head for Jost Van Dyke from Tortola's isolated West End. From there, ferryboats depart three times a day (25 minutes each way). The cost is $8 one-way, or $14 round-trip. Call the **Jost Van Dyke Ferryboat Service** (☎ **42997**) about departures from any of the points mentioned above. Of course, if all else fails, there are a handful of privately operated water taxis which for a fee will transport you, your entourage, and your luggage to Jost Van Dyke.

## WHERE TO STAY

Very casual types consider the simple accommodations offered by Rudy's under "Where to Dine," below.

### The Sandcastle

White Bay, Jost Van Dyke, BVI. ☎ **809/775-5262.** Fax 809/775-3590. 4 units (all with bath). Transportation: 20-minute private motor-launch from St. Thomas. Rates (including all meals): Jan 15–May 14, $255 single; $325 double. Off-season, $175–$195 single; $225–$265 double. Extra person $75–$95. MC, V.

A perfect retreat for escapists, this four-villa colony has octagonal-shaped cottages surrounded by flowering shrubbery and bougainvillea. Nestled among the palms, individual cottages take advantage of the tropical breezes and the view. This is a small, personalized place catering to only a handful of guests.

You're allowed to mix your own drinks at the beachside bar, the Soggy Dollar and keep your own tab. Visiting yachting people often drop in here for a while enjoy the beachside informality and order drinks called Painkillers See below for information about the dining room.

In the guest book, we found this endorsement: "I thought places like this only existed in the movies." For reservations and information from the U.S., call or write The Sandcastle, Suite 201, Red Hook Plaza, St. Thomas, USVI 00802 (☎ 809/775-5262).

# The British Virgin Islands/Sports

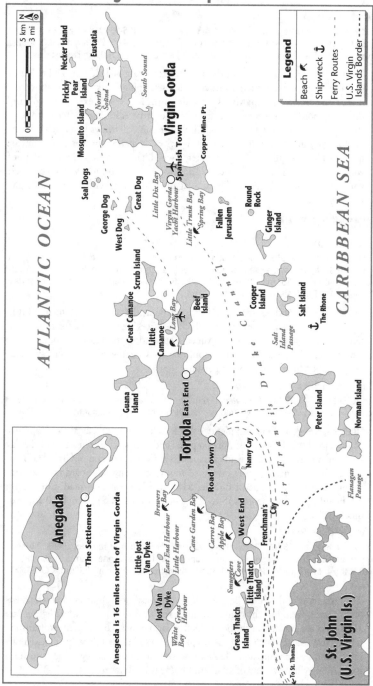

**Legend**

Beach
Shipwreck
Ferry Routes
U.S. Virgin Islands Border

ATLANTIC OCEAN

CARIBBEAN SEA

Necker Island
Eustatia
Prickly Pear Island
Mosquito Island
South Sound
North Sound
Virgin Gorda
Spanish Town
Copper Mine Pt.
Seal Dogs
George Dog
Great Dog
West Dog
Little Dix Bay
Virgin Gorda Yacht Harbour
Little Trunk Bay
Spring Bay
Fallen Jerusalem
Round Rock
Ginger Island
Scrub Island
Great Camanoe
Little Camanoe
Long Bay
Beef Island
Cooper Island
Salt Island
The Rhone
Salt Island Passage
Drake Channel
Guana Island
Tortola
East End
Road Town
Nanny Cay
West End
Frenchman's Cay
Sir Francis Drake Channel
Peter Island
Norman Island
Flanagan Passage
To St. Thomas

Anegada
The Settlement
Anegeda is 16 miles north of Virgin Gorda

Little Jost Van Dyke
Jost Van Dyke
White Bay
Great Harbour
Brewers Bay
East End Harbour
Little Harbour
Cane Garden Bay
Carrot Bay
Apple Bay
Smugglers Cove
Little Thatch Island
Great Thatch Island

St. John (U.S. Virgin Is.)

5 km
3 mi
0

## Sandy Ground

East End, Jost Van Dyke, BVI. ☎ **809/494-3391.** Fax 809/495-9379. 8 villas (all with bath). Transportation: Private water taxi from Tortola. Rates (weekly): Winter, $1,200 double; extra person $100–$150. Summer, $780 double; extra person $100. No credit cards.

Built on a 17-acre hill site on the northeastern part of Jost Van Dyke, Sandy Ground offers villas with self-sufficient housekeeping units under to those you might see along the Spanish Costa del Sol. The complex rents two- and three-bedroom villas. One of our favorites, constructed on a cliff, seems to hang about 80 or so feet over a good beach. If you've come all this way to reach this tiny outpost, you might as well stay a week, which is the period for which the rates are quoted. The airy villas are each privately owned, and each unit is fully equipped with refrigerators and stoves. You'll be directed to a store on Jost Van Dyke where you can purchase groceries. The managers help guests with boat rentals and water sports.

# WHERE TO DINE

### Abe's by the Sea

On Little Harbour. ☎ **59329.** Reservations recommended for groups of five or more. As you approach the harbor by private motor launch or boat from Tortola, you'll see Abe's on your right. Appetizers $3–$5; main dishes $12–$30. MC, V. Lunch daily noon–3pm; dinner daily 7–10pm. WEST INDIAN.

At this local bar and restaurant on Little Harbour, the cook offers a menu of fish, boiled lobster, conch, spareribs, and chicken. Prices are low, and a fungi band entertains. The main course is accompanied by peas, rice, green salad or coleslaw, and dessert. On Wednesday night in season, Abe's has a festive pig roast. Friday is barbecue night which costs $18 per person.

### Rudy's Mariner's Rendezvous

Great Harbour. ☎ **59282.** Reservations required by the afternoon of the night you expect to dine. Dinners $10–$22.50. No credit cards. Dinner daily 7pm–midnight. WEST INDIAN.

Rudy's serves good food and plenty of it. A welcoming drink awaits sea captains, and the food that follows is simply prepared and inexpensive. The catch of the day sometimes features lobster. Rudy's is located at the western end of Great Harbour.

Rudy's also rents 6 simply furnished rooms, charging full-board rates in winter of $75 to $125 single or double, $180 to $220 triple or quad. Off-season, full-board rates range from $55 to $75 single or double, $110 to $180 triple or quad.

### The Sandcastle

On White Bay. ☎ **55262.** Reservations required for lunch by 11am, for dinner by 4pm. Transportation: 20-minute private motor-launch from Tortola. Dinner from $30; lunch $15–$20. MC, V. Lunch daily, seating at 1:30pm; dinner daily seating at 7:30pm. CONTINENTAL.

The restaurant of this hotel (see "Accommodations," above) serves food which has often been frozen. Lunch is served in the open-air dining room, while lighter fare and snacks are available at the Soggy Dollar Bar. Dinner is by candlelight, featuring four to five courses, including such typical dishes as duck a l'orange, chicken tarragon, and grouper piccata. Meals are served with seasonal vegetables and fresh pasta, along with a variety of salads and homemade desserts.

## 3  Marina Cay

Near Beef Island, Marina Cay is a tiny private islet of 6 acres. Its claim to fame is that it was setting for the Robb White book *Our Virgin Isle*, which was made into a film in 1958 with Sidney Poitier and John Cassavetes.

The island lies only five minutes away by launch from Trellis Bay, adjacent to Beef Island International Airport.

## WHERE TO STAY

**Marina Cay Hotel**

Marina Cay, P.O. Box 76, Road Town, Tortola, BVI. ☎ **809/494-2174.** Fax 809/494-4775. 4 rms, 2 villas. Transportation: Private launch from Beef Island. Rates (including breakfast): Winter, $95–$125 double; $300 villa. Summer, $60–$75 double; $195 villa. AE, MC, V.

This small cottage hotel, opened in 1960 and extensively renovated, has preserved its original charm and conviviality. It houses guests in chalets, villas, and A-frames overlooking a reef and the Sir Francis Drake Channel, dotted with islands. Marina Cay is a tropical garden, with abundant frangipani, almond, tamarind, hibiscus, oleander, and bougainvillea. Dining is good yet casual; it features continental and West Indian dishes. Guests can remain active by snorkeling on adjacent Mother Turtle Reef; sailing on Sunfish, Windsurfers, and the J-24 sloop; scuba diving (certification courses are taught by a resident divemaster); kayaking; exploring on underwater safaris; taking castaway picnics on secluded beaches; and deep-sea fishing.

## 4  Peter Island

Half of this island, boasting a good marina and docking facilities, is devoted to the yacht club. The other part is deserted. Beach facilities are found at palm-fringed Deadman Bay, which faces the Atlantic but is protected by a reef. All goods and services are at the one resort (see below).

The island is so private that except for an occasional mason at work, about the only company you'll encounter will be an iguana or a feral cat whose ancestors were abandoned generations ago by shippers (the cats are said to have virtually eliminated the island's rodent population).

## GETTING THERE

A complimentary hotel-operated ferry, **Peter Island Boat** (☎ **52271**), picks up overnight guests who arrive at the Beef Island airport. It departs from the pier at Trellis Bay, near the airport, and requires a 45-minute crossing. Other boats depart eight or nine times a day from the CSY Dock in Road Town on Tortola for a 20- to 30-minute crossing. Passengers must communicate their plans to the hotel several hours in advance of their arrival or departure.

## WHERE TO STAY & DINE

**Peter Island Resort and Vacant Harbour**

Peter Island, P.O. Box 211, Road Town, Tortola, BVI. ☎ **809/494-2561,** or 800/346-4451. Fax 809/494-2313. 50 rms, one four-bedroom villa, two two-bedroom villas. A/C MINIBAR TEL Transportation: See above. Rates: Winter, $395–525 double; $675–875 Hawk's Nest two-bedroom villa for two; $3,220 Crow's Nest four-bedroom villa for up to eight guests.

Summer, $275–$385 double; $475–$675 Hawk's Nest two-bedroom villa for two; $1,230–$3,220 Crow's Nest four-bedroom villa for up to eight guests. MAP $65 per person extra. AE, MC, V.

Peter Island, which comprises only 1,800 acres, is the home of Peter Island Resort, solely dedicated to island guests and yacht owners who moor their craft here. After the destruction caused by the hurricane in 1989, the facilities and marina were restored and reopened in 1991. The island's tropical gardens and hillside are bordered by five private beaches.

The resort contains 30 units with oceanview or gardenview rooms facing Sprat Bay and Sir Francis Channel, and 20 larger beachfront units on Deadman Bay Beach. Casually elegant, the rooms include a terrace balcony, ceiling fan, and several other amenities. The Crow's Nest, a luxurious, four-bedroom villa, overlooks the harbor and Deadman Bay and offers its privileged guests a private swimming pool, hot tub, full kitchen, maid, gardener, personal steward, and island vehicle. The Hawk's Nest contains two two-bedroom villas situated on a hillside.

**Dining/Entertainment:** Tradewinds Restaurant serves breakfast and dinner featuring five-star gourmet cuisine throughout the year in fine Caribbean tradition. In a more casual setting, Deadman's Beach Bar and Grill serves sandwiches and salads beside the ocean. The main bar, Drakes Channel Lounge, is also open throughout the day and evening.

**Services:** Room service (breakfast only), laundry, massage, babysitting, guest launch transport to and from Beef Island airport.

**Facilities:** Fitness center, gift shop, freshwater pool, four tennis courts (two lit for night play), scuba-diving base, library, spa, conference facility, complete yacht marina. Complimentary use of Sunfish sailboats, basketballs, mountain bikes, sea kayaks, snorkeling gear, Windsurfers, and 19-foot Squib day-sailers.

## 5 Tortola

On the southern shore of this 24-square-mile island is **Road Town,** the sprawling capital of the British Virgin Islands. The landfill at Wickhams Cay, a 70-acre development and marina in the harbor, has brought in a massive yacht-chartering business and has transformed the sleepy capital into a bustling center.

The entire southern coast, including Road Town, is characterized by rugged mountain peaks with yellow cedar and frangipani. On the northern coast are white sandy beaches, banana and mango trees, and clusters of palms.

The **BVI Tourist Board** (☎ **809/494-3134**) is located in the center of Road Town near the ferry dock, lying south of Wickham's Cay. It is open Monday through Friday from 9am to 5pm.

### GETTING THERE

Close to Tortola's eastern end is **Beef Island,** the site of the main airport for passengers arriving in the British Virgins. The tiny island is connected to Tortola by the one-lane Queen Elizabeth Bridge.

### GETTING AROUND
#### BY TAXI

Taxis meet every arriving flight. Your hotel can also call a taxi. The fare from the Beef Island airport to Road Town is $15 for one to three passengers. A tour lasting 2¹/₂ hours costs $45 for one to three people. To call a taxi in Road Town, dial **42322;** on Beef Island, **52378.**

## BY CAR

Because of the volume of tourism on Tortola, you should reserve your rental car in advance, especially in winter. A handful of local companies rent cars, but because of the more lenient refund policies in case of billing errors, damage disputes, or insurance claims, we recommend using one of the U.S.-based giants, even if the cost is slightly higher. On Tortola, the local branch of **Budget** is at 1 Wickhams Cay, Road Town (☎ **809/494-5150,** or **800/527-0700**). **Avis** maintains offices opposite the police headquarters in Road Town (☎ **809/494-3322,** or **800/331-2112**). **Hertz** (☎ **809/495-4405,** or **800/654-3001**) has offices outside of Road Town, on the island's West End, near the ferryboat landing dock.

All three companies require that renters be at least 25 years old. You must also present a valid driver's license and purchase a temporary government-ordained BVI driver's license (which the car-rental company can sell you for $10; it's valid for three months).

At press time, Budget charged $210 per week for its least expensive car, a Nissan Sentra, a simple but peppy car with manual transmission suitable for four or five passengers. For an extra $18 a week, the same model was available with automatic transmission. A collision-damage waiver, eliminating all but $600 worth of financial responsibility in the event of an accident, cost an additional $8 per day. A 5% government tax was added to these prices. Rates at the other two companies were competitive.

These rates will almost certainly change before your departure. Call the companies for last-minute price adjustments at least 36 business hours before your intended pickup.

Remember to *drive on the left.* Because the island roads are notoriously dim at night, with few if any lines marking the shoulder of the sinuous and narrow roads, nighttime driving can be frightening. It's often a good idea to hire a taxi to take you to that difficult-to-find restaurant or nightspot.

## BY BUS

**Scato's Bus Service** (☎ **42365**) runs from the north end of the island to the west end, picking up passengers who hail it down. Fares are $1 to $3.

## WHAT TO SEE & DO

No visit to Tortola is complete without a trip to **Mount Sage,** Ridge Road, a national park rising 1,780 feet. On its slopes, you'll find traces of a primeval rain forest, the ideal spot for a picnic overlooking neighboring islets and cays. The mountain is reached by heading west from Road Town.

Before you head out, go by the tourist office and pick up a copy of a little brochure called *Sage Mountain National Park.* It has a location map, indicating directions to the forest (where there is a parking lot) and an outline of the main trails through the park.

Covering 92 acres, the park was established in 1964 to protect the remnants of Tortola's original forests which were not burned or cleared during the island's plantation era. From the parking lot, a trail leads to the main entrance of the park. The two main trails are the Rain Forest Trail and the Mahogany Forest Trail.

**Travel Plan Tours,** Waterfront Plaza, Road Town (☎ **42872**), oftens organized tours of Tortola. They will pick you up at your hotel (a minimum of four people is required) and take you on a 2¹/₂-hour tour of the island for $50 to $60. A **taxi tour** lasting 2¹/₂ hours costs $45 for up to three persons. To call a taxi in Road Town, dial **42322;** on Beef Island, **52378.**

## Hiking Trails

Life in the BVI centers on seafaring activities. In swimming, sailing, windsurfing, and simply sunning. If you suddenly experience a hankering for hiking along forested hillsides take a rented car (or a taxi if you don't mind the expense) northwest from Road Town to Sage Mountain National Park. In the park, 92 acres of protected, very hilly landscape are crossed by a network of hiking trails which are for the most part carefully designated with regard to time, difficulty, and destination.

The trails interconnect with one another at frequent intervals; all seem to converge at the BVI's tallest peak, Mount Sage. Little more than a hillock by North American standards, its 1,780-foot summit offers sweeping views of the surrounding islands and Sir Francis Drake Channel. Bring a picnic lunch for extended hikes. For data about current trail developments, stop in or contact BVI National Park Trust, Fishloch Road, P.O. Box 860, Road Town, Tortola, BVI.

## DRIVING TOUR
## Tortola's West End

**Start:**   Harbour Drive, in the center of Road Town.
**Finish:**   Harbour Drive, in the center of Road Town.
**Time:**   2 hours, not counting stops.
**Best Times:**   Any day before 5:30pm.
**Worst Times:**   Sunday, when many places close.

This tour concentrates on the West End, site of some of the lovelier beaches and vistas. Begin your tour at:

1. **Wickhams Cay,** which has the densest concentration of shops and restaurants, on Road Town. Less carefully planned than many other Caribbean capitals, Road Town seems at first glance to be a scattered sprawl of modern buildings which form a crescent along the harborfront and up the hillsides. At Wickhams Cay, however, some of the town's charm is more apparent.

From Road Town, head southwest along the coastal road, passing the capital's many bars and restaurants, including Pusser's, a popular watering hole. You'll also pass St. Paul's Episcopal Church (established 1937) and the Faith Tabernacle Church.

Less than 2 miles away on your left is the sandy peninsula containing:

2. **Nanny Cay Hotel and Marina.** There's an attractive restaurant here called Pegleg Landing (see "Where to Dine," below) and the opportunity to view some fine yachts bobbing at anchor.

Along the same road, 2$^1$/$_2$ miles southwest of Road Town, panoramic views on your left reveal the 5-mile-wide Sir Francis Drake Channel, loved by yachters throughout the world. You'll now traverse a curvy expanse of uncluttered road, one of the loveliest on the island, dotted with rocks, cays, inlets, and uninhabited offshore islands.

The crumbling antique masonry on the right side of the road (look through the creeping vegetation) is the ruins of a stone prison built by the English for pirates and unruly slaves. Lush St. John will appear across the distant channel.

Keeping the water constantly on your left, you'll come to the unpretentious hamlet of:

3. **West End and the pier at Soper's Hole.** Yachters and boaters report to the immigration and Customs officer stationed here. Turn left on the hamlet's only bridge to:

4. **Frenchman's Cay,** where there's a scenic view and, to the west, Little Thatch Island.

   Retrace your route toward Road Town. At the first major intersection, turn left up Zion's Hill. Tucked into a hollow in the hillside, is the:

5. **Zion Hill Methodist Church.** Boasting a devoted local following despite its rural isolation, it's one of many churches dotting the island.

   You'll soon be driving parallel to the island's northern coast, site of many of its least developed beaches, with imaginative names like Apple Bay, Little and Great Carrot Bays, and Ballast Bay. Stop at any of them to swim or snorkel wherever it looks safe; if in doubt, ask a local. Continuing along the coast, you'll pass the Methodist Church of Carrot Bay and the Seventh-day Adventist Church of Tortola.

☕ **TAKE A BREAK**      On the island's north coast, **Quito's Gazebo** is at Cane Garden Bay. Owned by Quito Rymer, one of the island's best musicians, it serves piña coladas (either virgin or laced with liberal quantities of Callwood's local rum) in an enlarged gazebo built almost directly above the waves.

   After Quito's, the road will cut inland, climbing dramatically through forests and fields; a sweeping view will unfold continuously behind you. Soon, you'll be forced to make a turn. Fork left, and continue for a short distance along the rocky spine that runs down the length of the island. A sign will point to a platform offering one of the finest views on Tortola:

6. **SkyWorld.** This eagle's-nest aerie has survived the most violent hurricanes. It offers unparalleled views of the entire island, as well as an array of food and drink. Many daytime visitors return to SkyWorld for a candlelit dinner.

   After passing SkyWorld, continue east for about 1 mile, forking right whenever possible. After the second right fork, the road will descend, passing houses, churches, suburbs, and schools, and eventually join the main road running beside the waterfront at Road Town.

## WHERE TO STAY

Many of the island's hotels are small, informal family-run guesthouses offering only the most basic amenities. Others are more elaborate, boasting a full range of resort-related facilities. None of them, however, is as big, splashy, and all-encompassing as the hotels in the U.S. Virgin Islands. Many of the island's repeat visitors seem to like that just fine.

   *Note:* All rates given within this chapter are subject to a 10% service charge and a 7% government tax.

   It is extremely difficult to divide hotels in the BVI into rigid price classifications, because some "inexpensive" hotels have a few "very expensive" rooms. Therefore, the following classifications are arbitrary and have many variations. In general, hotels ranked "expensive" charge from $195 to $295 for a double room. Those considered "moderate" ask from $140 to $195, although some rooms in this classification fall into the expensive category. Hotels ranked "inexpensive" ask less than $140 a night, although even in this category, there are some rooms in the "moderate" range. All the tariffs quoted are winter (high-season) rates. In summer, rates are discounted by 20% to as much as 60%.

---

### 🌐 In Their Footsteps

**Sir Francis Drake** (1543–96) English navigator and explorer famous for defeating the Spanish Armada in 1588. He's regarded as a notorious pirate throughout the Caribbean. Arriving in the Caribbean as the young captain of *The Judith* and a favored subject of Elizabeth I, Drake brought the swashbuckling adventures of the Elizabethan age to the Virgin Islands. A channel on Tortola now bears his name. He was the first Englishman to circumnavigate the globe.

**Birthplace:** Near Tavistock, England. **Residences:** He spent most of his life aboard ship, often in the Caribbean. **Resting Place:** Drake died aboard ship off Porto Bello on January 27, 1596, and was buried at sea.

---

## EXPENSIVE

### Frenchman's Cay Resort Hotel

P.O. Box 1054, West End, Tortola, BVI. ☎ **809/495-4844,** or 800/235-4077 in the U.S., or 800/463-0199 in Canada. Fax 809/495-4056. 9 villas (all with bath). A/C Directions: From Tortola, cross the bridge to Frenchman's Cay, turn left, and follow the road to the eastern tip of the cay. Rates: Winter, $195 one-bedroom villa for two; $295 two-bedroom villa for four. Summer, $115–$135 one-bedroom villa for two; $170–$200 two-bedroom villa for four. MAP $45 per person extra. AE, MC, V. Parking: Free.

This intimate, all-villa resort is tucked away on the windward side of Frenchman's Cay—the little island connected by bridge to Tortola. The 12-acre landscaped estate enjoys year-round cooling breezes and views of Sir Francis Drake Channel and the outer Virgins. The individual one- and two-bedroom villas are well furnished; each has a shaded terrace, full kitchen, dining room, and a sitting room. The two-bedroom villas have two full baths.

**Dining/Entertainment:** The Clubhouse Restaurant and lounge bar is located in the main pavilion, a typical island structure with a distinctive open-beam roof. The menu features continental and Caribbean cuisine. Every item is cooked to order. Try such dishes as island-style gazpacho, hot pumpkin soup, steak au poivre, or dolphin prepared West Indian style. A special island dinner costs $25.

**Services:** The following activities can be arranged: day-sail trips, horseback riding, scuba diving, island tours, and car rentals.

**Facilities:** Beach with snorkeling, freshwater swimming pool, tennis court, Sunfish sailboats, kayaks, Windsurfers.

### ✪ Long Bay Hotel

P.O. Box 433, Road Town, Long Bay, West End, Tortola, BVI. ☎ **809/495-4252;** 800/729-9599 in the U.S. or Canada; or 800/898-379 in Britain. Fax 914/833-3318 in Larchmont, N.Y. 62 rms, 20 two- and three-bedroom villas. A/C TEL Transportation: Taxi. Rates: Winter, $175–$265 single; $195–$295 double; from $600 two-bedroom villa for four. Summer, $55–$120 single; $110–$180 double; from $425 two-bedroom villa for four. MAP $37.50 per person extra. AE, MC, V. Parking: Free.

Located on the northwest shore about 10 minutes from the West End, this low-rise hotel complex is set in a 50-acre estate near the water. Escapists who want to stay on a faraway corner of a half-forgotten island come here. Regular and superior suites and cottages are available in a wide range of styles, shapes, and sizes. Accommodations are scattered along a hillside planted with shrubbery. Cottages come with two bedrooms (suitable for four guests), a bath and shower, a kitchen, and a living room overlooking the ocean. Beachfront deluxe rooms and cabañas, many benefiting from a massive rebuilding and upgrading following the 1989 hurricane, are set at the edge of the white sand overlooking the ocean.

**Dining/Entertainment:** The beach restaurant (within the stone ruins of a former distillery and sugar mill) offers breakfast and lunch, as well as informal à la carte suppers with delectable desserts. The Garden Restaurant serves dinner by reservation only, and the food is excellent.

**Services:** Room service, laundry, babysitting.

**Facilities:** Oceanside saltwater swimming pool, beach house.

### The Sugar Mill

P.O. Box 425, Apple Bay, Tortola, BVI. ☎ **809/495-4355,** or 800/462-8834. Fax 809/ 495-4696. 20 units (all with bath). 1 two-bedroom villa. Transportation: Taxi. Rates: Winter, $235 single; $250 double; $265 triple; $280 quad; $575 two-bedroom villa. Summer, $160–$175 single; $175 double; $190 triple; $220 quad; $390–$450 two-bedroom vila. Breakfast $9 extra. AE, MC, V. Parking: Free. Closed Aug–Sept.

Surrounded by lush foliage above the northwest shore of Tortola, this resort is a small inn of character with an acclaimed restaurant. Built on the site of a 300-year-old sugar mill, the cottage colony sweeps down the hillside to its own little beach. Jasmine, avocados, citrus trees, gardenias, bougainvillea, mangoes, bananas, pineapples, and sugar apples brighten the grounds. The estate is owned by former San Francisco residents Jeff and Jinx Morgan, who write about travel, food, and wine.

Comfortable apartments climb up the hillside, and at the center is a circular swimming pool. The contemporary well-planned accommodations range from cottages to suites; all accommodations are self-contained with kitchenettes and private terraces with views. Four of the units are suitable for families of four.

Lunch is served down by the beach, and dinner is served in the old Sugar Mill Restaurant, whose stone walls are decorated with Haitian paintings. Breakfast is offered on the terrace. The bars are open all day, and snorkeling equipment can be used for free.

## MODERATE

### The Moorings/Mariner Inn

P.O. Box 139, Wickhams Cay, Road Town, Tortola, BVI. ☎ **809/494-2332,** or 800/ 334-2435 for reservations. Fax 809/494-2226. 39 rms, 2 suites (all with bath). A/C TV TEL Transportation: Taxi. Rates: Winter, $150 single; $165 double; $230 suite. Summer, $80 single; $90 double; $125 suite. Extra person $15. Breakfast $7–$15 extra. AE, MC, V. Parking: Free.

The Caribbean's only complete yachting resort, this 8-acre complex contains shoreside accommodations, lanai hotel rooms, a dockside restaurant, a bar, a swimming pool, a tennis court, a gift shop, and a dive shop that has underwater video cameras for rent. Rooms are spacious, and all have kitchenettes. The inn is outfitted with 100 sailing yachts for rent, some worth hundreds of thousands of dollars. (See "Sports A to Z," below, for more information about renting yachts.)

### Nanny Cay Resort & Marina

P.O. Box 281, Nanny Cay, Road Town, Tortola, BVI. ☎ **809/494-4895,** or 800/786-4753. Fax 809/494-0555. 41 rms (all with bath). A/C MINIBAR TV TEL Transportation: Taxi. Rates: Winter, $140–$255 single or double. Summer, $45–$195 single or double. Extra person $20. Children under 12 stay free in their parents' room. Special diving, sailing, and windsurfing packages available. Breakfast $10 extra. AE, MC, V. Parking: Free.

Occupying a 25-acre site adjoining a 210-slip marina, the Nanny Cay is located 1¹/₂ miles southwest of the center of Road Town and 10 miles from the airport.

It offers rooms and studios with sitting areas, fully equipped kitchenettes, ceiling fans, and private balconies opening onto a view of the water, the marina, or the gardens. Accommodations, decorated in a West Indian motif, contain two big double or queen-size beds, along with many extras. Some of the accommodations are arranged around courtyards; others are on a strip of sandy land facing the distant end of the marina. When you're booking a room, ask about the hotel's package deals for everybody from divers to honeymooners. Built on stilts above the marina, the Pegleg Landing Restaurant serves both lunch and dinner daily, featuring international dishes with a Caribbean flair. More casual food is offered at the Plaza Restaurant.

## Prospect Reef Resort

P.O. Box 104, western end of Road Town, Tortola, BVI. ☎ **809/494-3311,** 800/356-8973 in the U.S. or 800/463-3608 in Canada. Fax 809/494-5595. 131 units (all with bath). TEL Transportation: Taxi. Rates: Winter, $147–$190 single or double; $ 410 two-bedroom villa for four. Summer, $88–$117 single or double; $274 two-bedroom villa for four. Continental breakfast $6 extra. AE, MC, V. Parking: Free.

Built by a consortium of British investors in 1979, Prospect Reef is the largest resort in the BVI. It's contained within a series of two-story cement-sided buildings scattered over 15 acres of steeply sloping terrain. It rises above a small, private harbor. The bedrooms encompass one of the most panoramic views of the Sir Francis Drake Channel. Each of the resort's buildings is painted inhibiscus-inspired shades of pink, peach, purple, and aquamarine. Each building contains up to 10 individual accommodations. Initially designed as condominiums, the buildings contains unique studios, town houses, and villas, in addition to guest rooms. All accommodations include private balconies or patios; larger units have kitchenettes, good-size living and dining areas, and separate bedrooms or sleeping lofts. About one third of the rooms are air-conditioned, while others are cooled by ceiling fans and the constant trade winds.

**Dining/Entertainment:** Food at the hotel's Upstairs Restaurant, offering a combination of continental specialties and island favorites, was praised by *Gourmet* magazine. Count on spending about $30 a person at dinner, more if you order wine and lobster. Light meals are served on the terrace of the Scuttlebutt Café or around the Seapool Bar and Grill.

**Services:** Guest services will advise you on day sailing, snorkeling, scuba diving, and sportfishing.

**Facilities:** Two pools, sand-terraced sea pools for snorkeling or fish-catching, six tennis courts, health-and-fitness center, pitch-and-putt course.

## ⑤ Treasure Isle Hotel

P.O. Box 68, Pasea Estate, east end of Road Town, Tortola, BVI. ☎ **809/494-2501,** or 800/ 334-2435 for reservations. Fax 809/494-2507. 39 rms. 2 suites (all with bath). A/C TEL Transportation: Taxi. Rates: Winter, $150 single; $165 double; $230 suite. Summer, $80 single; $90 double; $125 suite. Extra person $15. Breakfast $10–$12 extra. AE, MC, V. Parking: Free.

The most centrally located resort hotel on Tortola, Treasure Isle is located at the eastern edge of the capital, 1 mile from the center, on 15 acres of hillside overlooking the coastal road and a marina. The large, sunny bedrooms occupy two-storied angular buildings built along landscaped terraces. The other buildings on the site are suites.

Adjoining the hotel's free-form swimming pool area is a covered pavilion reminiscent of a West Indian clapboard-covered house. Overlooking the harbor, it serves barbecue and an à la carte menu. Every Wednesday, the restaurant offers one of the best-known West Indian buffets on the island, complete with music and dancing.

The hotel has a thoughtful staff and a fully equipped dive facility. Daily excursions are offered to nearby beaches, reefs, and secluded islands.

## INEXPENSIVE

### 🄂 Fort Burt Hotel

Fort Burt, Road Town, Tortola, BVI. ☎ **809/494-2587.** Fax 809/494-2002. 7 rms (all with bath), A/C TV Rates: Winter, $80 single; $110 double. Summer, $65 single; $85 double. Breakfast $8 extra. AE, MC, V. Parking: Free.

Covered with flowering vines, Fort Burt rents rooms but devotes most of its energy to its popular pub and restaurant (see "Where to Dine," below). Built in 1960 upon the ruins of a 17th-century Dutch fort, the rooms are set at a higher elevation than any others in Road Town, offering views from their private terraces to the waterfront below. Simple, sun-flooded, and cozy, they have a colonial charm and freewheeling conviviality. Guests must trek to the nearest beach, but there is a pool on the grounds.

### 🄂 Sebastians on the Beach

P.O. Box 441, Little Apple Bay, West End Tortola, BVI. ☎ **809/495-4212.** Fax 809/495-4466. 26 rms (all with bath). MINIBAR Transportation: Taxi to West End. Rates: Winter, $110–$180 single; $120–$190 double. Summer, $60–$140 single; $70–$150 double. Extra person $15. MAP $35 per person extra. AE, MC, V. Parking: Free.

Established in the 1970s, this hotel is located at Little Apple Bay, about a 15-minute drive from Road Town, on a long beach said to have some of the best surfing in the BVI. The rooms are housed in three buildings, only one of which is on the beach. The floral-accented units come with rattan furniture and have small refrigerators and private baths. Six units have air conditioning, balconies, and porches. The restaurant overlooks the bay and offers an international selection of cuisine; on Saturdays and Sundays, guests enjoy live entertainment in the bar. The hotel offers dive packages, as well as packages that include a MAP plan and other perks including a bottle of rum.

### Village Cay Hotel

Wickhams Cay, Road Town, Tortola, BVI. ☎ **809/494-2771.** Fax 809/494-2773. 20 rms (all with bath). A/C TV TEL Rates: Winter, $90–$300 single; $115–$400 double. Summer, $70–$230 single; $90–$300 double. Breakfast $3.50–$15. AE, DC, MC, V. Parking: Free.

Village Cay is the most centrally located full-service lodging facility in the British Virgin Islands. Set in the heart of Road Town, all rooms have been recently refurbished and many directly overlook a marina filled with yachts from around the world. Some of the rooms have balconies and patios, and room service and laundry are provided. You can get an inexpensive lodging here if you reserve one of the standard rooms. The most expensive rooms are in the waterfront accommodations, which are costly, especially in winter. The dockside restaurant is open daily from 7am to 11pm, serving breakfast, lunch, and dinner. Entertainment is featured during winter season.

Anything you need is available within a five-minute walk of the premises, including ferry service to other islands, secretarial services for traveling business clients, or taxi service to anywhere on Tortola.

**Readers Recommend**

*One of my delights on the island of Tortola was strolling into the authentic Italian café* **Cappricco di Mare** *for personal favorites such as lobster ravioli in rosé sauce, the sophisticated insalata mista with large leafy greens and slices of fresh parmesan, or, after one week in the tropics, an overdue cappuccino. [It] is just about as good as an oasis . . . .* —Donna M. Sianchuk, Westmount, Quebec, Canada

## WHERE TO DINE

Most guests dine at their hotels, but want to venture out, try one of our suggestions below.

Restaurants rated "expensive" ask around $30 to $35 for dinner, while a meal in a "moderate" place costs from $20 to $25. Restaurants serving meals for $20 or under are considered "inexpensive."

### EXPENSIVE

#### ✪ Brandywine Bay Restaurant

Brandywine Estate. ☎ **52301.** Reservations required. Transportation by taxi. Appetizers $6–$13; main dishes $21–$27. AE, MC, V. Dinner Mon–Sat 6:30–9:30pm. Closed Aug–Oct. FLORENTINE/CARIBBEAN.

Located on the south shore 3 miles east of the center of Road Town, this restaurant is set on a cobblestone garden terrace and overlooks Sir Francis Drake Channel. Chef Davide Pugliese and his wife, Cele McLachlan, have earned a reputation in Tortola for their outstanding Florentine and Caribbean food. Davide changes his menu daily based on the availability of fresh produce. Typical dishes include beef carpaccio, homemade lobster ravioli, and his own special calves' liver with cassis. When available, pheasant and venison might also be featured. Try the homemade mozzarella with fresh basil and tomatoes.

#### The Cloud Room

Ridge Road. ☎ **44429.** Reservations required. Transportation by private pickup from your hotel. Fixed-price menus $22–$30. AE, MC, V. Open Nov–May, dinner Mon–Sat 7:30–10pm. CONTINENTAL.

Dining at The Cloud Room is a unique experience. The restaurant/bar sits atop Butu Mountain, overlooking Road Town. When weather permits, which is practically every day of the year, the roof slides back, allowing you to dine under the stars. Unfortunately, the road here is bad and there's no place to park, so the owner, Paul Wattley, prefers to arrange to pick you up when you make your reservation for dinner. The selection includes juicy sirloin steaks, fresh fish in season, shish kebab (the house specialty), and shrimp in creole sauce.

#### ✪ Skyworld Restaurant

Ridge Rd. ☎ **43567.** Reservations recommended for dinner. Transportation by taxi. Appetizers $5.60–$7; main dishes $22–$28; six-course dinner $34–$40. AE, MC, V. Lunch daily 11:30am–3pm; dinner daily 6:30–9pm. Closed in Sept. INTERNATIONAL.

SkyWorld is all the rage, and it is certainly the worthiest excursion on the island, lying up "Joe's Hill," a mile north of Road Town. The route is signposted. On one of the loftiest peaks on Tortola, at a breezy 1,337 feet, it offers views of both the U.S. and British Virgins. The french fries and onion rings have been praised by

*Gourmet* magazine, and many consider the conch fritters the best on the island. Guests enjoy the view at lunch and dinner, when an elegant, classic French-inspired menu is offered. Main dishes include scallops, rack of lamb, lobster ravioli, and fresh local fish grilled to order. You can finish with a dish of homemade tropical ice cream.

## Sugar Mill Restaurant

Apple Bay. ☎ **54355.** Reservations required. Transportation by taxi. Appetizers $5–$7; main dishes $16–$28. AE, MC, V. Lunch daily noon–2pm; dinner daily 7–8:30pm. CALIFORNIA/CARIBBEAN.

At this restaurant, you'll dine in an informal room that was once a 300-year-old sugar mill (see "Where to Stay," above). Haitian paintings decorate stone walls alongside big copper basins once used for distilling rum and now filled with tropical flowers. Your hosts are Jeff and Jinx Morgan, who know a lot about food and wines. Together they write a monthly column, "Cooking for Friends" for *Bon Appétit.* They have also cowritten a cookbook. One of their most popular creations is curried banana soup.

Before you go to the dining room, we suggest a visit to the gazebo-inspired bar, open-air in true West Indian fashion. Jinx Morgan supervises the dining room, where specialties might include seafood creole, lobster crêpes, and a cold rum soufflé. Everything here is homemade, including many island specialties. Ingredients for the crisp salads come mostly from the hotel's extensive herb and vegetable garden. The small menu changes each evening. Lunch can be ordered by the beach at the second restaurant, Islands, where dinner is also served Tuesday through Saturday from 6:30 to 9pm, January through May. Islands features Caribbean specialties. Try the jerk ribs or stuffed crabs.

## MODERATE

### The Apple

Little Apple Bay. ☎ **54437.** Reservations recommended. Transportation by taxi. Appetizers $3.25–$8; main dishes $14–$30. AE. Lunch daily 11am–2:30pm; dinner daily 6:30–9:30pm. Closed Sept–Oct. WEST INDIAN.

You get West Indian fare with flair at this place on the northwest coast of Tortola at Little Apple Bay. Diners can begin with the bartender's special drink, a Virgin "souppy" made with soursop juice (from the famous Caribbean fruit) and rum, among other ingredients. For dinner, you can select from an array of seafood dishes, including whelks (large marine snails) in garlic butter, conch BVI style, or the catch of the day steamed and served with a creole sauce. Vegetarian meals are also featured. Call owner Liston Molyneaux, a native Tortolian, for a reservation; we will feed you well. In winter, local entertainment livens up the Apple from 7 to 10pm on Wednesday and Sunday.

### Captain's Table

Inner Harbour Marina, Wickhams Cay. ☎ **43885.** Reservations required for dinner. Appetizers $5–$14; main dishes $16.50–$20.50. AE, DC, MC, V. Lunch Mon–Fri 11:30am–3pm; dinner daily 6:30–10pm. CARIBBEAN/FRENCH.

This elegant restaurant is contained within a pastel-colored, low-slung building that was originally built as a disco in the early 1980s. Seating is available in a clean, high-ceilinged, and spacious dining room, but the more desirable tables are on a waterfront veranda with cane chairs and furnishings.

Lunch choices might include a salad of smoked salmon with asparagus, "wings of fire" (chicken wings in creole sauce), and sautéed flying fish. Dinner specialties often include linguine with seafood, stuffed crab, garlic-stuffed saltwater mussels, lobster pulled from the restaurant's holding tank, and several kinds of local fish, blackened and served with Cajun sauce. Kir Royale (champagne with crème de cassis) is a fine apéritif to cap off your meal.

### Fort Burt Restaurant and Pub

Fort Burt, Road Town. ☎ 42587. Reservation recommended for dinner. English breakfast $8; appetizers $4–$12; main dishes $4–$23. AE, MC, V. Breakfast daily 8–10am; lunch daily noon–3pm; dinner daily 6–11pm. Bar daily 10am–midnight. INTERNATIONAL.

This restaurant was built upon rocks mortared together with lime and molasses in the 17th century by the Dutch and the French. Lunches offer a selection of soups, salads, grilled fish, and sandwiches. Dinners are candlelit and more elaborate, with such dishes as fresh asparagus with aïoli sauce, conch fritters, shepherd's pie, pepper steak, and roast duck with orange and tarragon sauce.

### Mariner Inn Restaurant/Moorings

Wickhams Cay. ☎ 42332. Reservations recommended. Transportation by taxi. Appetizers $5–$6.50; main dishes $12.95–$30. AE, MC, V. Lunch daily 11:30am–2:30pm; dinner daily 6:30–9:30pm. FRENCH/CARIBBEAN.

This is one of the more sophisticated restaurants in the BVI, attracting a nautical crowd. Its open-air tables overlook the Moorings Marina lying east of Road Town. At lunch, you can drop in and enjoy light food at the Marina Inn Bar, including sandwiches, hamburgers, roti, and chef's salad. At night the candlelit dinners are more elegant, featuring such dishes as steak au poivre, dolphin, grouper, and lobster served Virgin Islands–style.

## INEXPENSIVE

### ⊗ Mrs. Scatliffe's Restaurant

Carrot Bay. ☎ 54556. Reservations required before 5:30pm for dinner. Transportation by taxi. Fixed-price menu $20–$27. No credit cards. Dinner daily 7–8pm (no later). WEST INDIAN.

For the best and most authentic West Indian fare (with an international touch), check out this restaurant. Mrs. Una Scatliffe offers meals on the open-air deck of her island home, and some of the vegetables come right from her garden. Begin with one of the best daiquiris on the island, made from fresh tropical fruit, while munching a breadfruit stick. Next you'll be served a soup, perhaps spicy papaya, which will be followed by curried goat or "ole wife" fish, perhaps chicken in a coconut shell. After dinner, the devoutly religious Scatliffe family often entertains with a fungi-band performance (Monday to Saturday only). Be aware that part of your experience at this place might be an exposure to the gentle and often humorous form of Christian fundamentalism that affects many aspects of Mrs. Scatliffe's life. A bible reading and a heartfelt rendition of a gospel song might follow your meal after the dessert is served. Advance reservations are absolutely essential before you head out on the rather arduous road toward this restaurant.

### Paradise Pub

Fort Burt Marina, Harbour Road. ☎ 42608. Reservations recommended. Appetizers $6–$12.50; main dishes $8.50–$21. AE, MC, V. Lunch Mon–Fri 11:30am–2:30pm; dinner daily 5:30–10pm. INTERNATIONAL.

Contained within a low-slung timbered building on a narrow strip of land between the coastal road and the southern edge of Road Town's harbor, this establishment has a grangelike interior and a rambling veranda built on piers over the water. Many of the island's sports teams celebrate here after their victories. The pub also attracts the boating crowd. In inventory are more than 25 different kinds of beer. Live entertainment begins at 10pm. If you're here for a meal, you can order Bahamian fritters, Caesar or Greek salads, pasta, four kinds of steaks, and burgers. The chef also prepares a catch of the day, perhaps wahoo. Different nights of the week are devoted to theme dinners, including all-you-can-eat pasta night, prime rib night, and baby back ribs night. Call to find out what the theme is on the night of your visit.

### Pegleg Landing

Nanny Cay Hotel and Marina, Road Town. ☎ **44895.** Reservations not required. Appetizers $6.75–$8; main dishes $18–$25. AE, MC, V. Lunch daily 11:30am–2pm; dinner daily 6–10pm. Bar daily 10am until closing. INTERNATIONAL.

Built in 1980, this restaurant lies $1^1/_2$ miles southwest of Road Town and overlooks the yachts of the Nanny Cay Marina. You'll find accents of stained glass, mastheads from old clipper ships, lots of rustic paneling, and a nautical theme enhanced by the views and breezes from the sea. Specialties include sautéed breast of chicken in a champagne and orange sauce, charbroiled New York strip steak with mushrooms, and fresh filets of fish.

### Pusser's Landing

Frenchman's Cay, West End. ☎ **54554.** Reservations not required. Transportation by taxi. Appetizers $4–$9; main dishes $13–$25; lunch $6–$8.75. AE, MC, V. Lunch daily 11am–3pm; dinner daily 6–10pm. CARIBBEAN/ENGLISH PUB/MEXICAN.

This second Pusser's (see below for the original Pusser's) is more desirably located than its predecessor, as it lies in the West End, opening onto the water. The well prepared dinners include fresh grilled fish and some English-inspired dishes, such as classic shepherd's pie with a potato crust. Begin with a hearty bowl of fresh soup with seasonal ingredients and follow it with filet mignon, West Indian roasted chicken, or a filet of swordfish. Mud pie is the classic dessert. Happy hour is daily from 5 to 6:30pm.

### Pusser's Ltd.

Main St., Road Town. ☎ **43897.** Reservations recommended. Appetizers $3–$7.95; main dishes $7–$13.95. AE, MC, V. Daily 9am–10pm. CARIBBEAN/ENGLISH PUB/MEXICAN.

The complete lunch and dinner menu here includes old-style English shepherd's pies, New York deli–style sandwiches, and even Mexican fare in the evening. *Gourmet* magazine asked for the recipe for the chicken and asparagus pie. Pusser's also serves John Courage draft ale. Of course, the drink to have here is the famous Pusser's Rum, the same blend of five West Indian rums that the Royal Navy has served to warm sailors for more than 300 years.

### Sebastians on the Beach

West End. ☎ **54212.** Reservations not required. Transportation by taxi. Breakfast $5–$7.50; lunch $4–$9; dinner appetizers $4–$6; dinner main dishes $15–$33. AE, MC, V. Breakfast daily 8–11am; lunch daily noon–6pm; dinner daily 6:30–9:30pm. Bar daily 10am–10:30pm. INTERNATIONAL.

The wooden tables and rush-buttomed chairs here are scattered, Polynesian style, beneath a rustic yet comfortable pavilion few feet from the waves of the island's

West End. Sun lovers sit within the open courtyard nearby. The lunch menu consists of burgers, sandwiches, and salads; it is replaced in the evening with a more elaborate choice of food including a selection of fresh fish and lobster, dolphin in an island creole sauce or lime butter, curried chicken, prime ribs, and grilled steaks.

### Quito's Gazebo

Cane Garden Bay. ☎ **54837.** Reservations not required. Transportation by taxi. Lunch $4–$8; dinner appetizers $4.50–$8; dinner main dishes $12–$16. No credit cards. Lunch Tues–Sun 11am–3pm; dinner Tues–Sun 6:30–9:30pm. Bar open Tues–Sun 11am–midnight. CONTINENTAL/WEST INDIAN.

Owned by Quito Rymer, one of the island's most famous and acclaimed musicians, this is the most popular of the several restaurants located along the shoreline of Cane Bay. Quito himself performs after dinner on Tuesday, Thursday, Friday, Saturday, and Sunday. Set directly on the sands of the beach and designed like an enlarged gazebo, the restaurant serves frothy rum-based drinks priced at from $4 each (ask for the house version of a piña colada, or a Bushwacker made with four different kinds of rum). Lunch includes sandwiches, salads, and platters. Evening meals might include conch or pumpkin fritters, mahi mahi with a wine-butter sauce, conch with Callwood rum sauce, chicken rôti, or steamed local mutton served with a sauce of island tomatoes and pepper.

### BUDGET

### Harbour Café

Prospect Reef Resort, Drake's Hwy. ☎ **43311** (ext. 229). Reservations not accepted. Sandwiches, platters, and salads $5–$14; breakfast omelets $6. AE, MC, V. Daily 7am–1am. INTERNATIONAL.

The café's greatest asset is its location 1 mile west of the center of Road Town beside the smallest and perhaps most charming marina in Road Town. Order your meal at the counter, then carry it to one of the picnic tables, which are sheltered from the sun but not from the breezes off the water. The simple setting here keeps prices down, and the food—especially breakfast—is plentiful and good. Specialties include lobster or beef crêpes, fried filets of fish, lobster or crabmeat salads, sandwiches, burgers, and a house drink that combines several kinds of rum into a lethal combination known as a Painkiller. The place is especially popular at breakfast, when eight different kinds of "rooster omelets" draw the yachters and construction workers alike.

## SPORTS A TO Z
### BEACHES

Beaches are rarely crowded on Tortola unless a cruise ship arrives. You can rent a car or a Jeep to reach these beaches, or else take a taxi (arrange for a return at an appointed time). There is no public transportation.

The finest beach is **Cane Garden Bay,** which some aficionados have compared favorably to the famous Magens Bay Beach on the north shore of St. Thomas. Cane Garden Bay lies directly west of Road Town, up and down some steep hills, but it's worth the effort to get there.

Surfers like **Apple Bay,** lying to the west of Road Town. A hotel on Apple Bay, Sebastians (see "Where to Stay," above), caters to a surfing crowd. January and February are the ideal time to visit.

**Brewers Bay,** site of a campground, lies northwest of Road Town. Both snorkelers and surfers are attracted to this beach.

**Smugglers Cove** is at the extreme western end of Tortola, opposite from the offshore island of Great Thatch. The American island of St. John is directly south of Smugglers Cove. This beach, also known as Lowre Belmont Bay, also attracts surfers.

**Long Bay Beach** is on Beef Island, east of Tortola, and the site of the major airport. This mile-long stretch of white sand beach is reached by taking the Queen Elizabeth Bridge and then going along a dirt road to the left before you come to the airport. From Long Bay, you'll have a good view of Little Camanoe, one of the rocky offshore islands around Tortola.

## SPORTS

**Boating**    The best place for this sport is **The Moorings,** P.O. Box 139, Wickhams Cay, Road Town, BVI (☎ **42332,** or **800/535-7289**) (this 8-acre waterside resort is also recommended under "Where to Stay," above). This resort, along with a limited handful of others, makes the British Virgins the cruising capital of the world. Charlie and Ginny Cary started the first charter service in the BVIs. You can choose from their fleet of sailing yachts, which can accommodate up to four couples in comfort and style. Depending on your skill and inclination, you can arrange a bareboat rental (with no crew); a fully crewed rental with a skipper, a staff, and a cook; or any variation in between. Boats usually come equipped with a portable barbecue, snorkeling gear, dinghy, linens, and galley equipment.

The Moorings has an experienced staff of mechanics, electricians, riggers, and cleaners. In addition, if you're going out on your own, you'll get a thorough briefing session about Virgin Island waters and anchorages.

**Horseback Riding    Shadow's Ranch,** Todman's Estate (☎ **42262**), offers horseback riding through Sage Mountain National Park or down to the shores of Cane Garden Bay. Call for details Monday through Saturday from 9am to 5pm. The cost is $25 per hour.

**Scuba**    The one dive site in the British Virgins that lures divers from St. Thomas is the wreckage of the RMS *Rhone*, which sank in 1867 near the western point of Salt Island. *Skin Diver* magazine called this "the world's most fantastic ship wreck dive." It teems with beautiful marine life and coral formations, and was featured in the motion picture *The Deep.*

Geared to everyone from the entry-level to the experienced diver, **Baskin in the Sun** (☎ **45854,** or **800/233-7938** in the U.S.), is a PADI five-star facility. Baskin in the Sun has three locations: Prospect Reef Resort, near Road Town; Sopher's Hole in Tortola's West End; and Village Cay Marina, also in Road Town. Baskin offers a discover scuba diving experience for $95, including a guided reef tour to give beginners a taste of diving under supervision. Daily trips are scheduled to such sites as the RMS *Rhone,* Painted Walls, and the "Indians."

**Underwater Safaris** (☎ **43235,** or **800/537-7032**), takes you to all of the best dive sites, including the RMS *Rhone,* Spyglass Wall, and Alice in Wonderland. Its offices, given the moniker Safari Base, are located in Road Town; the Safari Cay office is located on Cooper Island. (Call for directions.)

The center, located at The Moorings, offers a complete PADI and NAUI training facility. An introductory resort course and one dive costs $95; an open-water certification, with four days of instruction and four open-water dives, costs $385.

**Snorkeling**    Marina Cay off Tortola's East End is known for its good snorkeling beach. It also recommend the site at Cooper Island, across Sir Francis Drake

Channel. Underwater Safaris (see above) leads dive and snorkel expeditions to both sites frequently, weather permitting.

# SHOPPING

Most of the shops in the BVI are on Main Street, in Road Town on Tortola. British goods are imported without duty, and the wise shopper will be able to find some good buys among these imported items, especially in English china. In general, store hours are 9am to 4pm Monday through Friday and 9am to 1pm on Saturday.

### Bonker's Gallery
Main Street. ☎ **42535.**

Next to a bakery, this women's apparel store carries Java Wrap sarongs, although there are much larger Java Wrap collections in St. Thomas and St. Croix. The shop mainly sells bathing suits and accessories for women, including cotton and washable silk tops and bottoms, but there are also some shirts and pants for men as well.

### Caribbean Fine Arts Ltd.
Main St. ☎ **44240.**

This store has one of the most unusual collections of art from the West Indies. Not only does it sell original watercolors and oils, but it also offers limited edition serigraphs and sepia photographs from the turn of the century. The store also sells pottery and primitives.

### Caribbean Handprints
Main Street. ☎ **43717.**

This store features island handprints, all handmade by local craftspeople in Tortola. It also sells colorful fabric by the yard.

### Flamboyance
Soper's Hole. ☎ **54699.**

This is the best place to shop for duty-free perfume. Fendi purses are also sold here.

### J. R. O'Neal
Upper Main Street. ☎ **42292.**

Across from the Methodist church, this home accessories store sells the most extensive collection of decorative items on the island. You'll find terra-cotta pottery, wicker and rattan home furnishings, Mexican glassware, Dhurrie rugs, baskets, and ceramics. There is also a collection of fine crystal and china, including Royal Worcester.

### Kids in de Sun
Main Street. ☎ **43343.**

In the Abbot Building, this outlet carries the best collection of tropical wear for children, including T-shirts, shorts, and swimsuits, among other items.

### Little Denmark
Main Street. ☎ **42455.**

Little Denmark is your best bet for famous names in gold and silver jewelry and china such as Spode and Royal Copenhagen. Here you'll find many of the well-known designs from Scandinavian countries. The store also offers jewelry made in the BVI, a collection of watches, and even a large selection of fishing equipment.

### Pusser's Company Store
Main Street and Waterfront Road. ☎ **42467.**

Pusser's is both a long, mahogany-trimmed bar accented with many fine nautical artifacts and a souvenir store selling T-shirts, postcards, and upmarket gift items. Pusser's Rum is one of the best-selling items here.

### Sunny Caribbee Herb and Spice Company/Sunny Caribbee Art Gallery
Main Street. ☎ **42178.**

In a lovely old West Indian building that was the first hotel on Tortola, this store specializes in Caribbean spices, seasonings, teas, condiments, and handcrafts. Most of the products are blended and packaged on the island. You can buy two world-famous specialties here: West Indian hangover cure and Arawak love potion. A Caribbean cosmetics collection, Sunsations, is also available, including herbal bath gels, West Indian bay rum, and island perfume.

In the Sunny Caribbee Art Gallery, adjacent to the spice shop, you'll find an extensive collection of original art, prints, metal sculpture, and many other Caribbean crafts.

## TORTOLA AFTER DARK

Ask around to find out which hotel has entertainment on a given evening. Steel bands and fungi or scratch bands appear regularly, and nonresidents are usually welcome. Pick up a copy of *Limin' Times*, usually available at your hotel, which lists local events.

### ✪ Bomba's Surfside Shack
Cappoon's Bay. ☎ **54148.** Admission free. Bomba punch $3.50; beer $2; Wed and Sun barbecue $8 per person. Open daily 10am–midnight (or later).

The oddest, most memorable, and most uninhibited nightlife venue on the island sits on a 20-foot-wide strip of unpromising coastline near the West End. By anyone's standards, this is the "junk palace" of the island, covered with Day-Glo graffiti, and laced into a semblance of coherence with wire, rejected odds and ends of plywood, driftwood, and abandoned rubber tires.

Despite its makeshift appearance, the shack has all the electronic amplification anyone would need to create a really great party, which is exactly what happens every night from the first rum punch "until the last person is drunk and ready to go home." The place is at its wildest Wednesday and Sunday nights, when there's live music and an all-you-can-eat barbecue. The once-a-month "Full Moon" parties, assisted with an herbal tea brewed on the islands, are legendary.

### The Moorings/Mariner Inn
Wickhams Cay. ☎ **42332.** Admission free. Drinks $4. Open daily 11am–11pm.

This inn (see "Where to Stay," above) contains the preferred watering hole for some of the most upscale yacht owners in the islands. Open to a view of its own marina, and bathed in a dim and flattering light, the place is nautical and relaxed. A fungi band sometimes provides a backdrop to the socializing.

### Spyhouse Bar
Treasure Isle Hotel, eastern end of Road Town. ☎ **42501.** Drinks $2–$4. Open daily 10am–10pm.

This is one of the most popular bars on the island, lying in a little house designed with Haitian gingerbread and a sunken bar, set on a terrace overlooking the swimming pool and faraway marina facilities of this popular hotel (see "Where to Stay," above). Its specialties include "Treasure Trove" (Bailey's Irish Cream, brandy, crème de cacao, and milk) and "Virgin Decider" (vodka, gin, brandy, Benedictine, and pineapple juice).

## AN EXCURSION TO CANE GARDEN BAY

**Cane Garden Bay II,** one of the choicest pieces of real estate on the island, discovered long ago by the sailing crowd. Its white sandy beach with sheltering palms is a cliché of Caribbean charm, but it's sometimes crowded with cruise-ship passengers. The beach alone is reason to visit Cane Garden Bay. You can eat at Rhymer's Bar and Restaurant, where you can also rent snorkeling gear, hire a water taxi, and take a glassbottom boat to see the colorful underwater life offshore.

### Rhymer's

Cane Garden Bay. ☎ **54639.** Reservations not required. Transportation: Taxi. Appetizers $4–$6; main dishes $12–$20. AE, MC, V. Daily 8am–10pm. CARIBBEAN.

Rhymer's is the place to go for both food and entertainment. Skippers of any kind of craft are likely to stock up on supplies here. Conch and whelk show up regularly on the menu, as well as beer and refreshing rum drinks. If you're tired of fish, maybe James will make you some of his barbecued spareribs. On selected nights, a steel-drum band entertains, and maybe host James Rhymer himself will show you what a limbo dance is all about! You can rent Sunfish and Windsurfers, and ice and freshwater showers are available (towels are for rent, too).

## 6 Virgin Gorda

The second-largest island in the cluster of British Virgins, Virgin Gorda is 10 miles long and 2 miles wide, with a population of 1,400-odd people. It is located 12 miles east of Road Town and 26 miles from St. Thomas.

In 1493, on his second voyage to the New World, Columbus named the island Virgin Gorda or "Fat Virgin," after the mountain framing the island, which looks like a protruding stomach. Seen from a boat, its shape has also been compared to that of a pregnant woman lying on her back.

The island was a fairly desolate agricultural community until Laurance Rockefeller established the resort of Little Dix in the early 1960s, following his success with St. John and Caneel Bay in the 1950s.

He envisioned a "wilderness beach," where privacy and solitude reigned, and he literally put Virgin Gorda on the world map. Other major hotels followed in the wake of Little Dix, but privacy and solitude still reign supreme.

In 1971, the Virgin Gorda Yacht Harbour opened, accommodating 120 yachts. It is operated by Little Dix Bay Hotel.

## GETTING THERE & GETTING AROUND

**Speedy's Fantasy** (☎ **55240**) operates a ferry service between Road Town on Toriola and Virgin Gorda. Three ferries a day leave from Road Town Monday through Saturday; two run on Sunday. The cost is $10 one-way or $19 round-trip. From St. Thomas to Virgin Gorda, there is service three times a week (Tuesday, Thursday, and Saturday); the cost is $25 one-way and $45 round-trip.

**Air St. Thomas** (☎ **809/495-5935**) flies to Virgin Gorda daily from San Juan, Puerto Rico. The 40-minute flight costs $80 one-way.

There are so few roads on the island that you can detour from any of them and quickly recover the thread of your itinerary.

An aerial view of the island shows what looks like three bulky masses connected by two very narrow isthmuses. The most northeasterly of these three masses (which contains two of the most interesting hotels) is not even accessible by road at all, requiring ferryboat transit from the more accessible parts of the island.

One possibility for exploring Virgin Gorda by car is to drive from the southwest to the northeast along the island's rocky and meandering spine. This route will take you to The Baths (in the extreme southeast), Spanish Harbour (near the middle), and eventually, after skirting the mountainous edges of Gorda Peak, the most northwesterly tip of the island's road system, near North Sound. There, a cluster of houses and a mini-armada of infrequently scheduled ferryboats depart and arrive from Biras Creek and the Bitter End Yacht Club.

Independently operated open-sided **safari buses** run along the main road. Holding up to 14 passengers, these buses charge upwards from $3 per person to transport a passenger, say, from The Valley to The Baths.

## FAST FACTS

**American Express**   The local representative is Travel Plan, Virgin Gorda Yacht Harbour (☎ **55586**), open Monday through Friday 9am to noon and 1 to 3pm, Saturday from 9am to 1pm.

**Laundry and Dry Cleaning**   Stevens Laundry & Dry Cleaning, near the Virgin Gorda Yacht Harbour (☎ **55525**), is open daily from 8am to 9pm.

**Photographic Needs**   Try Kysk Tropix, Virgin Gorda Yacht Harbour (☎ **55636**), open Monday through Saturday from 9am to 5:45pm.

**Services and Supplies**   In Spanish Town, opposite Beef Island, stands the Yacht Harbour Shopping Centre where you can stock up on supplies and find various services. The shopping complex contains a supermarket, ice-cream parlor, a pub, a wine and liquor store, a dive shop, a bakery, a Laundromat, a drugstore, and a boutique.

## WHAT TO SEE & DO

The northern side of Virgin Gorda is mountainous, with one peak reaching 1,370 feet. However, the southern half is flat, with large boulders appearing at every turn. The best **beaches** are at The Baths, where giant boulders form a series of panoramic pools and grottoes flooded with sea water. Nearby snorkeling is excellent. Neighboring the The Baths is Spring Bay, one of the best of the island's beaches, with white sand, clear water, and good snorkeling. Trunk Bay is a wide sand beach accessible by boat or by a rough path from Spring Bay. Savannah Bay is a sandy beach north of Yacht Harbour. Mahoe Bay, at the Mango Bay Resort, has a gently curving beach with vivid blue water.

Virgin Gorda has a few attractions that merit a visit. **Coppermine Point** is the site of an abandoned copper mine and smelter. Because of loose rock formations, it can be dangerous, and you should exercise caution if you explore it. Legend has it that the Spanish worked these mines in the 1600s; however, the only authenticated document reveals that the English sank the shafts in 1838 to mine copper.

✪ **The Baths** is a justly famous tourist spot known for its snorkeling. Equipment can be rented on the beach. The Baths are a phenomenon of tranquil pools and caves formed by gigantic house-size boulders. As these boulders toppled over one another, they formed saltwater grottoes, suitable for exploring. The pools among the boulders provide excellent places for swimming.

The **Devil's Bay National Park** can be reached by a trail from the Baths Roundabout. The walk to the secluded coral sand beach through a setting of boulders and dry coastal vegetation takes about 15 minutes.

The Baths and surrounding areas are part of a proposed system of parks and protected areas for the BVI. The protected area encompasses 682 acres of land, including sites at Little Fort, Spring Bay, The Baths, and Devil's Bay on the east coast.

If you grow jaded of too constant a diet of sun, sea, and sand, consider hiking up the stairs and paths that crisscross Virgin Gorda's largest stretch of undeveloped land—the Virgin Gorda Peak National Park. To reach the best point of departure for your uphill trek, drive north of The Valley on the only road leading to North Sound for about 15 minutes. (Use of a four-wheel-drive vehicle is preferable on these hilly roads.) Stop at the base of the stairway leading steeply uphill, where there's a sign pointing to the Virgin Gorda Peak National Park.

It takes between 25 and 40 minutes to reach the summit of Gorda Peak, the highest point on the island, where views of many scattered islets of the Virgin archipelago await you. There's a tower at the summit which you can climb for enhanced views. Along the way, you're likely to encounter to encounter birds, lizards, and non-venomous snakes, consider bringing a picnic; there are picnic tables scattered amid the network of hiking trails.

The best way to see the island if you're over for a day trip is to call Andy Flax at Fischers Cove Beach Hotel (☎ **55252**). He runs **Virgin Gorda Tours Association,** which will give you a tour of the island for about $50 for one to three persons. The tour leaves twice daily. You can be picked up at the ferry dock.

**Kilbrides Underwater Tours** (☎ **59638,** or **800/932-4286**), is located at the Bitter End Resort at North Sound. The outfit is a recipient of the prestigious NOGI award—the Oscar of the diving industry. Kilbrides offers the best diving in the BVI at more than 15 to 20 dive sites, including the wreck of the RMS *Rhone*. Prices range from $80 to $90 for a two-tank dive on one of the coral reefs. Tanks and weighted belts are supplied at no charge, and videos of your dives are available.

# WHERE TO STAY
## VERY EXPENSIVE

### ✪ Little Dix Bay Hotel
P.O. Box 70, Virgin Gorda, BVI. ☎ **809/495-5555,** or 800/928-3000. Fax 809/495-5661. 98 rms, 4 one-bedroom suites. TEL Transportation: Private ferry service operating between Beef Island airport and the resort. Rates (including breakfast): Winter, $450–$790 single or double; $1,200 suite. Summer, $225–$560 single or double; $750–$930 suite. Third person in room $65. All meals $70 extra. AE, DC, MC, V. Parking free.

Understatedly luxurious, this resort, launched in 1964, is set discreetly along a crescent-shaped private bay on a 500-acre preserve in the northwest corner of the island. It has the same quiet elegance as its fellow resort, Caneel Bay on St. John. All rooms, built with woods of purpleheart, mahogany, locust, and ash, have private terraces with a view of the sea or the gardens. Some units are two-story rondavels raised on stilts to form their own breezeways. The decor is contemporary with all the conveniences. Trade winds come through louvers and screen walls and are circulated by ceiling fans. All the guest rooms have been renovated with new furnishings and fabrics. Forty-four of the rooms contain air conditioning. In the rondavels, hammocks swing from stilts.

**Dining/Entertainment:** Four interconnected, Polynesian-style pyramids tilted to face the sea comprise the roof of the Pavilion, venue for lunch buffets, afternoon teas, and candlelit dinners. The cuisine is international, featuring Caribbean specialties using fresh seafood. For drinks, guests sit on the restaurant's terrace where a band performs nightly. The Sugar Mill is elegant but casual, specializing in fresh grilled fish, lobster, and steaks. During the day, splashes of bougainvillea cover the rooftops as guests dine under the sun; at night, guests eat at tables under the stars beside the sea. On the edge of the beach, The Beach Grill is an informal choice for breakfast, a light lunch, or dinner. The menu features local grilled lobster, which can be ordered in the evening at candlelit tables overlooking the beach alight with blazing torches.

**Services:** Unequalled service with a staff-to-guest ratio of one-to-one.

**Facilities:** Seven all-weather outdoor tennis courts; Sunfish sailboats; Windsurfers; snorkeling; scuba diving; waterskiing; boat rentals; deep-sea fishing; diving excursions; and the Virgin Gorda Yacht Harbour, $^1/_2$ mile from the resort (owned and operated by Little Dix Bay).

## EXPENSIVE

### ✪ Biras Creek Estate

North Sound, P.O. Box 54, Virgin Gorda, BVI. ☎ **809/494-3555,** or 800/223-1108. Fax 809/494-3557. 16 cottages, 32 suites (all with bath). Transportation: Hotel's private motor launch. Rates (including all meals): Winter, $465–$685 suite for two; $840 cottage for two; $998 cottage for four. Summer, $340–$550 suite for two; $575 cottage for two; 710 cottage for four. AE, MC, V.

This private and romantic resort, located at the northern end of Virgin Gorda, is accessible only by boat. Perched on a hill, the fortress is surrounded by a 100-acre estate with its own marina, and it occupies a narrow neck of land with the sea on three sides. To create their Caribbean hideaway, Norwegian shipping interests carved this resort out of the wilderness, out wisely protected the surroundings. A greenhouse on the grounds provides a steady supply of foliage and flowers.

The guest accommodations (doubles and suites only) are along the shore. Rates include three meals a day, plus use of facilities and equipment. Cooled by ceiling fans, each suite has a well-furnished bedroom, a sitting room, a private patio, and a refrigerator.

**Dining/Entertainment:** Biras Creek's main open-air dining room is located in the hilltop stone castle and commands a 360-degree view. The restaurant is noted for its service and its cuisine: An imaginative menu features continental cooking and Caribbean specialties and offers fresh lobster every night. Biras Creek also boasts an extensive wine list. Cheerful by day and romantic by night, with candlelit tables and soft background music, the restaurant serves three meals daily. On Sunday, Biras Creek offers its popular curry luncheon buffet and, twice a week, guests are treated to the resort's outdoor beach barbecues. The dining room seats 120 people, with limited reservations accepted from nonhouseguests. A combo, with vocal performances, plays every Saturday night, from 9pm to midnight, on the stone terrace overlooking the water. On Thursday evening, a ballad singer entertains guests at the castle.

**Services:** Free trips to nearby islands, taxi service in Virgin Gorda to hotel's motor launch.

**Facilities:** Swimming pool, snorkeling gear, Sunfish sailboats, two tennis courts, Boston whalers, dinghies.

## ✪ Bitter End Yacht Club

John O'Point, North Sound, P.O. Box 46, Virgin Gorda, BVI. ☎ **809/494-2746**, or 800/872-2392 for reservations. Fax 809/494-4756. 92 units, 6 suites (all with bath). Transportation: From Beef Island airport, take NSX ferry to Bitter End Dock ($^1/_2$ hour). Rates (including meals): Winter, $300–$415 single; $350–$515 double; from $950 suite. Summer, $240–$290 single; $325–$395 double; from $495 suite. AE, DC, MC, V. Parking: Free.

Guests at this rendezvous point for the yachting set have included treasure-hunter Mel Fisher and Jean-Michel Cousteau. Bitter End offers an informal yet elegant life, as guests settle into one of the marina rooms, hillside chalets, or well-appointed beachfront and hillside villas overlooking the sound and yachts at anchor. Each room is suitable for two or more.

For a novel vacation, you can stay aboard one of the *Freedom 30* yachts, yours to sail, with dockage. The yachts include daily chamber service, meals in the yacht club dining room, and overnight provisions. Marina rooms go for the same rates as live-aboard yachts. Marina rooms and yacht rooms are the cheaper prices given in the rates above.

**Dining/Entertainment:** Dining is in the Clubhouse Steak and Seafood Grille or the English Carvery. The social hub of the place is the bar.

**Services:** Free sailing instruction, expeditions to neighboring cays.

**Facilities** (all included in rates): Lasers, Sunfish Sailboats, Rhodes 19s, J-24s, Windsurfers, outboard skiffs, snorkeling equipment.

## MODERATE

### ⑤ Fischers Cove Beach Hotel

The Valley, P.O. Box 60, Virgin Gorda, BVI. ☎ **809/495-5252.** Fax 809/495-5820. 12 rms, 8 cottages. Transportation: Taxi. Rates: Winter, $125–$130 single; $145–$150 double; $170–$180 one-bedroom cottage. Summer, $90 single; $100 double; $125–$135 one-bedroom cottage. MAP $40 per person extra. AE, MC, V. Parking: Free.

This group of cottages, nestled near the beach of St. Thomas Bay, offers swimming at its doorstep. Built of native stone, each house is self-contained; the one- and two-bedroom units have a combination living and dining room with a kitchenette. If you want to do your own cooking, you can stock up on provisions at a food store near the grounds. In addition to the cottages, a two-story unit has 12 pleasant but simple rooms that have private balconies with a view of Sir Francis Drake Channel.

**Dining/Entertainment:** There is lunch daily from 11am to 3:30pm and dinner daily from 6 to 10:30pm. Lunch runs from $7 to $15, and dinner from $14 to $32. Special features include a beach buffet, occasional reggae band, and an all Caribbean dinner.

### ✪ The Olde Yard Inn

The Valley, P.O. Box 26, Virgin Gorda, BVI. ☎ **809/495-5544,** or 800/633-7411. Fax 809/495-5986. 14 rms (all with bath). Transportation: Taxi. Rates: Winter, $130 single; $180 double; $205 triple; $230 quad. Summer, $80 single; $95 double; $120 triple; $140 quad. MAP $45 per person extra. AE, MC, V.

This little Caribbean inn is charming. Owner Carol Kaufman offers her guests good food, good beds, and hospitality that ranks among the best in the British Virgins. The renovated rooms are located in a tropical garden facing the sea; each has its own patio. Four of the rooms are air-conditioned. The inn maintains one of the best libraries on Virgin Gorda; it is stocked with books and video tapes.

**Dining/Entertainment:** the French-accented meals, served under a cedar roof, are another reason for staying here. Steaks cut at the inn are from the finest fresh sirloin. If you're just visiting for the day, you can enjoy a lunch from noon to 2pm, at a cost of $10. Dinner, served from 6:30 to 9pm, begins at $18. There is live entertainment twice a week in the dining room during the winter season.

**Services:** You can go for a sail on a yacht or go snorkeling at one of 16 beaches with a picnic lunch (perhaps lobster, pâté, champagne, or for simpler tastes, peanut-butter sandwiches.

## INEXPENSIVE

### ⑤ Guavaberry Spring Bay Vacation Homes

Spring Bay, P.O. Box 20, Virgin Gorda, BVI. ☎ **809/495-5227.** Fax 809/495-5283. 16 units (all with bath). Rates: Winter, $135 one-bedroom house for two; $200 two-bedroom house for four. Summer, $90 one-bedroom house for two; $140 two-bedroom house for four. Extra person $20. No credit cards. Parking: Free. Closed three weeks in Sept.

The homes are made up of clusters of hexagonal white-roofed redwood houses built on stilts. They are available for daily or weekly rentals. Staying here is like living in a tree house with screened and louvered walls to let in sea breezes. Each of the unique vacation homes has one or two bedrooms, small kitchenettes and dining areas, and a private elevated sundeck overlooking Sir Francis Drake Channel.

Within a few minutes of the cottage colony, is the beach at Spring Bay, and it's possible to explore. The Baths nearby. Your hosts can arrange for day charters for scuba diving or fishing, island Jeep tours, and horseback riding.

# WHERE TO DINE
## EXPENSIVE

### Chez Michelle

The Valley. ☎ **55510.** Reservations recommended. Appetizers $6–$7.50; main dishes $16–$28. MC, V. Dinner daily 6:30–9:30pm. Closed in Sept. CONTINENTAL.

Established on the ground floor of a clean and modern breeze-filled house by Michelle Noevere and her French-Canadian husband, Eric, Chez Michelle is considered the most sophisticated privately owned restaurant on the island. Menu specialties change frequently, but might include lobster-Rémy (flambéed with a sauce of cognac, cream, and tomatoes); conch à la meunière (with a sauce of shallots, white wine, garlic, and lemon); a pasta of the day; and steaks. Desserts are considered one of the high points of a meal here, with a separate menu of their own. You'll find Chez Michelle in Spanish Town just a short walk north of the yacht harbor.

## MODERATE

### ⑤ Teacher Ilma's

The Valley. ☎ **55355.** Reservations required for dinner; call before 3pm. At Spanish Town, turn left at the main road past the entrance to Fischers Cove Hotel; the sign to Teacher Ilma's is about two minutes-drive ahead and to the right. Full meals $18–$25. No credit cards. Lunch daily 12:30–2pm; dinner daily 7–8:30pm. WEST INDIAN.

Mrs. Ilma O'Neal, who taught youngsters at the island's public school for 43 years, began her restaurant by cooking privately for tourists and island construction workers. Main courses might include chicken, local goat meat, lobster, conch, pork, or fish (your choice of grouper, snapper, tuna, dolphin, swordfish, or triggerfish), followed by such desserts as homemade coconut, pineapple, or guava pies. Teacher Ilma emphasizes that her cuisine is not creole but local in its origin and flavors.

## INEXPENSIVE

### Bath and Turtle Pub

Virgin Gorda Yacht Harbour, Spanish Town. ☎ **55239.** Reservations recommended. Appetizers $6; main dishes $16–$25; snacks, sandwiches, salads, and platters $5–$25; tropical drinks $3–$6.50. AE, MC, V. Daily 7am–midnight. INTERNATIONAL.

This is the most popular bar and pub on Virgin Gorda, with an active local trade that is enhanced by its twice-daily happy hours (10:30 to 11:30am and 4 to 6pm). There's live music every Wednesday and Sunday (also Saturday in season) from 8pm to midnight (no cover charge).

At its handful of indoor and courtyard tables, you can order fried fish fingers, nachos, very spicy chili, pizza, Reubens or tuna melts, and an array of daily seafood specials such as conch fritters listed on an oversize blackboard.

### The Crab Hole

The Valley. ☎ **55307.** Reservations required for dinner. Head south along the road to The Baths, and turn left at the sign to the Crab Hole. Appetizers $4–$5; main dishes $10–$15. No credit cards. Lunch Mon–Sat 11:30am–2pm; dinner Mon–Sat 7–10pm. WEST INDIAN.

This is a clean and decent West Indian restaurant contained within the private home of Kenroy and Janet Millington. Built in 1986, it occupies the ground level of a concrete house surrounded by fields and other houses.

Order your food from the blackboard posted above the bar. The menu changes daily, but might include stewed whelk with a creole sauce made from local spices and tomatoes, bullfoot soup, curried chicken, fried fish, stewed oxtail, or hamburgers. Beer costs $2.50 a bottle.

### Mad Dog

The Baths, The Country. ☎ **55830.** Reservations not required. Sandwiches $4; piña coladas $3.50. No credit cards. Open daily 10am–7pm. PIÑA COLADAS/SANDWICHES.

Established in 1989, this is the most skillful and charming reconstruction of a West Indian cottage on Virgin Gorda. A wide veranda and the brightly painted 19th-century wooden timbers and clapboards create a cozy and convivial drink and sandwich bar where the piña coladas are absolutely divine. The owner and supervisor of this laid-back corner of heaven is London-born Colin McCullough, a self-described mad dog who sailed the BVI for almost 30 years before establishing his domain here.

### Thelma's Hideout

The Valley. ☎ **55646.** Reservations required for dinner. Lunches $8; fixed-price dinner $18–$20. No credit cards. Breakfast daily 7–10am; lunch daily 11:30am–2:30pm; dinner daily (only upon notification before 3pm) 6–10pm. Bar daily 11am–midnight. WEST INDIAN.

Located in concrete house whose angles are softened by ascending tiers of verandas, one of the most outspoken *grandes dames* of Virgin Gorda, Mrs. Thelma King (who worked in Manhattan for many years before returning to her native BVI) runs a convivial gathering place for the island's West Indian community. Food choices include grilled steaks, fish filets, and West Indian stews containing pork, mutton, or chicken. Limeade or mauby are available, but many clients stick to rum or beer. Several evenings a week, live music is presented.

## VIRGIN GORDA AFTER DARK

**Andy's Chateau de Pirate**
Spanish Town. ☎ **55252.** Free most nights, $5 Fri–Sun. Drinks $2–$3. Open daily 11am–
midnight. The club lies one-half mile south of yacht harbor.

Solidly built of poured concrete in 1985, this sprawling, sparsely furnished local
hangout has a simple stage, a very long bar, and huge ocean-front windows which
almost never close. The complex also houses the Lobster Pot Restaurant, the
Bucaneer Bar, and the nightclub EFX. The Lobster Pot is open from 7am to
10pm; dinners cost from $15 to $25.

The place is a famous showcase for the island's musical groups, which perform
Wednesday through Sunday from 8pm to midnight; lots of people congregate to
listen and kibitz.

# 7  Mosquito Island (North Sound)

The sandy, 125-acre Mosquito (also spelled Moskito) Island just north of Virgin
Gorda wasn't named for those pesky insects we all know and hate. It took its name
from the tribe who inhabited the small landmass before the arrival of the Spanish conquistadors in the 15th century. Archeological relics of these peaceful people
and their agricultural pursuits have been found here.

## GETTING THERE

You must take a plane to Virgin Gorda, then a taxi to Leverick Bay Dock. A boat
will meet you and take you on the five-minute ride from the dock to the resort.
The island lies north of Virgin Gorda.

## WHERE TO STAY

**Drake's Anchorage Resort Inn**
P.O. Box 2510, North Sound, Virgin Gorda, BVI. ☎ **809/494-2254,** or 800/624-6651;
**617/969-9913** in Massachusetts. 8 rms, 2 suites, 2 villas (all with bath). Rates (including
meals): Winter, $412–$423 double; $485 suite; $595 villa. Summer, $311–$338 double;
$343–$373 suite; $490–$515 villa. Single $218 year-round. AE, MC, V.

Privately owned Mosquito Island is uninhabited except for this resort, which many
patrons consider their favorite retreat in the British Virgins. The hotel offers comfortable rooms and two well-furnished villas that all have seaview verandas. The
tropical restaurant faces the water and serves a cuisine featuring local and continental dishes, including lobster and the fresh fish of the day.

The resort provides free use of Windsurfers, snorkeling equipment, and bicycles.
For additional fees, you can go scuba diving, deep-sea fishing, day sailing,
or you can visit The Baths at Virgin Gorda. The snorkeling and scuba here are
considered so good that members of the Cousteau Society once came here to
explore. There are four beaches on the island, each with different wave and water
conditions.

# 8  Guana Island

This 850-acre island, a nature sanctuary, is one of the most private hideaways in
the Caribbean. Don't come here seeking action; come only if you want to retreat
from the world. Guana Island lies right off the coast of Tortola. The small island

contains seven virgin beaches and nature trails and an abundance of unusual species of plant and animal life. The island is great for hiking. Its highest point is Sugarloaf Mountain at 806 feet, which offers a panoramic view. Arawak relics have been found on the island. It is said that the name of the island came from a jutting rock that resembled the head of an iguana.

**To get there,** take the Guana Island Club boat, which meets visitors at Beef Island airport (10 minutes) near Tortola.

## WHERE TO STAY

### Guana Island

P.O. Box 32, Road Town, Tortola, BVI. ☎ **809/494-2354,** or 800/544-8262. Fax 914/967-8048. For reservations write or call Guana Island, 10 Timber Trail, Rye. NY 10580 (☎ **914/967-6050,** or 800/54-GUANA). 15 rms (all with bath), 1 cottage. Transportation: Private launch from Tortola. Rates (including meals): Nov 1–Dec 15, $435 double; $660 cottage. Dec 16–Mar 31, $595 double; $890 cottage. Apr 1–Aug 31, $435 double; $660 cottage. No credit cards. Closed Sept-Oct.

Guana Island, the sixth or seventh largest of the British Virgin Islands, was bought in 1974 by Henry and Gloria Jarecki, dedicated conservationists who run this resort.

After your arrival on the island, a Land Rover will transport you up one of the most scenic hills in the region, in the northeast of Guana. You arrive at a cluster of white-walled cottages that were built as a private club in the 1930s on the foundations of a Quaker homestead. The stone-trimmed bungalows (with only two telephones) never hold more than 30 guests, and since the dwellings are staggered along a flower-dotted hillside, privacy is almost absolute. The airy accommodations all have ceiling fans, private terraces, and attractive bathrooms; the decor emphasizes rattan and wicker. The panoramic sweep from the terraces is spectacular, particularly at sunset.

When guests want company, they seek out the convivial atmosphere at the rattan-furnished clubhouse. Dinners by candlelight are served on the veranda, with menus that include homegrown vegetables and continental and mainland specialties. While dinner is a casually elegant sit-down affair, lunch is served buffet style every day. The self-serve bars charge guests according to the honor system.

Sports lovers and beachcombers will find seven beaches, some of which require a boat to reach. There are two tennis courts (one clay and one all-weather), and fishing and snorkeling. There is an abundance of nature trails on the island.

# Index

**Now Save Money on All Your Travels by Joining**

## The Advantages of Membership:

1. Your choice of any **TWO FREE BOOKS.**

2. Your own subscription to the **TRIPS & TRAVEL** quarterly newsletter, where you'll discover the best buys in travel, the hottest vacation spots, the latest travel trends, world-class events and festivals, and much more.

3. A **30% DISCOUNT** on any additional books you order through the club.

4. **DOMESTIC TRIP-ROUTING KITS** (available for a small additional fee). We'll send you a detailed map highlighting the most direct or scenic route to your destination, anywhere in North America.

## Here's all you have to do to join:

Send in your annual membership fee of $25.00 ($35.00 Canada/Foreign) with your name, address, and selections on the form below. Or call 815/734-1104 to use your credit card.

Send all orders to:

---

### FROMMER'S TRAVEL BOOK CLUB
P.O. Box 473 • Mt. Morris, IL 61054-0473 • ☎ 815/734-1104

YES! I want to take advantage of this opportunity to join Frommer's Travel Book Club.

[ ] My check for $25.00 ($35.00 for Canadian or foreign orders) is enclosed.
　　**All orders must be prepaid in U.S. funds only. Please make checks payable to Frommer's Travel Book Club.**

[ ] Please charge my credit card: [ ] Visa or [ ] Mastercard

　　Credit card number: _____

　　Expiration date: ___ / ___ / ___

　　Signature: _____

　　Or call 815/734-1104 to use your credit card by phone.

Name: _____

Address: _____

City: _____ State: _____ Zip code: _____

Phone number (in case we have a question regarding your order): _____

Please indicate your choices for TWO FREE books (*see following pages*):

　　Book 1 - Code: _____ Title: _____

　　Book 2 - Code: _____ Title: _____

For information on ordering additional titles, see your first issue of the *Trips & Travel* newsletter.

Allow 4–6 weeks for delivery for all items. Prices of books, membership fee, and publication dates are subject to change without notice. All orders are subject to acceptance and availability.

AC1

The following Frommer's guides are available from your favorite bookstore, or you can use the order form on the preceding page to request them as part of your membership in Frommer's Travel Book Club.

## FROMMER'S COMPLETE TRAVEL GUIDES

*(Comprehensive guides to sightseeing, dining and accommodations, with selections in all price ranges—from deluxe to budget)*

| | | | |
|---|---|---|---|
| Acapulco/Ixtapa/Taxco, 2nd Ed. | C157 | Jamaica/Barbados, 2nd Ed. | C149 |
| Alaska '94-'95 | C131 | Japan '94-'95 | C144 |
| Arizona '95 | C166 | Maui, 1st Ed. | C153 |
| Australia '94-'95 | C147 | Nepal, 3rd Ed. (avail. 11/95) | C184 |
| Austria, 6th Ed. | C162 | New England '95 | C165 |
| Bahamas '96 (avail. 8/95) | C172 | New Mexico, 3rd Ed. | C167 |
| Belgium/Holland/Luxembourg, | | New York State, 4th Ed. | C133 |
| 4th Ed. | C170 | Northwest, 5th Ed. | C140 |
| Bermuda '96 (avail. 8/95) | C174 | Portugal '94-'95 | C141 |
| California '95 | C164 | Puerto Rico '95-'96 | C151 |
| Canada '94-'95 | C145 | Puerto Vallarta/Manzanillo/ | |
| Caribbean '96 (avail. 9/95) | C173 | Guadalajara, 2nd Ed. | C135 |
| Carolinas/Georgia, 2nd Ed. | C128 | Scandinavia, 16th Ed. | C169 |
| Colorado '96 (avail. 11/95) | C179 | Scotland '94-'95 | C146 |
| Costa Rica, 1st Ed. | C161 | South Pacific '94-'95 | C138 |
| Cruises '95-'96 | C150 | Spain, 16th Ed. | C163 |
| Delaware/Maryland '94-'95 | C136 | Switzerland, 7th Ed. | |
| England '96 (avail. 10/95) | C180 | (avail. 9/95) | C177 |
| Florida '96 (avail. 9/95) | C181 | Thailand, 2nd Ed. | C154 |
| France '96 (avail. 11/95) | C182 | U.S.A., 4th Ed. | C156 |
| Germany '96 (avail. 9/95) | C176 | Virgin Islands, 3rd Ed. | |
| Honolulu/Waikiki/Oahu, 4th Ed. | | (avail. 8/95) | C175 |
| (avail. 10/95) | C178 | Virginia '94-'95 | C142 |
| Ireland, 1st Ed. | C168 | Yucatán '95-'96 | C155 |
| Italy '96 (avail. 11/95) | C183 | | |

## FROMMER'S $-A-DAY GUIDES

*(Dream Vacations at Down-to-Earth Prices)*

| | | | |
|---|---|---|---|
| Australia on $45 '95-'96 | D122 | Ireland on $45 '94-'95 | D118 |
| Berlin from $50, 3rd Ed. | | Israel on $45, 15th Ed. | D130 |
| (avail. 10/95) | D137 | London from $55 '96 | |
| Caribbean from $60, 1st Ed. | | (avail. 11/95) | D136 |
| (avail. 9/95) | D133 | Madrid on $50 '94-'95 | D119 |
| Costa Rica/Guatemala/Belize | | Mexico from $35 '96 | |
| on $35, 3rd Ed. | D126 | (avail. 10/95) | D135 |
| Eastern Europe on $30, 5th Ed. | D129 | New York on $70 '94-'95 | D121 |
| England from $50 '96 | | New Zealand from $45, 6th Ed. | D132 |
| (avail. 11/95) | D138 | Paris on $45 '94-'95 | D117 |
| Europe from $50 '96 | | South America on $40, 16th Ed. | D123 |
| (avail. 10/95) | D139 | Washington, D.C. on $50 | |
| Greece from $45, 6th Ed. | D131 | '94-'95 | D120 |
| Hawaii from $60 '96 (avail. 9/95) | D134 | | |

# FROMMER'S COMPLETE CITY GUIDES

*(Comprehensive guides to sightseeing, dining, and accommodations in all price ranges)*

# FROMMER'S FAMILY GUIDES

*(Guides to family-friendly hotels, restaurants, activities, and attractions)*

# FROMMER'S WALKING TOURS

*(Memorable strolls through colorful and historic neighborhoods, accompanied by detailed directions and maps)*

# FROMMER'S AMERICA ON WHEELS

*(Guides for travelers who are exploring the U.S.A. by car, featuring a brand-new rating system for accommodations and full-color road maps)*

# FROMMER'S SPECIAL-INTEREST TITLES

# FROMMER'S BEST BEACH VACATIONS
*(The top places to sun, stroll, shop, stay, play, party, and swim—with each beach rated for beauty, swimming, sand, and amenities)*

# FROMMER'S BED & BREAKFAST GUIDES
*(Selective guides with four-color photos and full descriptions of the best inns in each region)*

# FROMMER'S IRREVERENT GUIDES
*(Wickedly honest guides for sophisticated travelers and those who want to be)*

# FROMMER'S DRIVING TOURS
*(Four-color photos and detailed maps outlining spectacular scenic driving routes)*

# FROMMER'S BORN TO SHOP
*(The ultimate travel guides for discriminating shoppers—from cut-rate to couture)*